Human Rights in European Criminal Law

Stefano Ruggeri
Editor

Human Rights in European Criminal Law

New Developments in European Legislation and Case Law after the Lisbon Treaty

Springer

Editor
Stefano Ruggeri
Department of Law
University of Messina
Messina
Italy

ISBN 978-3-319-12041-6 ISBN 978-3-319-12042-3 (eBook)
DOI 10.1007/978-3-319-12042-3

Library of Congress Control Number: 2014958750

Springer Cham Heidelberg New York Dordrecht London

Printed on acid-free paper

Springer is part of Springer Science+Business Media (www.springer.com)

Acknowledgements

This book contains the results of a conference organised in 2013 by my chair of Italian and European criminal procedure at the University of Messina on the main developments occurred over the last years in European criminal law from human rights perspective. This initiative was financially supported by the same University of Messina and the *Assemblea Regionale Siciliana* (ARS), for which I am truly grateful.

A special thank goes, again, to Springer Verlag and in particular to Dr. Brigitte Reschke for her interest in publishing our academic works. I am very grateful to all my distinguished colleagues who have written for this book. Moreover, this work constitutes the second step of a wider project (after *Transnational Evidence and Multicultural Inquiries in Europe. Developments in EU Legislation and New Challenges for Human Rights-Oriented Criminal Investigations in Cross-border Cases*, also published by Springer Verlag), aimed at promoting both young scholars and students of our University to research activities. This is a very demanding task, which certainly requires many efforts and time by all people involved, but I must admit that watching the results of this work, with all its imperfections, fills me with satisfaction and joy.

Finally, as always, I wish to conclude thanking my family, my wife Norma and my two little daughters, Anna Lucia and Maria Isabel, for accompanying me in all the steps of my research path.

Thank you all very much!
10 July 2014

Tindari, Italy Stefano Ruggeri

Abbreviations

AFSJ	Area of Freedom, Security and Justice
CCP	Code of Criminal Procedure
CISA	Convention Implementing the Schengen Agreement
CNAV	French National Council for Assistance to Victims
DAL	Directive on the right of Access to a Lawyer
D. l.	Decree-Law
D. lgs.	Legislative Decree
EAW	European Arrest Warrant
ECHR	European Convention on Human Rights
ECJ	Court of Justice of the European Union
ECMACM	European Convention on Mutual Legal Assistance in Criminal Matters
ECtHR	European Court of Human Rights
EEW	European Evidence Warrant
EIO	European Investigation Order
EPPO	European Public Prosecutor Office
EU	European Union
EUCMACM	Convention on Mutual Assistance in Criminal Matters between the Member States of the European Union
EU FRCh	Charter of Fundamental Rights of the European Union
GIP	Italian Judge in Charge of Preliminary Investigations
IACMACM	Inter-American Convention on Mutual Assistance in Criminal Matters
ICCPR	International Covenant on Civil and Political Rights
INAVEM	French National Institute for Assistance to Victims and Mediation
JHA	Justice and Home Affairs
MLA	Mutual Legal Assistance
MR	Mutual Recognition
OFPE	Execution in the EU of Orders Freezing Property or Evidence
OJEU	Official Journal of the European Union

OCTA	Organized Crime Threat Assessment
PD	Proposal for a Directive
SAP ECMACM	Second Additional Protocol to European Convention on Mutual Legal Assistance in Criminal Matters
TEU	Treaty on European Union
TFEU	Treaty on the Functioning of the European Union
UN MTMACM	United Nations Model Treaty on Mutual Assistance in Criminal Matters
UN CTOC	United Nations Convention against Transnational Organized Crime

Contents

The Development of Individual Rights Protection in European Criminal Law After the Lisbon Treaty

Bernd Hecker

Contents

Abstract The lecture provides an overview of the development of individual rights protection in European Criminal Law after the enforcement of the Lisbon Treaty especially considering the EU's accession to the ECHR.

1 Introduction

Having been asked to speak about the development of individual rights protection in European Criminal Law after the entry into force of the Lisbon Treaty, it is essential to clarify the term "European Criminal Law" first.

B. Hecker (✉)
Fachbereich Rechtswissenschaft, Law School, University of Trier, Universitätsring No. 15, Trier, Germany
e-mail: hecker@uni-trier.de

S. Ruggeri (ed.), *Human Rights in European Criminal Law*,
DOI 10.1007/978-3-319-12042-3_1

1.1 Meaning of the Term "European Criminal Law"

The term seems to imply a normative structure that resembles a domestic criminal law system as found in Germany, Italy, France, the UK or other member states of the EU. This would mean that we would be looking at a set of criminal offences that derive from a single European source of law that is directly applicable in all member states as supranational law. At this time such a European Criminal Code does not exist, and there are no criminal rules that are uniformly applicable in all member states. According to the principle of conferral of competences that is provided in Article 5(1–2) TEU, the European Union's competence to create supranational criminal law is limited to certain well-defined fields—namely fraud affecting the financial interests of the EU [see Art. 325(4) TFEU]. Besides those, the EU cannot enact new supranational criminal law applicable in all member states to supplement or even replace existing domestic criminal law.

In a broader sense, every legal rule of the European legal order with criminal law content can be considered a part of European Criminal Law. This would also include EU measures aiming at the harmonisation of the member states' criminal law. Under the new treaties, Article 83 TFEU provides now a general competence provision for the approximation of substantive criminal law by means of directives. The provision distinguishes between the approximation of particular serious crimes with a cross-border dimension on one hand (see par. 1) and the approximation to ensure the effective implementation of Union policy in an area that has been subject to harmonisation measures, the so-called annex competence, on the other hand (see par. 2). Finally, Article 83(3) TFEU establishes an "emergency break", which enables individual member states to veto any draft directive if they fear its enactment would affect fundamental aspects of their criminal justice system.

Furthermore, international treaties within the framework of the Council of Europe with implications for the national criminal procedural law, such as the European Convention of Human Rights, are part of the "European Criminal Law" as well.

Finally, we can define "European Criminal Law" as an instrument encompassing all rules of national criminal law as embraced, modified and complemented by EU law. These rules may be termed "Europeanized national criminal law". Last but not least, "European Criminal Law" includes the judicial cooperation in criminal matters on the basis of the principle of mutual recognition (see Art. 82 TFEU).

1.2 Principle of Mutual Recognition

The classical instrument of international cooperation in criminal matters is mutual assistance, which has been and still is shaped by various bilateral and multilateral conventions. The traditional law of judicial assistance is based on the sovereignty of states. For this reason, the traditional concepts are not suitable for the cooperation between states that, like the EU member states, aim for the creation of a common area of justice. This aim would be hindered if one, for example, were to cling to the classical prerequisite of double criminality within the law of extradition or to categorically refuse to extradite one's own citizens. In the EU, the law of extradition is soon to be replaced by the principle of mutual recognition. The fundamental meaning of this principle is now also outlined in Article 82(1) TFEU.

The principle of mutual recognition was originally developed by the Commission for the establishment of the internal market in order to achieve the marketability of goods without a time-consuming and difficult process of harmonisation of national provisions. Applied to criminal procedural law, this principle would mean that a judicial decision that was lawfully reached in one member state has to be recognised in every other member state. Legislative acts on the basis of the principle of mutual recognition are, for example, the European arrest warrant, the European evidence warrant and the transnational *ne bis in idem* principle (see Art. 54 CISA, Art. 50 EU FRCh).

The European Criminal Law after the entry into force of the Lisbon Treaty is characterised by strong tendencies towards harmonisation and enhanced judicial cooperation under the principle of mutual recognition. In the light of the above, the question arises how fundamental rights of a person pursued can be guaranteed.

2 Protection of Individual Rights in Europe

2.1 General Remarks

Different levels of the protection of fundamental rights were developed within the context of European integration.

At national level, the protection of fundamental rights is ensured by national constitutional law and national criminal procedure law. Here, the law enforcement bodies as well as the criminal courts have to respect the fundamental rights, which are enshrined in national criminal procedure and constitutional law. In this sense, national fundamental rights engage and restrict the exercise of public authority directly. For example, in Germany, decisions of the highest federal criminal court can be challenged by constitutional complaint if the person affected claims the violation of her fundamental rights.

At European level, the protection of fundamental rights is guaranteed, first, by the European Court of Justice (ECJ) on the basis of European Union law and, second, by the European Court of Human Rights (ECtHR) on the basis of the European Convention of Human Rights (ECHR). Here, the Fundamental Rights of the Union provide fundamental rights standards for a well-structured supranational system of government.

The system of the Union's Fundamental Rights protection includes the Charter of Fundamental Rights (CFR), which now became legally binding by Article 6 par.

1 TEU. As a consequence, the Charter now is part of the EU primary law. Guarantees of Fundamental Rights can also be found in some instruments of European Union legislation, such as in Article 54 CISA, that provides for a prohibition of transnational double jeopardy.

As expressed in Art. 53 ECHR, the European Convention of Human Rights establishes only a common minimum standard for all contracting parties that has to be implemented into national law. It does not conflict with those rights either granted by domestic law or other international instruments that exceed the guarantees of the Convention—irrespective of the rank the ECHR enjoys in domestic jurisdictions. The individual rights embodied in Arts. 47–50 CFR merely provide an absolute minimum standard.

2.2 The EU's Accession to the ECHR

Mainly for two reasons the EU could not become a party to the ECHR in the past. First, the EU did not have the competence to accede to the ECHR under EU law. Second, membership to the convention was reserved to members of the Council of Europe pursuant to Article 59(1) ECHR. This membership, in turn, was open to states only. Recent developments on December 2009 and January 2010 have changed the legal parameters. The Lisbon Treaty amended the EU Treaty, assigning the required competence for accession in Article 6(2) TEU and the Russian State Duma approved Additional Protocol No. 14 to the ECHR on 15 January 2010. It entered into force on 1 June 2010, 3 months after the deposit of the Russian instrument for ratification, and amended (*inter alia*) Article 59 ECHR by providing that the EU may accede to this Convention.

However, even after Additional Protocol No. 14 has entered into force, further obstacles have to be overcome. First, the member states to ECHR and the EU have to negotiate an accession treaty. Several amendments to the ECHR will also be necessary, for instance, concerning the appointment of an EU judge to the ECtHR and the admissibility of interstate applications by member states against the EU. Second, the Lisbon Treaty establishes a complicated procedure in Article 218 TFEU for accession treaties. Pursuant to Article 218(6) TFEU, it is the Council that adopts a decision concluding the agreement but has to obtain the consent of the European Parliament before doing so. The council must then act unanimously. Finally, the decision concluding the agreement will only enter into force if it is approved by all member states in accordance with their respective constitutional requirements. The ECHR, as an international treaty, would be incorporated into EU law and rank below the TEU and the TFEU (and also the CFR) but above ordinary secondary legislation within the EU framework.

Regardless of the accession of the EU to the ECHR, the convention already influences European Criminal Law today.

2.3 The Charter of Fundamental Rights (EU FRCh)

Since the Lisbon Treaty has entered into force, the ECHR and the case law of the ECtHR have become indirectly binding for the EU through the Charter of Fundamental Rights because of the reference in the Charter's preamble and the coherence clause in Article 52(3) EU FRCh. This provision states that the meaning and scope of those rights in the Charter that correspond to rights in the ECHR shall be the same as those laid down by the Convention. The EU FRCh in turn has become legally binding with the entry into force of the Lisbon Treaty. According to Article 6(1) TEU, the Charter is legally equivalent to the Treaties and is therefore binding for the EU. Due to Article 51(1) EU FRCh, its provisions are addressed to the institutions, bodies, offices and agencies of the Union as well as to the member states when implementing EU law. Additionally, Article 6(3) TEU incorporates the rights guaranteed by ECHR into EU law as they are constitutional traditions common to the member states. This provision in effect codifies the ECT's practice to "extract" common European fundamental rights by way of comparison of the member states' legal systems. The Court considered especially the ECHR a common denominator for fundamental rights because it is (and has been) legally binding on all EU member states.

2.4 The Relationship Between ECtHR and ECJ

EU organs are therefore indirectly bound by the ECHR. Within EU law, however, the scope of its relevance is determined by the European Court of Justice (ECJ). The ECtHR does not have any direct jurisdiction over EU law as long as the EU does not have access to the ECHR. This raises the question of how to deal with diverging interpretations of the ECHR by the ECJ and the ECtHR, although both courts have so far tried to interpret the Convention consistently.

The accession treaty will finally resolve the difficult question as to which court is competent to decide on fundamental rights issues in cases in which national authorities and courts of the member states apply EU law. Domestic authorities are like EU organs bound by the fundamental rights of European law when implementing EU law. Since these fundamental rights have to be interpreted in the light of the convention, domestic authorities are therefore bound by the ECHR through the fundamental rights of Union law as interpreted by the ECJ. At the same time, they have to comply with the Convention as organs of contracting parties to the ECHR. This raises the question as to whether the ECtHR had the competence to review whether a contracting party had violated its responsibilities under the Convention while implementing Union law and whether it could consequently claim (indirect) jurisdiction over EU law. The ECtHR has answered this question in a practical manner. As a starting point, the contracting parties remain bound to the Convention even when they act in the process of fulfilling European Union's obligations. However, state action taken in compliance with such legal obligations is justified as long as the relevant organisation is considered at least equivalent to that for which the Convention provides. By "equivalent" the Court means "comparable". In this case the presumption will be that a state has not departed from the requirements of the Convention. However, any such presumption can be rebutted if it is considered that the protection of Convention was manifestly deficient. The ECtHR presumes that the protection of fundamental rights exerted by the ECJ is equivalent to the protection provided by the ECtHR. As long as this presumption is not rebutted, the ECtHR will assume that the obligations imposed on contracting parties by the ECHR are met.

Thus, the development of the individual rights protection in European Criminal Law, especially the relationship between the ECtHR and the ECJ, will remain an exciting field of open questions for lawyers in practice and science.

Part I
Developments in European and Domestic Case Law in Criminal Matters

"Dialogue" Between European and National Courts, in the Pursuit of the Strongest Protection of Fundamental Rights (with Specific Regard to Criminal and Procedural Law)

Antonio Ruggeri

Contents

Abstract The paper highlights that the so-called dialogue between the Courts represents, at the same time, a *fact* and a *value*, and that the methodological

A. Ruggeri (✉)
Department of Law, University of Messina, Piazza Pugliatti, 98168 Messina, Italy
e-mail: Antonio.Ruggeri@unime.it

S. Ruggeri (ed.), *Human Rights in European Criminal Law*,
DOI 10.1007/978-3-319-12042-3_2

perspective best suited to revealing its essence is *axiological-substantial* in nature. It is a question in fact of establishing in the individual cases what *rule*, not *source* (Constitution or international charter of rights), is best suited in ensuring the "strongest" protection of fundamental rights. The parameter according to which this test is carried out is that of the dignity of the human person, a "super-constitutional value", contextualised yet also universally applicable. We then take into consideration some selected cases, specifically relating to criminal and procedural law, that show the commitment of the Courts in making their respective case law trends converge, without however renouncing the specificity of the legal system of provenance and with it the identity of the Courts themselves.

Keywords Convergences • Criminal and procedural law • "Dialogue" between European and national courts • Divergences in case law trends

1 The "Dialogue" Between the Courts: Notes on Method and Constitutional Theory

1.1 The Dual Value—Objective-Existential *and* Axiological-Normative—*of the "Dialogue" Between the Courts*

There has for some time been a heated debate on the "dialogue" between national and European Courts, with widely varying and even diametrically opposed views, with some commentators feeling that it may represent extremely serious risks for constitutional rights (some in particular, such as social rights[1]), which could suffer, and others conversely considering it a precious resource, which we can no longer do without, guaranteeing those same constitutional rights, both those expressly provided for and other "new" ones, which also, thanks to the aforementioned "dialogue", could enjoy appropriate protection.[2]

In terms of opportuneness, all these opinions are clearly legitimately sustainable, and therefore I would not like here to add my voice to one camp of scholars or the

[1] On this subject, see variously the proceedings of the conference on "I diritti sociali dopo Lisbona. Il ruolo delle Corti. Il diritto del lavoro fra riforme delle regole e vincoli di sistema", Reggio Calabria 5 November 2011, and *ivi*, in particular, Spadaro (2011); Salazar (2012); Panzera (2012); Rauti (2011); Guazzarotti (2011); Gambino (2012); Gargiulo (2011); Mezzetti and Morrone (2011); Romeo (2011a), pp. 487 ff. Also by Romeo (2011b). Other references, also *infra*.

[2] See, respectively, in the first camp, de Vergottini (2010) and Troilo (2011); in the second, amongst many, Conti (2011). Useful indications from a comparative perspective have recently been made in Martinico and Pollicino (2012), and Repetto (2013).

other. I will simply limit myself to showing that the "dialogue" in question is in any case a *fact*, in my opinion with a dual value, being both *objective-existential* and *axiological-normative*. In other words, it is, at the same time, a *fact* and a *value* or, rather, a fact that may (and must) be translated into a value. This may take place on the condition that the "dialogue" itself takes certain forms (and not others), stays within certain limits, and is directed and developed in a certain way.

In other terms, it is a question of establishing a theoretical framework within which the "dialogue" itself can take place and bear fruit. Straying outside this framework could end up having the opposite result, an inter-case-law conflict with unforeseeable outcomes and that, also for this reason, is harmful to rights or—which is basically the same thing—the incommunicability between those speaking different languages

That "dialogue" is an unconfutable objective fact is testified already by the fact that the European courts increasingly often mutually refer to each other,[3] as they also do to the most significant rulings of national courts (some in particular) from whose case law they draw on those "common constitutional traditions" that are seen as an inexhaustible reservoir for an effective, renewed protection of rights. At the same time, also in the rulings of national courts (both constitutional and ordinary[4]) there are now frequent references to the case law of European courts, especially in view of the fulfilment of those "new" rights that, in a growing number and demand, are to be safeguarded.[5]

It is, nevertheless, true that all the aforementioned references have a multiple value and respond to various needs: sometimes (even often) they are instead used as rhetorical artifices to support a decision that, with the mere use of parameters and criteria borrowed from the original legal system, the court maintains it can easily reach. These are thus artifices that serve at best to reinforce an argument that, even without them, is in any case considered solid. On other occasions, meanwhile, we have the impression that without the contribution offered by the international charters of rights (as far as regards the issue at hand here, the European Convention on Human Rights and the EU Charter of Fundamental Rights), the case would have had a different outcome.[6]

---

[3] ... as well as to non-European courts, as Groppi and Lecis Cocco-Ortu (2013) have rightly highlighted.

[4] In this paper, "ordinary case law" and "ordinary courts" are intended as referring to all courts or case law that ordinarily administer justice according to the organisation of jurisdiction in the legal system concerned. The role that ordinary courts play in Italy in the multilevel protection of fundamental rights is stressed with particular force in the aforementioned work by Conti, who has moreover dedicated a large number of studies to the issue (and, most recently among these, Conti 2014). *Adde* Ceccherini (2013), pp. 467 ff.

[5] This explains the increasingly insistent reference made in courtrooms to the dignity of the human person, regarding which see, albeit from a perspective different to that adopted here, Sperti (2013).

[6] Moreover, on various occasions, the Constitutional Court has made it clear that, due to the faulty way in which an issue of constitutional legitimacy has been presented (without reference to a violation of the European Convention on Human Rights), it has not been able to accept it, consequently leading to the cancellation of the rule of law at the basis of the dispute itself.

Highly indicative of the changing direction of case law is a ruling, albeit not very recent, of the Italian Constitutional Court, which, on one hand, admits the reciprocal support that the Constitution and Charter of Fundamental Rights give each other, contributing to their constant regeneration of meaning, and, on the other, states that the former, in any case (and, it would seem, for any right), offers a protection of rights that is no weaker than that provided by the Charters. Thus, in judgment no. 398 1999, the Constitutional Court argues that the Constitution and the Charters of Rights "integrate each other, mutually completing each other in interpretation"; just before, however, there is a warning that "human rights, also guaranteed by universal or regional conventions signed by Italy, are also expressed, *and guaranteed to no lesser extent*, in the Constitution" (there follows a reference to Constitutional Court no. 399 of 1998). Commenting on this, I saw the need to note how it expressed "a state of mind ... which was uncertain, not to say disturbed, vacillating between supranational openness and a retreat into naive and unproductive constitutional nationalism or patriotism".[7]

This sort of constitutional case law in Italy is extremely illuminating and leads us to reflect, both in terms of method and theory, on the various, immediate implications for the object of study here.

1.2 The Way in Which the Constitution and the International Charters of Rights Relate to Each Other, at the Service of the Dignity of Man: The Alternative Between a Total Constitution *and a* Partial Constitution

The answer to the issue concerned with these "dialogues" in fact raises further general questions that precede and determine the former, starting with the fundamental issue, which questions the very theory of the Constitution. In fact, we find ourselves having to choose between an idea of *total Constitution*, which says everything on everything and is thus able to satisfy man's every elementary need, and a *partial Constitution*, which acknowledges its own limits and seeks support from other Charters, since it is unable alone to provide full satisfaction.

The former is an almost sacred idea of Constitution, which starts with the assumption of its perfection and self-sufficiency, and originates from the idea, vigorously supported by the French revolutionaries, that the constituent power is an unlimited power, founding and not founded, able to create from nothing a new constitutional order based on fundamental principles untouchable by any act that is an expression of constituted power, even a law theoretically suitable to modify the Constitution. This is a theoretical framework, which increasingly intense international relations and the advanced process of supranational integration (which in turn

[7] Ruggeri (2013c), § 4.

has further highlighted the crisis of national sovereignty)[8] prove to be obsolete. Despite this, it is slavishly followed and repeated also by those who show that they are aware of the deep changes that have taken place in constitutional reality.

The other, conversely, is an idea that acknowledges the limited nature of the Constitution and is aware of the dual role performed by the Charters of Rights in the way they relate to the Constitution itself. In fact, on one hand, they contribute to the constantly updated interpretation of the declarations of the Constitution, while, on the other, they help compensate for its shortcomings and are thus applied in its place to protect those fundamental rights that it does not envisage.

I have already tried to point out that in this way, precisely when it seems to buckle under and retreat in the face of Charters of external origin, the Constitution is actually exalted, and fully realised.[9] The former Charters, in fact, in any case may demand to be held valid and to be implemented internally insofar as they excellently serve, in the objective conditions of the context, those trans-epochal, if not fully universal, values of freedom and equality that compose the fundamental axiological couple, both of the national legal system and of the relations between different legal systems. The *Grundnorm*, which is also an authentic *Grundwert*, is in fact provided by both the aforementioned values, each conceptually and positively non-independent, unable to demand enforcement if lacking the support offered by the other,[10] from whose combination justice is created. All together they form a sort of *trinity value*, which seems to reflect and translate the real *super-constitutional value*, namely the dignity of the human person.[11]

Expressed in another way, the Charters of Rights may influence the practice of legislative production and interpretation-application solely on the condition that they ensure a greater protection of freedom, equality, justice (and, ultimately, dignity) than would have been achieved by applying solely the Constitution, which in this way is thus taken to its utmost realisation, namely *magis ut valeat*.

Here is the heart of the question once more being dealt with, and here—as we see—there converge the indications from the Constitution and from the Charters of Rights themselves, the former and the latter having their *raison d'être*, the purpose that justifies their adoption and lasting application, in providing the greatest protection possible to rights.

There is an apparent (but it is, in fact, merely apparent) difference between the way in which the Charters relate to the Constitution and the way in which the Constitution in turn relates to them. The former, in fact, expressly acknowledge their "subsidiary" role with regard to the safeguards provided to rights in the

[8] We need merely think of the ultimatums imposed by the European Union on those states whose public accounts are not in order during the extremely serious current economic-financial crisis.

[9] ... also in the work last mentioned.

[10] On the mutual implications between the values in question, see, among many, Silvestri (2009).

[11] The idea of dignity as a *super-constitutional value* began to be discussed by Ruggeri and Spadaro (1991), pp. 343 ff.; this was followed, among others, by Drigo (2011), pp. 239 ff., and Salazar (2013a).

national sphere (see Article 53 of the Charter of Nice-Strasbourg and the ECHR), while the latter instead does not always explicitly profess such humility with regard to the former. This silence is very often intended rather as an implicit confirmation of the primacy of the national Charter, of its unquestionable "sovereignty".

In this way, we however make a serious mistake, not only of theoretical reconstruction, but above all of methodical perspective, by ignoring the basic fact that the Constitution, on a par with any other legislative document, should always be *construed in its entirety*, due to the way in which the statements that compose it create a "system".[12]

Thus, with specific regard to the Italian Constitution, in this way we unduly throw into shade the crucial meaning of the value of peace and justice between Nations, in whose name under Article 11 the limitation of state sovereignty is justified (and moreover imposed). This meaning is informed and justified—as we have seen—through the necessary reference to the axiological couple of liberty and equality (and, ultimately, dignity).

1.3 The Alternative Between a Systematic Approach Based on a Formal-Abstract or Axiological-Substantial Approach

On this crucial point, constitutional case law (and I shall refer here specifically to that of the Italian Constitutional Court regarding the role and condition of the ECHR in the Italian legal system) still oscillates between two opposite approaches to reconstructing the relations between the sources—at times formal-abstract, at others axiological-substantial.

On one hand, the Constitutional Court (starting with the famous "twin" judgments, judgment nos. 348 and 349 of 2007) argues that the ECHR (but this holds true for every other Charter and international law instrument in general[13]) has a "sub-constitutional" nature, thus establishing itself, certainly, as a parameter of the validity of the common laws, while being in turn obliged to comply with every constitutional rule (and not only the fundamental principles). On the other hand, however, the Constitutional Court admits that national laws, even if they fail to comply with the Convention, may nevertheless be applied, if it can be demonstrated that they lead to a more "intense" protection of rights (see, in particular, judgment no. 317 of 2009). This is an affirmation of extraordinary significance, perhaps not

[12] The most recent constitutional case law has insisted on the need to regard the Constitution as a "system", albeit in a theoretical-reconstructive context noticeably different from that which I personally espouse: see, therefore, the decisions of the Constitutional Court nos. 264 of 2012 and 1, 170 and 202 of 2013.

[13] . . . with the sole exception perhaps of agreements in a simplified form, whose binding force with regard to common laws is, as is known, questioned by many scholars.

yet appreciated in all its possible repercussions, since this is no longer a comparison between *sources*, on the basis of their formal connotations or origin, but is rather direct and exclusive, between *rules*, being a question in fact of establishing which of them offers the best service to rights. Upon closer examination, moreover, this affirmation, taken to its ultimate consequences, inevitably ends up involving the Constitution itself, since it cannot *a priori* rule out that it is precisely the norms of the Charters of external origin that provide that service *in place of the Constitution* and is also—as has been seen—in view of the optimal realisation of the *Constitution itself.*

The choice is therefore basically one of method, since it is necessary at the end to establish whether we should adopt a systematic approach, which is formal-abstract or—as here once again suggested—axiological-substantial in nature. And it is thus a question of verifying the implications of a theoretical-reconstructive nature that derive from one or the other methodical option. Thus, it is clear—at least, it seems to me—that, if we adopt the latter point of view, we cannot in theory place any limitation on the inclusion into the domestic constitutional order of rules that, even where they seem to depart from the very rules of the Constitution (even in its fundamental principles![14]), prove in reality to be even better suited to serving the values of freedom and equality (and, for this reason, of dignity), therefore raising even higher the point of synthesis of the constitutional values at stake.[15]

2 Order of the *Rules* (Rather Than *Sources*), in View of the Realization of the *Constitution as System*, Every Source (Constitution Included!) Possessing Vigour Conditioned to the Affirmation of Dignity, as *Contextualized Value* and, at the Same Time, *Universal Vocation*

The first of these implications, consequent to the adoption of a formal-abstract perspective, is the *static nature of the order of sources*, precisely since it is an order of *sources* and not of *rules*: each source is given its own "place" in the system, which derives from formal connotations and therefore does not vary depending on

[14] Contrary to an accredited and widespread opinion, the fundamental principles do not resist possible change, whenever this aims at the further promotion of the values expressed by the principles themselves, remaining in any case faithful to their original mould.

[15] The result is, for example, that the so-called doctrine of "counter-limits" against the entrance of norms of the European Union that are incompatible with the fundamental principles of the constitutional system, in the terms in which it is usually presented, may not be accepted, since no legal system may have *as its basis* a mixture of internal rules and rules of external origin. Rather, the system itself has to establish from time to time the way in which the rules themselves, whatever their form or origin, relate to the values of liberty and equality (and, ultimately, dignity).

the cases. On the contrary, the order of rules changes—as we know—by virtue of the cases themselves and of the interests that emerge in them.

The former approach, specifically because of the way in which domestic case law is created, leads at the same time to the *primacy of the Constitution* and to the *primacy of the Constitutional Court*. In this light, law in force is transformed into and expressed in the consistent case law (the so-called *diritto vivente*), which precisely the Constitutional Court is qualified to interpret, albeit not solely, since it also has to take into account the trends of ordinary case law. Unlike the order of rules, which—as we will immediately see—is circular in nature, the order of sources reveals a reconstruction of a pyramidal type, at whose apex stands in sovereign solitude a single Constitution and a single Court. The terrible risk inherent in such a methodical-theoretical approach, however, is to make the Constitutional Court a sort of monstrous *permanent constituent power*, whose "truths" of constitutional law are incontrovertible and, therefore, resistant to any other "truth" pronounced by other courts (and, in particular, by European courts). We are thus faced again with the disturbing question posed by Juvenal: *quis custodiet ipsos custodes*?

On the contrary, the order of rules admits that the "game" can allow continuously changing results: now to the benefit of this rule, then to that of another (or, therefore, this court and then another). The stabilisation of trends in case law, as a suitable guarantee for containing (albeit not entirely protecting from) this risk, may be precisely a result of the convergence, even practically identification in some cases, of the trends displayed by the European courts and those by national courts, which naturally fuel each other. And it is clear that, when bodies administering justice (whether of ordinary or constitutional nature[16]) are forced to take into account the legal systems of other bodies that also guarantee rights, the risk of sudden changes in case law trends is reduced, compared to what may often be seen in the rulings of constitutional courts that hide behind the principle of the unquestionability of their decisions, insofar as they are viewed as the first and ultimate guarantors of constitutional legality.

The "dialogue" between the case law of the various systems is then the best resource we have for preserving, in the practices in which the consistent case law is formed and renewed, the idea of the *Constitution as system.*

This statement can be fully understood, in its multiple applications to cases, when we return to considering that the comparison between rules, for the purposes of establishing where the most "intense" protection of rights is found, should be

[16] In the latter I include, although somewhat straining the point, also what happens in the European courts, which, while not abandoning their particular typical origin and nature, are de facto increasingly becoming materially constitutional courts, since they also are called to ensure compliance with those fundamental rights for whose protection the struggle was fought for the birth of Constitutions, in the meaning espoused in liberal legal systems. On the tendency of European courts to "constitutionalize themselves", see, among others, Pollicino (2010).

made in light of the fundamental and unifying value of the dignity of the human person.[17]

Dignity possesses, in my opinion,[18] a double value or, to say better, a double vocation, being at the same time a *contextualised value* and a *value with universal demands*. It is the former if we agree (as we must) that the notion of dignity varies from place to place and over time; it is, however, also the latter if we admit (as equally we must) that at its core it can be reduced to (and entirely coincides with) the *humanitas* of each person, which needs to be in every circumstance of their life, treated in fact as a person,[19] regardless of their merits or demerits.[20]

Through this way, we can thus obtain a constitutional notion of dignity, which largely coincides with the notion that can be derived from the Charters of Rights and results from the idea of the *Constitution as a system* that has in its fundamental positivised values its maximum and most genuine expression. A worthy person for the Constitution is someone who identifies with a model of organised political society profoundly characterised by democratic values (in all their forms and manifestations, such as direct democracy, representative and participatory democracy or—as it has also been called[21]—"pluralist" democracy); a society in which the differences (of all kinds: colour of one's skin, language, religion, gender or sexual orientation, social conditions in general) not only are not a cause of discrimination but are, on the contrary, seen as precious resources for the growth and enrichment of each individual and the entire community; a society in which each of its members is put in a position to be able to realise their life projects, without however compromising those of others; a society, in brief—as we have been saying—in which freedom and equality are the core around which the most important experiences of social life revolve and are linked to.

Dignity—as we can see—is then fuelled by liberty and equality, but the latter two draw strength from the former, together with their direction and the way in

[17] Scholarship for some time has been debating without however achieving consensus of opinion, on the criterion in application of which it may be possible to establish, without excessive uncertainties, which Charter from time to time provides the most "intense" protection of the rights at stake. Among the many others and variously, in addition to Conti (2011); Butturini (2/2010), pp. 1816 ff.; Panzera (2011), pp. 299 ff., espec. pp. 303 ff.; Randazzo (2011), pp. 313 ff.; Salazar (2013a), section II. Lastly, see also Ruggeri (2011b).

[18] Information on the issue can be found in Ruggeri (2011a).

[19] Among others, Camerlengo (2007), espec. pp. 338 ff., has greatly insisted on this latter point.

[20] Silvestri (2013), § 2 observed that dignity "does not need to be 'deserved' by the individual person and may not ever be lost". It has been effectively argued by Glendon (2007), p. 98, that, from a Christian point of view, "human rights are based on the duty of each person to fulfil their own dignity, which in turn obliges them to respect the 'donated' spark of dignity present in others, whatever they may have done". According, instead, to Zagrebelsky (1995), p. 34, "if human rights are founded on the value of man, and if we admit that not all men have the same value, ... it will be necessary to say: not the same rights for everyone, but for everyone the rights they have deserved".

[21] I would like here, once again, to refer to my late teacher, Martines, who dedicated memorable works to this connotation of democratic value, still today with theoretical significance and incredibly relevant (among many, see Martines 1957, 2000, pp. 239 ff.).

which they are implemented, in a sole constitutional circular process that recharges and renews itself without respite.

In such a theoretical-reconstructive context, opening up to the international order and to supranational legal systems (specifically to the European Union) plays a role of prime importance and acts as a vehicle for that introduction of external rules in a national context whose first and most fundamental *raison d'etre* is precisely the need to fulfil the demands of dignity. This phenomenon—as we have seen—reveals a *conditioned force of the sources of law* (of *all* the sources, including the Constitution therefore), which can be expanded or contracted like an accordion to achieve the optimal solution in a given case, *according to value*, i.e., by virtue of their capacity to provide from time to time the most intense protection of rights. No source, basically, may presume that it is *always* valid, *in any case*; it is, rather, valid if and insofar as it demonstrates that it serves the fundamental needs of man and, in the final analysis, his dignity.

3 Converging and Diverging Trends in Case Law in the Field of Criminal Law and the Decision-Making Techniques Used by the Constitutional Court to Free Itself from the Pressure Applied by the European Courts (in Particular, Circumscribing the Obligation to Observe European Case Law to Mere "Substance" and the Need to Enforce in Any Case the *Constitution as System*)

Case law in criminal matters represents an ideal test bench for checking how watertight the approach summarily described here actually is.

The overall picture seems to be full of relevant case law,[22] as well as being particularly articulated, and shows that we are still at an early stage in the process of the mutual integration of the Charters in terms of interpretation and the service of fundamental rights. We will here highlight only some of the most important aspects of this picture, taking examples here and there from European and Italian case law (and, in particular, constitutional case law[23]), solely for the purpose of identifying elements that may be useful for reconstructive ends.

---

[22] And this moreover is confirmed by the constant monitoring of the developments in case law in Italy and Europe, found in www.penalecontemporaneo.it (see, for example, in the latter, Romeo 2013).

[23] Reasons of space force me to sacrifice here ordinary case law, and this is a real shame, since it too, especially in its most advanced manifestations, represents a precious asset if we wish to describe (I won't say comprehensively, but almost) as faithfully as possible the level achieved in the mutual acknowledgment of the system of the Constitution and the Charters of Rights. Moreover, in quite a few cases, ordinary case law has not merely passively followed the indications given to it by European and Italian constitutional case law, but rather it has given an active,

On one hand, the convergence of the Charters, as takes place in consistent case law through the work performed on a daily basis by their Courts, is undeniable and can be seen clearly. This should therefore be favourably welcomed, also due to the influence that it has already had and may have in the future in view of greater supranational integration and the growing intensification of bonds of solidarity between the states in the international community.

On the other hand, however, it is difficult to eliminate the resistance resulting from the aspiration of each Court—an aspiration that remains unappeased and from time to time clearly re-emerges—to reaffirm its primacy over the other Courts. We can thus say, wishing to anticipate a conclusion that will become even clearer shortly, that the "model" summarily presented here of the relationships between Charters (and between Courts) ends up being confirmed and then refuted: both the former and the latter are temporary, are inconstant and may be used to support or reject the model itself, for the way in which it is translated into experience.

To be sure, we should rather perform an analysis by distinct material fields and even typed for the same field, by virtue of the cases studied and the interests at stake.

Case law, moreover, as is known, is created and constantly renewed; it is therefore no surprise if even with regard to the same right, in its various applications to the events of life, we see one kind of result and then another.

The Courts have a wide range of techniques for decision-making (which, as is known, they have wisely and elegantly moulded themselves, for themselves), which allow them to distance themselves from a trend in the case law of other courts if they consider it "inconvenient" or embarrassing, especially if the trend appears to be excessively overpowering.

I will restrict myself here to merely mentioning a couple of these, which have been encountered a number of times in experience, and refer specifically to the use made of them by the Italian Constitutional Court, before going on to mention some of the main occasions in which the divarication of the positions between this Court and European Courts has emerged, albeit ably disguised.

The first technique is the recognition of the obligation deriving from the case law of the Court of Strasberg but limited to its mere "substance". The court then, when it has to interpret national laws in line with the Convention (and, therefore, all things considered, with its Court), is not obliged to apply European case law in every part but only to take into consideration its "substance". What all this means, in terms of theory and practice, is not yet clear, and I fear that it will not become so in the future either. To be sure, the criterion of "substance" can be used for selections of case law

---

and not secondary, contribution to its renewal. Unfortunately, as far as I am aware, there is so far no organic study that clarifies the relationship of mutual *give and take* that has existed (and continues to) between the two types of case law, although there are some specific sectorial studies of certain interest (for example, with regard to criminal law, the monograph by Manes 2012a, in which we find perceptive observations of a theoretical-reconstructive type; also by Manes 2012b, pp. 839 ff.).

I feel that this gap urgently needs to be filled.

according to convenience, regardless of how difficult it may be to discard case law that is in line with a consolidated trend based on a significant number of rulings all in the same direction.

The second technique is the guarantee provided not so much to the individual right as to the rights in their joint creation of a "system", not only among themselves but also related to other constitutionally protected assets or interests. This is perhaps an even more refined technique than the previous one, since, while it is not clear what the basis of the former is,[24] the latter may be supported by reference to a concept, that of the "system", which, albeit requiring specification, nonetheless belongs to the tradition of legal studies, and therefore possesses a theoretically suggestive evocative force.

4 Selected Cases from European and Constitutional Case Law in the Criminal and Procedural Fields: Agreements and Conflicts

Here, we can also find the most significant differences between the international Charters and the national Charter of rights, since, while the former mostly contain the acknowledgment exclusively, or prevalently, of rights alone, the latter also provides "cover" for interests of another nature, such as those referring to problems of financial equilibrium, which the States, especially in the current economic crisis, are obliged to take into account.

Contrary to the opinion manifested by the scholarship mentioned at the beginning of this paper, particularly concerned about the destiny of social rights, comprehensively protected by the Constitution but instead lacking similar protection under the European Charters (specifically the ECHR and the EU Charter itself), on some occasions even greater attention has been given to the rights themselves by European judges than by the Constitutional Court, which has not infrequently balanced (in an *unbalanced*, penalising way) the rights in question against the strict needs of financial equilibrium.[25]

In this regard, the so-called laws of authentic interpretation (*leggi di interpretazione autentica*) offer an enlightening example: the Strasbourg Court has judged them as unsuitable for interfering with trials in progress,[26] whereas

---

[24] Why on earth, we may wonder, should the obligation be reduced only *by half* (or even less), to the "hard core" of European case law, even if we suppose that the "substance" can be identified and entirely dealt with in reference to it?

[25] See, on this point, of crucial importance for my position, Ruggeri (2013a) and the views of Cappuccio (2012), pp. 65 ff.; Caretti (2012); Tega (2012); and Guazzarotti (1/2013), pp. 9 ff. Most recently, perceptive observations have been made in Salazar (2013c). Other indications can be found in the works referred to above in note 1.

[26] I am referring in particular to the well-known cases *Agrati v. Italy* and *Maggio v. Italy*, which—as is known—have attracted a real tidal wave of comments.

priority has been given by Italian constitutional judges[27] in the name of those "imperative reasons of public interest" that also the European Court deems worthy of being taken into consideration. The point, however, is that the Italian Constitutional Court maintains that it has exclusive and unquestionable competence with regard to the question of whether or not to acknowledge them,[28] basically coming to the conclusion that they must always (or almost always[29]) be given priority when performing balancing operations. This is due to the fact that one of these reasons is precisely the value of legal certainty, a value that—as is known—is *per tabulas* cited to justify the adoption of the aforementioned laws.

In the concrete case, the hidden (yet clearly visible) value was given by the expenditure of significant sums of money that should have been sustained by the state treasury in order to satisfy the demands of claimants damaged by the adoption of laws that clearly did not "interpret" but rather innovated the laws that embodied damage to the rights of the claimants themselves.[30]

Constitutional case law expressed a different meaning and equally different significance to legal certainty in ruling no. 113 of 2011, which declared as unconstitutional the failure of Article 630 of the Italian Code of Criminal Procedure to include as a justification for review of a trial the existence of a ruling by the European Court, which has found a violation of the ECHR during the trial itself. This well-known decision has been subject to comments of various kinds,[31] showing the emblematic "loyal cooperation" offered by the Italian Constitutional Court to European courts. It is obviously not important here to report the merit or assess

[27] For example, in judgment no. 311 of 2009 and others.

[28] This, however, may not be taken lightly by the European Court, and in fact this is the source of the conflict.

[29] We can exclude the presence of the imperative reasons mentioned above in the case recently settled in judgment no. 170 of 2013, which declared the constitutional illegitimacy of legislation that, with a retroactive effect, went beyond the *res judicata* in the field of bankruptcy proceedings (the so-called *giudicato endo-fallimentare*), in violation of the principles of equality and reasonableness, as well as of the European Convention on Human Rights. This is a ruling in which we see an effort to highlight the affinity of the case law trends of the Court of Strasbourg with that of the Italian Constitutional Court itself, which however—as I will try to demonstrate here—while encountering the circumstance in question, does not seem to possess general applicability.

[30] Another question, which however we cannot deal with here, regards the nature, at any rate innovative, of the so-called "interpretative laws", which, as is known, has been discussed in perceptive scholarship (references can be found in Laneve 2012, pp. 201 ff.). What this nonetheless means here is that, albeit with all good will, the legislative discipline referred to in the text did not fall within the linguistic-conceptual framework drawn by the previous discipline but clearly extended outside it. The confines marked by the text—as is known—remain, in some places marked and resistant, in others less so; in the cases mentioned above, they are quite frankly strained.

[31] Among which I mention here only those at the round table on "Giudicato 'europeo' e giudicato penale italiano: la svolta della Corte costituzionale", in Legislazione penale, 2/2011, pp. 463 ff., with contributions by Canzio, Kostoris, Chiavario and Ruggeri, the latter of which contains some observations also taken up here. The most organic treatment in Italian scholarship, in which an attentive study is made of the numerous, serious issues regarding judgments in the face of supervening rulings by the European Court, is that of Sciarabba (2013).

the solidity of the arguments adduced to support it.[32] It is important only to observe that, according to a large number of scholars, the value of legal certainty has been balanced against the right of defence, with priority given to the latter, in the name of ensuring a fair trial.

To be sure, once again what was at stake here was a taking of sides, in terms of method, choosing between a formal-abstract approach and an axiological-substantial one. The latter in particular may profitably allow us to observe the assets at stake (and the rules that regard them), in their mutual combinations in given cases.

For those who, like me, are used to reconstructing the dynamics of regulation and the "system" based on them, starting with the latter of the perspectives mentioned above, the conclusion is simple, unavoidable. Namely, the only *legal certainty in an objective sense*, recognised by case law on many occasions as being a supreme constitutional value, entitled to affirm itself, is the *certainty of constitutional rights*, in other words those rights that, as the unsurpassed lesson of the French Revolution tells us, are the essence of the *Constitution in a material sense* (note the well-known definition of Article 16 of the Declaration of 1789).

It is thus not appropriate, in my opinion, *from the perspective of constitutional law*,[33] in the situation just mentioned, to talk of a reduction in the extent or significance of legal certainty, consequent to its being used in operations of balancing, in the course of which it has, all things considered, a recessive nature. On the other hand, we can (and must) talk of its affirmation, completely appreciable in an axiological perspective, resulting from an adequate assessment of the rights *of the* trial and of the rights *in the* trial, as always assuming as a necessary parameter for judges the inviolable dignity of the human person.

In this field we clearly see the different methodical-theoretical approach to the trend of Court of Justice case law, which recently has included significant expressions in the criminal and procedural field with the famous *Melloni* ruling, regarding performance of the European arrest warrant.[34] Specifically, in points 57 et seq. of the ruling, there in fact emerges a conception that dangerously places the guarantee of fundamental rights after other interests, such as the mutual trust among the Member States of the Union in implementing their decisions, thus allowing the Union itself to become a "space of liberty security and justice".[35]

---

[32] Important support for the rulings of the Court of Strasbourg has now come from judgment no. 210 of 2013 of the Constitutional Court, then taken up in order no. 235 of the same year, which recognised the value of pilot judgments and thus placed the basis for their effective and widespread observance by judges (on the rulings, see the notes by di Viganò 2013a, b; Romeo 2013).

[33] . . ., or rather, from an *axiologically orientated* perspective, which in other words sees the Constitution, in its essence, as being composed of a handful of positivised fundamental values, in the light of which therefore both the dynamics of regulation and those of interpretation-application may receive their correct collocation and organisation.

[34] Grand Chamber, 25 February 2013.

[35] Recently, also Epidendio (2013), pp. 451 ff., urges us to consider the point; cf. Vecchio (2013), pp. 454 ff., and the perceptive comments of De Amicis (2013) and Conti (2013), pp. 109 ff.

The point is that here the real thing at stake—as made clear by the commitment proceedings of the Spanish Constitutional Court—was the importance to give to the principle of the primacy of EU law: in other words, whether this held true unconditionally or whether it was itself subject to axiologically informed balancing. The Luxembourg judges had no hesitation whatsoever in taking sides with the aforementioned principle, aware of the fact that, once the protective net of supranational law had been widened, the terrible risk it would be exposed to would have been that of having to stand by and helplessly witness the loss of interests whose protection is the very condition of the maintenance of the Union, even more than its further advancement along the path of full supranational integration.

When making an initial comment on the decision in question, I felt it is appropriate to point out that the result of the reasoning may have been similar but following a different line of argument.[36] The Court in fact seems strangely to neglect the provisions of Article 4 of the TEU as reformed by the Lisbon Treaty, which—as is known—solemnly affirms the Union's obligation to respect the structural principles of the national legal systems, including—it is superfluous to mention here—that of safeguarding as "intensely" as possible the objective conditions of the context, the inviolable rights of man (and, in the final analysis, of his dignity).[37] There is no explicit reference, adequately argued, to the aforementioned provision, whatever is stated in widespread scholarship, which argues that in any case it can be read between the lines of the grounds for the decision in question.

Thus, the right to defence, which however may be balanced against the interest in the functionality of the trial, does not seem in this circumstance to have been compromised, since the measure restricting liberty had been notified to the counsel of the defendant who had decided not to attend the trial. The principle of a fair trial, on the other hand, has multiple expressions, all equally deserving protection, and in any case has to reconcile subjective positions with needs of an objective nature, linked to the carrying out of the trial according to schedules and methods that in any case guarantee the fruitful pursuit of truth and satisfy the demands for justice that lie at its basis.

With regard to the right to defence (and, in general, to the safeguard of subjective positions), the position of the Italian Court, in relation to that on the point adopted by the European Courts, is complex and inconstant. This further confirms the changeable nature of case law, which is extremely difficult to pin down in terms of a given "direction" in the strict sense of the term (which suggests linearity and continuity over time).

On one hand, the Constitutional Court has not hesitated, on various occasions (even recently), to base its decisions on European case law, without highlighting—

[36] See, therefore, Ruggeri (2013b).

[37] On the principle referred to in Article 4, see recently Guastaferro (2012), pp. 263 ff., and Vecchio (2012).

at least explicitly—any difference in the way of intending the law itself.[38] On the other hand, however, subjecting the principle of the retroactivity of criminal law to different and further limits than those deducible from Article 6 ECHR visibly circumscribes the guarantees provided to the person, with repercussions on their expectations of protection (and therefore, ultimately, of dignity).[39]

We have here a further example of that reference to the "system", with the variety of the interests expressed in it, all in theory deserving consideration and thus entitled to participate in balancing operations, which however not infrequently result in a marked restriction of rights.

Upon close examination—as mentioned above and we are now able fully to grasp—fundamentally (and, at least up to certain point, understandably) the *cultural moulds* that inform and justify the "directions" consolidated in the courts administering Italian and non-Italian laws respectively are different. The very conception of law and the role, serving it, that judges in their respective spheres of operation and duties are called to perform is clearly different.

We need merely think of the different notions of the principle of *nulla pena sine lege*, which seem to be adopted by the ECtHR and the Italian Constitutional Court. That emerging from the case law of the former is clearly wider ranging,[40] insofar as it is extended not only to the right of legislative production but also to that of case law production,[41] while that of the latter Court is more restricted,[42] being anchored to an older (but by now inexorably obsolete) tradition affirmed in positive systems of *civil law*, which considers that the *verum ius* should be restricted to legislative law alone.[43]

Yet also in relation to such an important issue there are, once again, some evident vacillations and contradictions that make the Italian constitutional case law extremely unstable. We need merely think of the fact that shortly before the adoption of the ruling just referred to, the Constitutional Court, on another

---

[38] For example, in judgment no. 143 of 2013, with regard to interviews with the lawyers of defendants or convicted offenders held according to special detention rules (see, for all, the comment by Manes and Napoleoni 2013). A reference to Strasbourg case law (in particular the *Torreggiani* case) was also seen in judgment no. 235 of 2013, in the penitentiary field (and on this, the note by Della Bella 2013).

[39] See, for example, the approach taken in judgment no. 236 of 2011, compared to that emerging from the cases *Scoppola v. Italy*, *Morabito v. Italy*, *Agrati v. Italy* and, most recently, *Maktouf and Damjanovi v. Bosnia-Herzegovina*, as defined by the Strasbourg Court. Extensive references to the *Scoppola* case have most recently been found in judgment no. 210 and in order no. 235 of 2013, which highlight an effort to move closer to the positions of the European courts, of which, however, we await further confirmation.

[40] See, in particular, the cases *Sud Fondi v. Italy* and *Previti v. Italy*.

[41] This is explained by the vastness of the territories and variety of legal systems to which the Convention is applied, with recipients operating in contexts of both common and civil laws.

[42] See, especially, judgment no. 230 of 2012 (and, among the many comments on it, Colombi 2013; Falcinelli 2013; Mazza 2012, pp. 3464 ff.; Manes 2012c, pp. 3474 ff.; Ruggeri 2012b, c).

[43] A general reflection on the principle of legality, together with perceptive observations of a theoretical-reconstructive nature, can be seen in Salazar (2013b).

occasion,[44] in a certain way assimilated case law with statutory law, while not in terms of its legal nature, at least on the level of its effects, resubmitting certain issues of constitutional legitimacy to the original authorities for a new assessment of their relevance, in the light of an innovative (with respect to the moment they were originally submitted) direction in European case law. It has, then, basically treated the latter exactly as it usually does in the presence of *ius superveniens*, whose adoption justifies the possible rethinking of the procedural initiative implemented by ordinary courts that seek a decision from the Constitutional Court.[45]

5 A Brief Final Observation: Confirmation of the Courts' Efforts to Establish a Fruitful Reciprocal "Dialogue" While at the Same Time Safeguarding Their Legal Systems of Provenance and Individual Identity

The conclusion of this quick review, circumscribed, as mentioned, solely to some cases taken by way of a sample, in which constitutional case law is combined with that of the European courts, seems to confirm that the effort to initiate and bring to fruition a constructive "dialogue" has been made by all the courts to an appreciable extent, while at the same time each one of them is concerned with safeguarding the specificity of the legal system of provenance and with this, their identity. Convergences and divergences should thus be seen in this light, and, apart from the overall lack of argument to be found in some rulings and the varyingly satisfying results achieved on the basis of them, it remains true that the former and the latter can be explained by the need, felt by all those working in the legal field, to pursue the most suitable forms for their convergence, while also maintaining and further transmitting over time the traits typical of each legal system.

This confirms the conclusion, which I have already discussed in other contributions, of the equal legal status of the international charters of rights and the Constitution, which mainly implies that we are currently witnessing an *interconstitutional order in progress*,[46] i.e., an order in which there is not, nor may be, the undisputed, sole "sovereignty" of the Constitution as *fons fontium*, the only point holding up the entire system, also in terms of its relations with other legal systems. This is due to the simple fact that the very Constitution is—if we can put it this way—an *interconstitution*, as is evident in its expressive identifying trait, namely

[44] See order no. 150 of 2012 (and, on it, among the many comments, Repetto 2012, pp. 2069 ff.; Romboli 2013, and writings referred to there, as well as, if wished, also Ruggeri 2012a).

[45] I will omit here to observe that in general the Constitutional Court recognises that the constant case law, which is created in courtrooms, is the subject of judgments of constitutionality, even though it is frequently set aside in the name of consistent interpretation.

[46] I began to discuss this in Ruggeri (2001), pp. 544 ff.

the principle whereby it is "open" to international and supranational laws and creates a "system" with the remaining fundamental principles. This principle ensures that the Constitution embraces and to a certain extent internalises all the rules of an external origin (and, among them, first of all those that acknowledge and safeguard fundamental rights) that have been proved to serve the principles of liberty, equality, justice and, last of all (or first of all...), dignity.

The inverse is also true, i.e., that the international charters themselves may aspire to their full "constitutionalisation" on the sole condition that they deem themselves to be servants of rights, and therefore prepared to measure themselves against national Constitutions, to give way to the latter if necessary, to be influenced by them and semantically regenerated by them, continuously and profoundly.

The best guarantee that the specificities particular to each Charter (and, more widely, to each system of norms, whether internal or external) will not be lost, but rather further, substantially preserved, is given by the fact that no charter (or Court) may—as said—insanely boast that it is the "Charter of Charters" (or the "Supercourt"), since even if the process of supranational integration should finally reach full maturation, the *interconstitutional order* we are talking about will not only not be superseded but moreover will finally have achieved its firmest rooting and maximum development.

This alone is therefore the true meaning of the "dialogue": the healthy competition between the Charters (or Courts) to see who can offer more and better to protect fundamental rights (and, ultimately, dignity). The fruits that each of them is able to make available to the courts should remain distinct but harmoniously unifiable, in order to satisfy (despite the difficult conditions of the present) the pressing and deserving needs (and, ultimately, the dignity) of each human being.

References

Butturini D (2010) La partecipazione paritaria della Costituzione e della norma sovranazionale all'elaborazione del contenuto indefettibile del diritto fondamentale. Osservazioni a margine di Corte cost. n. 317 del 2009. Giurisprudenza costituzionale, pp 1816 ff

Camerlengo Q (2007) Contributo ad una teoria del diritto costituzionale cosmopolitico. Giuffrè, Milano

Cappuccio L (2012) Differenti orientamenti giurisprudenziali tra Corte EDU e Corte costituzionale nella tutela dei diritti. In: Decaro C et al (eds) La "manutenzione" della giustizia costituzionale. Il giudizio sulle leggi in Italia, Spagna e Francia. Giappichelli, Torino, pp 65 ff

Caretti P (2012) I diritti e le garanzie. www.rivistaaic.it. Accessed 19 Nov 2012

Ceccherini E (2013) L'integrazione fra ordinamenti e il ruolo del giudice. Diritto pubblico ed europeo: II, pp 467 ff

Colombi F (2013) Gli strumenti di garanzia dei diritti fondamentali fra Costituzione e CEDU: riserva di legge e base legale. Riflessioni a margine di un *obiter dictum* di Corte cost. sent. 8 ottobre 2012, n. 230. www.rivistaaic.it. Accessed 13 Sept 2013

Conti R (2011) La Convenzione europea dei diritti dell'uomo. Il ruolo del giudice. Aracne, Roma

Conti R (2013) Il caso Melloni: Corte Giust. Unione Europea 26 febbraio 2013 (Grande Sezione) C-399/11. Un'occasione da non perdere per alimentare il dialogo fra Giudici. Cultura e diritti, pp 109 ff

Conti R (2014) I giudici ed il biodiritto. Un esame concreto dei casi difficili e del ruolo del giudice di merito, della Cassazione e delle Corti europee. Aracne, Roma

De Amicis G (2013) All'incrocio tra diritti fondamentali, mandato d'arresto europeo e decisioni contumaciali: la Corte di giustizia e il "caso Melloni". www.penalecontemporaneo.it. Accessed 7 June 2013

de Vergottini G (2010) Oltre il dialogo tra le Corti. Giudici, diritto straniero, comparazione. Il Mulino, Bologna

Della Bella A (2013) La Corte costituzionale stabilisce che l'Amministrazione penitenziaria è obbligata ad eseguire i provvedimenti assunti dal Magistrato di sorveglianza a tutela dei diritti dei detenuti. www.penalecontemporaneo.it. Accessed 13 June 2013

Drigo C (2011) La dignità umana quale valore (super)costituzionale. In: Mezzetti L (ed) Principî costituzionali. Giappichelli, Torino, pp 239 ff

Epidendio TE (2013) Il caso *Melloni*: il nodo irrisolto del massimo standard di tutela dei diritti fondamentali. Quaderni costituzionali, pp 451 ff

Falcinelli D (2013) In nome della legge penale italiana. Giudici d'Europa, custodi del diritto penale (appunti sulla sentenza della Corte costituzionale n. 230/2012). Focus *Human Rights*. www.federalismi.it. Accessed 16 Sept 2013

Gambino S (2012) Constitutionnalismes nationaux et constitutionnalisme européen: les droits fondamentaux sociaux, la Charte des droits de l'Union Européenne et l'identité constitutionnelle nazionale. www.federalismi.it. Accessed 21 Mar 2012

Gargiulo P (ed) (2011) Politica e diritti sociali nell'Unione europea. Quale modello sociale europeo? Jovene, Napoli

Glendon MA (2007) Il fondamento dei diritti umani: il lavoro incompiuto, ora in Carozza P G, Cartabia M Tradizioni in subbuglio. Rubbettino, Soveria Mannelli

Groppi T, Lecis Cocco-Ortu AM (2013) Le citazioni reciproche tra la Corte europea e la Corte interamericana dei diritti dell'uomo: dall'influenza al dialogo? www.federalismi.it. Accessed 25 Sept 2013

Guastaferro B (2012) Beyond the *exceptionalism* of constitutional conflicts: the *ordinary* functions of the identity clause. Yearbook of European Law 31:263 ff

Guazzarotti A (2011) The European Court of Human Rights as counterbalance: looking for synergies between the ECHR, ILO and ESC case law. www.europeanrights.eu. Accessed 14 Nov 2011

Guazzarotti A (2013) I diritti sociali nella giurisprudenza della Corte europea dei diritti dell'uomo. Rivista trimestrale di diritto pubblico, pp 9 ff

Laneve G (2012) Le leggi interpretative nella centralità dell'attività d'interpretazione. In press in Studi in onore di Loiodice A. I. Cacucci, Bari, pp 201 ff

Manes V (2012a) Il giudice nel labirinto. Profili delle intersezioni tra diritto penale. Aracne, Roma

Manes V (2012b) I principi penalistici nel network multilivello: trapianto, palingenesi, *cross-fertilization*. Rivista italiana di diritto e procedura penale, pp 839 ff

Manes V (2012c) Prometeo alla Consulta: una lettura dei limiti costituzionale all'equiparazione tra 'diritto giurisprudenziale' e 'legge'. Giurisprudenza costituzionale, pp 3474 ff

Manes V, Napoleoni V (2013) Incostituzionali le restrizioni ai colloqui difensivi dei detenuti in regime di "carcere duro": nuovi tracciati della Corte in tema di bilanciamento dei diritti fondamentali. www.penalecontemporaneo.it. Accessed 3 July 2013

Martines T (1957) Contributo ad una teoria giuridica delle forze politiche. Giuffrè, Milano

Martines T (2000) La democrazia pluralista. In Opere, I, Teoria generale. Giuffrè, Milano, pp 239 ff

Martinico G, Pollicino O (2012) The interaction between Europe's legal systems. Judicial dialogue and the creation of supranational laws, Elgar E, Cheltenham – Northampton

Mazza A (2012) Il principio di legalità nel nuovo sistema penale liquido. Giurisprudenza costituzionale, pp 3464 ss

Mezzetti L, Morrone A (eds) (2011) Lo strumento costituzionale dell'ordine pubblico europeo. Nei sessant'anni della Convenzione per la salvaguardia dei diritti dell'uomo e delle libertà fondamentali (1950–2010). Giappichelli, Torino

Panzera C (2011) Un passo alla volta. A proposito della più recente giurisprudenza costituzionale sulla CEDU. In: Dal Canto F, Rossi E (eds) Corte costituzionale e sistema istituzionale. Giappichelli, Torino, pp 299 ff

Panzera C (2012) Per i cinquant'anni della Carta sociale europea. www.gruppodipisa.it. Accessed 28 Feb 2012

Pollicino O (2010) Allargamento ad est dello spazio giuridico europeo e rapporto tra Corti costituzionali e Corti europee. Verso una teoria generale dell'impatto interordinamentale del diritto sovranazionale? Giuffrè, Milano

Randazzo A (2011) Alla ricerca della tutela più intensa dei diritti fondamentali, attraverso il "dialogo" tra le Corti. In: Dal Canto F, Rossi E (eds) Corte costituzionale e sistema istituzionale, Giappichelli, Torino, pp 313 ff

Rauti A (2011) La "giustizia sociale" presa sul serio. Prime riflessioni. www.forumcostituzionale.it. Accessed 22 Dec 2011

Repetto G (2012) Corte costituzionale, fecondazione eterologa e precedente CEDU "*superveniens*": i rischi dell'*iperconcretezza* della questione di legittimità costituzionale. Giurisprudenza costituzionale, pp 2069 ff

Repetto G (ed) (2013) The constitutional relevance of the ECHR in domestic and European law. An Italian perspective. Intersentia, Cambridge

Romboli R (2013) Lo strumento della restituzione degli atti e l'ordinanza 150/2012: il mutamento di giurisprudenza della Corte Edu come *ius superveniens* e la sua incidenza per la riproposizione delle questioni di costituzionalità sul divieto di inseminazione eterologa. www.giurcost.org. Accessed 26 Feb 2013

Romeo G (2011a) Civil rights v. social rights nella giurisprudenza della Corte europea dei diritti dell'uomo: c'è un giudice a Strasburgo per i diritti sociali? In: Mezzetti L, Morrone A (eds) Lo strumento costituzionale dell'ordine pubblico europeo. Nei sessant'anni della Convenzione per la salvaguardia dei diritti dell'uomo e delle libertà fondamentali (1950–2010). Giappichelli, Torino

Romeo G (2011b) La cittadinanza sociale nell'era del cosmopolitismo: uno studio comparato. Cedam, Padova

Romeo G (2013) Giudicato penale e resistenza alla *lex mitior* sopravvenuta: note sparse a margine di Corte cost. n. 210 del 2013. www.penalecontemporaneo.it. Accessed 1 Oct 2013

Ruggeri A (2001) Sovranità dello Stato e sovranità sovranazionale, attraverso i diritti umani, e le prospettive di un diritto europeo "intercostituzionale". Diritto pubblico comparato ed europeo, pp 544 ff

Ruggeri A (2011a) Dignità *versus* vita? www.rivistaaic.it

Ruggeri A (2011b) Rapporti tra Corte costituzionale e Corti europee, bilanciamenti interordinamentali e "controlimiti" mobili, a garanzia dei diritti fondamentali. www.rivistaaic.it

Ruggeri A (2012a) La Corte costituzionale, i parametri "conseguenziali" e la tecnica dell'assorbimento dei vizi rovesciata (a margine di Corte cost. n. 150 del 2012 e dell'anomala restituzione degli atti da essa operata con riguardo alle questioni di costituzionalità relative alla legge sulla procreazione medicalmente assistita). www.giurcost.org. Accessed 12 June 2012

Ruggeri A (2012b) Penelope alla Consulta: tesse e sfila la tela dei suoi rapporti con la Corte EDU, con significativi richiami ai tratti identificativi della struttura dell'ordine interno e distintivi rispetto alla struttura dell'ordine convenzionale ("a prima lettura" di Corte cost. n. 230 del 2012). www.diritticomparati.it. Accessed 15 Oct 2012; Consulta Online Accessed 16 Oct 2012

Ruggeri A (2012c) Ancora a margine di Corte cost. n. 230 del 2012, *post scriptum*. www.diritticomparati.it. Accessed 29 Oct 2012; Consulta Online Accessed 29 Oct 2012

Ruggeri A (2013a) Il futuro dei diritti fondamentali: viaggio avventuroso nell'ignoto o ritorno al passato? www.federalismi.it. Accessed 15 Feb 2013

Ruggeri A (2013b) La Corte di giustizia, il primato incondizionato del diritto dell'Unione e il suo mancato bilanciamento col valore della salvaguardia dei principi di struttura degli ordinamenti nazionali nel loro fare "sistema" (nota minima a Corte giust., Grande Sez., 26 febbraio 2013, in causa C-399/11, *Melloni c. Ministerio Fiscal*). www.diritticomparati.it. Accessed 2 Apr 2013

Ruggeri A (2013c) CEDU, diritto "eurounitario" e diritto interno: alla ricerca del "sistema dei sistemi". www.giurcost.org. Accessed 19 Apr 2013

Ruggeri A, Spadaro A (1991) Dignità dell'uomo e giurisprudenza costituzionale (prime notazioni). Politica del diritto, pp 343 ff

Salazar C (2012) *A Lisbon story*: la Carta dei diritti fondamentali dell'Unione europea da un tormentato passato ... a un incerto presente? www.gruppodipisa.it. Accessed 21 Dec 2012

Salazar C (2013a) I princìpi in materia di libertà. In: Ventura L (ed) I principi costituzionali (at press)

Salazar C (2013b) Il principio di legalità. In: Ventura L (ed) I principi costituzionali, Giuffrè, Milano (forthcoming)

Salazar C (2013c) Crisi economica e diritti fondamentali. www.rivistaaic.it Accessed 11 October 2013

Sciarabba V (2013) Il giudicato e la CEDU. Profili di diritto costituzionale, internazionale e comparato. Cedam, Padova

Silvestri G (2009) Dal potere ai princìpi. Libertà ed eguaglianza nel costituzionalismo contemporaneo. Laterza, Roma-Bari

Silvestri G (2013) I diritti fondamentali nella giurisprudenza costituzionale italiana: bilanciamenti, conflitti e integrazioni delle tutele. In: Ventura L (ed) I principi costituzionali, Giuffrè, Milano (forthcoming)

Spadaro A (2011) I diritti *sociali* di fronte alla crisi (necessità di un nuovo "modello sociale europeo": più sobrio, solidale e sostenibile). www.rivistaaic.it. Accessed 6 Dec 2011

Sperti A (2013) Una riflessione sulle ragioni del recente successo della dignità nell'argomentazione giudiziale. www.costituzionalismo.it. Accessed 18 June 2013

Tega D (2012) I diritti in crisi. Tra Corti nazionali e Corte europea di Strasburgo. Giuffrè, Milano

Troilo S (2011) (Non) di solo dialogo tra i giudici vivranno i diritti? Considerazioni (controcorrente?) sui rapporti tra le Corti costituzionali e le Corti europee nel presente sistema di tutela multilivello dei diritti fondamentali. www.forumcostituzionale.it. Accessed 13 Apr 2011

Vecchio F (2012) Primazia del diritto europeo e salvaguardia delle identità costituzionali. Effetti asimmetrici dell'europeizzazione dei controlimiti. Giappichelli, Torino

Vecchio F (2013) I casi *Melloni* e *Akeberg*: il sistema multilivello di protezione dei diritti fondamentali. Quaderni costituzionali, pp 454 ff

Viganò F (2013c) La Corte costituzionale sulle ricadute interne della sentenza Scoppola della Corte EDU. www.penalecontemporaneo.it. Accessed 19 July 2013

Viganò F (2013b) Prosegue la 'saga Scoppola': una discutibile ordinanza di manifesta inammissibilità della Corte costituzionale. www.penalecontemporaneo.it. Accessed 26 July 2013

Zagrebelsky G (1995) Relazione. In: Associazione Italiana dei Costituzionalisti (ed) I diritti fondamentali oggi. Cedam, Padova

The Principle of *Nullum Crimen Sine Lege* in the Construction of European Criminal Law

Giuseppe Toscano

Contents

Abstract This paper investigates the role played by the rule of law in the construction of an EU criminal law. The analysis, also from a historical perspective, of the rule of law shows how it is tremendously flexible and adaptable to the changing socioinstitutional contexts in which it is considered. It is necessary to assess whether the process of Europeanization can be considered a "risk factor" for its stability or whether, on the contrary, it requires only simple adaptations that do not detract from its essence.

Keywords Accessory competence • Civil rights • Democracy • Direct competence • Directives • Europeanization • Framework decisions • Principle of assimilation • Rule of law • Treaty of Lisbon

---

G. Toscano (✉)
Department of Law, University of Messina, Piazza Pugliatti No. 1, Messina, Italy
e-mail: toscanop89@libero.it

S. Ruggeri (ed.), *Human Rights in European Criminal Law*,
DOI 10.1007/978-3-319-12042-3_3

1 Introduction

The concept of Europeanization, in a generic sense, indicates the slow, gradual and problematic attempt at bringing closer together the national cultures of the old continent, now called upon to mutually cooperate to provide adequate answers to the problems posed by modern society. Legal professionals now unavoidably have to deal with this need, and are called upon to rewrite the very hierarchy of sources, taking into account these new institutional systems.[1] Unlike scholars in disciplines for some time accustomed to dealing with supranational sources, we find a more prudent attitude in criminal law scholars, who tend to be more statist and self-referential.[2]

Having laid these general premises, this paper aims to analyze the phenomenon of the Europeanization of criminal law from the perspective of the rule of law, the first and irreplaceable source of legitimacy of the entire criminal system. The genesis of the rule of law, as is well known, responds to needs above all of a political nature. It in fact started out as a guarantee of civil liberties and as a connecting element between the law of the sovereign and the rights of the subject.[3] The analysis of the rule of law thus requires assessments also of a nonlegal nature, necessary for a comprehensive examination of the topic.[4]

This paper will therefore have to take account of this dual aspect: historical-cultural and technical-legal, hence the need for a separate discussion of the two types of problems, in order to fully assess the critical issues regarding legality in the current historical context and to engage in an evaluation of the process of Europeanization in a *de lege ferenda* perspective.[5]

The path followed in this paper first examines the rule of law from a historical perspective, to better understand its content and values. Having identified the key aspects and verified the real content of the principle of *nullum crimen sine lege*, we will try to establish the possible role of the rule of law in the new European institutional framework outlined by the Lisbon Treaty. The route is extremely circuitous, and the investigative method chosen does nothing to help simplify matters. However, an examination of the historical-dogmatic aspects of the problem is absolutely unavoidable.

---

[1] On the theory of the plurality of sources and systems, cf. Romano (1977), p. 27.

[2] For a general overview of the theoretical difficulties involved in traditional legal reasoning "by source" in the new European context, see Ruggeri (2010), pp. 125 ff.

[3] Note Article 8 of the Declaration of the Rights of Man and the Citizen of 1789, where it is stated: "The law must establish only penalties that are strictly and evidently necessary, and no one may be punished except by virtue of a law established and promulgated prior to the offence, and legally applied."

[4] Regarding the axiological rule of law, cf. Fiandaca (2003), pp. 53 ff.

[5] Interesting observations have been made on this point by Picotti (2008), p. 331, who splits the relationship between criminal law and European legal system into three phases, identifying a relationship of inverse proportionality between the progress of cooperation between the Member States and the discretion of domestic legislators.

2 The Form and Substance of the Rule of Law: A Brief Historical Overview

As mentioned in the introduction, the first necessary step in this survey is to retrace, albeit briefly, the main stages of the history of the rule of law, to see how it has adapted over time to the socioinstitutional changes affecting Europe.

Although the formula *nullum crimen, nulla poena sine lege* goes back to the second-century AD politician and jurist Ulpian, it was only in the second half of the eighteenth century that the rule of law became clearly defined and conceptually independent.[6] This was especially true after the fall of the *Ancien Régime*, when it became a symbol of the Enlightenment (which saw the law as a guarantee of rationality) and liberal culture (which aimed to build a punitive system free from the arbitrariness and the abuse of power).[7]

From the early stages of this new vision of things, there thus emerged a conception of the rule of law that made it the cornerstone of a new sociopolitical system based on new distinctive traits that marked a sharp break with the past.

In this process, the principle of *nullum crimen sine lege* played a primary and indispensable role, since the law is an expression of sovereignty illuminated by the light of reason, the instrument able to distinguish between the lawful and the prohibited and to attribute to each offense the corresponding punishment.[8]

In the liberal era, the rule of law therefore expressed a purely *formal* characterization of the concept: in accordance with the principle of *favor libertatis* of the citizens, the express legislative provision was the sole point of reference for verifying criminal conduct.

Corollaries of the principle being considered here are the principle of the *reserve of law*, under which the monopoly of criminalization rests only with state legislative power; the principle of *nonretroactivity*, whereby the criminal law is valid only for the future and may not apply to acts prior to its entry into force; that of its *mandatory nature*, whereby general abstract legislative propositions in criminal matters must fulfill the requirements of clarity, precision and comprehensiveness;

---

[6] Pre-Republican and Republican Roman law, in fact, based on case law, rejected codification and allowed the use of analogy both for crimes and punishment, thus disregarding the concept of the rule of law. Subsequently, during the monarchy, criminal law was administered by the king, while in the Republican age there was a shift to *iurisdictio* by investiture of a magistrate, who had absolute power to determine the sentence and also and, above all, to bring someone to trial for an offense. For a full discussion on the regulation of crimes in Roman law, refer to Santalucia (1998).

[7] It was the scholars of the Enlightenment, all concerned with safeguarding the citizens' rights of freedom vis-à-vis the king, who reflected on a postulate essential to the very nature of law: you cannot punish *a posteriori* conduct that at the time of its performance was not considered a crime, however ethically questionable the conduct in question may be.

[8] We cannot fail to quote the observation of Paul Anselm Feuerbach, who wrote: "The infliction of a penalty always presupposes a criminal law (*nulla poena sine lege*). In fact, only the threat of harm by the law underpins the concept and the legal legitimacy of a penalty"; cf. Feuerbach (1986), p. 41.

and finally, the *prohibition of analogy*, which prevents the court from subsuming within the scope of a given provision a case not provided for on the basis of an alleged relationship of similarity with that expressly being considered.

Behind this apparent clarity and solidity, the formal rule of law conceals elements of fragility that emerged subsequently in the first half of the last century, when dictatorial regimes dramatically violated precisely those individual rights that the rule of law seemed to guarantee.

There thus gradually emerged the need to ensure the rule of law through new contents that went beyond rigid formalism.

The crisis of legality in the formal sense therefore gave rise to a question reminiscent of that expressed in Juvenal's *Satires*: *quis custodiet ipsos custodes*?

This need was felt by all the Constitutional Charters after the Second World War, which would enrich the rule of law with new contents, necessary to give it renewed strength. The rule of law thus found an ally in "constitutionalised" civil and political liberties that, in an approach based on *mutual trust*, became in turn the guardians of legality.[9]

The close link between the rule of law and fundamental rights presupposes in the first place a new relationship between *civil rights* and *democracy*, which will become the two key concepts of the issue in question.[10]

In this perspective, *substantial* legality in fact indicates primarily a mode of production of democratic and dialectic law, such as to ensure, through parliamentary debate and discussion, the consensus of all the political and social groups present in Parliament. It is only from Parliament, as the representative body of society as a whole, that we can expect a nonabusive exercise of regulatory authority in criminal matters. Consequently, criminal law could never be arbitrary, since it is always created in the interests of society and respectful of individual liberties.

However, the substantial dimension of the rule of law is manifested through various contents, of which that relating to the democratic method of producing law is only one aspect.

In addition to the democratic method of producing the criminal law and the criteria of compulsoriness, uniformity, precision and certainty with which criminal rules must be made, we must remember that in their formulation account should be taken of the distinctive elements of the offense, such as the materiality of the action, the seriousness of the offense, the possibility of attributing guilt and procedural safeguards in the assessment of criminal liability.

In assessing whether the new forms of prosecution from supranational sources are compatible with the rule of law, these are the variables that will be taken into

[9] Emblematic in this regard is the ruling of the Italian Constitutional Court no. 50/1980, which states: "The rule of law applied to criminal penalties, as provided for under Article 25(2) of the Constitution, establishes a system whose content and approach derives from other substantive principles and in which the implementation of a restorative distributive justice requires differentiation more than uniformity."

[10] For a comprehensive and documented reconstruction of the process that led to Italy not to "constitutionalise" the principle of *nulla poena sine lege*, cf. Lucifredi (1962), pp. 1632 ff.

account. They will thus allow us to determine whether the process of Europeanization can be said to be compatible with the basic principles of criminal law.

3 The Rule of Law in the European Context

3.1 General Attempts at Harmonization: The Technique of Assimilation and Framework Decisions

The reconstruction of the history of the rule of law makes it clear why the national states, traditionally reluctant and cautious about implementing forms of *horizontal cooperation*, have proved to be even more reluctant to accept a *vertical transfer of competence* in criminal matters to supranational entities. The "mercantile" connotation of the European Economic Community, as set out in the Treaty of 1957, and the traditional willingness on the part of States to maintain a monopoly on criminal law had meant that the Treaty itself contained no rule conferring criminal competence to the Community. In particular, the institutional architecture of the EC and the procedures for the approval of regulatory acts did not meet the standards of democracy that the principle of the reserve of law in criminal matters presupposes.[11]

Therefore, in light of the already existing principle of attribution, under which the EC could only legislate on matters for which it had been assigned competence by the Member States, both direct and indirect criminal jurisdictions were excluded.

Over time, this system proved to be wholly inadequate, to the point that it was almost counterproductive, especially considering the specific needs of the process of European development. The increasingly close integration between the Member States in fact meant that it was no longer possible to put off more active coordination between national criminal systems.[12]

More specifically, the development of an internal market characterized by the free movement of people, goods and capital ended up offering new opportunities for organized crime, especially following the agreement of Shenghen (1985), which required the adoption of "compensatory measures" designed to break down all the boundaries between the judicial authorities and police of the various States.

Beyond formal forecasts, the overlap between the state system and supranational legal systems in the same legal space had in any case made interaction between the

[11] On one hand, there was a European Parliament not elected by universal suffrage by the citizens of the Member States but composed of representatives of national parliaments and appointed by them; on the other, there was a procedure for the adoption of EU policies characterized by a clear prevalence of the Community's "executive" bodies.

[12] For an overview of the "original" state of criminal matters within the EU, refer to Sgubbi (1990), p. 90.

sources of Community law and domestic regulations inevitable. The absence of direct or indirect competence in criminal matters on the part of the European Community soon clashed with the fundamental need to ensure the effectiveness of the rules of Community origin through a system of penalties.[13]

A leading player in this reunification between Community and national sources in criminal matters was, in the first place, the Court of Justice, which repeatedly held that, even in the absence of an independent punitive power in the hands of the European Community, the Member States, according to the principle of *loyal cooperation*, were still obliged to harmonize their national rules and to take all appropriate measures to ensure compliance with Community legislation.[14]

The so-called *principle of assimilation*—whereby violations of Community law should be punished in the Member States with penalties similar to those applicable to infringements of national law of a similar nature and gravity—was stated for the first time in the late 1980s, in the historic judgment on the "Greek corn" case.[15] The

[13] It should be noted that the emerging needs of the fight against transnational organized crime had led the European states, already in the decades following the establishment of the EEC (albeit outside the Community's institutions and sources, namely in the context of international treaty law), to introduce embryonic forms of cooperation and convergence of legislation in criminal matters. Examples include the Council of Europe Conventions on extradition, the recognition of judgments in criminal matters and the transfer of convicted persons. These convention-based sources, on one hand, did not constitute "threats" to domestic criminal autarchy in the same way as EC sources, since as they required unanimous rather than majority approval, they had no direct effect (since they required a ratification law), and were not accompanied by a procedure to regulate their infringement. On the other hand, they were the first embryonic attempts at bringing closer to each other national criminal justice systems and encouraging cooperation between state authorities, able to break down the barriers built on the absence of mutual trust and a stubborn will to preserve autonomy in criminal matters.

In the same perspective, almost all the Member States of the Community signed and ratified various international conventions enshrining the common adherence to certain general principles of law, especially with regard to fundamental rights (e.g., the European Convention on Human Rights, the International Covenant on Civil and Political Rights of 1966), as well as numerous international conventions aimed at harmonizing national criminal systems in particularly sensitive sectors (UN conventions on terrorism and racial discrimination). There thus emerged a hard core of values (especially those related to the respect of the fundamental rights of the individual), common to all the legal systems of the Member States.

[14] On the possibility that, in the presence of highly diversified punitive disciplines among EU Member States, criminal activities of an economic nature may be concentrated in those characterized by less severe regulations, cf. Sevenster (1992), p. 30.

[15] See sent. September 21, 1989, *Commission v. Greece*, 68/88, Coll. 1989, p. 2985. Soon after, with the "Zwarteld" order (Case C-2/88 Imm, Coll. I, p. 3365), there was support for the possibility of Member States to provide criminal penalties to ensure the effectiveness of Community law and safeguard its direct or secondary interests. Along the same lines, we also find the well-known ECJ judgment regarding Unilever (Case C-77/97), which envisages a nucleus of criminal sanctions for the infringement of Community law by imposing a strict obligation on Member States to penalize infringements of Community interests. It was, however, a purely indirect competence of the Community and subject to the Member State's approval of the "appropriateness" of the protection. The result was that domestic legislation had absolute and unquestionable discretion in deciding which penalties to apply to specific cases resulting from requests for protection of Community origin.

assimilation model, as a tool for transposing Community law into domestic law, made it possible to equalize, in terms of safeguards, the legal interests protected at the national and Community levels.[16]

Having established that the European Community, albeit lacking direct legitimacy to enact criminal laws, could however oblige Member States to provide criminal law protection for the Community's interests, the compatibility of this model with the rule of law remained doubtful. It is important to remember that this principle is relevant not only for the constitution but also for the community, seeing that it belongs to the constitutional traditions of the Member States, as well as being found in international law.[17]

It is in fact obvious that such forms of interaction between EU and national legislators significantly reduce the discretionary contribution of the latter in the definition of criminal offenses, in establishing both unlawful conduct and penalties.[18]

Such a mechanism, given the democratic deficit characterizing Community institutions, appeared problematic with respect to the rule of law, especially regarding the use that was made of it. Without carrying out preliminary work of identifying individual national instances in the field of legislation under consideration, Community provisions often contained only a general reference to the domestic laws in force in that specific sector. The various legal systems of the Member States in fact display different characteristics in terms of structure and articulation of legislation, and it is therefore impossible to refer to specific national incriminating standards or to particular legal instruments or categories. The standard of reference will therefore inevitably display a degree of generality.

It should be noted, however, that in the meantime the changing legal and political context, together with the aforementioned need for greater coordination between national criminal systems, resulted in the approach found in the Treaty of Maastricht (1992), which instituted the European Union, creating the so-called three-pillar structure.

More specifically, in the framework of the third pillar of the EU, there was an assignment of specific skills also in the field of cooperation in criminal matters, which did not imply the assignment to the European institutions of regulatory powers identical to those of the Community scope (first pillar), i.e., exercisable by means of regulations and directives. The third pillar in fact represented a hybrid, an intermediate solution between the "Community" method typical of the first pillar and the "intergovernmental" method typical of international conventions.

---

[16] As for the obligations of assimilation, attention was given to Article 280(2) EC Treaty, according to which "The Community and the Member States shall counter fraud and any other illegal activities affecting the financial interests of the Community through measures to be taken in accordance with this article."

[17] This principle was in fact already enshrined in Article 7 ECHR, in Article 15(1) ICCPR and would subsequently be confirmed by Article 49 (1) EU FRCh.

[18] For a complete discussion of issues of compatibility between assimilation clauses and the rule of law, refer to Panebianco (2007), pp. 62ff.

The differences between the sources of the two pillars can be seen by analyzing the characteristics of the most significant source adoptable in the framework of the third pillar, namely *framework decisions*.[19]

The harmonizing effect of framework decisions on national criminal systems is based on the mechanism of *compulsory incrimination*. These sources require Member States to envisage criminal penalties for certain types of behavior described in the European source, which often also lays down some instructions on the *type* of penalty (e.g., penalties restricting personal liberty) and on the *severity* of the penalty itself. It is therefore a form of *indirect* criminal jurisdiction, through the imposition of an obligation to bring charges, which however is not supported by EU-imposed penalties in the event of nonimplementation, meaning that its actuation displays disturbing margins of uncertainty.[20]

Despite the less binding nature of framework decisions compared to instruments of the first pillar, their adoption has however brought the criminal legislation of the states significantly closer in many areas.[21]

Similar tools were also joined by the increasingly widespread practice of the so-called double text, i.e., a technique of standardization that envisaged the simultaneous recourse to Community law and to EU law, on one hand, to establish the type of violation and interest protected and, on the other, to lay down constraints on Member States in the choice of what conduct to criminalize. This model, however, was cumbersome and would in fact be abandoned as a result of ECJ case law, which established that already in the scope of the first pillar it was possible to decide what conduct to criminalize and to envisage the type of penalty applicable.[22]

However, alongside the growing conviction that an effective European criminal policy in the fight against organized crime was indispensable, the characteristics of framework decisions and instruments of assimilation, which had initially made it possible to overcome the traditional resistance of states to the allocation of powers in criminal matters to the EU, were later perceived as critical points. In particular,

---

[19] The features of framework decisions have made these sources, on one hand, more easily "tolerable" compared to the sources of the first pillar by those states most reluctant to the devolution of powers in criminal matters to the European institutions; on the other hand, they are more easily adopted than international conventions. They are in fact, considering the first point, taken by unanimity (i.e., the dissenting opinion of just one Member State is enough to prevent their adoption), they have no direct effect (and thus always require domestic implementing legislation), and their violation does not result in infringement proceedings (making them less stringent than regulations and directives). Considering the second point, their entry into force does not require approval or ratification by individual Member States but occurs *ipso facto* as a result of the unanimous resolution of the Council.

[20] On the democratic coefficient of framework decisions, cf. Bernardi (2007), pp. 1171 ff.

[21] On the impact of framework decisions on national sources, see Manes (2006), pp. 1150 ff.

[22] We should note in particular the judgment of the Grand Chamber of the Court of Justice of 13 September 2005 in Case 176/03.

the absence of an infringement procedure made it impossible to punish late fulfillment or nonfulfillment of the obligations to prosecute by some Member States.[23]

3.2 Recognition of the EU's Competence to Harmonize Criminal Law in the Treaty of Lisbon

The rapprochement between the disciplines of different Member States, after a first failed attempt together with plans for a European Constitution, would be fully consecrated by the Treaty of Lisbon. Coming into force with effect from December 1, 2009, it did away with the three-pillar structure and reduced the democratic deficit from which Community institutions had always suffered by giving the EU autonomous competence in the harmonization of criminal law.[24]

In particular, Article 83 TFEU provides that the European Parliament and the Council "may [...] establish minimum rules concerning the definition of criminal offences and sanctions in the areas of particularly serious crime with a cross-border dimension resulting from the nature or impact of such offences or from a special need to combat them on a common basis."

To this end, the process of harmonization of criminal law is no longer entrusted to the somewhat ineffective instrument of the framework decision, but to that of the directive, so that the new form of European criminal jurisdiction, while remaining indirect,[25] now obliges the Member States to implement its provisions with the threat of proceedings for noncompliance and conviction by the Court of Justice.[26]

The awareness of the need to fight transnational crime in a European context by means of sufficiently homogeneous penalties has led to the EU criminal jurisdiction being seen as *autonomous*. On one hand, in fact, this jurisdiction does not require the prior existence of European noncriminal legislation in need of protection, since it may at any time legitimize itself in function of the fight against the most serious forms of transnational crime. On the other hand, the aforementioned EU criminal jurisdiction has assumed a marked "functionalist autonomy," since it is no longer primarily aimed at the need to coordinate crime-fighting authorities (while,

[23] It should not be forgotten, however, that the individual state's failure to comply with a framework decision constitutes a violation of the principle of "sincere cooperation" under Article 10 TEC. On this point, cf. Militello (2000), pp. 3 ff.

[24] On the subject of the reserve of law in relation to Community legislation, there is extensive literature. Specifically on the legislative powers of the European Union in criminal matters, see Sotis (2007).

[25] The minimal penal provisions contained in the harmonization directives, in fact, have no direct effect and, depending on their level of detail, postulate implementation and clarification by the Member States.

[26] Paonessa (2007), p. 409, however stresses the limited remedies available in the event of a breach of EU obligations in terms of criminal law protection, since they are not subject to specific performance.

conversely, in accordance with Articles 29 and 31 TEU previously in force, such needs formed the basis of the criminal jurisdiction of the third pillar).[27] This evolution towards the autonomy of European criminal jurisdiction thus expresses the desire to give new vigour and teleological scope to the recent European rules aimed at tackling serious cross-border crime, pursuing aims other than those considered in the past.[28]

It is in this spirit that we must read Article 83(1)(1) TFEU, and subparagraph 2 of the Article moves in the same direction, containing a list of areas of crime intervention with marked political-criminal importance. This importance is certainly not set to diminish in the future but rather to increase if, pursuant to the following subparagraph 3, in the light of developments in crime, the Council decides unanimously to adopt a decision aimed at identifying further areas of crime destined to fall within the *independent* criminal jurisdiction of the Union.[29]

A necessary condition so that the Union may adopt "minimum standards" aimed at bringing closer together the laws and regulations of the Member States in criminal matters is their *indispensability*. It is clear that the technique of drawing up minimum shared standards will impact significantly on what are considered the typical elements of a crime, on the identification of the objective and subjective elements of the case in question and also, and especially, on the type of penalty to be applied.[30]

The Lisbon Treaty also provides for the attribution of another form of indirect criminal jurisdiction to the Union, which aims to ensure the *useful effect* of the precepts of a community origin and at the same time to prevent some EU countries—in the absence of adequate national punitive measures aimed at striking the most serious violations of those precepts—from being transformed into a real criminal paradises able to frustrate the criminal prevention activities carried out by other EU countries.[31] Taking account of those needs, Article 83(2) TFEU

[27] Cf. D'Amico (2009), p. 76.

[28] Consider the instances contained in the so-called *Stockholm Programme* (2010–2014) aimed at drawing up strategic guidelines for legislative and operational planning within the area of freedom, security and justice. Starting with the observation that organized crime is increasingly assuming an alarming global dimension, this program insists on the adoption of a structured approach to the fight against this form of crime, putting it at the heart of the Union's priorities and identifying the types of crime against which it will deploy the tools at its disposal. See the Stockholm Programme, An open and secure Europe serving and protecting citizens (2010/C 115/01), in EU Off. Gazz., 4 May 2010, C 115/4.

[29] Cf. Grasso (2011), p. 2326.

[30] However, it should be noted that the same Article 83(3) of the Treaty of Lisbon provides a guarantee for the individual criminal law systems of the EU member states in the form of the so-called emergency brake, a procedure whereby, if a member of the Council considers that a draft directive would affect fundamental aspects of its criminal justice system, it may request the European Council to assess the matter, resulting in the suspension of the legislative procedure for adoption of the directive.

[31] On the principle of the so-called useful effect, which requires states to allow the achievement of the objectives of Community legislation, cf. Scorrano (2006), pp. 349 ff.

envisages, again through directives, the introduction of minimum rules concerning the definition of criminal offenses and sanctions in the areas that have been subject to harmonization measures, when the laws and regulations of the Member States in criminal matters need to converge to ensure the effective implementation of EU policy in these areas.

Such criminal jurisdiction is usual called *accessory*, since it does not express the core of European criminal policy, which should probably deal with the efforts to fight transnational crime governed by Article 83(1) TFEU.[32] Of course, this accessory nature also remains where the criminal jurisdiction provided for by Article 83 (2) TFEU intervenes to harmonize penalties, both in areas of exclusive EU competence and in areas of shared competence, subject to unification measures.[33]

The influence of European criminal law on national criminal law is not limited, however, to the obligations to prosecute arising from the directives provided for in Article 83 TFEU. Apart from the aspect of the substantial repeal of the incriminating provision due to its conflict with a directly applicable supranational rule, there is the question of finding *exonerating* regulations in a broad sense in the various sources of European law. We are talking about regulations that are incompatible with domestic incriminating regulations and may thus rule out or limit the applicability of the latter in relation to certain types of conduct, thanks to the hierarchical superiority generally attributed to European over domestic legislation. It is clear that this issue involves the conflict of laws, in this case only apparent because of the primacy of European law, which also excludes as a criterion for the solution of the conflict the "chronological" profile: a European law takes precedence over an internal one even if passed prior to the latter.[34] There can be no doubt, therefore, that the *lawfulness* of a given conduct, resulting from a regulation or a provision of

[32] Unlike autonomous criminal jurisdiction, accessory jurisdiction did not have to wait for the Lisbon Treaty to come into force to become operational, since it had been explicitly recognized by the Court of Justice in the aforementioned ruling of 13 September 2005 (case C-176/03, Commission v. Council) and the judgment of 23 October 2007 (in Case C-440/05, Commission v. Council), conferring indirect criminal jurisdiction on the first pillar. In this regard, we need merely recall that in paragraph 48 of the first of those judgments, the Court used a language very similar to that now found in Article 83.2 TFEU, stating that "when the application of effective, proportionate and dissuasive criminal penalties by the competent national authorities is an essential measure for combating serious environmental offences, [the Community legislature is not prevented] from taking measures which relate to the criminal law of the Member States which it considers necessary in order to ensure that the rules which it lays down on environmental protection are fully effective." As is known, in the light of this case law, the first Directive harmonizing criminal law was introduced, no. 2008/99/EC of the European Parliament and of the Council of 19 November 2008, on protection of the environment from criminal activity.

[33] Interesting findings on this issue can be found in Sotis (2002), pp. 44 ff., who emphasizes that accessory criminal jurisdiction may involve an excessive recourse to criminal laws of European origin, contrary to the principle of *extrema ratio* in the light of the different views of the EU and individual Member States on the intrinsic gravity of criminal conduct.

[34] Already well before the Treaty of Lisbon, various scholars made this point, including Mazzini (2000), p. 361, and Panebianco (2007), pp. 59 ff.

the Treaties themselves, functions as a cause of justification with regard to typical conduct.[35]

4 Prospects for the Principle of *Nullum Crimen Sine Lege* in the New European Context

Our analysis has revealed an attitude of progressive abandonment of the statist conception of the production of rules for prosecution. It is, however, a slow process still in its early stages, since mutual distrust of any form of erosion of the state monopoly in the production of law continues to persist.

In terms of the obligations to prosecute, in particular, there is an alleged incompatibility between the Europeanization of criminal law and the substantive spirit of the rule of law, which would require a guarantee of the genuine democratic legitimacy of criminal policy decisions and not their automatic devolution to supranational institutions.[36]

On closer reflection, moreover, this approach, although it promotes the rule of law, provides an excessively "static" view of it, which certainly does not seem to reflect the dynamism that the rule of law has shown to have.

Today, once again, the rule of law has to deal with a radically changed institutional and cultural context, in which the sources of law diversify, multiply and intertwine well beyond the classic framework of a clear hierarchy. In this context, therefore, the rule of law in criminal matters cannot be stressed *sic et simpliciter*, but requires conceptual reinvigoration, without however compromising its essential contents.

It should be borne in mind that the ordinary legislative procedure governed by Article 294 TFEU, envisaged today for the majority of European legal sources, fully satisfies the requirement of "democracy" laid down by the substantial rule of law. This procedure implies that the Union's legislative instruments (regulations, directives and decisions) are adopted jointly by the European Parliament and the Council, at the proposal of the Commission. The requirement of democracy is also ensured by the powers both of veto and amendment that are held by the European

---

[35] What instead is problematic is the attribution of the same justification to provisions contained in directives, since these sources do not as a rule have direct effect on national law but require domestic legislative intervention. A well-established trend shows the existence within this category of European sources of "detailed" or "analytical" directives, which identify with a high degree of accuracy the elements that may cause a certain type of conduct, already considered typical under domestic criminal provisions, not to be seen as criminal in nature. Precisely this feature should make the provision of Community law immediately operational, with an "exonerating" effect, even if the national legislature has failed to implement it, and precisely in order not to unjustly burden the accused with the negative consequences of such a failure.

[36] For wider discussions on compliance with the rule of law in criminal legislation deriving from harmonization directives, see Bernardi (2009), p. 48.

Parliament with respect to EU legislative proposals.[37] Concerns related to the democratic failings of the legislative process can thus be considered to a large extent overcome.

The reasons for the so-called crisis of legality do not therefore depend on the phenomenon of the Europeanization of criminal law itself, or on the relationships between the European institutions, but must undoubtedly be sought elsewhere.[38]

It cannot be denied, however, that the explicit recognition in the TFEU of EU criminal jurisdiction, given the absence of a genuine European *demos*, however constitutes an experiment still beset by uncertainty, whose outcome is unsure.[39] The intervention of the European legislature still seems to be excessively fragmentary, to the extent that it is not only insufficient, but may actually potentially destabilize the logical and rational order that should characterize any criminal law system.[40] Nevertheless, the identification of common strategies in criminal matters is a crucial step in the ongoing construction of Europe.[41]

We have to take into account that similar harmonization measures for criminal law might be considered indispensable in the near future in delicate areas such as the safety of workers and public health.[42] In this context, the rule of law is far from being a barrier to the introduction of European obligations to criminalize certain conducts. It instead becomes an unavoidable (though not exhaustive) scrutiny of

---

[37] It should however be noted that, as part of the autonomous criminal jurisdiction of the EU, directives are always undertaken in accordance with the ordinary legislative procedure. On the other hand, in cases of the accessory criminal jurisdiction of the European Union, within the meaning of the last part of Article 83.2, TFEU, criminal law harmonization directives may also be adopted in accordance with a special legislative procedure, where the European Parliament has a merely "advisory" role and therefore does not have the power of veto. The problem of the democratic legitimation of accessory criminal harmonization directives is, however, mitigated in practice due to the fact that today recourse is almost always made to the ordinary procedure.

[38] Among the "risk factors," we should mention in the first place national laws and practices that seem to conflict with the democratic component of the rule of law. As noted by De Vero (2012), p. 256, from the Italian perspective, it is enough to consider that the whole subject of the transposition of the directives was settled in domestic legislation with Law 11/2005, which stipulated that each year a special "Community law" would provide for adjusting the domestic legal system to bring it in line with the European directives of the previous year, specifically mentioned in a list drawn up for this purpose. This resulted in a situation in which Parliament ended up filling *community law* with legislative delegations to the Government, moreover characterized by vague and generic principles and directive criteria (so-called carte-blanche delegations). Consequently, even though national legislative instruments implementing European sources have for many years now represented almost half of the state's legislative production, Parliament's contribution to their definition is somewhat limited.

[39] On this issue, Paonessa (2009), p. 272, observes that the predominantly economistic nature of the Union could lead the European legislature to make extensive use of punishment for economic offenses.

[40] On this point, cf. Sicurella (2011), pp. 2624 ff.

[41] On the possibility that, in the presence of strongly inhomogeneous punitive disciplines among EU Member States, criminal activities of an economic nature may be concentrated in those characterized by less severe regulations, cf. Riondato (1996), p. 142.

[42] On the need to protect what are now supranational interests, cf. Sicurella (2008), p. 225.

their constitutional compliance and a valid guiding criterion that can lead to the construction of a Europe seen no longer as an organization of zealous bureaucrats but as a political and legal entity that becomes a marriage of cultural identities with a view to harmonization.[43]

References

Bernardi A (2007) Il ruolo del terzo pilastro UE nella europeizzazione del diritto penale. Un sintetico bilancio alla vigilia della riforma dei Trattati. Rivista italiana diritto pubblico comparato, pp 1171 ff

Bernardi A (2009) All'indomani di Lisbona: note sul principio europeo di legalità penale. Quaderni costituzionali, p 48

Bernardi A (2013) Interpretazione conforme al diritto UE e costituzionalizzazione dell'Unione europea. Diritto penale contemporaneo

D'amico M (2009) Trattato di Lisbona: principi, diritti e "tono costituzionale". In: Bilancia P, D'amico M (eds) La nuova Europa dopo il Trattato di Lisbona. Giuffrè, Milano, p 76

De Vero G (2012) Corso di diritto penale. Giappichelli, Torino

Feuerbach PA (1986) Lehrbuch des gemeinen. In: Deutschland gültigen peinlichen Rechts, 14th edn. 1847, rist. 1986, § 20, p 41

Fiandaca G (2003) Diritto penale sostanziale. In: Fiandaca G, Di Chiara V (eds) Una introduzione al sistema penale. Per una lettura costituzionalmente orientata. Jovene, Napoli, pp 53 ff

Grasso G (2011) Il Trattato di Lisbona e le nuove competenze penali dell'Unione. In: Studi in onore di Mario Romano. Jovene, Napoli, p 2326

Lucifredi R (1962) Note sulla rilevanza costituzionale del principio *"nulla poena sine lege"*. Giurisprudenza costtituzionale, pp 1632 ff

Manes V (2006) L'incidenza delle "decisioni-quadro" sull'interpretazione in materia penale: Profili di diritto sostanziale. Cassazione Penale 3:1150 e ff

Mazzini G (2000) Prevalenza del diritto comunitario sul diritto penale interno ed effetti nei confronti del reo. Diritto dell'Unione europea, p 361

Militello V (2000) Agli albori di un diritto penale comune in Europa: il contrasto al crimine organizzato. In: Militello V et al (eds) Aa.Vv. Il crimine organizzato come fenomeno transnazionale. Milano, pp 3 ff

Panebianco G (2007) La giurisprudenza della Corte di Lussemburgo. In: De Vero G, Panebianco G (eds) Delitti e pene nella giurisprudenza delle Corti Europee. Giappichelli, Torino, pp 62 e ff

Paonessa C (2007) La discrezionalità del legislatore nazionale nella cornice dei vincoli comunitari di tutela. Criminalia, p 409

Paonessa C (2009) Gli obblighi di tutela penale. La discrezionalità legislativa nella cornice dei vincoli costituzionali e comunitari. Ets, Pisa, p 272

Picotti L (2008) Superamento della tecnica del "doppio testo" e tutela penale degli interessi europei. In: Grasso G, Sicurella R (eds) Per un rilancio del progetto europeo. Esigenze di tutela degli interessi comunitari e nuove strategie di integrazione penale. Milano, p 331

Riondato S (1996) Competenza penale della Comunità europea. Problemi di attribuzione attraverso la giurisprudenza. Cedam, Padova, p 142

Romano S (1977) L'ordinamento giuridico. rist., Firenze, p 27

Ruggeri A (2010) Dimensione europea della tutela dei diritti fondamentali e tecniche interpretative. Diritto dell'Unione Europea, pp 125 ff

Santalucia B (1998) Diritto e processo penale nell'antica Roma. Giuffrè, Milano

[43] On the process of the constitutionalization of the European Union, see Bernardi (2013).

Scorrano MG (2006) Il principio dell'effetto utile. In: Mangiameli S (ed) L'ordinamento europeo, II, L'esercizio delle competenze. Giuffrè, Milano, pp 349 ff
Sevenster HG (1992) Criminal law and EC law. Common Market Law Rev 29:30
Sgubbi F (1990) Diritto penale comunitario. Digesto delle discipline penalistiche, 4th vol. Torino, pp 90 ff
Sicurella R (2008) "Eppur si muove!": alla ricerca di un nuovo equilibrio nella dialettica tra legislatore comunitario e legislatore nazionale per la tutela degli interessi dell'Unione europea. In: Grasso G, Sicurella L (eds) Per un rilancio del progetto europeo. Milano, p 225
Sicurella R (2011) Questioni di metodo nella costruzione di una teoria della competenza dell'Unione europea in materia penale. In: Studi in onore di Mario Romano, vol IV. Jovene, Napoli, pp 2624 ff
Sotis C (2002) Diritto comunitario e meritevolezza di pena. In: De Francesco GA, Venafro E (eds) Meritevolezza di penale logiche deflattive. Giappichelli, Torino, pp 44 e ff
Sotis C (2007) Il diritto senza codice. Uno studio sul sistema penale europeo vigente. Milano

The *Nulla Poena Sine Culpa* Principle in European Courts Case Law

The Perspective of the Italian Criminal Law

Giuseppina Panebianco

Contents

Abstract Although the *nulla poena sine culpa* principle is not clearly recognised by the ECHR or in the Charter of Fundamental Rights of the European Union, several judgments acknowledge it in a more or less wide sense. European Courts identify the legal basis of the *nulla poena sine culpa* principle in the presumption of innocence, as provided by Article 6(2) ECHR as well as by Article 48 of the Nice Charter. However, the presumption of innocence is a principle regarding procedural criminal law and does not seem suitable as the basis for the *nulla poena sine culpa*

G. Panebianco (✉)
Department of Law, University of Messina, Piazza Pugliatti No. 1, Messina, Italy
e-mail: gpanebianco@unime.it

S. Ruggeri (ed.), *Human Rights in European Criminal Law*,
DOI 10.1007/978-3-319-12042-3_4

principle, which pertains to substantive criminal law. The inadequacy of Article 6 ECHR as a basis for the principle of culpability forces the ECtHR to reason on the burden of proof at the procedural level. The suspected offence of absolute liability is thus turned into a presumption of liability that the defence needs to rebut. A similar approach can be found in the latest ECJ case law, which refers to Article 6 (2) ECHR. To be more precise, the ECtHR case law shows a new hermeneutical approach relating the principle of culpability to the *nulla poena sine lege* principle, and from this perspective the legal basis of the principle is identified in Article 7 ECHR. In relation to the justiciability of the *nulla poena sine culpa* principle after the Lisbon Treaty, it seems appropriate to identify the basis of this principle in Article 49 of the Nice Charter or, to refer once again to the presumption of innocence, in Article 48. Whatever legal basis is referred to, the recognition of the *nulla poena sine culpa* principle also in the EU law system, through the Nice Charter, would multiply the chances of safeguard increasing the justiciability means. Basing the principle of culpability on the Charter of Fundamental Rights of the European Union implies its binding nature for the EU institutions as well as for Member States, since Article 6(1) TEU attributes to the Nice Charter "the same legal value as the Treaties".

Keywords Case law of Court of Justice of the European Union • Case law of European Court of Human Rights • Justiciability • Legal basis • *Nulla poena sine culpa* principle

1 Fundamental Guarantees of Substantive Criminal Law in the Case Law of the European Courts

Before the Lisbon Treaty came into force, one of the main debated issues in criminal law doctrine was related to the EU competence to legislate in the area of criminal law. Thus, particular attention was paid to one constitutional principle governing criminal matters, namely the *nulla poena sine lege* principle. However, the case law of the Court of Justice of the European Union (from now on ECJ) prior to 2009 also deals with criminal matters that take into account further guarantees provided by the principle of offensiveness (combined with the principles of proportionality and necessity) and the principle of culpability. Furthermore, in the ECJ case law prior to the Lisbon Treaty, the principle of offensiveness appeared as a duty to provide criminal punishments for conducts prejudicial to Community legal values. This in turn led back to the *nulla poena sine lege* principle: it cannot be denied that assessments regarding the need for criminal law are thus taken away from the Member States' sovereignty. A similar situation is found in the *nulla poena sine culpa* principle in the jurisdiction of the European Court of Human

Rights (from now on ECtHR). As will be shown further,[1] this principle, as theorised by scholarship and formulated by the case law of the Italian Constitutional Court, inevitably leads back to the *nulla poena sine lege* principle, albeit from a different perspective, that of the sufficient certainty of criminal law, corresponding to the principle of precision.

A comparative analysis of ECJ and ECtHR case law—the latter by definition related to criminal matters—shows the need to enact the *nulla poena sine culpa* principle at supranational level.[2] It cannot be denied, however, that the ECtHR has always been in a better position to define fundamental guarantees that should govern substantive criminal law, thanks to a more favourable legal basis compared to the European Union context prior to the *recognition* of the Charter of Fundamental Rights of the European Union (known as the Nice Charter) in the TEU. The European Convention on Human Rights (from now on ECHR), even at a basic level, inevitably evokes the safeguard of guarantees informing the use of criminal law. These include the *nulla poena sine lege* principle, as provided by Article 7, starting with its heading, embodying the *nulla poena sine lege* maxim.[3] Not surprisingly, there are numerous references to criminal law guarantees in the ECtHR case law, since Strasbourg Judges operate in a more favourable normative context. As previously shown in relation to the ECJ case law, the principle of offensiveness is once again intended from the perspective of the duty to provide for criminal sanctions to punish conducts prejudicial to fundamental rights in the ECtHR case law. In a legal context that tends to guarantee such principles, an earlier recognition of the *nulla poena sine culpa* principle by the Strasbourg Judges would have been appropriate, given that this guarantee does not seem to have been fully recognised until quite recently, as in the case of the Italian Constitutional Court. This means that for a long time in the ECtHR case law, this principle was not subject to the circularity mentioned above, leading almost intuitively to the *nulla poena sine lege* principle.

Such late identification of the *nulla poena sine culpa* principle in the case law of the European Courts is largely caused by the lack of an explicit provision not only in the EU treaties, whose originally *mercantile vocation* justifies such a lack in terms of fundamental guarantees, but also in the ECHR. In both contexts, the only, albeit approximate, reference seems to be the *presumption of innocence*, provided by Article 48 of the Nice Charter, to which Article 6(1) of the Treaty on European Union recognises the same legal value as the Treaties, as well as by Article 6 (2) ECHR.[4]

---

[1] See below, Sect. 4.2.

[2] For a comparative analysis of the European Courts' case law on the *nulla poena sine culpa* principle, see Maugeri (2011), pp. 120 ff.; Maugeri (2008), pp. 130 ff.; Maugeri (2007), pp. 163 ff.

[3] This is the heading of Article 7 ECHR in the Italian translation, corresponding to the expression "No punishment without law" and "Pas de peine sans loi" of the English and French versions.

[4] See below, Sect. 3.

2 The *Nulla Poena Sine Culpa* Principle in the Italian Context

Before examining the legal basis influencing the European Courts, I shall focus on some specific issues related to the *nulla pena sine culpa* principle in national law. To this end I shall adopt the viewpoint of the Italian criminal law, because of the high development of this principle in the Italian criminal law system.

Article 27(1) of the Italian Constitution identifies the principle of individual criminal responsibility without hesitation. Despite such a precise definition in the Constitution, the doctrine, and even the Constitutional Court, has minimised this constitutional principle, identifying it with the more obvious *prohibition on the attribution of responsibility for the actions of others*. This is why the Constitutional Court considered absolute liability pursuant to Article 27(1) of the Constitution for a long period of time.[5]

As commonly known, only thanks to the hermeneutic approach in Italian constitutional case law in the late 1980s, was the principle of individual criminal liability interpreted as *prohibition on punishing a person for a wrongful act without mens rea*.[6] According to this perspective, the principle provided by Article 27(1) of the Italian Constitution requires a conduct linked to the accused as the author of the action by a nexus of material causality "but also and above all by the *mens rea* which must characterise—at least in the form of negligence—the most significant elements of the typical *actus reus*".[7] The committed crime should thus reveal a clear hostile behaviour or at least an *indifference* to the legal interest safeguarded by the criminal law provision.

The peculiarity of this new hermeneutic approach by the Italian Constitutional Court is that such interpretation of the principle of personal criminal liability has been related to the rehabilitation purpose of punishment provided by Article 27 (3) of the Italian Constitution, thus revealing a further aspect, or rather the true meaning that criminal liability should acquire to be constitutionally compliant. To apply the most severe sanction provided by the Italian legal system, the offence through which the offender's *mens rea* has been expressed should be *attributed* to the latter; in other words, the offender should be aware of the social impact of his/her conduct and that he/she has not complied with the duty of abstention from committing an offence imposed on citizens to encourage their responsible and personal contribution to a common project of social coexistence. Such awareness is jeopardised every time the meaning of the violated criminal law provision is not *socially understandable*, and as a consequence the lack of knowledge of the law

---

[5] For an overview of the different approaches in the doctrine regarding Article 27(1) of the Italian Constitution, see Alessandri (1991), pp. 24 ff.

[6] Italian Constitutional Court, Judgment no 364 of 1988, which was developed in the following Judgment no 1085 of 1988.

[7] This is a quotation from Italian Constitutional Court, Judgment no 364 of 1988.

provision becomes a further limit to criminal liability, and the offence cannot be attributed to the offender.

The reasoning of the Constitutional Court judges, based on a connection between the individual and the criminal provision that can be blamelessly ignored, inevitably leads to *mala prohibita* offences, which do not refer to the social harmfulness of the punished conduct. However, such an approach does not imply the incontrovertible *reproach* of the author of offences whose social harmfulness can be assessed on the phenomenal level. The offender might not be aware of the social harmfulness of his/her conduct due to limited mental capacity, to which the application of a punishment should be subject, as provided by the Criminal Code.[8] On the constitutional level, the *nulla poena sine culpa* principle, therefore, involves a whole series of conditions allowing an offence to be attributed to the offender and a process of re-education to be legitimised.

3 The European Legal Basis of the *Nulla Poena Sine Culpa* Principle

As previously shown, the *nulla poena sine culpa* principle is not intended here as *prohibition on punishing a person for a wrongful act without mens rea*. Rather, it is seen from a perspective of assuming the greatest possible involvement of the offender. The offence can be attributed to its author only when he/she is capable of understanding the social harmfulness of his/her conduct; this means that a punishment can be applied only when, besides intent or negligence, the mental capacity of the offender can be assessed, together with his/her access to the criminal provision in the case of *mala prohibita* offences.[9]

However, despite the fact that such interpretation of the *nulla poena sine culpa* principle is widely accepted in the Italian legal system, the same cannot be said for the European context where the ECJ and ECtHR operate. As previously argued, neither the EU Treaties nor the ECHR explicitly refer to this principle.[10] More precisely, a reference can be found in EU law, in Article 6(3) TEU, which recognises as "general principles of the Union's law" the fundamental rights as they emerge from the constitutional traditions common to the Member States. However, the *principle of culpability*, in its narrow sense as *prohibition on the attribution of responsibility for the actions of others*, cannot be found in the Constitutions of the countries originally forming the European Community (France,

[8] See Panebianco (2012) on juvenile offenders, p. 94.

[9] For this interpretation of the *guilt principle* in the Italian Constitution, see de Vero (2012), pp. 175 ff.

[10] See Sicurella (2002), p. 18. Grasso (2007), pp. 662 f.; Maugeri (2008), p. 130; Maugeri (2011), p. 121; Maugeri (2007), pp. 171 ff., criticise the lack of this principle in the EU FRCh.

Germany, Belgium, Luxembourg and Holland),[11] except for Italy; among the countries that joined the EU later, only the Portuguese Constitution explicitly refers to this principle intended as *prohibition on the attribution of responsibility for the actions of others*, since according to Article 30(3) "Criminal liability is not transferable". The principle (of procedural criminal law) of the presumption of innocence is widely recognised, whereas the *nulla poena sine lege* principle is predominant and variously interpreted to the extent of including the *lex mitior principle*.[12] Equally significant is a constant reference to the prohibition of torture and inhuman or degrading treatment or punishment.[13]

The reason for the lack of an explicit constitutional provision on the *nulla poena sine culpa* principle could be that this principle should be immanent in a rule of law as a fundamental principle of legal civilisation. This could also explain why the Constitutional Charters of Contracting States do not include *prohibition on the attribution of responsibility for the actions of others*.[14] As far as a narrow definition of the principle is concerned, no comparison can be made with national criminal legislation, where criminal offences based on absolute liability are commonly found despite the fact that they are even less compatible with the more complex *nulla poena sine culpa* principle, interpreted as a series of conditions that allow the offender *to be reproached*. This is largely testified to by the slow appearance of the *nulla poena sine culpa* principle in its wide sense in the Italian Constitutional court case law, which is still reluctant to strongly intervene even in the case of offences based on lawful conduct.[15]

---

[11] *Contra*, Manes (2012b), p. 844, footnote 24, argues that the *nulla poena sine culpa* principle belongs to the constitutional traditions common to the Member States. Similarly, Maugeri (2007), p. 172.

[12] The *lex mitior principle* can be found in the Constitutions of Portugal (Art. 29), Estonia (Art. 23), Czech Republic (more specifically Article 40 of the Charter of Fundamental Rights and Freedoms, which is considered as part of the constitutional legal system), Slovenia (Art. 28) and Slovakia (Art. 50).

[13] It should be noted, however, that the reference to the constitutional traditions common to the Member States to include this principle among the EU fundamental rights should not be interpreted as a unanimous recognition, since the criteria of the *maximum standard* is sufficient: see Sicurella (2002), p. 32; more recently, Grasso (2011), p. 2321.

[14] See, however, Article 30(3) of the Portuguese Constitution (mentioned above in the main text), which together with Article 27 of the Italian Constitution in recognising the *nulla poena sine culpa* principle, codifies it in its narrow sense of *prohibition on the attribution of responsibility for the actions of others*.

[15] The reference here is to the history of Article 609 *sexies* (previously Article 539) of the Italian Criminal Code, which has only recently been *adapted* by the legislature to the Constitution (with law no. 172/2012). Before the 2012 reform, if the sexual offences provided for under Articles 609-*bis*, 609-*ter*, 609-*quater* and 609-*octies* were committed against a minor under the age of 14, or for offences falling under Article 609-*quinquies*, the guilty party could not invoke ignorance of the age of the injured party in his defence. See Risicato (2007), pp. 1465 ff., on the latest constitutional judgment in terms of *error aetatis*, once again cautious in relation to Article 609 *sexies* of the Criminal Code.

The lack of a clear constitutionalisation does not prevent the principle of culpability from *existing* in the criminal law pertaining to the requirements of liability, in the wide sense attributed to it by the Italian Constitutional Court in 1988. Paragraph 17 of the German Criminal Code,[16] Article 122-3 of the French Criminal Code and Article 14(3) of the Spanish Criminal Code are clear examples of this. Moreover, there are several instances whereby this principle has been given a constitutional identity, as testified to by the recent judgment of the *Bundesverfassungsgericht* of 30 June 2009 (known as *Lissabon Urteil*),[17] which has some precedents and relates the principle of culpability to the guarantee of human dignity under Article 1 of the German Basic Law, thus considering it as "part of the constitutional identity which is unassailable due to Article 79.3 of the Basic Law and which is also protected against encroachment by supranational public authority".[18]

The lack of an explicit constitutional provision on this principle inevitably encourages its violation; suffice to think about the hypothesis of absolute liability in the criminal laws of Member States, included even in Italian criminal law, despite the clear constitutionalisation of this principle. The French case is emblematic, since absolute liability for misdemeanours was abolished following the reform of the Criminal Code in 1994 but was maintained for petty offences.

The Spanish experience is different since, as provided by Article 5 in the Preliminary Title of the Criminal code,[19] "No punishment whatsoever shall be imposed in the absence of either *mens rea* or negligence", despite the fact that such categories are not expressed anywhere else.[20]

The normative basis of national constitutions seems, therefore, to prevent the recognition of the *nulla poena sine culpa* principle as a general principle of the Union's law.

4 The *Nulla Poena Sine Culpa* Principle in ECtHR Case Law

Having examined the legal context of the European Courts' judgments, we can now try to assess whether the *nulla poena sine culpa* principle is applied in the jurisdictions mentioned above.

---

[16] Anticipated by the decision of the *Großer Senat* of the *Bundesgerichtshof* of 18 March 1952.

[17] For a critical analysis of this important judgment of the *Bundesverfassungsgericht*, see Böse (2009), pp. 267 ff.

[18] This is a quotation from § 364 of the judgment of 30 June 2009 *Bundesverfassungsgericht*.

[19] The Preliminary Title of the Spanish Criminal Code, "On penal guarantees and on the application of the Criminal Law", particularly focuses on the principles codified in it to the point of revealing a certain "constitutional vocation", Palazzo and Papa (2013), p. 183.

[20] See Palazzo and Papa (2013), p. 183.

Despite the lack of an explicit reference to the *nulla poena sine culpa* principle in the ECHR, the ECtHR has identified the violation of the principle of the personal criminal liability, intended as *prohibition on the attribution of responsibility for the actions of others*, relying on the principle of the presumption of innocence, as provided by Article 6(2) ECHR.[21]

This was the case of the heirs of a Swiss entrepreneur sentenced to a fine for tax evasion of their bequeather. According to Article 130(1) of the Ordinance on Direct Federal Tax, "If the evasion is discovered only after the death of the taxpayer, proceedings shall be brought against his heirs. Irrespective of personal guilt, the heirs shall be jointly liable for the deceased person's evaded taxes and the fine incurred by him up to an amount not exceeding their share in the estate". The heirs applied to the ECtHR invoking, among other things, the violation of the presumption of innocence. The applicants contended that they had been compelled by a legal presumption to assume criminal liability for tax evasion allegedly committed by the deceased entrepreneur. More precisely, the Court argued that "It is a fundamental rule of criminal law that criminal liability does not survive the person who has committed the criminal act", thus declaring the infringement of Article 6 (2) ECHR.[22]

Despite the ECtHR's good intentions aimed at filling the gap regarding substantive criminal law guarantees provided by the ECHR, the reference to the presumption of innocence appears to be inadequate.[23] However, Article 6(2) ECHR is often referred to as a legal benchmark to report the punishment of conducts that are not based on the offender's awareness. The leading case here is *Salabiaku v. France*[24]: the issue submitted to the ECtHR was related to the application of a criminal offence based on the simple possession of given goods that did not imply the offender's criminal intention. The judgment followed the application proposed by a Zaïrese national convicted of smuggling prohibited goods after having taken possession of a truck with 10 k of drugs at the airport of Paris, despite the fact that he was unaware of the trunk's contents.[25] The applicant had in fact gone to the airport to collect a suitcase that some relatives from Zaire had sent to him but found a trunk coming from the same country without any indication of its addressee, while

[21] See Chenal and Tamietti (2012); Meyer-Ladewig (2011), para 211 ff., on Article 6(2) ECHR. On the presumption of innocence, see also Trechsel (2005), pp. 153 ff.

[22] ECtHR, Judgment of 29 August 1997, *A.P., M.P. and T.P. v. Svizzera*, Application no. 19958/92, § 48.

[23] See de Vero (2007), p. 55. Trechsel (2005), p. 171, agrees with the Strasbourg Judges' conclusions.

[24] ECtHR, Judgment of 7 October 1988, *Salabiaku v. France*, Application no. 10519/83. See also Nicosia (2006), pp. 83 ff. on the lack of reference to the *nulla poena sine culpa* principle in the Strasbourg jurisdiction.

[25] To be more precise, he was even accused of the criminal offence of the illegal importation of narcotics, although the national judges decided that the facts alleged against the accused were not sufficiently proven: ECtHR, Judgment of 7 October 1988, *Salabiaku v. France*, Application no. 10519/83, § 14.

a few days later he was informed that the suitcase that he was waiting for had wrongly been delivered to Bruxelles airport. Convicted of smuggling prohibited goods (as provided by the general clause of Article 392(1) of the French Customs Code, under the terms of which "the person in possession of contraband goods shall be deemed liable for the offence"), the applicant reported the violation of the presumption of innocence, since he had been convicted of a customs offence even though he was unaware of the luggage's content, and the French Customs law pertaining to smuggling does not require any assessment of *mens rea*.

Given that it was not possible to assess the compatibility (*in abstracto*) of the national provision with the ECHR, the ECtHR simply verified whether the related offence had been applied in compliance with the presumption of innocence reported by the applicant.[26]

The negative conclusion of the European judges was preceded by some general statements, often referred to in subsequent case law. According to the ECtHR, Contracting States "may, under certain conditions, penalise a simple or objective fact as such, irrespective of whether it results from criminal intent or from negligence".[27]

Furthermore, the Strasbourg Court has acknowledged that

> Article 6 §§ 1 and 2 do not prevent domestic criminal law from providing for presumptions of fact or law to be drawn from elements proved by the prosecution, thereby absolving the prosecution from having to establish separately all the elements of the offence, provided such presumptions remain within reasonable limits which take into account the importance of what is at stake and maintain the rights of the defence.[28]

As the ECtHR has had the opportunity to explain in other judgments, the means employed have to be reasonably proportionate to the legitimate aim sought.[29] This implies that there should be a balance between the political-criminal assessment and the subsequent sanctions applied in the case in question.

Such statements seem to strongly deny the *nulla poena sine culpa* principle as a fundamental right guaranteed by the ECHR; however, the effort made by the European judges in assessing the offender's guilty mind in order to deny the

---

[26] ECtHR, Judgment of 7 October 1988, *Salabiaku v. France*, Application no. 10519/83, § 30.

[27] ECtHR, Judgment of 7 October 1988, *Salabiaku v. France*, Application no. 10519/83, § 27; with the same meaning, see ECtHR, Judgment of 23 July 2002, *Västberga Taxi Aktiebolag and Vulic v. Sweden*, Application no. 36985/97, § 112; ECtHR, Judgment of 23 July 2002, *Janosevic v. Sweden,* Application no. 34619/97, § 100.

[28] More recently, see ECtHR, Judgment of 30 August 2011, *G. v. United Kingdom*, Application no. 37334/08, § 26, referred to later in the main text.

[29] ECtHR, Judgment of 23 July 2002, *Västberga Taxi Aktiebolag and Vulic v. Sweden*, Application no. 36985/97, § 113; ECtHR, Judgment of 23 July 2002, *Janosevic v. Sweden,* Application no. 34619/97, § 101; ECtHR, Decision of 19 October 2004, *Falk v. Netherlands*, Application no. 66273/01.

violation of the presumption of innocence indicates a tendency towards the fundamental guarantees of substantive criminal law.[30]

In this case, the Court denied the violation of the presumption of innocence since the applicant, having realised that the luggage did not correspond to what he expected, should have verified its contents, rather than identifying himself as its owner. He had even been warned by an airport official not to take possession of the trunk unless he was sure that it belonged to him, since the luggage might have had illegal contents. Thus, the national judges, despite the fact that they could have referred to the presumption provided for by the Customs Code, assessed a *certain é lément intentionnel* in the specific circumstances,[31] similar to the risk-taking characterising recklessness in the Italian legal system.

As previously argued, the reference to Article 6(2) ECHR does not seem coherent as the legal basis of the *nulla poena sine culpa* principle.[32] The use of the presumption of innocence has forced European judges to turn the hypothesis of absolute liability, implied in this specific case, into a hypothesis of (rebuttable) presumptions of liability, which could be overcome through evidence of the mental element. It is the procedural value of the principle provided by Article 6(2) ECHR that facilitates this hermeneutical approach: assessments by the national judges in relation to the guilty verdict of the offender are sufficient for the verdict to be considered compatible with Article 6(2) ECHR,[33] regardless of the structural *deficit*s of the criminal offence considered *in abstracto*. It cannot be denied that the vocation of the ECtHR jurisdiction to express its opinion on a specific case contributes to this formulation of the judgment.

4.1 Some Similarities with the Hermeneutical Approaches of the Italian Constitutional Court

The hermeneutical approach based on the presumption of innocence has led the ECtHR to the point of excluding key aspects of the harmfulness of a criminal offence from its constituent elements. Marginalising the requisites of the offence, which might involve absolute *criminal liability*, thus allows the ECtHR to guarantee compatibility with the ECHR of punishment imposed for conducts that do not imply intrinsic unlawfulness. From this perspective, not only is the Prosecutor

[30] According to Sicurella (2002), pp. 20 f., the judgment quoted in the main text reveals a tendency of Strasbourg case law towards the principle of guilt. Abbadessa's (2011), p. 394, view is even stronger, and starting from the leading case *Salabiaku v. France*, he supports the recognition of the principle of guilt in ECtHR case law.

[31] ECtHR, Judgment of 7 October 1988, *Salabiaku v. France*, Application no. 10519/83, § 30.

[32] *Contra* Trechsel (2005), p. 158, for whom the principle *nullum crimen sine culpa* embodies a fundamental right whose violation should be considered an infringement of the presumption of innocence.

[33] See Abbadessa (2011), pp. 380 f. on this.

relieved of the burden of proof, while the defendant cannot compensate for it, but the defendant State can also avoid compliance with the reasonable limits that, according to the ECtHR, Article 6(2) ECHR imposes in the use of presumptions.[34]

The issue that has allowed the ECtHR to have a further hermeneutical approach pertains to the relevance of mistake regarding the victim's age in the offence of rape of a child under 13.[35]

In the instant case, the complaint concerning the infringement of Article 6 ECHR is related to a conviction of rape of a 15-year-old boy for sexual intercourse with a 12-year-old girl. The applicant argued that he was wrongly convinced that the victim was the same age as him and that she had consented to sex. As in the Italian law, *Sexual Offences Act 2003* does not recognise any value to the victim's consent to sexual intercourse when the victim is a child under 13.[36] Once again, the inadequacy of Article 6 ECHR in basing the principle of culpability forces the ECtHR to reason on the burden of proof at the procedural level. Confirming the statements of the *leading case Salabiaku v. France*,[37] the ECtHR has argued that, if it is true that the presumption of innocence places the burden of proving the elements of the offence on the prosecution, Article 6 ECHR does not prevent the lawgiver from relieving the prosecution of the burden of proof through presumptions of fact or law, provided such presumptions remain within reasonable limits that take into account the importance of what is at stake and maintain the rights of the defence.[38] Having emphasised that "Contracting States remain free to apply the criminal law to any act which is not carried out in the normal exercise of one of the rights protected under the Convention", and given that it cannot interfere with the political-criminal choices of the national lawgiver regarding the constituent elements of the offences,[39] the ECtHR has focused on the national discipline involved in the instant case. To this aim, the European judges have argued that the offence identified by the domestic criminal law requires an *actus reus*, represented by the sexual intercourse as described by law, and a *mens rea*, interpreted as the intention of carrying out the forbidden sexual intercourse, whereas knowledge of, or recklessness as to, the age of the child or as to the child's unwillingness to take part in the sexual activity do not constitute elements of the offence,[40] and as a consequence the prosecution is not required to provide proof of it. This is why the principle of the

[34] On the reasonable limits in the use of presumptions in the national legislation, see ECtHR, Judgment of 7 October 1988, *Salabiaku v. France*, Application no. 10519/83, § 28.

[35] ECtHR, Decision of 30 August 2011, *G. v. United Kingdom*, Application no. 37334/08.

[36] In Italian Criminal Law, the age of sexual consent is 14 years. The age of consent rises to 16 if the offender is a family member or is in a position of trust in relation to the victim. The age of consent rises to 18 if a family member or a person who is in a position of trust in relation to the victim abuses his power related to his position. Even the *Sexual Offences Act 2003* provides an increase of the age of sexual consent in these cases.

[37] See above in the main text.

[38] ECtHR, Decision of 30 August 2011, *G. v. United Kingdom*, Application no. 37334/08, § 26.

[39] *Ibid.*, § 27.

[40] *Ibid.*, § 28.

reasonable limits considered in *Salabiaku v. France* would not be applicable here.[41]

In the attempt at *self-restraint* to guarantee the Sovereignty of the Contracting States, the ECtHR has not tried to verify the balance between the safeguard needs expressed by the sexual inviolability of juveniles and the principle of culpability, even though the latter is linked back to the presumption of innocence. The exclusion of the victim's age and her consent from the constituent elements of the offence allows the European judges to avoid assessing the *reasonable limits*, delimiting the legitimacy of presumptions.

In this sense, one cannot but help making a comparison with the history of the *nulla poena sine culpa* principle, in terms of the protection of the sexual inviolability of juveniles, which prevailed on the guarantees expressed by the principle of culpability, in the case law of the Italian Constitutional Court. According to the Constitutional Court's approach, which assigned to Article 27 of the Italian Constitution the narrow sense of *prohibition on the attribution of responsibility for the actions of others*, constitutional judges have noted that, even considering any mental nexus between the conduct and the harm as an essential requisite of personal criminal liability, the discipline on *error aetatis* (formerly Article 539, today 609 *sexies* Criminal Code) appeared to be compatible with the Constitution. In an outdated interpretation of the Italian Constitutional Court, the criminal offence needed to include a mental ingredient, since *awareness* and *volition* would have affected sexual intercourse only, rather than the age of the victim, considered "a prerequisite for the offence and more specifically a (non-objective) condition of liability for punishment".[42] This means that the European judges' recent interpretative *stratagem* to exclude the victim's age from the constituent elements of the offence of the performance of sexual acts with a minor was already being applied in less recent Italian constitutional case law.

Returning to the case law of the Italian Constitutional Court, the change of approach shown by judgments no. 364 and no 1085 in 1988 inevitably affected its subsequent case law, which has recently returned to this issue. In judgment no. 322 of 2007,[43] the Italian Constitutional Court relates the principle of culpability to the principles of the *nulla poena sine lege* and non-retroactivity in criminal law, principles that all share the same aim "to guarantee to those subject to the criminal law the freedom to choose (judgment No. 364 of 1988) on the basis of assessments made in advance (*calculability*) of the legal consequences of their own conduct".[44] Thus, if the lawgiver was in the position of totally disregarding the *mens rea* in the structuring of the offences, the balance between the principle of culpability and other values with constitutional status—whose safeguard requires the use of criminal law—would be left to the legislator's discretion, "with the

---

[41] *Ibid.*, § 29.

[42] Italian Constitutional Court, Judgment no. 107 of 1957.

[43] See Risicato (2007).

[44] This is a quotation from Italian Constitutional Court, Judgment no 322 of 2007.

resulting encroachment on the presumption of innocence and 'underlying' goals of the principle of blame".[45]

As opposed to the ECtHR, the Constitutional Court does not prevent itself from balancing the interests at stake, since it is facilitated by a different legitimation of its jurisdiction. However, the delicate issues involved in the criminal law provision suspected of unconstitutionality has proved to be an obstacle for a more effective decision of the Constitutional Court, which has ruled the issue of constitutionality to be ineligible.[46]

4.2 *The Variable Solidity of the Strasbourg Judges' Reasoning*

It would be superficial to blame the ECtHR for the hermeneutical approaches that have prevented the *nulla poena sine culpa* principle from having its role recognised among the fundamental rights identified by the ECHR. The ECtHR has the hard task of ensuring the safeguard of fundamental rights within the context identified by the submissions of law of applicants and by rebuttals carried out by representatives of the Contracting States. This is why the value of given principles is affected by the role that they have in the legal system of the State involved and by the applicants' ability to identify an adequate legal basis in the ECHR. The more a national legal system guarantees a given principle on a formal level and in terms of its dogmatic formulation, the more will be the resources used to safeguard it even on a supra-national level, providing the ECtHR with a stronger reasoning. It is no coincidence that a better formulation of the *nulla poena sine culpa* principle and of its legal basis can be found in a more recent judgment of the ECtHR concerning Italy.

This is the well-known *Punta Perotti* case, which led to the *Sud Fondi srl v. Italy* judgment on the European level.[47] Taking advantage of the importance of the *nulla poena sine culpa* principle in the national law system, where it is constitutionally recognised and distinguished from the principle of the presumption of innocence (concerning procedural criminal law),[48] applicants refer to the *nullum poena sine lege* principle (concerning substantive criminal law) to report the incompatibility with the ECHR of the sentence they have received. The reference to Article 7 ECHR allows us to emphasise a fruitful connection between the *nulla poena sine culpa* principle and the *nullum poena sine lege* principle, a connection that was immediately perceived by the Strasbourg Judges. Having emphasised that the

---

[45] *Ibid.*

[46] More recently, the Italian legislature has modified Art. 609 *sexies* Criminal Code (by Law no 172 of 2012), which today focuses on the unavoidable mistake regarding the minor's age.

[47] ECtHR, Judgment of 20 January 2009, *Sud Fondi srl v. Italy*, Application no. 75909/01. See Mazzacuva (2009), pp. 1540 ff.

[48] See above, Sect. 2.

notion of *law*, as provided by Article 7 ECHR, includes both that of legal origin and that of case law origin, the Court specified that it implies the qualitative conditions of *accessibilité* and *prévisibilité*.[49] Furthermore, the ECtHR argues that

> l'article 7 ne mentionne pas expressément le lien moral entre l'élément matériel de l'infraction et la personne qui en est considérée comme l'auteur. Cependant, la logique de la peine et de la punition ainsi que la notion de 'guilty' (dans la version anglaise) et la notion correspondante de 'personne coupable' (dans la version française) vont dans le sens d'une interprétation de l'article 7 qui exige, pour punir, un lien de nature intellectuelle (conscience et volonté) permettant de déceler un élément de responsabilité dans la conduite de l'auteur matériel de l'infraction.[50]

In this sense, it would not be coherent to expect the *accessibilité* and *prévisibilité* of the law while at the same time letting a person being considered guilty and punished even though he/she is not in a position to know the criminal law due to an unavoidable mistake he/she is not responsible for.[51] The principle of culpability is, thus, related to the *nulla poena sine lege* principle. A legal system preventing the accused from knowing *le sens et la portée* of the criminal law not only fails to meet the qualitative requirements of a law, but it is also lacking in terms of specific needs pertaining to the *nullum poena sine lege* principle in criminal matters.[52] It could be argued that the unavoidable ignorance of the criminal law implies that the law provision itself does not exist for the offender at the time when the offence was committed.

To be precise, such a development in the reasoning on the principle of culpability had already been inherent in the ECtHR case law based on the *nulla poena sine lege* principle, as provided by Article 7 ECHR for a long time, particularly in terms of the precision of the offence, implying the requisite of the predictability of the penal consequences of one's behaviour. If it is true that the *nulla poena sine lege* principle forces the legislator to formulate the criminal law provision in a sufficiently clear manner, in order to make its content recognisable and therefore allow citizens to foresee the penal consequences of their conduct, the addressees of the *message* of the criminal law provision have the duty to be informed about the law regulating the activities that they might want to carry out. This makes it possible to assess the *prévisibilité* of the criminal law provision in relation to the possibility of demanding such a duty, thus revealing a sort of circularity between the *nulla poena sine lege* principle and the principle of culpability.[53]

The leading case of this important hermeneutical development is the judgment *Cantoni v. France*.[54] In this case submitted to the European judges, the manager of

---

[49] ECtHR, Judgment of 20 January 2009, Application no. 75909/01, *Sud Fondi srl v. Italy*, § 108.

[50] *Ibid.*, § 116.

[51] *Ibid.*, § 116.

[52] *Ibid.*, § 117.

[53] See the ECtHR, Judgment of 25 July 2013, *Khodorkovskiy and Lebedev v. Russia*, Applications nos. 11082/06 and 13772/05, § 779.

[54] ECtHR, Judgment of 11 November 1996, *Cantoni v. France*, Application no. 17862/91.

a French supermarket reported the infringement of Article 7 ECHR subsequent to a sentence for unlawfully selling pharmaceutical products. The applicant's submissions of law concerned the national law on health issues, particularly the provision of the French Public Health Code, according to which the definition of *medicament* is considered extremely imprecise, leaving wide margins to the judges' opinion on some *borderline* products. The applicant's submissions of law allowed the ECtHR to focus on the compliance with Article 7 ECHR of the techniques of regulation by rules founded on the use of general categorisations. The Strasbourg Judges remarked that such techniques of regulation by rules are a "logical consequence of the principle that laws must be of general application".[55] However, the *nulla poena sine lege* principle requires that the law provision has a core of certainty wide enough for its application to be sufficiently clear in the large majority of cases, while the clarification of the *borderline hypothesis*, included in the grey areas at the fringes of the definition, is left to the judges.[56] In the instant case, the Strasbourg Judges considered vital the jurisprudence of the French Court of Cassation, which tended to recognise the medicinal value of para-pharmaceutical substances. To assess its *prévisibilité*, the ECtHR emphasised that the latter is not affected by the fact that (within reasonable limits) "the person concerned has to take appropriate legal advice to assess, to a degree that is reasonable in the circumstances, the consequences which a given action may entail", particularly in the case of professional activities that require a high degree of caution.[57] From this perspective, the Strasbourg Judges put the requisite of the foreseeability of the law provision, as identified by French case law, in relation to the duty to keep oneself informed, neglected by the applicant, who could have consulted an expert to be informed of the penal consequences of his/her conduct.

On a general level, the ECtHR case law based on Article 7 ECHR shows similarities with the line of case law stemming from the Italian Constitutional Court in judgment nos. 364 and 1085 of 1988. However, in the previous line of ECtHR case law mentioned above, the submissions of law made by the parties prevent the principle of culpability, and its relation with the *nulla poena sine lege* principle, from standing out, due to the fact that the references to Article 7 ECHR focus exclusively on the *nulla poena sine lege* principle rather than on the principle of culpability. Moreover, the Strasbourg Judges' focus on the requirements of *accessibilité* and of *prévisibilité* in assessing a violation of Article 7 ECHR reveals only a moderate attention to the principle of culpability. To be more precise, the assessment of the qualitative requirements of criminal law reveals its need to be compatible with different constitutional systems of various Contracting States, and

---

[55] *Ibid.*, § 31.

[56] *Ibid.*, § 32.

[57] *Ibid.*, § 35.

this would be rather difficult if European judges focused on the sources of a criminal law provision.[58]

5 ECJ Case Law

A comparison with ECJ case law is surprising if we consider that the experience of the EU, which did not originally have *competence* to legislate in the area of criminal law, has been marked for a long time by the principle of personal *punitive* liability, both in the sense of *prohibition on the attribution of responsibility for the actions of others* and in the sense related to the principle of culpability, typical of substantive criminal law.

Given the complex legal context of the EU, it is worth examining the hermeneutical approaches of the ECJ on the *nulla poena sine culpa* principle, keeping separate the different forms of safeguard of the European legal interests, whose normative transposition generates the issues submitted to the European judges.

As commonly known, the safeguard of legal interests relevant to the EU can be expressed with varying intensity, depending on the degree of involvement of the national legislature.[59] A first level, which is certainly more significant in terms of impact on the Member States' legal systems, includes offences provided for and punished by Regulations.[60] At the level of the national legislature, instead, there are offences that, despite being provided for by EU law, are sanctioned by the Member States' legal systems.

It is obvious that it is possible to trace judgments of the ECJ pertaining to the issue of criminal liability only in relation to offences of a European origin at the second level. The lack of a direct criminal law competence of the EU[61] prevents a

[58] See Palazzo (2013), p. 99, defining the *accessibilité* of the criminal law provision as the more *universalist* core of the *nulla poena sine lege* principle, compared to its interpretation as a discipline of the sources of law. See also Manes (2012a), pp. 278 ff.

[59] On the techniques of protection of Community legal values, see Grasso (1989), pp. 41 ff.; see also Grasso (2008), pp. 9 ff. On the different forms of harmonisation of penalties, in the *three-pillar* European context, see also Bernardi (2008), pp. 381 ff.; Sicurella (2007), pp. 245 ff. For a recent analysis of the European legal values, see Salcuni (2011), pp. 11 ff.

[60] For a distinction, at the level of the EU direct punitive authority, between (*Community*) *centralised* and *decentralised* sanctions, the former marked by the Union's exclusive competences pertaining to their provision and imposition, the latter, instead, provided for by the European legislature but imposed by the national administrative bodies, see Bernardi (2008), pp. 444 ff.; see also Maugeri (2011), pp. 71 f.; Maugeri (2007), pp. 100 ff.

[61] On this point, the interpretation excluding the EU direct criminal law competence, even after the Lisbon Treaty came into force, is preferable. See Grasso (2011), pp. 2344 ff.; Maugeri (2011), pp. 73 f.; Sicurella (2011), p. 2604, footnote 57. *Contra*, Sotis (2010), pp. 1164 ff., which, focusing on Art. 86(2) TFEU identifies a direct criminal law competence of the EU pertaining to financial interests, albeit limited only to infringements, rather than being extended to penalties. For an opposite view, see also Bernardi (2006), Bernardi (2004), pp. 8 f., and Picotti (2004), pp. 80 f. and 85 ff., on Articles III-274 and III-415 (or Articles III-175 and III-321 of the *Draft*) *Treaty establishing a Constitution for Europe*, whose content has been transferred with due changes and integrations to Articles 86 and 325 TFEU.

definition of criminal offences and sanctions from being expressed in a comprehensive manner in the EU sources of law without any intervention of the Member States. However, the ECJ's more civil-rights-oriented positions can be found in the case law pertaining to offences provided for and punished by Regulations, whose administrative nature is undeniable.[62] As will be further shown, the type of competence of the European institutions to ensure the safeguard of European legal interests largely affects the ECJ's reaction and the subsequent recognition of the *nulla poena sine culpa* principle in the related judgments.

5.1 The **Nulla Poena Sine Culpa Principle** *and the EU's Punitive Authority*

In terms of administrative offences expressing EU *punitive authority*, that is to say offences that are directly sanctioned on a supranational level, ECJ judgments are definitely more effective than those originating from a request for a preliminary ruling, involving a national punitive provision. In the first case, in fact, the ECJ judgment pertains to the *punitive* jurisdiction (which is administrative by nature) typical of the EU, without any involvement of national legislation. The lack of a necessary comparison with domestic legislation and with its principles certainly makes the argumentative approaches of European judges smoother and more effective.[63]

As previously argued, despite the administrative nature of offences regulated by EU law, there are past ECJ judgments concerning the applications subsequent to the decisions imposing pecuniary penalties, adopted by the Commission, that recognise the principle of blame, besides the guarantee of the individual punitive liability, interpreted as *prohibition on the attribution of responsibility for the actions of others* and *prohibition on the absolute liability*.

The civil rights vocation of this ECJ case law is undoubtedly facilitated by the supranational law involved in the case law informing the European Court's judgments. As commonly known, the EU mainly performs its *punitive authority* on the issue of competition[64]; to this aim, Regulation (EC) No 1/2003, on the implementation of the rules on competition laid down in Articles 81 and 82 of the Treaty (currently Articles 101 and 102 TFEU), includes the necessary intention or negligence of the infringement, which means that no *reproach* can be made to the European legislature on the structuring of the law provisions pertaining to the

[62] On the administrative nature of penalties following first level offences, see Bernardi (2008).

[63] On the different content that the principles may have in ECJ case law depending on the context of application, see Sotis (2007), pp. 18 ff.

[64] This issue is regulated by the EU provisions providing for the so-called *centralised* sanctions; see footnote 60 above.

infringements of UE competition law.[65] More precisely, complaints on the violation of the principle of personal liability do not concern law provisions but rather their practical application by the Commission. In particular, in terms of the conducts of participation in cartel practices, undertakings usually involved on various levels in anti-competitive practice—and therefore penalised by the Commission—are deemed liable for the entire infringement, regardless of the intensity, in terms of duration and severity, of their role. The Court has more than once recognised personal liability for the cartel practice, considered as a single infringement, despite the fact that it results from a series of conducts of varied severity, arguing that all these conducts have a common aim. Complaints on the violation of the principle of individual punitive liability, considering it as a single infringement, are overcome by the awareness that in such practices an undertaking can be considered responsible for the anti-competitive behaviour of other undertakings taking part in the cartel, "where it is established that the undertaking in question was aware of the offending conduct of the other participants or that it could reasonably have foreseen it and that it was prepared to take the risk".[66]

On the contrary, the principle of individual punitive liability seems to be undermined in the case law on the hypothesis of participation in cartel practices by companies linked to others through a parent company–subsidiary company relationship. In this sense, the ECJ, according to a consolidated approach of its case law, considers compliant with the principle of individual punitive liability the conviction of a parent company for its participation in cartel practices through its subsidiaries, although these are separate incorporated entities, when they do not autonomously determine their commercial policy and follow instead the indications of their parent company.[67] The limit imposed by the principle of individual liability, which in this case would already be violated in its narrow sense of *prohibition on the attribution of responsibility for the actions of others*, is not disregarded by the European judges, who take it for granted, to a certain extent, but is rather eluded by extending the definition of the subjects that can be considered offenders. According to the ECJ, the parent company and its subsidiaries are part of the same *economic unit*—and therefore of a single undertaking under the European law of competition—"even if in law that economic unit consists of several persons, natural or legal".[68] As a consequence, the Commission "may address a decision imposing fines on the parent company, without having to establish the personal involvement

---

[65] On the doubts raised in scholarship by Article 23(4) of Regulation No 1/2003, in relation to the principle of culpability, see Maugeri (2007), p. 173, and the related footnote 244. Even Regulation No 2988/95, on the protection of the European Communities' financial interests, provides in Article 5 for the intention or negligence of the infringement.

[66] ECJ 8 July 1999, *Commission v. Anic Partecipazioni SpA*, Case C-49/92 P, § 83.

[67] See, among the most recent, ECJ 19 July 2012, *Alliance One International Inc. and Others v. Commission*, Case C-628/10 P and C-14/11 P, § 43.

[68] See ECJ 12 July 1984, *Hydrotherm Geräetebau GmbH v. Ditta Compact del Dott. Ing. Mario Andreoli & c. sas*, Case 170/83, § 11; more recently, ECJ 18 July 2013, *Schindler Holding Ltd and Others v. Commission*, Case C-501/11 P, § 103.

of the latter in the infringement".[69] To be more precise, the extension of the concept of an undertaking—and therefore of offenders—does not appear to be totally inappropriate if one takes into account the relationship between the parent company and its subsidiaries, related to the former through economic, organisational and legal links.[70] Furthermore, if the parent company wholly or almost wholly owns the subsidiary's capital, Luxembourg Judges claim a (rebuttable) presumption according to which the parent company exercises a decisive influence over the conduct of the subsidiary.[71] It is therefore sufficient for the Commission to prove that the subsidiary is wholly owned by the parent company for the latter to be considered jointly and severally liable together with the former for the fine imposed for the infringement of European competition rules.[72] Thus, the burden of proof lies with the parent company[73] that can rebut the presumption of liability by providing sufficient supporting evidence to demonstrate the autonomous nature of the commercial policy of its subsidiary.[74]

According to the ECJ, the presumption of the exercise of decisive influence over the subsidiary's commercial policy is intended to strike a balance between, on one hand, the importance of the objective of combatting and preventing conduct contrary to the competition rules and, on the other hand, the requirements flowing from certain "general principles of the European Union law, such as the principle of the presumption of innocence, according to which penalties should be applied solely to the offender, as well as the principle of legal certainty and the rights of the defence, including the principle of equality of arms".[75] This would explain why

[69] Among the most recent, see ECJ 9 July 2012, *Alliance One International Inc. and Others v. Commission*, Case C-628/10 P and C-14/11 P, § 44; ECJ 29 September 2011, *Elf Aquitaine SA v. Commission*, Case C-521/09 P, § 55.

[70] Suffice to recall judgments quoted in the previous footnote.

[71] See, among many, ECJ 10 September 2009, *Akzo Nobel NV and Others v. Commission*, Case C-97/08 P, § 58; ECJ 29 September 2011, *Elf Aquitaine SA v. Commission*, Case C-521/09 P, §§ 56 and 88.

[72] ECJ 29 September 2011, *Elf Aquitaine SA v. Commission*, Case C-521/09 P, § 57; ECJ 10 September 2009, *Akzo Nobel NV and Others v. Commission*, Case C-97/08 P, § 61. In some ways, the ECJ's approach in case of imposition of fines where undertakings succeed each other is similar: see ECJ 11 December 2007, *Autorità Garante della Concorrenza e del Mercato and Others v. Ente tabacchi italiani - ETI SpA e a.*, Case C-280/06, § 52. In the instant case, the ECJ expressed its judgment within the *mediated safeguard* of EU interests: see below, Sect. 5.2.

[73] It is worth noting that under Article 2 of Regulation No 1/2003, the burden of proving an infringement of Article 81(1) or of Article 82 TEC (now 101 and 102 TFEU) shall rest on the party or the authority alleging the infringement.

[74] Similar reasoning has not prevented the European judges from considering insufficient, to overcome the controversial presumption, the existence of behaviour codes adopted by the parent company to prevent violations of the discipline in terms of competition by its subsidiaries: see ECJ 18 July 2013, *Schindler Holding Ltd and Other v. Commission*, Case C-501/11 P, §§ 113 and 114.

[75] See ECJ 18 July 2013, *Schindler Holding Ltd and Other v. Commission*, Case C-501/11 P, § 108; ECJ 29 September 2011, *Elf Aquitaine SA v. Commission*, Case C-521/09 P, § 59.

the presumption is rebuttable.[76] It cannot be denied that the functional efficacy of the presumption mechanism, which by exempting the Commission from the burden of proof of the parent company's liability makes it possible to spare the European bodies the costs of a difficult verification. It is in the sphere of the parent company's operations that it would be more effective to carry out an investigation of the elements necessary to show the lack of the actual decisive influence exercised on the subsidiaries' conduct on the market[77]; it is clear that the *probatio diabolica* is less so if entrusted to subjects with whom the presumption lies. In this sense, the views of the Judges in Luxembourg correspond at times to the hermeneutical approaches of the Strasbourg Court, constantly referred to, concerning the limits of the use of the presumptions of liability: the latter would be applicable if proportionate to the legitimate aim pursued, if evidence to the contrary could be submitted and if the rights of the defence were preserved.[78] Having taken into account the aim of the presumption, that is to say to strike a balance between, on one hand, the importance of the objective of combatting and preventing conduct contrary to the competition rules and, on the other hand, the need to protect guarantees that can be affected by the presumptions, the ECJ considers the presumption to be proportionate "to the legitimate aim pursued".[79]

The case law analysed here shows that more attention is given to the procedural implications of the presumption of innocence than to the substantial nature of the individual punitive liability. As shown above, the issues submitted to the ECJ do not concern the offence envisaged under legislation, but its implementation by the Commission, usually shared by the Luxembourg Judges. The presumption mechanism applied by the Commission and supported by the ECJ pertains to the judicial guarantees of the defence regarding the imposition of a sanction whose prerequisites in terms of substantive law include a necessary mental link between the offence and the offender.[80]

However, it cannot be denied that the ECJ's precision in reacting to the remarks concerning the violation of the principle of individual punitive liability indicates a full formal recognition of the guarantee.[81] Sometimes the Luxembourg Judges'

---

76 ECJ 29 September 2011, *Elf Aquitaine SA v. Commission*, Case C-521/09 P, § 59.

77 *Ibid.*, § 60.

78 See ECJ 18 July 2013, *Schindler Holding Ltd and Others v. Commission*, Case C-501/11 P, § 107; ECJ 29 September 2011, *Elf Aquitaine SA v. Commission*, Case C-521/09 P, § 62, referring back to the ECtHR Judgment of 23 July 2002, *Janosevic v. Sweden*, Application no. 34619/97.

79 ECJ 18 July 2013, *Schindler Holding Ltd and Other v. Commission*, Case C-501/11 P, § 108.

80 See Article 23(4) of Regulation No 1/2003.

81 See Maugeri (2007), pp. 166 ff., on the conclusions of scholarship pertaining to the ECJ judgments that define the relevant *force majeure* for the exclusion of the liability for the committed infringement. The reference, in particular, is to judgment ECJ 18 March 1980, *SpA Ferriera Valsabbia and Others v. Commission*, Joined Cases 154, 205, 206, 226–228, 263 and 264/78, 39, 31, 83 and 85/79, § 140, in which the ECJ considers necessary that "the external cause relied on by individuals has consequences which are inexorable and inevitable to the point of making it objectively impossible for the persons concerned to comply with their obligations and, in this case, leaving them no alternative but to infringe" the Community law.

statements refer to the *nulla poena sine culpa* principle, intended in the wide sense of the principle of blame, taking into account the possibility of knowing the law provisions. The ECJ takes into account the error caused by the Commission's communications, concerning the conformity of the conducts penalised to European law, or by practices tolerated, and therefore misleading, of the EU institutions, without disregarding the necessary offender's precaution to be exempt from the *reproach* for the infringement.[82]

The ECJ, however, usually refuses to justify the undertaking sanctioned for the unawareness of the unlawfulness of conduct, even when the undertaking asserts that it had the support of *reassuring* legal opinions on the compatibility of its market practice with EU law.[83] In this sense, the ECJ considers that a conduct intrinsically offensive to the EU interests does not allow the infringement of the ban imposed by the EU law to be excused. Particularly in relation to the ban of anti-competitive practices, it is sufficient for the subject in question to be aware that the company's market practice leads to a restriction of competition, regardless of his/her awareness of infringing the Treaty rules on this matter, to be held responsible for the infringement.[84] Some ECJ's judgments deny even the undoubted punitive nature of given sanctions that thus fall back onto the level of guarantees, implying the compliance of the hypothesis of absolute liability with EU law.[85]

---

[82] See Sotis (2007), p. 22. Sotis argues that in terms of safeguarding EU interests, the ECJ has the highest degree of freedom in determining the principle since it is EU law that is creating the principle to limit its own power.

[83] ECJ 1 February 1978, *Miller International Schallplatten GmbH v. Commission*, Case 19/77, § 18. It is worth noting that the Community rules on competition, in force at the time of the judgment quoted above, provided for a consultation procedure of the Commission to obtain clarifications on the undertakings' position (see Regulation no 17/1962). Trusting in a legal opinion, given that there was not a request for a "negative clearance" by the Commission, tended to make the error of the undertaking regarding the lawfulness of its own commercial conduct avoidable.

[84] See ECJ 8 November 1983, *NV IAZ International Belgium and Others v. Commission*, Joined Cases 96–102, 104, 105, 108 and 110/82, § 45; more recently, ECJ 14 October 2010, *Deutsche Telekom AG v. Commission*, Case C-280/08 P, §§ 124 f., pertaining to a hypothesis of violation of competition rules allowed by the national authorities: "As regards the question whether the infringements of the competition rules were committed intentionally or negligently and are, therefore, liable to be punished by a fine in accordance with the first subparagraph of Article 15 (2) of Regulation No 17, that condition is satisfied where the undertaking cannot be unaware of the anti-competitive nature of its conduct, whether or not it is aware that it is infringing the competition rules of the Treaty. This is so in the case of an undertaking in the telecommunications sector which could not have been unaware that, notwithstanding the authorisation decisions of the regulatory authority for telecommunications and post, it had genuine scope to set its retail prices for end-user access services and, moreover, the margin squeeze entailed serious restrictions on competition, particularly in view of its monopoly on the wholesale market in local loop access services and its virtual monopoly on the retail market in end-user access services" (Summary n. 6 of the judgment quoted above).

[85] ECJ, 11 July 2002, *Käserei Champignon Hofmeister GmbH & Co. KG v. Hauptzollamt Hamburg-Jonas*, Case C -210/00. See Riondato (2002), pp. 1557 ff.; ECJ, 18 September 2003, *Volkswagen AG v. Commission*, Case C-338/00 P, § 96.

5.2 The Diverse Solidity of the **Nulla Poena Sine Culpa Principle** *in the Protection of European Interests Mediated by National Laws*

At the second level of safeguard of relevant interests within the EU, where national sources of law are involved, as shown earlier, the Luxembourg Court displays a more cautious approach. In this case, the protection of supranational interests is mediated by national legislatures that often apply criminal sanctions to restrain conducts infringing European regulations. It should be noted, however, that the national law provision punishing infringements of European regulations with criminal sanctions, treating them as offences of absolute liability, is not necessarily considered to conflict with the principles of EU law. The main adopted criteria are the principle of loyal cooperation between the EU and the Member States, now provided for in Article 4(3) TEU, and the subsequent duty of Member States to "ensure that infringements of EU law are penalized under procedural and substantive conditions analogous to those applicable to infringements of national law of a similar nature and importance". This means that the compliance of offences of absolute liability with the Union law is determined by the degree of juridical sensitivity of the national law involved in the instant case.[86]

The ECJ's lack of interest towards the *nulla poena sine culpa* principle is therefore not surprising, given that some (apparently) isolated judgments show that the EU judges are not particularly concerned about the compliance with the Union law of the principle that the mistake of law cannot be excused.[87]

The ECJ's caution in expressing its role in the context of protection of the EU's interests mediated by national laws is perhaps imposed by the necessary involvement of national legislation. The cause of the uneasiness of EU judges is probably related to the fact that the *nulla poena sine culpa* principle is not common to the constitutional traditions of all Member States[88] and therefore cannot be used as a limit to national laws. If one considers that the unavoidable mistake of law excluding liability is hardly ever recognised in the national legislation pertaining to criminal matters, the EU judges' approach towards the *nulla poena sine culpa* principle in administrative law is not surprising.[89]

It is, however, worth noting that an emphasis on the mental ingredient of crime can be found in the ECJ judgments aimed at assessing the proportionality of the sanctions applied by Member States on the basis of the duty to protect the EU's

---

[86] See ECJ 10 July 1990, *Anklagemyndigheden v. Hansen & Søn I/S*, Case C-326/88. On this, see Panebianco (2007), p. 117.

[87] See ECJ 25 November 1998, *Manfredi v. Puglia*, Case C-308/97, § 34.

[88] See Sotis (2007), p. 22.

[89] Even though a study on the administrative and criminal system of sanctions of Member States funded by the Commission seems to indicate a growing relevance of the principle of culpability in administrative law, see Maugeri (2008), p. 131.

interests.[90] It is common knowledge that such duties imposed by the EU force Member States to adopt "effective, proportionate and dissuasive" penalties. This is related to the principle of loyal cooperation also implemented in European secondary legislation. The assessment of the proportionality of penalties, as provided by the involved Member State, is carried out in relation to rights and freedoms safeguarded by the EU, particularly *the freedom of movement of persons*, a freedom of paramount value clearly affected by criminal sanctions and, more specifically, by custodial sentences.[91]

The assessment of the proportionality of criminal sanctions is usually entrusted to national courts, which are given guidelines and recommendations by the ECJ. More specifically, the national court is required to take into account factors related to the extent of the damage and danger and the offender's *good or bad faith* when balancing the specific safeguard needs, as requested by the EU.[92]

More recently, the ECJ has referred to the presumption of innocence, as interpreted by ECtHR case law with reference to Article 6 ECHR. In a judgment dating back to a few years ago, the ECJ considered compliant with the presumption of innocence, as provided by Article 6(2) ECHR, a directive pertaining to insider dealing that defined practices that are prohibited without any clear indication of an awareness of the forbidden action, although such awareness was required by previous Community law.[93] More precisely, the ECJ specified that the constituent elements of insider dealing allow intention to be assumed, provided that this presumption is open to rebuttal.[94]

Insider dealing is, in actual fact, an offence marked by intent.[95] It is clear in the arguments of the Luxembourg Judges that the national context described by the legislature makes it possible to rule out, *in principle*, that the *insider* can act without being aware of his/her own actions and ignoring the inside information he/she has received. Moreover, it is the mental element that requires an indirect assessment through an analysis of external factors that can be supported by experience. However, if the intentionality of the conduct were inferred from a combination of the (objective) constituent elements of the offence, excluding completely the

---

[90] On the ECJ case law pertaining to proportionality of the sanctions, see Panebianco (2007), pp. 122 ff.

[91] See ECJ 7 July 1976, *Lynne Watson and Alessandro Belmann*, Case C 118-75, § 21; ECJ 3 July 1980, *Regina v. Pieck*, Case 157/79, § 19.

[92] ECJ 17 October 1995, *Leifer and Others*, Case C-83/94, § 40; ECJ 4 October 1991, *Richardt and "Les Accessoires Scientifiques" SNC*, Case C-367/89, § 25.

[93] ECJ 23 December 2009, *Spector Photo Group NV and Chris Van Raemdonck v. Commissie voor het Bank-, Financie- en Assurantiewezen (CBFA)*, Case C-45/08.

[94] *Ibid.*, §§ 36, 38 and 44.

[95] Under Article 2(1) of Directive 2003/6/EC, "Member States shall prohibit any person referred to in the second subparagraph who possesses inside information from using that information by acquiring or disposing of, or by trying to acquire or dispose of, for his own account or for the account of a third party, either directly or indirectly, financial instruments to which that information relates".

assessment of the mental element, it would be detrimental to the guarantees protecting the accused. This unfortunately occurs in Italian case law, which allows forms of *dolus in re ipsa* in criminal matters, with the alibi of the possibility to rebut the presumption.

To be more precise, the ECJ does not insist on the legitimacy of such a presumption mechanism precisely because of the presumption of innocence, guaranteed by the ECHR as a fundamental right. The ECJ refers to its own constant case law that recognises fundamental rights as "an integral part of the general principles of Community law", whose compliance is a condition of the lawfulness of Community acts.[96] Since Article 6(2) ECHR is confined to criminal matters, the ECJ specifies that, although Community rules suspected of unlawfulness do not oblige the Member States to provide for criminal sanctions against the authors of their infringements, the nature of the infringements at issue and the degree of severity of the sanctions that may be imposed allow them to be qualified as criminal for the purposes of the application of Article 6(2) ECHR.[97] At this point of the ECJ's hermeneutical approach, a reference to the Strasbourg Court's case law becomes inevitable, more precisely to the judgment *Salabiaku v. France*, on the limits in the use of the presumptions of liability.[98] This reasoning is behind the declaration of compatibility of EU discipline involved in the instant case with Article 6(2) ECHR, taking into account the possibility of rebutting the presumption and the subsequent safeguard of the right to defence.

The suspected offence of absolute liability is thus turned into a presumption of liability that the defence needs to rebut, as already occurred in the Strasbourg Court's case law. It cannot be denied that the Luxembourg Judges' reference to Article 6 ECHR to bridge the gap, on the procedural level, of a suspected *deficit* of culpability of the substantive law provision testifies to a fairly explicit recognition of the principle of personal punitive liability in EU law.

5.3 The Contribution of the Advocates General of the ECJ to the Supranational Recognition of the **Nulla Poena Sine Culpa** *Principle*

While the ECJ's case law does not exclude *a priori* the recognition of the *nulla poena sine culpa* principle as an EU law principle, the strongest positions can be found in the arguments of the Advocates General, even in the more complex context of the mediated protection of EU interests. Besides the recurrent recognition of the

[96] ECJ 23 December 2009, *Spector Photo Group NV and Chris Van Raemdonck v. Commissie voor het Bank-, Financie- en Assurantiewezen (CBFA)*, Case C-45/08, §§ 40 and 41.

[97] *Ibid.*, § 42. It is interesting to note that the judgment was passed right after the Lisbon Treaty came into force.

[98] See above, Sect. 4.

principle of personal liability, imposed as a limit to the exercise by public authorities of the *jus puniendi*,[99] which can be transferred, with due caution, to the administrative law,[100] the most interesting interpretations focus on the wide sense of the *nulla poena sine culpa* principle, intended as the principle of blame,[101] more precisely in relation to the excusable nature of the unavoidable mistake of law.[102]

The issue has been recently addressed by the Advocate General Kokott following a request for a preliminary ruling, relating once again to a case of participation in cartel practices. In the main proceedings, the undertakings were supported by the unavoidable mistake about the lawfulness of the conduct on the market, based on a legal advice that later turned out to be wrong, and on an order of the national competition authority, which had concluded for the lawfulness of conduct of the undertakings, albeit assessed from the perspective of the national law. The Advocate General opened his legal analysis of the question, wondering "whether the concept that an error of law as to the wrongfulness of an act precludes liability, which is familiar from general criminal law, is recognised in European competition law". A question barely considered and never fully addressed by the European judges,[103] despite the ECJ's case law's recognition of the validity of the *nulla poena sine culpa* principle in EU law.[104]

The logical premises of the recognition of the mistake of law excluding liability in the EU legal system are the assessment of the nature of antitrust law, unrelated to the "core area of criminal law", albeit undoubtedly with a "character similar to criminal law".[105] As a consequence, the Advocate General considers the antitrust

[99] Opinion of Advocate General Bot delivered on 26 October 2010, *ThyssenKrupp Nirosta GmbH*, formerly *ThyssenKrupp Nirosta AG*, formerly *ThyssenKrupp Stainless AG v. Commission*, Case C-352/09 P, §§ 161 f.; Opinion of Advocate General Ruiz-Jarabo delivered on 11 February 2003, *Aalborg Portland A/S v. Commission*, Case C-204/00 P, § 63, both regarding the liability for infringement of competition rules.

[100] Opinion of Advocate General Ruiz-Jarabo delivered on 11 February 2003, *Aalborg Portland A/S v. Commission*, Case C-204/00 P, § 64.

[101] See above, n. 2.

[102] See the Opinion of Advocate General Reischl delivered on 19 September 1978, *Hoffmann-La Roche & Co. AG v. Commission*, *European Court Reports 1979*, Case 85/76, p. 596 f., regarding the recognition of the mistake of law excluding liability in the Community law.

[103] Opinion of Advocate General Kokott delivered on 28 February 2013, *Schenker & Co. AG and Others*, Case C-681/11, § 38.

[104] *Ibid.*, § 41.

[105] *Ibid.*, § 40. There seems to be an agreement among the European Courts on this matter: even the Strasbourg Court has recognised the criminal nature of a financial penalty imposed by a national competition authority basing on the *Engel criteria*: see ECtHR, Judgment of 27 September 2011, *Menarini Diagnostics v. Italy*, Application no. 43509/08, §§ from 38 to 44. As commonly known, in the *Engel* Judgment the Strasbourg Court indicates the following three criteria to identify a *criminal charge*: (1) the legal classification of the offence under national law, (2) the nature of the offence, (3) the degree of severity of the penalty that the person concerned risks incurring: see ECtHR, Judgment of 8 June 1976, *Engel and Others v. The Netherlands*, Application no. 5100/71; 5101/71; 5102/71; 5354/72; 5370/72. On the notion of *criminal matter* in the ECtHR's case law, see Nicosia (2006), pp. 39 ff.

law as being subordinate to the compliance of principles typical of criminal law, including the *nulla poena sine culpa* principle,[106] considered as a fundamental right common to the constitutional traditions of the Member States.[107] Having taken into account the lack of an explicit reference to the principle in the Charter of Fundamental Rights of the European Union and in the ECHR, the Advocate General considers it as a necessary precondition for the presumption of innocence, and therefore as implicitly included both in Article 48(1) of the Nice Charter[108] and in Article 6(2) of the ECHR, which are "the expression in procedural law of the principle of *nulla poena sine culpa*".[109] This interpretation makes it possible to relate to the compliance with the principle of culpability, not only the imposition of penalties expressed by the *EU punitive authority* in terms of competition—as provided by Article 23(2) of Regulation No 1/2003[110]—but also the imposition of penalties applied on a national level in compliance with the supranational duties of protection, given that when they exercise their powers national authorities must comply with general principles of EU law.[111]

The supranational recognition of the *nulla poena sine culpa* principle thus allows the Advocate General to acknowledge that an unavoidable mistake of law excludes liability,[112] and therefore an undertaking may not be held liable when "all possible and reasonable steps to avoid its alleged infringement of EU antitrust law had been taken",[113] whereas the fact that the mistake of law could be avoided causes at least a negligent infringement, which *may* (but not *must*) lead to a reduced fine.[114]

However, none of the interesting statements of the Advocate General has led to even moderate ECJ judgments acknowledging that the unavoidable mistake of law excludes liability in EU law. In the concluding judgment, where the Advocate General provided his opinion, the most significant meaning of the *nulla poena sine culpa* principle is once again recognised only implicitly to the extent that the ECJ emphasises the denial of the relevance of the legal advice given by a lawyer or of the national competition authorities' orders since they do not have the power to adopt a decision concluding that there is no infringement of Treaty rules on competition.[115]

---

[106] Opinion of Advocate General Kokott delivered on 28 February 2013, *Schenker & Co. AG and Others*, Case C-681/11, § 41.

[107] *Ibid.*

[108] On the presumption of innocence in the Charter of Fundamental Rights of the European Union, see Eser (2011a), pp. 589 ff.

[109] Opinion of Advocate General Kokott delivered on 28 February 2013, *Schenker & Co. AG and Others*, Case C-681/11, § 41.

[110] See above, Sect. 5.1.

[111] See Opinion of Advocate General Kokott delivered on 28 February 2013, *Schenker & Co. AG and Others*, Case C-681/11, § 43, and the judgments quoted in it.

[112] *Ibid.*, §§ 44 and 45.

[113] *Ibid.*, § 46.

[114] *Ibid.*, § 47.

[115] *Ibid.*, §§ 41 and 42.

6 Developments and Justiciability of the *Nulla Poena Sine Culpa* Principle After the Lisbon Treaty

It cannot be denied that the destiny of the *nulla poena sine culpa* principle in the two European law systems would have been different if the ECHR and the Charter of Fundamental Rights of the European Union had explicitly recognised it.

However, the repeated borrowings from the ECtHR's case law by Luxembourg Judges could be further developed through the wider interpretation of the *nulla poena sine culpa* principle formulated by the Strasbourg Judges. Through the connection offered by Article 6(3) TEU,[116] the most open interpretation of Article 7 of the ECHR, recently applied in the ECtHR case law and aimed at relating the *nulla poena sine culpa* principle with the *nulla poena sine lege* principle,[117] could indicate that this normative parameter should inform the issues submitted to the ECJ involving the principle of culpability.[118] Such a hermeneutical approach would, among other things, be facilitated by Article 49 of the Nice Charter, overlapping with Article 7 of the ECHR and to a certain extent going beyond it, since it also explicitly provides for the *lex mitior* principle[119] and the principle of proportionality of criminal offences and penalties.

More precisely, a clear reference to the Charter of Fundamental Rights of the European Union offers a simpler approach to the recognition and binding nature of the principle of culpability in the EU law system. Rather than following the problematic *procedure* provided by Article 6(3) TEU, guaranteeing the *nulla poena sine culpa* principle through a mediated connection with the ECHR, a direct reference could be made to Article 49 of the Nice Charter[120] in the implementation of EU law.[121] It is true that in ECJ case law an interpretation similar to the one

---

[116] Under Article 6(3) TEU, "Fundamental rights, as guaranteed by the European Convention for the Protection of Human Rights and Fundamental Freedoms and as they result from the constitutional traditions common to the Member States, shall constitute general principles of the Union's law". Grasso suggests exploiting the connection with the ECHR proposed by Article 6(3) TEU to overcome the ECJ's approach aimed at denying the recognition of the principle of culpability as a fundamental right, Grasso (2011), pp. 2319 ff.

[117] See ECtHR, Judgment of 20 January 2009, *Sud Fondi srl v. Italy*, Application no. 75909/01. On this, see above, Sect. 4.2.

[118] See Maugeri (2011), p. 124. She argues that the change marked by the Judgment *Sud Fondi srl v. Italy* in the ECtHR's case law should lead to an appreciation of the principle of culpability also by the Luxembourg Judges.

[119] As commonly known, the *lex mitior principle* has been derived from Article 7 ECHR in the Judgment of 17 September 2009, *Scoppola v. Italy*, Application no. 10249/03.

[120] For a detailed analysis of Article 49 of the Charter of Fundamental Rights of the European Union, see Eser (2011b), pp. 602 ff.

[121] Under Article 51(1) of the Charter of Fundamental Rights of the European Union, "The provisions of this Charter are addressed to the institutions and bodies of the Union with due regard for the principle of subsidiarity and to the Member States only when they are implementing Union law. They shall therefore respect the rights, observe the principles and promote the application thereof in accordance with their respective powers." According to Grasso (2011), p. 2322, Article 51(1) should be applied every time there is a connection with EU law.

offered by the Strasbourg Court, pertaining to Article 7 of the ECHR in the Judgment *Sud Fondi srl v. Italy*, is lacking; however, the Nice Charter guarantees fundamental rights corresponding to rights guaranteed by the ECHR, with the same meaning and the same scope laid down by the said Convention, even allowing a more extensive protection.[122] From this perspective, the meaning currently attributed to the *nulla poena sine culpa* principle in its relation to the *nulla poena sine lege* principle will become a minimum *standard* of safeguard that can be implemented.

The ECJ judges, moreover, do not seem ready for such a hermeneutical approach, nor is it possible to rely on the effectiveness of more decisive interpretations by the Advocates General.[123] In a recent opinion in which Advocate General Kokott openly addresses the issue whether the mistake of law precludes liability in EU law,[124] the *nulla poena sine culpa* principle is once again based on the presumption of innocence, albeit through the combined reference to Articles 6 ECHR and 48 of the Charter of Fundamental Rights of the European Union.

Whatever legal basis is invoked, the recognition of the *nulla poena sine culpa* principle even in the EU law system, through the Nice Charter, would multiply the *chances* of safeguard by increasing the means of justiciability. Basing the principle of culpability on the Charter of Fundamental Rights of the European Union implies the certainty of its binding nature on the EU institutions as well as on Member States, since Article 6(1) TEU attributes to the Nice Charter "the same legal value as the Treaties". On the contrary, Contracting States to the ECHR, which include all EU Member States, must comply with the ECHR, although the latter does not have a binding effect on the EU since accession to the ECHR announced in Article 6 (2) TEU has not yet been completed.

An overview of the justiciability approaches of the *nulla poena sine culpa* principle within EU law–which cannot be exhaustive—according to an interpretation excluding the direct criminal law competence of the EU,[125] should be based on the hypothesis of a national implementing legislation (both implicit and explicit) of EU rules, whereby one or the other or both are contrary to the principle of

---

[122] According to Article 52(3) of the Nice Charter, "In so far as this Charter contains rights which correspond to rights guaranteed by the Convention for the Protection of Human Rights and Fundamental Freedoms, the meaning and scope of those rights shall be the same as those laid down by the said Convention. This provision shall not prevent Union law from providing more extensive protection." For a detailed analysis of this provision, see Borowsky (2011), para 29 ff.

[123] See above, Sect. 5.3. The European institutions seem to be going in the opposite direction: in the conclusions of the Justice and Home Affairs Council of 30 November 2009 *on model provisions, guiding the Council's criminal law deliberations*, there is an explicitly negative approach to the hypothesis of absolute liability that "should not be prescribed in EU criminal legislation", as provided by point 8 of the Council Conclusions, which can be found on the EU Council official website. See Sicurella (2011), pp. 2636 ff.

[124] See above, Sect. 5.3.

[125] See above, footnote 61.

culpability, which here is assumed as recognised by the Charter of Fundamental Rights of the European Union.

According to this perspective, if the national legal system recognises the *nulla poena sine culpa principle*, as in the case of Article 27 of the Italian Constitution, and this is violated (only) by the national law provision, both the unconstitutionality of the national law provision and the incompatibility with EU law of the national law provision transposing a European rule follow. In this case, a more direct and effective safeguard in terms of a reinstatement of the principle with *erga omnes* efficacy should be provided by the national Constitutional Court[126]; however, the necessary primacy of EU law over national law seems to direct towards a solution based on the reference to the ECJ for a preliminary ruling.[127] The national court, to which a violation of the *nulla poena sine culpa* principle is reported, should refer to the ECJ to require an interpretation of the European rule applied at the national level. In the case where the ECJ should find the national law provision to be incompatible with EU law, the national law provision would be subsequently inapplicable in this specific case. Moreover, individuals would have the right, after all domestic remedies have been exhausted, to apply to the ECtHR to report the infringement of the European Convention, involving the Contracting State whose law has damaged the principle of culpability. This approach to justiciability should also be applied when the national legal system does not recognise the principle of *nulla poena sine culpa*.

A more problematic example is the case when the European rule, which is transposed into the national law provision, is not compliant with the principle of culpability, as recognised by the national legal system. Besides the unconstitutionality of the national law provision, the illegality of the European rule itself, in relation to EU law, also comes into play, and the national court should probably first refer to the ECJ to ask for clarification on the interpretation of the European rule. In the case where the ECJ should supply an interpretation confirming the illegality of the European secondary legislation rule—arguing, for example, that such a Directive does not preclude national legislation from considering the specific behaviour as a criminal offence, even though there was no intention or negligence—the national court could raise the question of the constitutionality of the national law provision before the National Constitutional Court.[128] The exclusion of the national law provision, however, would not prevent the European rule from having effect in the other Member States to the point where an action for annulment will make the illegal European rule void.

If the case mentioned above were to be made worse by a failure to recognise the principle of culpability by the National Constitution, despite an ECJ preliminary ruling that considers once again the European rule of secondary legislation not as an obstacle to the national criminal law providing for an absolute liability, and after all

[126] See Sotis (2007), pp. 202 f.

[127] See Ruggeri (2011), pp. 167 ff.

[128] See Sotis (2007), pp. 202 f.

domestic remedies have been exhausted, it would still be possible to apply to the ECtHR for the infringement of the European Convention. However, the assessment of an infringement within the ECtHR jurisdiction would not exclude the illegal law provision from the national legal system, resulting once again in the justice of a specific case.[129]

As argued at the beginning, possible hypotheses of violation of the *nulla poena sine culpa* principle have been examined focusing on the level of protection of EU interests mediated by national laws on the basis of a lack of direct EU criminal law competence. However, we cannot rule out that more decisive interpretations of the ECJ might lead us to recognise a *mainly penal* character in the sense indicated by the ECtHR in the *Engel* judgment,[130] even to the law provisions expressing the *EU punitive authority* ensuring the safeguard of the *nulla poena sine culpa principle* in the EU administrative punitive law. As previously argued, basing the principle of culpability on the Charter of Fundamental Rights of the European Union can ensure a stronger normative support rather than basing it on a connection with the ECHR when applying Article 6(3) TEU, and more importantly in comparison with the legitimisation of the principle as a common denominator in the constitutional traditions shared by the Member States.

References

Abbadessa G (2011) Il principio di presunzione di innocenza nella CEDU: profili sostanziali. In: Manes V, Zagrelbesky V (eds) La Convenzione europea dei diritti dell'uomo nell'ordinamento penale italiano. Giuffrè, Milano, pp 377–410

Alessandri A (1991) I – Il 1° comma dell'art. 27. In: Branca G, Pizzorusso A (eds) Commentario della Costituzione. Rapporti civili. Art. 27–28. Zanichelli, Bologna - Società Editrice del Foro Italiano, Roma, pp 1 ff

Bernardi A (2004) Europeizzazione del diritto penale e progetto di Costituzione europea. Diritto penale e processo 1:5–12

Bernardi A (2006) "Riserva di legge" e fonti europee in materia penale. In: Annali dell'Università di Ferrara, Scienze giuridiche, Nuova serie, XX

Bernardi A (2008) L'armonizzazione delle sanzioni in Europa: linee ricostruttive. In: Grasso G, Sicurella R (eds) Per un rilancio del progetto europeo. Esigenze di tutela degli interessi comunitari e nuove strategie di integrazione penale. Giuffrè, Milano, pp 381–454

Borowsky M (2011) Artikel 52. In: Meyer (ed) Charta der Grundrechte der Europäischen Union, 3rd edn. Nomos, Baden-Baden, pp 667 ff

Böse M (2009) La sentenza della Corte costituzionale tedesca sul Trattato di Lisbona e il suo significato per la europeizzazione del diritto penale. Criminalia 267–301

[129] According to the *Final report* on the fifth negotiation meeting, held in Strasbourg on 5 April 2013, on the Accession of the European Union to the European Convention on Human Rights, the EU can be held responsible by the ECtHR as the main respondent, or as a co-respondent together with a Member State, for the violations of the Convention or its Protocols deriving from the application of EU law by Member States.

[130] See above, footnote 105.

Chenal R, Tamietti A (2012) Art. 6. §§ IX–XXIII. In: Bartole S, De Sena P, Zagrebelsky V (eds) Commentario breve alla Convenzione europea per la salvaguardia dei diritti dell'uomo e delle libertà fondamentali. Cedam, Padova, pp 181–245

de Vero G (2007) La giurisprudenza della Corte di Strasburgo. In: de Vero G, Panebianco G (eds) Delitti e pene nella giurisprudenza delle Corti europee. Giappichelli, Torino, pp 11–58

de Vero G (2012) Corso di diritto penale. I, 2nd edn. Giappichelli, Torino

Eser A (2011a) Artikel 48. In: Meyer J (ed) Charta der Grundrechte der Europäischen Union, 3rd edn. Nomos, Baden-Baden, pp 588 ff

Eser A (2011b) Artikel 49. In: Meyer J (ed) Charta der Grundrechte der Europäischen Union, 3rd edn. Nomos, Baden-Baden, pp 602 ff

Grasso G (1989) Comunità europee e diritto penale. I rapporti tra l'ordinamento comunitario e i sistemi penali degli Stati membri. Giuffrè, Milano

Grasso G (2007) La protezione dei diritti fondamentali nella Costituzione per l'Europa e il diritto penale: spunti di riflessione critica. In: Grasso G, Sicurella R (eds) Lezioni di diritto penale europeo. Giuffrè, Milano, pp 633–672

Grasso G (2008) Relazione introduttiva. In: Grasso G, Sicurella R (eds) Per un rilancio del progetto europeo. Esigenze di tutela degli interessi comunitari e nuove strategie di integrazione penale. Giuffrè, Milano, pp 1–49

Grasso G (2011) Il Trattato di Lisbona e le nuove competenze penali dell'Unione Europea. In: Studi in onore di Mario Romano. IV. Jovene, Napoli, pp 2307–2350

Manes V (2012a) Art. 7 §§ I–XV. In: Bartole S, De Sena P, Zagrebelsky V (eds) Commentario breve alla Convenzione europea per la salvaguardia dei diritti dell'uomo e delle libertà fondamentali. Cedam, Padova, pp 258–288

Manes V (2012b) I principi penalistici nel *network* multilivello: trapianto palingenesi, *cross-fertilization*. Rivista italiana di diritto e procedura penale 3:839–874

Maugeri AM (2007) Il sistema sanzionatorio comunitario dopo la Carta europea dei diritti fondamentali. In: Grasso G, Sicurella R (eds) Lezioni di diritto penale europeo. Giuffrè, Milano, pp 99–244

Maugeri AM (2008) I principi fondamentali del sistema punitivo comunitario: la giurisprudenza della Corte di giustizia e della Corte europea dei diritti dell'uomo. In: Grasso G, Sicurella R (eds) Per un rilancio del progetto europeo. Esigenze di tutela degli interessi comunitari e nuove strategie di integrazione penale. Giuffrè, Milano, pp 83–162

Maugeri AM (2011) Il principio di proporzione nelle scelte punitive del legislatore europeo: l'alternativa delle sanzioni amministrative comunitarie. In: Grasso G, Picotti L, Sicurella R (eds) L'evoluzione del sistema penale nei settori d'interesse europeo alla luce del Trattato di Lisbona. Giuffrè, Milano, pp 67–132

Mazzacuva F (2009) Un "hard case" davanti alla Corte europea: argomenti e principi nella sentenza su Punta Perotti. Diritto penale e processo 12:1540–1552

Meyer-Ladewig J (2011) EMRK. Europäische Menschenrechtskonvention, 3rd edn. Nomos, Baden-Baden

Nicosia E (2006) Convenzione europea dei diritti dell'uomo e diritto penale. Giappichelli, Torino

Palazzo F (2013) Corso di diritto penale. Parte generale, 5th edn. Giappichelli, Torino

Palazzo F, Papa M (2013) Lezioni di diritto penale comparato, 3rd edn. Giappichelli, Torino

Panebianco G (2007) La giurisprudenza della Corte di Lussemburgo. In: de Vero G, Panebianco G (eds) Delitti e pene nella giurisprudenza delle Corti europee. Giappichelli, Torino, pp 59–130

Panebianco G (2012) Il sistema penale minorile. Imputabilità, pericolosità ed esigenze educative. Giappichelli, Torino

Picotti L (2004) Il Corpus Juris 2000. Profili di diritto penale sostanziale e prospettive d'attuazione alla luce del Progetto di Costituzione per l'Europa. In: Picotti L (ed) Il Corpus Juris 2000. Nuova formulazione e prospettive di attuazione. Cedam, Padova, pp 3–91

Riondato S (2002) Un negativo "giro di vite" in rema di responsabilità "personale". Diritto penale e processo 12:1557–1562

Risicato L (2007) L'errore sull'età tra *error facti* ed *error iuris*: una decisione "timida" o "storica" della Corte costituzionale? Il commento. Diritto penale e processo 11:1465–1475
Ruggeri A (2011) "Itinerari" di una ricerca sul sistema delle fonti, XIV, Studi dell'anno 2010. Giappichelli, Torino
Salcuni G (2011) L'europeizzazione del diritto penale: problemi e prospettive. Giuffrè, Milano
Sicurella R (2002) Nulla poena sine culpa: un véritable principe commun européen? Revue de science criminelle 1:15–33
Sicurella R (2007) La tutela "mediata" degli interessi della costruzione europea: l'armonizzazione dei sistemi penali nazionali tra diritto comunitario e diritto dell'Unione europea. In: Grasso G, Sicurella R (eds) Lezioni di diritto penale europeo. Giuffrè, Milano, pp 245–393
Sicurella R (2011) Questioni di metodo nella costruzione di una teoria delle competenze dell'Unione europea in materia penale. In: Studi in onore di Mario Romano, vol IV. Jovene, Napoli, pp 2569–2644
Sotis C (2007) Il diritto senza codice. Uno studio sul sistema penale europeo vigente. Giuffrè, Milano
Sotis C (2010) Il Trattato di Lisbona e le competenze penali dell'Unione europea. Cassazione penale 3:1146–1166
Trechsel S (2005) Human rights in criminal proceedings. Oxford University Press, New York

Part II
Defence and Language Rights in Criminal Procedures

The Right to Information in EU Legislation

Serena Quattrocolo

Contents

Abstract This paper analyzes EU Directive 2012/13 on the right to information in criminal proceedings. This is the second step in the implementation of the EU Roadmap, settled after the Treaty of Lisbon entered into force, aimed at strengthening some of the guarantees envisaged under the ECHR. The aim of the present study is to reflect, first of all, on the meaning of the measures adopted and, second, on the impact that these may have on national systems. This reflection is intended as being general, since its goal is not to constitute a comparative study among the 28 EU domestic legal systems. Many provisions, in fact, although appearing to have highly innovative potential, may be interpreted restrictively.

Keywords Consequences of a lack of information • Information regarding the charge • Right to be informed on procedural rights

S. Quattrocolo (✉)
Department of Law, University of Torino, Lungo Dora Siena 100, 10153 Torino, Italy
e-mail: serena.quattrocolo@unito.it

S. Ruggeri (ed.), *Human Rights in European Criminal Law*,
DOI 10.1007/978-3-319-12042-3_5

1 The Fair Trial in the Post-Lisbon Era

The title of this paper suggests, foremost, a preliminary question. Why is it necessary to reflect, today, on EU legislation regulating the right to information in criminal proceedings?

It is in fact well known that this is a fundamental aspect of the general principle of the right to a fair trial, traditionally provided under the covenants and conventions on human rights.

We are used to referring to the procedural rights of individuals involved in criminal proceedings, starting with the general right to a trial,[1] within the scope of the regional conventions on human rights and, especially in Europe, of the European convention on human rights, signed in Rome in 1950.[2] We are also used to the topic of procedural rights in the area of the constitutional Charters of our countries.[3]

But the "post-Lisbon era" we now live in has brought with it a new perspective on EU legislation.[4] The reference to the post-Lisbon era is not only due to the new legislative framework, which has abolished the third-pillar system, introducing standard legislative tools into the AFSJ. Of course, as we will see below, the adoption of directives and the "other measures" mentioned in article 82(2) and (1) of the standing TFEU will have important consequences. Alongside these developments, furthermore, the particular significance of the post-Lisbon era may seem to derive—as extensive scholarship suggests[5]—from the implementation of the Tampere program, which led to the introduction of instruments mostly aimed at improving the fight against crime. As has been noted,[6] the major aim—not the only one, of course—of EU legislation in the first decade of the 2000s was to speed up police and judicial cooperation.

Probably because the coming into force of the Lisbon Treaty gave binding legal force to the EU FRCh—whose article 47 provides for the right to a fair trial—a new cohesion on the issues of procedural safeguards has finally been achieved among the EU Member States.

Of course, we have to remember that an important initiative by the EU Commission was launched in 2004, aimed at a Council framework decision "on certain procedural rights."[7] This proposal referred to the right to legal assistance (including legal aid), the right to free interpretation and translation, the right to communicate with other persons and to receive consular assistance and the right to information.[8]

---

[1] See Chiavario (1982), *passim*; see also Renucci (2013), p. 309.

[2] See Hecker (2012), p. 10.

[3] See Pollicino and Rando (2013), pp. 53 ff.

[4] See Herlin-Karnell (2009), p. 242; Miettinen (2013), pp. 85 ff.; Vergès (2012), pp. 635 ff.

[5] Van Puyenbroeck and Vermeulen (2011), pp. 1018 ff. See Vogler, in this book.

[6] See Ambos (2005), p. 235.

[7] Commission of the European Communities, COM(2004) 328 final, Bruxelles 28 April 2004.

[8] See Rafaraci (2013), The right to defence, pp. 333 ff.

One could thus argue that this is not such a novelty, but this brings us on to the central issue being dealt with in this paper. When the proposal in question was submitted, one of the most frequent arguments against it was that laying down rules on procedural rights would be useless, since these were already set out and established by the ECHR. It was the general opinion that the European system had already strengthened that set of rules through Strasbourg case law.

2 Ineffectiveness in the ECHR System

Since the second half of the first decade of the 2000s, a growing consciousness emerged. Some studies, requested by the EU Commission,[9] reported an unsatisfactory level of effectiveness in the Strasbourg system. The main reason for this turned out to be, foremost, the increasing number of Member States to the Council of Europe, which led to a backlog of cases. As a consequence, the number of "repetitive cases" grew enormously, i.e., cases in which the Court had to decide on matters that had already been dealt with.[10] This was due to the fact that ECtHR judgments are often not properly executed by the States.[11] In fact, only in a few cases did the Court require national countries to modify their legal systems, which are rarely declared as incompatible with the Convention itself.

This has created a vicious circle, in that the Strasbourg system does not seem to be able to adequately enforce "practical and effective rights."

This does not mean that the ECtHR has been insensitive to the effectiveness of the Convention rights, especially with regard to the topic of the present study. Even if the Convention provides "core rights"—i.e., the guarantee of a fair trial—Strasbourg case law also gives attention to the tools that can help implement these rights, such as the right to be informed about them. For example, in the cases of *Mattoccia v. Italy*[12] and *Salduz v. Turkey*,[13] the Court (the Grand Chamber, in the latter case) underlined that the Convention does not acknowledge rights that are "theoretical or illusory but rights that are practical and effective," as had already been stated in the case of *Artico v. Italy*.[14]

---

[9] Van Puyenbroeck and Vermeulen (2011), pp. 1022 ff.; Spronken and de Vocht (2011), pp. 437 ff. See also Morgan (2007), pp. 27 ff.

[10] Spronken and de Vocht (2011), p. 443. See the Brighton Declaration, 19 April 2012; see also the European Council Committee of Ministers' 2012 annual report, finally showing a decrease of repetitive cases submitted to the ECtHR.

[11] Cf. Imbert (2003), pp. 10 ff.

[12] ECtHR, 25 July 2000, *Mattoccia v. Italy*, Application No. 23969/94.

[13] ECtHR, Grand Chamber, 27 November 2008, *Salduz v. Turkey*, Application No. 36391/02.

[14] This was one of the first judgments given against Italy, which accepted quite late the individual jurisdiction of the ECtHR: ECtHR, 13 May 1980, *Artico v. Italy*, Application No. 6694/74.

Since the 2004 general initiative failed, the new post-Lisbon approach to procedural rights was conduced step by step.[15] In 2009, the Roadmap, first, and the Stockholm Program, second, focused on several steps to be taken to further implement the enormous impact that the ECHR system had already produced in the field of procedural rights.

Measures from A to F of the Roadmap pointed out six topics on which the EU bodies will submit normative proposals. Among them, measure A dealt with translation and interpretation,[16] while measure B dealt with information on rights and information on charges.

The Commission proposal on measure B—under article 82(2) TFEU and considering articles 47 and 48 of the Charter—was submitted in 2010[17] and finally approved in 2012. During this somewhat long period, some fundamental changes were made to the original text.

3 Reflecting on EU Directive 2012/13

As far as the 2012/13 directive is concerned, it would be superfluous here to set forth its contents, as they are well known. Rather, we should analyze it from the point of view that was adopted at the very beginning of this study: how and to what extent can this new legislative tool effectively implement the rights already enshrined in the ECHR system?

To begin, it must be stressed that, although the original draft proposal only concerned transborder procedures, the solution adopted in the directive concerns all types of criminal proceedings, regardless of the legal status, citizenship, or nationality of the accused person, as written in recital no. 16.

The aim of the directive is multiple:

- ensuring the right to information on the procedural rights of the suspected and accused persons, as well as of the arrested and detained persons in domestic proceedings;
- ensuring the same information to the persons under EAW proceedings;
- ensuring the right to information on charges.

[15] See Spronken and de Vocht (2011), pp. 453 ff.; Herlin-Karnell (2009), pp. 229 ff.; Spencer (2009), pp. 447 ff.

[16] See Rafaraci, in this book; Bargis (2013), pp. 91 ff.; Cras and De Matteis (2010), pp. 153 ss.

[17] See the European Commission Proposal for a Directive of the Parliament and of the Council on the right to information in criminal proceedings COM(2010) 392 final, submitted on 20 July 2010.

3.1 *Dies a Quo* of the Right to Be Informed

A preliminary element that helps test the effectiveness of the guarantees laid down in the directive regards when the duty of MS judicial authorities to inform arises. Articles 2, 3 e and 6 are relevant from this point of view.

Article 2 states that the directive applies "from the time persons are made aware that they are suspected or accused" to the end of the proceedings, until a final decision is made, including any appeal.[18]

Therefore, the duty to inform arises promptly—according to article 3—after the person is made aware of being suspected or accused.[19]

Under the term "suspect," the text includes all those who have not yet been officially charged.[20]

In this first stage, the person is to be informed at least of his/her right to access to a lawyer; of the right to free legal advice; of the right to be informed of the accusation, according to following article 6; of his/her right to interpretation; and, of course, of the right to remain silent.

It is worth noting that the directive proposal launched by the Commission contained no reference to the right to remain silent, a reference that was added in the course of the Council examination.[21] Moreover, the Committee on Legal Affairs, to which the draft was submitted, stressed the importance of providing further information[22]: namely, to inform the suspect of "any implications there may be in exercising that right under the national law," because of the different consequences related to silence in each domestic system. By the way, this last amendment was not approved.

Concerning the procedural stage at which the suspect must first be informed, it is worth noting that this may vary enormously under the different domestic systems. In fact, under national law, there may be a considerable delay before a suspect is informed that he/she is under investigation.[23] Some systems,[24] of course, might prefer to safeguard the interest of the secrecy of the pretrial investigation phase,

[18] See Ciampi (2013), pp. 21 ff.

[19] Amalfitano (2014b), p. 19.

[20] This lexical choice was highly appreciated in those national systems in which human rights guarantees depend on the individual investigative act rather than on a person's status as a suspect. See, for example, Vergès (2012), p. 638.

[21] See the debate in Council on 7 October 2010 (2010/0215 (COD)), during which the Council asked the preparatory bodies to add the right to remain silent.

[22] RR\885029EN.doc; PE452.900v03-00, rapporteur J.P. Albrecht, submitted on 27 January 2011.

[23] See Vergès (2012), p. 639.

[24] The Italian system, for instance, provides a very low level of information on the charge during the pretrial phase (see arts. 335, 369, 369-*bis*, 415-*bis* CCP-Italy): it might happen that the suspect will not be informed of his/her situation until the end of the investigation, if the prosecutor does not decide to assume one of those investigative acts that make the counsel's presence mandatory. For an extensive overview, see Ciampi (2010), *passim*. See also Candito, in this book.

allowing a long delay in informing the accused of the fact that he/she is actually accused!

If the directive, especially its article 2, was interpreted in the sense that the duty of information needs not be anticipated, information provided under article 3 would lose much of its effectiveness.[25]

3.2 Letters to Arrested Persons

The new directive attaches special attention to the peculiar situation of the arrested person. The limitation of personal liberty requires the accused to be granted stronger guarantees than in normal cases; as provided by article 4, an arrested or detained person must be given further information in writing, by means of a letter in a simple and accessible form, in a language he/she understands. It is noteworthy that the linguistic requirement of information (see art. 4 § 5) must be strictly interpreted in line with the guarantees laid down under directive 2010/64.[26] Furthermore, the importance of the linguistic aspect is evident under article 5, which provides the right of the person arrested under an EAW to receive a special letter. This must report the rights and guarantees of the person according to the national law implementing the EAW Framework Decision.[27]

Of course, the need for additional information is due to the particular situation of the persons who are deprived of their liberty, who, principally, might be in a troubled state of mind and might not understand or remember correctly the information they were given orally. It is thus of great importance that the arrested can keep the letter throughout the detention period, during which the elapse of time makes the single guarantees increasingly important.

The directive contains two annexes, providing indicative models for the two different letters. Although their adoption is not mandatory, the Member States, in following these models, will certainly comply with the obligations set down by the directive.

Analyzing the "minimum" content of the letters, an important innovation seems to be the duty of Member States to expressly inform the arrested or detained person of his/her right to access to urgent medical assistance. Some Member States already provide for this, such as France,[28] but others

[25] In this sense, see Vergès (2012) p. 641: "cette ambigüité est dommageable. Elle crée un conflit d'interprétation et pourrait entraîner une transposition a minima."

[26] Amalfitano (2014b), p. 20.

[27] Ciampi (2013), p. 23.

[28] See the recent reform of the very discussed *garde à vue*, entered into force since April 2011 (l. no. 93–2011, 14.4.2011); according to the new article 63–1 CCP-France, the person submitted to *garde à vue* must be immediately informed of his right—among others—to be visited by a doctor, as provided under article 63–3 CCP-France, which was introduced in 1993 and integrated by Law no. 93–2011. See, among others, Mauro (2012), pp. 73 f.; Vergès (2011), p. 3005; Alix

do not.[29] Furthermore, another very important feature of the letter is the provision of informing the arrested of the means to challenge the lawfulness of the arrest or to obtain provisional release. This is of fundamental importance in allowing an effective defense but is probably not common practice in all the Member States.

In general terms, the information contained in article 4 does not seem to raise controversial interpretation.

3.3 *The Right to Information Regarding the Charge*

This is not the case of article 6, concerning the right to information on the accusation. In fact, this provision establishes two different forms of information: (1) general information about the criminal act, which defendants must be promptly given, in such detail necessary to safeguard the fairness of the proceedings and the effective exercise of the rights of the defense, and (2) a second level of information under paragraph 3, which provides that "at the latest before the submission of the merits of the accusation to a Court," detailed information is to be given about the nature, the legal classification and the nature of participation. It seems that the former type of information is to be given only in factual terms, while the latter regards legal aspects.[30]

By the way, as far as concerns the contents of such information, it is hard to imagine what differences there could be between the elements under paragraphs 3 and 1, starting with the premise that the latter aims at granting the defendant information sufficiently detailed to safeguard both the fairness of the proceedings and the effectiveness in exercising his/her defense rights. Without the basic elements provided under paragraph 3, both the fairness and effectiveness of the defense envisaged under paragraph 1 would be meaningless.

Can the introductory recitals help clarify this part of the text? Recitals no. 19 and no. 28 establish, respectively, the moment when the different sets of information laid down in articles 3 and 6 must be given. Even though no express reference can be found in article 3, recital 19 establishes that information on procedural rights must be provided "before the first interview by the police or by other competent authority." With regard to the information about the accusation, laid down in article 6, recital 28 seems to confirm the hypothesis of two different formal levels. The first regards information on the criminal act, which must be given, according to recital 28, "at the latest before the first interview by the police or by another competent authority," that is to say within the same time limit established for information under article 3. The second involves a description of the facts, including, whenever

(2011), p. 1703; Gindre (2011), p. 298; Roujou de Boubée (2011), p. 1128; Matsopoulou (2011), p. 3039.

[29] For a comparative point of view, see Ruggeri (2012), p. 185 ff.

[30] See Vergès (2012), p. 642.

known, the time and place of the offense. Moreover, various details—according to the current stage of the proceeding—should be given "to safeguard the fairness of the proceeding and the effective exercise of the rights of the defence."

A close examination of this recital makes it even more difficult to distinguish between the contents of the two forms of information. Moreover, we can exclude that the distinction between paragraphs 1 and 3 of article 6 is based upon a possible modification of the charge. Paragraph 4 of article 6 expressly provides for this by establishing that "any change in the information given" in accordance with article 6 must be communicated to the accused.[31] This seems to relate to any possible changes, both on the material side and on the legal side of the description of the facts.

The referral in recital 28 to the "different stage of the proceeding" seems to confirm that the effectiveness of the right to be informed about the accusation will depend, even in the future, on the peculiar structure of the national pretrial phase. In some of the 28 domestic systems, such as the Italian one, pretrial investigation can last for a considerable time, even up to 18 or 24 months.[32] This can have a strong impact on the issue at hand, as well as on the problem of access to the case file, provided under article 7 of the directive.

3.4 The Right to Access the File

Another important aspect of the right of information is the "right to access to the materials of the case." This issue, regulated by article 7, is strictly linked with the right to information about the accusation. During the preparatory sessions of the directive, the original referral to the "case file" was changed into "materials of the case," in accordance with the observation that not all the domestic legislation shares the concept of "case file."

Preliminarily, article 7(1) grants arrested or detained people access to the materials, in order to allow remedies against unlawful detention. In fact, the letter of rights, under article 4, must contain, as has been noted, information about the means and the opportunities of challenging the arrest or obtaining provisional release.

Paragraph 2 of article 7 grants access to the file also to suspects and accused persons who have not been arrested.

The extent of access, in such a case, depends on the need for discovery in respect to all those documents and elements—in favor of or against the person—that are useful to prepare the defense and to safeguard the fairness of the proceedings. However, the time elapsing before this right comes into force can be very long, as the provision states that discovery must take place "at the latest upon submission of

[31] See Ciampi (2013), p. 26.

[32] See arts. 407 and 406 CCP-Italy.

the merits of the accusation to the judgment of a Court." Again, the different structure of the pretrial phase of domestic proceedings can give rise to considerable differences among national countries as to the effectiveness of the right to access the file.

Furthermore, paragraph 4 provides for some situations allowing the national authorities to delay or deny—the expression used in the text is "refuse"—access to some parts of the file. After clarifying that this must not have a negative impact on the fairness of the proceedings, article 7 points out two different sets of relevant situations:

- a threat to the life or other fundamental rights of a person other than the accused;
- the safeguard of an important public interest, such as ensuring that ongoing investigations are not compromised or that the national security of the Member States in which the proceeding is led is not put at risk.

The denial to access must be pronounced by the judicial authority or, at least, must be subject to judicial review.

Once more, the text is very flexible in considering situations that allow the Member States' authorities to refuse or delay access to the file, especially because the interests of the ongoing investigations and national security are just two examples of what may be considered "important public interest."[33]

3.5 The Recording of Information

A further subject needs to be analyzed to complete the path introduced at the beginning of this paper. Article 8 of the directive requires Member States to record the information given under articles 3 and 6, according to domestic procedures. This means that a written or taped record of the information must be available in the file, to prove that the person received it. This provision aims at satisfying the practical need to increase the effectiveness of the rights established by the directive.

However, the directive does not establish any consequences for a failure to effectively provide the information in question. A possible solution might be to establish procedural sanctions in the event of no record of the information being available in the file. Only recital 36 refers to such a situation, submitting to national law the right of the defense to challenge the failure or denial to give information. Of course, providing procedural sanctions in the text of the directive would have been a drastic move on the part of the EU legislator. Although it would not have changed

[33] See the opinion of the Committee on Legal Affairs (fn. 10), in which the rapporteur affirms "on the whole, your rapporteur for opinion considers the Commission proposal to be strong and worthy of support. Unfortunately, the Council, in its general approach contained in Document No. 17503/10 dated 6 December 2010, would severely weaken it by including several references to national law and adding more conditions for the giving of the Letter of Rights."

the content or extent of the rights established under the directive, it would have ensured that national systems effectively implemented them.

What would happen, in fact, if, after the national implementation of the directive, the judicial authorities of a Member State avoided or completely failed to give information on the procedural rights of a suspected person or to give the letter to the arrested person? Being unaware of his/her right to be informed about his/her procedural rights, the accused would not be able to face the infringement of his/her rights. Faced with the inactivity of the judicial authorities, he/she would not be able to challenge the unlawfulness of the situation, having no act of refusal to appeal against or challenge.[34]

Moreover, we can imagine that, when counsel takes on the defense of the accused, the former will ask the latter if he/she has received the information provided for under articles 3, 4, 6 of the directive, as transposed into national rules. The accused will explain that no information was actually received, and counsel will be able to check this in the case file, where no record will be found. However, what will be the consequences of such a discovery? The risk is that no consequence will derive from this unlawful situation, because implementation of the directive will be adequately satisfied by providing the burden to inform, whereas no procedural measures are in place to deal with the event of no information being given at all. If the national legislation is sensitive enough, it will introduce rules—or will specify existing rules—correlating the duty to inform to a procedural "sanction" in the event of its infringement. This procedural sanction will affect the acts accomplished in a total lack of information on procedural rights. This is exactly what the ECtHR affirmed in the *Salduz* doctrine, establishing that the general provision to access to a lawyer is in effect infringed when the accused is not able to rely on the presence of counsel during those investigative acts unlawfully applied against him/her, in which he/she risks self-incrimination.

Thus, how could the directive improve the existing Strasbourg case law from this point of view? One solution would be to establish a general provision of procedural sanctions in the event of the total infringement of the duty to inform the accused of his/her rights, leaving national legislators free to determine the best form to choose, according to the individual national system.

4 Conclusions

At the end of this discussion, some questions need to be addressed. Does it seem that the second measure of the EU Roadmap may contribute to implementing the Stockholm program, aimed at strengthening the protection of human rights already provided by the Strasbourg system? Is it possible to say that, when the directive is

[34] Ciampi (2013), p. 23.

implemented by the Member States, greater mutual trust in the criminal justice systems of the Member States (recital no. 7) will be achieved?

It is probable that a certain approximation among the legislation of the "new EU Member States" and the "traditional EU Member States" will be achieved, even if the former have already been Member States of the Council of Europe for a long time. This standardization will also strictly depend on the new directive on the right to defense and to communicate with the lawyer after arrest, recently approved.[35]

In any case, the general impression is that the EU system does really dispose of the means to definitively improve the protection of human rights in the interest of all EU citizens and of any persons in EU territory. In order to achieve such a goal, we would probably need to set aside the general limit that article 82(2) establishes as a "fence" that cannot be trespassed,[36] i.e., that EU competence in the procedural field is submitted to the need of implementing mutual recognition.[37] Article 83 TFEU, which deals with intervention in substantive criminal law, does not provide this fence.

According to the imminent access of the EU to the ECHR, as the fifth negotiation was accomplished just few months ago, we may say that major results could be achieved if the goal of improving ECHR standards was directly pursued. In other words, also in accordance with the EU Charter, we should recognize that EU legislation in the field of criminal proceedings aims at protecting fundamental human rights.

These are crucial months for the future of the EU. The economic crisis is casting shadows on the monetary Union, while some political parties in the Mediterranean area are proposing that their countries leave the EU. The UK Prime Minister—even if the House of Lords does not seem to agree—is trying to loosen bonds to the EU.

We could perhaps adopt a different perspective, affirming that everything has changed in the post-Lisbon Treaty era. EU tools—which were less effective under the third pillar—have become much more incisive. They can satisfy the aim of mutual confidence in order to implement judicial cooperation in the AFSJ, but they can also satisfy another aim—an aim that was, until now, mostly related to the ECHR system, namely that of introducing the culture of the defense of human rights in criminal proceedings. This has already happened in other fields. For example, the former EC had no direct competence in workers' rights, but we must recognize that over the last 30 years, EC and EU legislation on the free circulation of goods and workers has produced a statutory compendium of workers' rights, especially those of women workers. Consequently, the workers of all European countries can now rely on a common compendium of guarantees.

Might this also happen with fundamental rights in criminal proceedings? The expression of this hope is certainly the most fitting way to end this analysis.

---

[35] See Bachmaier Winter, in this book.

[36] Böse (2011), p. 45; Amalfitano (2014a), pp. 12 ff.

[37] See Rafaraci (2013), p. 340 f.

References

Alix J (2011) Les droits de la défense au cours de l'enquête de police après la réforme de la garde à vue: état des lieux et perspectives. Recueil Dalloz, pp 1699–1707

Amalfitano C (2014a) Art. 82 TFEU. In: Tizzano A (ed) Le fonti del diritto italiano. Trattati sull'Unione europea, 2nd edn. Giuffrè, Milano, pp 866–896

Amalfitano C (2014b) Le prime direttive sul ravvicinamento "processuale": il diritto all'interprete, alla traduzione e all'informazione nei processi penali. In: Pistoia E, Del Coco R, Lo straniero dinanzi alla giustizia penale. Cacucci, Bari, pp 1–34

Ambos K (2005) Mutual recognition versus procedural guarantees? In: de Hoyos Sancho M (ed) Criminal proceedings in the European union: essential safeguards. Lex Nova, Valladolid, pp 235 ff

Bargis M (2013) L'assistenza linguistica per l'imputato: dalla direttiva europea 64/2010 nuovi inputs alla tutela fra teoria e prassi. In: Bargis M (ed) Scritti in memoria di Maria Gabriella Aimonetto. Giuffrè, Milano, pp 91–118

Böse M (2011) Der Grundsatz der gegenseitigen Anerkennung unter dem Vertrag von Lissabon. In: Ambos K (ed) Europäisches Strafrecht post-Lissabon. Universitätsverlag Göttingen, Göttingen, pp 45–63

Chiavario M (1982) Processo e garanzie delle persone, vol I and II. Giuffrè, Milano

Ciampi S (2010) L'informazione dell'indagato nel procedimento penale. Giuffrè, Milano

Ciampi S (2013) Il commento. Diritto Penale e Processo, pp 21–27

Cras S, De Matteis L (2010) The directive on the right to interpretation and translation in criminal proceedings. EuCrim, pp 153–162

Gindre E (2011) Une réforme en urgence: la loi n. 2011–392 du 14 avril 2011, relative à la garde à vue. Revue Pénitentiaire et de Droit penal, pp 297–309

Hecker B (2012) Europäisches Strefrecht, 4th edn. Springer, Heidelberg

Herlin-Karnell M (2009) Waiting for Lisbon... constitutional reflections on the embryonic general part of EU criminal law. Eur J Crime Crim Law Crim Justice 17:222–242

Imbert PH (2003) L'exécution des arrêts de la Cour européenne des droits de l'homme. Le role du Comité des ministres du Conseil de l'Europe. In: AA.VV., La Corte europea dei diritti umani e l'esecuzione delle sue sentenze. Atti del Convegno della S.I.O.I., E.S., Napoli, pp 20–39

Matsopoulou H (2011) Les dispositions de la loi du 14 avril 2011 sur la garde à vue declarées conformes à la Constitution. Recueil Dalloz, pp 3034–3039

Mauro C (2012) La garde à vue: sotto pressione la procedura penale francese. La Legisalzione penale 32:73–83

Miettinen S (2013) Criminal law and policy in the European Union. Routledge, Oxford

Morgan M (2007) Are Art. 6 ECHR and ECtHR enough to protect defense rights? J Eur Crim Law 27–35

Pollicino O, Rando G (2013) Judicial cooperation and multilevel protection of the right to liberty and security in criminal proceedings. The influence of European courts' case-law on the modern constitutionalism in Europe. In: Ruggeri S (ed), Transnational inquiries and the protection of fundamental rights in criminal proceedings. Springer, Heidelberg, pp 53 ff

Rafaraci T (2013) The right to defence in EU judicial cooperation in criminal matters. In: Ruggeri S (ed) Transnational inquiries and the protection of fundamental rights in criminal proceedings. Springer, Heidelberg, pp 331–344

Renucci JF (2013) Droit européen des droits de l'homme, 5th edn. Lextenso, Paris

Roujou de Boubée G (2011) La réforme attedue de la garde à vue. Recueil Dalloz, pp 1128–1229

Ruggeri S (2012) Personal liberty in Europe. A comparative analysis of pre-trial precautionary measures in criminal proceedings. In: Ruggeri S (ed) Liberty and security in Europe. V&R Unipress, Osnabrück, pp 185 ff

Spencer J (2009) EU fair trail rights – progress at last. New J Eur Crim Law 1(4):447 ff

Spronken T, de Vocht D (2011) EU policy to guarantee procedural rights in criminal proceedings: "Step by Step". North Carol J Int Law Commer Regul 37:436–488

Van Puyenbroeck L, Vermeulen G (2011) Towards minimum procedural guarantees for the defense in criminal proceedings in the EU. Int Comp Law Q 60:1017–1038

Vergès E (2011) Garde à vue: le rôle de l'avocat au coeur d'un conflit de normes nationales et éuropéennes. Recueil Dalloz, pp 3005–3006

Vergès E (2012) Émergence européenne d'un régime juridique du suspect, une nouvelle rationalité juridique. Revue de Science Criminelle et de droit penal comparé 3:635–647

Lost in Translation: Language Rights for Defendants in European Criminal Proceedings

Richard Vogler

Contents

Abstract This chapter examines the growing need for interpretation and translation in criminal proceedings and the emergence of new ideas about the communicative rights of defendants. It evaluates the case law of the European Court of Human Rights in this area, concluding that there have been significant advances in recent years in the protection of persons who are unable to speak the language of the country in which they have been arrested. Some important weaknesses remain, however, notably in respect of the translation of documents and the qualifications and independence of interpreters. The new regime under the European Union Directive 2010/64/EU on the Right to Interpretation and Translation in Criminal Proceedings is also considered. It is argued that, taken together, these two important initiatives represent a model for the establishment of more general European process rights.

R. Vogler (✉)
Sussex Law School, University of Sussex, Falmer, Brighton BN1 9QQ, UK
e-mail: R.K.Vogler@Sussex.ac.uk

S. Ruggeri (ed.), *Human Rights in European Criminal Law*,
DOI 10.1007/978-3-319-12042-3_6

Keywords Case law • Communicative rights • Directives • European Court of Human Rights • European Union • Interpretation • Translation

1 Introduction

There are approximately 7,000 distinct languages spoken around the world, and over 260 of these are native to Europe. Taking into account the impact of inward migration, the number of spoken languages in our continent is much greater still, and the UK National Centre for Languages calculates, for example, that over 300 different languages can be heard in London alone.[1] We may therefore consider our European Area of Freedom, Security and Justice,[2] in which free movement is so warmly encouraged, as a linguistic Babel. These population movements also have profound implications for criminal justice, as criminological research from the 1920s Chicago School onwards has shown that mobile, displaced communities are statistically much more likely to be involved with the police.[3] In the UK, 10 % of all criminal prosecutions and 20 % of all serious crime prosecutions for rape and murder involve non-nationals.[4] More worryingly still, non-nationals comprise 12.6 % of the UK prison population, a figure that rises to 17.8 % in France, 26.7 % in Germany, 33.2 % in Spain and 35.6 % in Italy.[5] Many of these non-nationals will have great difficulty in understanding the language of the country in which they are incarcerated. Peter Jan Honigsberg has argued that linguistic isolation in detention is a brutal form of solitary confinement with consequences that can amount, in some circumstances, to inhumane and degrading treatment or even torture. He compares the experience with that suffered by stroke victims.[6] Such feelings can be even more terrifying in the phases of the criminal investigation and trial itself, where the consequences of a failure to understand the allegations and the process can be catastrophic, a horror recalling the imagined scenarios of authors such as Kafka or Koestler.[7]

Dramatic increases in global mobility and the advent of the International Criminal Trials since the 1990s[8] have contributed to a growing awareness of the

[1] CILT, http://www.cilt.org.uk/research_and_statistics.aspx, accessed 8th September 2013.

[2] Kaunert (2005).

[3] Mears (2001).

[4] *The Telegraph*, 13 May 2013.

[5] World Prison Brief, at http://www.prisonstudies.org/info/worldbrief/, accessed 8th September 2013.

[6] Honigsberg (2013), p. 16.

[7] Gottlieb (2001).

[8] Giridhar (2010).

importance of communicative rights in criminal justice. This awareness has been reinforced in the same period by the work of Sociolinguist activists, such as Skutnabb-Kangas[9] and Paulston,[10] who have championed language rights as general human rights. The criminal trial is an act of communication, and some scholars have argued that communicative rights in the face of state authority comprise an important new and hitherto undeveloped terrain for human rights protection.[11] Namakula has situated language and communication guarantees at the heart of the right to fair trial,[12] while Abayesekara has pointed out the chronic difficulties of providing accurate interpretation and translation in the highly technical area of law.[13]

An emerging realisation of the scale of the problem has resulted in some significant developments in Europe[14] in recent years, with enormous significance for marginal and displaced migrant populations. The first is the increasingly robust case law of the European Court of Human Rights (ECtHR), which in decisions such as *Cuscani v United Kingdom* in 2002 and *Şaman v. Turkey* in 2011 has begun to establish the parameters of a universal communicative right as an aspect of a fair trial just as, in cases such as *Salduz v Turkey*[15] and *Panovits v Cyprus*[16] in 2008, it is developing the parallel right to legal assistance.[17] This jurisprudence was highly influential in the creation by the European Union (EU) of Directive 2010/64/EU on the Right to Interpretation and Translation in Criminal Proceedings. The Directive has been described by Hodgson as "a landmark, as the first criminal justice measure to be adopted by the co-decision procedure and the first to address safeguards for the accused".[18] Although, as will be argued below, there are serious defects in the protections offered by both the ECtHR jurisprudence and the EU Directive, nevertheless, taken together, they constitute nothing less than a breakthrough, not just in communication rights but also in wider attempts to establish baseline fair trial rights across Europe. For the first time, we can witness the spectacle of the ECtHR and the EU working together to provide agreed pan-European guidelines that are protective of the rights of defendants in the criminal process.

---

9 Skutnabb-Kangas and Phillipson (1995).

10 Paulston (1997).

11 Lubbe (2009).

12 Namakula (2012).

13 Abayasekara (2010).

14 It is not just in Europe that attempts have been made to address these problems, and the American Bar Association in 2012 adopted its *Standards for Language Access in Courts*, available at http://www.americanbar.org/groups/legal_aid_indigent_defendants/initiatives/language_access.html (accessed on 9 September 2013), which cover much of the same ground, although not on a mandatory basis.

15 ECtHR, decision of 27 November 2008. Application no. 6391/02 [Grand Chamber].

16 ECtHR, decision of 11 December 2008. Application no. 4268/04.

17 Hodgson (2011), pp. 656–662.

18 *Ibid.*, p. 651.

2 The Right to Interpretation/Translation under the European Convention on Human Rights (ECHR)

The right to interpretation/translation appears in two Articles of the European Convention on Human Rights[19] once in relation to detention in Article 5 and once in relation to fair trial rights in Article 6. Under Article 5(2):

> Everyone who is arrested shall be informed promptly, in a language which he understands, of the reasons for his arrest and of any charge against him.

Under Article 6(3):

> Everyone charged with a criminal offence has the following minimum rights: (a) to be informed promptly, in a language which he understands and in detail, of the nature and cause of the accusation against him; . . . (e) to have the free assistance of an interpreter if he cannot understand or speak the language used in court. . . .

These are, of course, minimum rights, and the ECtHR has elaborated this framework into a much more comprehensive provision, addressing questions that include, who exactly is entitled to interpretation help? which are the phases of the proceedings where an interpreter is required? and does this help extend to the translation of documents? Finally, questions of the adequacy of interpretation and translation and its funding have been considered. In evaluating the effectiveness of the ECtHR case law in this area, it will be helpful to consider these issues in turn.

3 Who is Entitled to Interpretation Assistance?

The answer to this first question is entirely dependent on an accurate assessment of the specific language skills of the defendant, who may be reluctant to reveal his or her level of language competency or to speak at all. This is always a subjective and probabilistic judgement, reached by unqualified individuals, often without guidance and under difficult and pressured circumstances. In *Ladent v Poland*, there was a breach of Article 5(2) when a French national, albeit travelling with his Polish wife, was informed of the reasons for his arrest and the charges against him in Polish, whereas the authorities clearly knew, because they had served translated papers on him after his release, that he spoke only French.[20] However, there was no breach in *Galliani v Romania* where the Italian defendant in a deportation case, although by no means fluent, "could engage in dialogue with the police officers and had no difficulty in understanding what was said to her and expected from her".[21]

[19] See also Article 14(3) of The International Covenant on Civil and Political Rights (ICCPR).

[20] ECtHR decision of 18 March 2008. Application no. 11036/03, § 64.

[21] ECtHR decision of 10 September 2008. Application no. 69273/01, § 54.

The defendant's own declarations on the subject may be highly relevant. In 1975, Mr. Brozikec, a Czech national, tore down some flags erected for a political party event in Pietra Ligure. He was investigated by the local police who sent him a judicial notice in Italian to which he replied (in French):

> I have always expressly requested that either the mother tongue of the persons concerned or one of the international official languages of the United Nations be used, in order to avoid from the outset any risk of misunderstanding.[22]

The Italian authorities ignored this letter and carried on to judgement in Italian, asserting that, in their belief, Mr. Brozikec actually spoke Italian. The ECtHR found that they should have provided interpretation

> unless they were in a position to establish that the applicant in fact had sufficient knowledge of Italian to understand from the notification the purport of the letter notifying him of the charges brought against him.[23]

In other words, the burden of proving that an interpreter is needed falls on the prosecuting authority (once they are alerted to a problem) and not on the defendant, notwithstanding that this appears to be the reverse of the practice in many European states, including Italy.[24]

Haphazard arrangements that may seem appropriate at the time in the interests of expediency may prove to be inadequate. Mr Cuscani, a Sicilian, opened an Italian restaurant in Newcastle, which he named, perhaps rashly, "The Godfather". Such bravado may have proved irresistible to the tax authorities who eventually charged him with tax fraud.[25] At the trial, for the first time, his counsel pointed out that he could manage only very simple concepts in English and even his Italian was "very southern". Rather than adjourning the case to find a qualified interpreter, the judge acceded to counsel's proposal that Mr. Cuscani's brother, present in court and of unspecified ability as an interpreter, should translate the proceedings. Mr Cuscani was duly sentenced to 4 years of imprisonment. The ECtHR concluded:

> The onus was thus on the judge to reassure himself that the absence of an interpreter at the hearing ... would not prejudice the applicant's full involvement in a matter of crucial importance for him. In the circumstances of the instant case, that requirement cannot be said to have been satisfied by leaving it to the applicant, and without the judge having consulted the latter, to invoke the untested language skills of his brother.[26]

It would be otherwise where a defendant had specifically waived the right of interpretation,[27] but the waiver had to be clear and unequivocal and ideally in

[22] ECtHR decision of 19 December 1989, *Brozicek v Italy*, Application no. 10964/84, § 16.

[23] *Ibid.*, § 41.

[24] See Cape et al. (2010).

[25] ECtHR decision of 24 December 2002, *Cuscani v United Kingdom*. Application no. 32771/96.

[26] *Ibid.*, § 38.

[27] ECtHR decision of 10 April 2007, *Berisha & Haljiti v. former Yugoslav Republic of Macedonia*. Application no. 18670/03.

writing.[28] Otherwise, the domestic court has the responsibility itself to establish whether the defendant has an adequate level of linguistic competency—a task that a judge may be ill-equipped to perform, and in any event there are no clear guidelines established by the ECtHR. However, as emphasised by the Court in *Hermi v Italy*:

> ... while it is true that the conduct of the defence is essentially a matter between the defendant and his counsel, ... the ultimate guardians of the fairness of the proceedings – encompassing, among other aspects, the possible absence of translation or interpretation for a non-national defendant – are the domestic courts.[29]

How they are expected to carry out such a technical and onerous task as assessing language competency is not made clear. In *Sandel v. the former Yugoslav Republic of Macedonia*, the applicant in a fraud case had insisted on a Hebrew interpreter, and as the rules of the court required all interpreters to be Macedonian nationals, proceedings were delayed for several years while one was sought. However, although this delay was clearly a breach of Article 6(1) for which the domestic court was responsible,[30] there was no breach of the interpretation requirement in Article 6(3) since it was clear from the start that the applicant had a working, if not a perfect, knowledge of Serbian, English and Bulgarian, for which interpreters were readily available.[31]

4 When is Interpretation Assistance Available?

Despite the wording of Article 6(3), which refers specifically to an inability to understand the "language used in court", protection has been specifically extended to all phases of the procedure, and especially the pre-trial. In *Şaman v. Turkey*, an illiterate Kurdish-speaking woman with a very limited command of Turkish, who had been found in possession of false identity documents in Turkey was convicted and sentenced to 12 years and 6 months for membership of the PKK.[32] She had been assisted by a lawyer and interpreter at court but not at the police station where complex matters had been put to her. The court found that "the issue of the defendant's linguistic knowledge is vital" and the authorities have an obligation to assess whether the case is sufficiently complex to require a detailed knowledge of the language used. Here there was a clear breach of Article 6(3). An interpreter should always be provided in the investigation stage for a defendant with language difficulties unless there were compelling reasons not to do so,[33] a point that had been forcefully made in the case of *Diallo v Sweden*, the year before.[34]

---

[28] See ECtHR decision of 8 January 2004, *Sardinas Albo v Italy. Application no.* 56271/00.

[29] ECtHR decision of 28 June 2005, *Hermi v Italy*. Application no. 18114/02, § 72.

[30] ECtHR decision of 27 May 2010. Application no. 21790/03, §§ 40–45.

[31] *Ibid.* §§ 46–56.

[32] *Partiya Karkerên Kurdistan*, Kurdish Worker's Party, opposed to the Turkish state.

[33] ECtHR decision of 5 April 2011, *Şaman v. Turkey*. Application no. 35292/05, § 30.

[34] ECtHR decision of 5 January 2010, *Diallo v. Sweden*. Application no. 13205/07, § 25.

In *Amer v Turkey*, a Sudanese-Bulgarian national was able to speak in Turkish but couldn't read text. Thus, although he could respond effectively in a police interview, he was unable to read a statement that he was given to check and sign. As the ECtHR emphasised:

> the right guaranteed by Article 6 § 3 (e) of the Convention to the free assistance of an interpreter is not only applicable when making oral statements at hearings in the course of a trial, but also to documentary material and the pre-trial proceedings.[35]

5 The Translation of Documents

The availability of translation for documents presents a further problem. It would clearly defeat the intentions of Article 6(3) if the words "free assistance of an interpreter" were construed so as to exclude the translation of documents. In those circumstances, a defendant in a primarily written procedure would be at a considerable disadvantage compared with one where the evidence was mostly oral. This principle was stated most clearly in the case of *Kamasinski v Austria*, where a US citizen went to trial without having a translation of the indictment or pre-trial witness statements. Moreover, the final judgement in the case was also not fully translated at any time, even after the event. The ECtHR took the opportunity to insist unequivocally that Article 6(3) applied not only to oral statements made at the trial hearing but also to documentary material.[36] This does not mean that every piece of writing must be translated, but there should be sufficient documents "to enable the defendant to have knowledge of the case against him and to defend himself, notably by being able to put before the court his version of the events".[37] The list of such documents may or may not include the indictment and the judgement, depending on the circumstances. Sometimes an oral translation or summary will be adequate, as in *Vikoulov v Latvia*, where it was held that this provided sufficient information to enable a detention order to be appealed.[38]

This point of view was also emphasised in the decision in the case of *Husain v Italy*, which arose out of the *Achille Lauro* hijacking. Here the applicant had been tried *in absentia*, and on his final transfer to Italy he was given a copy of his committal order that was written only in Italian, which he, as an Arabic speaker, wasn't able to understand. It was orally translated at the time, but

> he had just been transferred to Italy from a foreign prison and was in no condition to pay attention to the interpreter's words or to understand their technical meaning. He stressed that he was unfamiliar with the complexities of the Italian legal system and had believed the committal warrant to be a list of offences and statutory provisions.[39]

---

[35] ECtHR decision of 6 July 2009, *Amer v Turkey*. Application no. 25720/02, § 77.

[36] ECtHR decision of 19 December 1989, *Kamasinski v Austria*. Application no. 9783/82, § 74.

[37] *Ibid.*

[38] ECtHR decision of 25 September 2012. Application no. 16870/03.

[39] ECtHR decision of 24 February 2005, *Husain v Italy* Application no. 18913/03.

Nevertheless, it was held, somewhat harshly, that "oral linguistic assistance may satisfy the requirements of the Convention"[40] and that the complaint was in this case manifestly ill-founded.

Whether or not documents must be translated will depend critically on the complexity of the case. In *Herni v Italy*, which involved a French and Arabic speaker who nevertheless understood spoken Italian and who was accused of drug dealing, the Lower Chamber pointed out:

> It has not been established, either, whether and to what extent the applicant understood Italian and was capable of grasping the meaning of a legal document of some complexity. In that context, the financial, social and cultural situation of the person concerned, and the language difficulties likely to be encountered in a foreign country, are of relevance. . . .[41]

Such an assessment has to be made on a case-by-case basis, a point underlined by the fact that whereas the Lower Chamber found that there had been a breach of Article 6(3), the Grand Chamber took a different view.[42]

6 The Adequacy of the Interpretation

There is little guidance available on the question of how the court should assess the competency of the interpretation provided. In *Čonka v. Belgium*, a large group of Roma asylum seekers, fleeing from skinhead attacks in Slovakia, were provided with only one interpreter who did not accompany them to the closed transit centre. However, there was no breach of Article 5 § 2 of the Convention (although there were breaches of other Articles) because the interpreter in fact managed to convey to them all the grounds for their detention.[43] In *Kamasinski v Austria*, the ECtHR took the view that an assessment of the adequacy of the Austrian registration scheme for approved court interpreters was not necessary and the only relevant question was whether the interpretation was in fact adequate.[44]

It appears that there are no specific requirements of impartiality. In a case where an interpreter spoke only Turkish and not Kurdish and openly argued with the Kurdish defendant, went red in the face and became angry, pointing her finger at him and calling him a liar, the ECtHR felt that it had no duty to enquire into impartiality. It said that since the domestic court had been satisfied with the professional skills of the interpreter and no complaint had been made at the time:

> ... it is not appropriate under Article 6 § 3(e) to lay down any detailed conditions concerning the method by which interpreters may be provided to assist accused persons. An interpreter is not part of the court or tribunal within the meaning of Article 6 § 1 and

---

[40] *Ibid.*

[41] *Hermi v Italy*, (fn. 29).

[42] 18 October 2006.

[43] ECtHR decision of 5 February 2002. Application no. 51564/99, § 52.

[44] *Kamasinski v Austria* (fn. 36), § 73.

> there is no formal requirement of independence or impartiality as such. The services of the interpreter must provide the accused with effective assistance in conducting his defence and the interpreter's conduct must not be of such a nature as to impinge on the fairness of the proceedings.[45]

In *Ozcan v Turkey*[46] and *Baka v Romania*,[47] the defendants were held to have waived their right to insist on a trained interpreter when they accepted the services of a police officer and a court clerk, respectively. Nevertheless, where the defendant drew attention to the inadequacies of the interpretation, the court was obliged to investigate and to take action if necessary.[48]

The defendant will receive little help in communicating with a legal representative who does not speak his language. In *X v Austria*, the court noted that the translation of communications was necessary only between the court and the defendant, who in this case spoke only French:

> ... the applicant must be taken to be responsible for that situation. It was indeed for him either to appoint another lawyer with a good knowledge of French or to call for an interpreter he would have remunerated.[49]

7 Free Assistance?

Article 6(3) refers specifically to the "free assistance of an interpreter", and this provision has been rigorously enforced by the ECtHR. Retrospective attempts to recover the cost of interpretation or to means test the beneficiaries have all been decisively rejected. In *Luedicke, Belkacem and Koç v. Germany*, it was pointed out that even if reimbursement was sought only after conviction, "the risk remains that in some borderline cases the appointment or not of an interpreter might depend on the attitude taken by the accused, which might in turn be influenced by the fear of financial consequences".[50] As a result of this judgement, both France and Germany were forced to amend their legislation on the recovery of costs for translation services. However, this principle does not apply in respect of the reimbursement of translation fees that are unconnected with the applicant's defence.[51]

---

[45] ECtHR decision of 24 January 2002, *Uçak v the United Kingdom* Application no. 44234/98, § 2.

[46] ECtHR decision of 20 February 2007. Application no. 45906/99.

[47] ECtHR decision of 16 July 2009, *Baka v Romania*, Application no. 30400/02.

[48] *Kamasinski v Austria*, (fn. 36).

[49] 6185/73, 29 May 1975, DR 2 § 68.

[50] ECtHR decision of 28 November 1978, *Luedicke, Belkacem and Koç v. Germany*. Applications nos. 6210/73; 6877/75, § 42.

[51] See, e.g., ECtHR decision of 18 November 2004, *Akbingöl v. Germany* (decision). Application no. 74235/01.

8 Directive 2010/64/EU on the Right to Interpretation and Translation in Criminal Proceedings

This jurisprudence clearly represents a considerable achievement, unmatched anywhere else in the world.[52] The responsibility of the domestic courts and authorities to ensure adequate interpretation, including in the pre-trial, has been emphatically asserted and the requirements of free assistance emphasised. Nevertheless, serious deficiencies remain, and it cannot yet be affirmed that the network of linguistic safeguards, especially for vulnerable defendants, is complete. Weaknesses include a serious lack of clarity regarding the requirements to guarantee the availability of competent and impartial interpreters both for the court and for legal representatives and in the translation of documents. There are also well-known practical limitations to the protections offered. In the first place, access to the ECtHR is now obstructed by a considerable backlog of cases. Cases that do not proceed to trial are diverted or are dealt with by way of guilty plea or where there are "compensating" factors in the procedure as a whole, fall outside the net. Extradition proceedings and proceedings under the European Arrest Warrant (EAW) are not included, whereas the margin of appreciation doctrine sometimes allows extraordinary departures from acceptable practice.[53]

In 2003, in belated recognition of the fact that most EU legislative effort to date had been invested in prosecutorial strategies such as the EAW, the European Commission decided to address the need for common European minimum standards of protection for those suspected or accused of crime. Its Green Paper entitled *Procedural Safeguards for Suspects and Defendants in Criminal Proceedings Throughout the European Union*[54] expressed the view that the right to interpretation and translation was "fundamental" to this project.[55] Much of the motivation for the inclusion of Interpretation and Translating came from two Grotius Projects,[56] which considered how equivalent standards could be effectively promoted. The resulting publication *Aequitas – Access to Justice Across Language and Culture* set out good practice guideline proposals in this area,[57] which were to form the basis for subsequent initiatives.

As Morgan has pointed out, the research phase for the proposals revealed that there was a serious problem arising from the varying standards of legal interpreting and translation available in criminal proceedings throughout the EU.[58] These

[52] Although see the 2012 ABA Guidance (fn. 14) and Abel (2013).

[53] Hodgson (2011), pp. 648–650.

[54] European Commission, *Green Paper from the Commission. Procedural Safeguards for Suspects and Defendants in Criminal Proceedings throughout the European Union*, COM(2003) 75 final (19 February 2003, Brussels).

[55] *Ibid.*, para. 5.2.

[56] 98/GR/131 and 2001/GRP/015.

[57] Hertog (2001).

[58] Morgan (2011), p. 5.

concerns were represented forcefully in meetings of the Linguist-Jurist groups in preparation for the new proposals. The first attempt, in response to the Green Paper, to establish a common baseline right of interpretation and translation was as part of the 2004 Framework Document, which encompassed an array of the five recommended procedural rights.[59] As a result of opposition, largely from the UK, this co-ordinated plan was abandoned in 2007 and was replaced by a more cautious "step by step" approach as part of the "Roadmap" developed within the Stockholm Process.[60] This "Roadmap", which called for the progressive enactment of a series of procedural rights, was adopted by the Council on 30 November 2009, 1 day before the entry into force of the Lisbon Treaty.

In view of the unhappy history of the previous proposals, the first "step" to be proposed was a Directive on the right to interpretation and translation, on the grounds that it was the "least controversial right in the discussions on the 2004 proposals and that information and research was already available."[61] However, for various technical reasons that are explored at length by Cras and de Mattias,[62] two competing versions of the proposed Directive were produced. One was submitted on 8 December 2009 by a group of 13 Member States,[63] while a second version was delivered by the European Commission on 9 March 2010.[64] As Cras and Mattias point out, this was a "fight over competencies" between the Member States anxious to preserve their prerogatives under the *Treaty on the Functioning of the European Union* (TFEU) and the Commission, keen to assert its primary role in the aftermath of the Lisbon Treaty.[65] Referee in this dispute was to be the European Parliament's Committee on Civil Liberties, Justice and Home Affairs chaired by Baroness Sarah Ludford. In the event, the Ludford Committee opted decisively for the Member States' proposals, for a variety of reasons, not unconnected with the support already expressed by the Council and by significant Member States such as the UK and Ireland.[66] The Member States' proposal also called for lower standards of protection than the Commission version. It was considered of paramount importance that the Directive should be fully compliant with ECtHR case law, and the Council of Europe was invited to submit its detailed recommendations in this respect.[67] After further amendments and consultations between the Trilogue parties and with the

[59] COM(2004) 328 final. Council Doc 9318/04, inter-institutional file no 2004/0113 (CNS).

[60] Spronken and de Vocht (2011), pp. 11 and 12.

[61] European Commission, *Proposal for a Council Framework Decision on the Right to Interpretation and to Translation in Criminal Proceedings*, COM(2009) 338 final (Brussels, 8 July 2009), p. 2.

[62] Cras and De Matteis (2010), pp. 154 and 155.

[63] O.J. C 69, 18.3.2010, p. 1; inter-institutional file no 2010/0801 (COD).

[64] COM(2010) 82 final.

[65] *Ibid.*, p. 155.

[66] Committee on Civil Liberties, Justice and Home Affairs, *Report on the Draft Directive of the European Parliament and of the Council on the Rights to Interpretation and to Translation in Criminal Proceedings*, A7-0198/2010 (Brussels, 10 June 2010) (Ludford Committee).

[67] Council Doc. 5928/10.

Linguist-Jurists, a final version was agreed and signed at Strasbourg on 20 October 2010.[68] Although the piecemeal approach of the Stockholm Process was, as the Ludford Committee put it, "second best" to the Big Bang approach of the 2004 initiative,[69] given the entrenched resistance to the original Framework Directive, this was a considerable achievement.

Article 2 of the Directive lays down the following as a fundamental principle:

> Member States shall ensure that suspected or accused persons who do not speak or understand the language of the criminal proceedings concerned are provided, without delay, with interpretation during criminal proceedings before investigative and judicial authorities, including during police questioning, all court hearings and any necessary interim hearings.

It is worth noting that the Directive applies only to criminal proceedings (but not minor proceedings such as road traffic violations[70]) and to EAW proceedings, which might otherwise be considered as exempt extradition proceedings.[71]

Article 1(3) also provides the welcome assurance that Member States must ensure that "interpretation is available for communication between suspected or accused persons and their legal counsel". Reflecting ECtHR case law, interpretation must also be of a quality sufficient to safeguard the fairness of the proceedings, in particular by ensuring that suspected or accused persons have knowledge of the case against them and are able to exercise their right of defence.[72] Articles 1(5) and 1(6), respectively, require Member States to set up a mechanism to discover whether interpretation is necessary and for any refusal to provide it to be susceptible of challenge.

As far as documents are concerned, the Directive limits translation to those "which are essential to ensure that (defendants) are able to exercise their right of defence and to safeguard the fairness of the proceedings".[73] "Essential" is defined for this purpose as "any decision depriving a person of his liberty, any charge or indictment, and any judgment",[74] omitting passages "which are not relevant for the purposes of enabling suspected or accused persons to have knowledge of the case against them".[75] Unfortunately, on grounds of cost, the Member States refused to allow the inclusion of "essential documentary evidence" within the elements to be translated,[76] and it is hard to see how a right of defence could be fully exercised without this. Moreover, Article 3(7) allows "an oral translation or oral summary" of

---

[68] Directive 2010/64/EU of the European Parliament and of the Council of 20 October 2010 on the Right to Interpretation and Translation in Criminal Proceedings.

[69] Ludford Committee (fn. 66), p. 18.

[70] Article 1(3) of the 2010 Directive (fn. 68).

[71] Article 1(1) *Ibid.*

[72] Article 1(8) *ibid.*

[73] Article 3(1) *ibid.*

[74] Article 3(2) *ibid.*

[75] Article 3(4) *ibid.*

[76] Cras and De Matteis (2010), p. 159.

essential documents, but only as an exception to the general rules and where this does not prejudice the fairness of the proceedings. Although this is in conformity with ECtHR jurisprudence, it still offers the potential for abuse and contrasts sharply with the much more liberal approach to the translation of evidence adopted by the international criminal tribunals.[77] The defendant must, however, have the opportunity to challenge any decision taken in relation to the translation of documents.[78] There are quality assurance provisions in Articles 2(8) and 3(9), and the competency of a particular interpreter must be reviewable under Articles 2(5) and 3 (5). Member States are encouraged to set up a system of certification of competency,[79] but the Directive has no provisions regarding independence or impartiality. The costs of all interpretation and translation must be met by the Member State.[80]

Each Member State must ensure that provisions giving effect to these requirements are enacted by transposing the Directive into their internal legal orders by 27 October 2013.[81] It is encouraging to see that these proposals not only reflect the spirit and the intentions of the case law of the ECtHR but also go beyond it in a number of significant respects.

9 Remote Translation and the Technological Revolution in Interpreting

One of the more radical departures of the Directive is contained in Article 2(6), which holds that

> Where appropriate, communication technology such as videoconferencing, telephone or the Internet may be used, unless the physical presence of the interpreter is required in order to safeguard the fairness of the proceedings.

There is abundant research evidence, notably from the AVIDICUS Project in 2011, indicating that what Braun describes as "double mediation" (through language and through video) has serious implications for participants.[82] Haas has emphasised that "video-mediated personal interactions are perceived as significantly different by the participants and observers than in-person interactions"[83] and remote interpretation is very unpopular with interpreters.[84] However, better

[77] Giridhar (2010).

[78] Article 3(5) 2010 Directive (fn. 68).

[79] Article 5(2) *ibid.*

[80] Article 4, *ibid.*

[81] A failure to do so will result in infringement procedure by the Commission under Art. 258 TFEU, as well as the possible imposition of executive measures and penalties under Art. 260 TFEU. For an assessment of implementation in Romania, see Damaschin (2012).

[82] Braun (2011), p. 265.

[83] Haas (2006), p. 61.

[84] Braun (2011), p. 266. See also Fowler (2013).

technology, better training and codes of conduct that require the consent of the parties can all help to overcome these difficulties. The international tribunals have pioneered e-courts and have considerable experience with the routine incorporation of remote interpretation and translation facilities into proceedings.[85] Equally, London's Metropolitan Police has introduced an Interpreters Deployment Team (IDT) as a single point of contact to access interpreter services. In 2011, the IDT serviced nearly 35,000 requests, of which 85 % were assigned to an interpreter in less than 30 min, using Remote Interpreting Hubs, which dramatically reduced travelling time and increased the availability of interpretation in minority languages.[86] Such developments also assist in the monitoring and quality assurance of translation facilities.

10 Conclusion

The two initiatives described above represent an impressive attempt to establish a robust and universal regime for interpretation and translation in criminal process across the European continent, which can provide a model for the wider world. Beyond this, it is hard to tell whether such parallel developments in Strasburg and Brussels represent the significant first steps in a wider attempt to establish Europe-wide baseline procedures on which the mutual recognition of investigatory and detention measures can be safely established. It is certainly encouraging to witness over recent years the progressive broadening of the concept of a "trial" for the purposes of Article 6 of the ECHR to include the pretrial and the incremental achievement of a Europe-wide culture of rights protection in this phase of the procedure. Translation rights, because they are relatively uncontroversial and operate in essentially the same way in countries that adopt both adversarial and an inquisitorial methodologies, represent an ideal experimental guinea pig for more ambitious rights-based Directives. Much will depend on the success of this radical new departure.

References

Abayasekara S (2010) A dog without a bark: a critical assessment of the international law on language rights. Aust Int Law J 17:89–111

Abel LK (2013) Language access in the Federal courts. Drake Law Rev 61:593–913

Braun S (2011). Recommendations for the use of video-mediated interpreting in criminal proceedings. Videoconference and remote interpreting in legal proceedings, Braun S. Guildford, University of Surrey, Surrey

[85] Giridhar (2010) and Hepburn (2012).

[86] Braun and Taylor (2011).

Braun S, Taylor J (2011) Videoconference and remote interpreting in legal proceedings. Videoconference and remote interpreting in legal proceedings, University of Surrey, Guildford

Cape E, Namoradze Z et al (2010) Effective criminal defence in Europe. Intersentia, Mortel

Cras S, De Matteis L (2010) The directive on the right to interpretation and translation in criminal proceedings. Eucrim 4:153–162

Damaschin N (2012) The right to interpretation and translation in criminal proceedings. The exigencies imposed by the European Union. National standards. Juridica 8:31–43

Fowler Y (2013) Non-English-speaking defendants in the Magistrates court: a comparative study of face-to-face and prison video link interpreter-mediated hearings in England. Aston University, Birmingham

Giridhar KR (2010) Justice for all: protecting the translation rights of defendants in international war crime tribunals. Case West Reserve J Int Law 43:799–829

Gottlieb E (2001) Dystopian fiction east and west: universe of terror and trial. McGill-Queen's Press-MQUP, Montreal

Haas A (2006) Videoconferencing in immigration proceedings. Pierce Law Rev 5:59–109

Hepburn P (2012) The translation of evidence at the ICTY: a ground-breaking institution. Translation Interpreting Stud 7:54–71

Hertog E (2001) *Aequitas*. Access to justice across language and culture in the EU. Lessius Hogeschool, Antwerp

Hodgson JS (2011) Safeguarding suspects' rights in Europe: a comparative perspective. New Crim Law Rev 14:611–665

Honigsberg P (2013) Alone in a sea of voices: recognizing a new form of isolation by language barriers. University of San Francisco Law Research Paper 2013-11. Available at SSRN http://ssrn.com/abstract=2208749 or http://dx.doi.org/10.2139/ssrn.2208749

Kaunert C (2005) The area of freedom, security and justice: the construction of a 'European public order'. Eur Secur 14:459–483

Lubbe HJ (2009) The right to language in court: a language right or a communication right? Língua e Cidadanía Global, Direito

Mears DP (2001) The immigration-crime nexus: toward an analytic framework for assessing and guiding theory, research, and policy. Sociol Perspect 44:1–19

Morgan C (2011). The new European directive on the rights to interpretation and translation in criminal proceedings. Videoconference and remote interpreting in legal proceedings, Braun S. Guildford, University of Surrey, Surrey

Namakula CS (2012) Language rights in the minimum guarantees of fair criminal trial. Int J Speech Lang Law 19:73–93

Paulston CB (1997) Language policies and language rights. Annu Rev Anthropol 26:73–85

Skutnabb-Kangas T, Phillipson R (1995) Linguistic human rights – overcoming linguistic discrimination. Mouton de Gruyter, Berlin

Spronken TNBM, de Vocht DLF (2011) EU policy to guarantee procedural rights in criminal proceedings: "Step by step". The future of the adversarial system. University of North Carolina at Chapel Hill School of Law, Chapel Hill

The EU Directive on the Right to Access to a Lawyer: A Critical Assessment

Lorena Bachmaier Winter

Contents

Abstract After lengthy discussions, several drafts and numerous amendments, on 22 October 2013 the final text of the Directive on access to lawyer, right to have a person informed and right to communicate with a third person while deprived of liberty was adopted. This study analyses in detail the provisions of the European Directive of Access to Lawyer of 22 October 2013 from a critical perspective. Apart from analysing this legal instrument, it aims to assess how far this new Directive serves to harmonise the defence rights in a European single space of justice and to

---

L.B. Winter (✉)
Faculty of Law, University Complutense Madrid, Avda Complutense s/n, 28040 Madrid, Spain
e-mail: L.Bachmaier@der.ucm.es

S. Ruggeri (ed.), *Human Rights in European Criminal Law*,
DOI 10.1007/978-3-319-12042-3_7

guarantee adequately the rights of the defendants in transnational criminal proceedings.

Keywords European Arrest Warrant • European criminal procedure • European Public Prosecutor • Human rights right of access to lawyer • Procedural safeguards • Protection of suspects • Right to communicate • Rights of defence • Transnational criminal proceedings

1 Introduction

After the failure in moving forward and approving the Proposal for a Framework Decision on certain procedural rights of suspects,[1] the EU Commission opted for a piecemeal approach, dealing with each of the procedural rights separately, as a way to overcome the stalemate situation on the negotiations. The Roadmap on Procedural Rights, adopted by the Council of the European Union on November 2009, sets out the guidelines to be followed in strengthening the rights of suspects and accused persons and enhances mutual trust necessary for the implementation of the principle of mutual recognition.[2] Executing this Roadmap has not been easy, and the EU began presenting and passing those Directives regarding the guarantees of defendants in criminal proceedings where the agreement could be achieved easier, as, for example, the Directive on the right to interpretation and translation in criminal proceedings[3] or the Directive on the right to information in criminal proceedings.[4] The negotiations on the right to access to lawyer and legal aid should follow.

On 8 June 2011, the EU Commission presented a proposal for a directive on access to lawyer. Shortly after the presentation of this text, a group of Member States expressed their opposition to the Commission's approach, stating that the

[1] Proposal for a Council Framework Decision on certain procedural rights in criminal proceedings throughout the EU, COM (2004) 328 of 28 April 2004. Prior to this Proposal of FD, the Commission presented the Green Paper on Procedural safeguards [COM (2003) 75 final, of 19.2.2003].

[2] 2009/C 295/01. This Roadmap was incorporated into the Stockholm Programme "An open and secure Europe serving and protecting the citizen" adopted December 2009. See, generally, Jimeno-Bulnes (2009), pp. 157 ff.; Spronken (2011), pp. 213 ff.; Blackstock (2012), pp. 23 ff.; Morgan (2012), pp. 73 ff.

[3] Directive 2010/64/EU of the European Parliament and of the Council of 20 October 2010 on the right to interpretation and translation in criminal proceedings.

[4] Directive 2012/13/EU of the European Parliament and of the Council of 22 May 2012 on the right to information in criminal proceedings.

proposal would "present substantial difficulties for the effective conduct of criminal proceedings" by their investigating, prosecuting and judicial authorities,[5] because the rights enshrined in the proposal were not adequately balanced with the needs of the criminal prosecution. The initial text was subject subsequently to several amendments, and different texts were elaborated during the negotiations until the final text of the Directive on access to lawyer, right to have a person informed and right to communicate with a third person while deprived of liberty (hereinafter DAL) was adopted on 22 October 2013.[6]

The objective of this study is not only to analyse in detail the provisions of this Directive from a critical perspective but also to assess in how far the Directive serves to harmonise the defence rights in a European single area of Freedom, Security and Justice (AFSJ) and to guarantee adequately the rights of the defendants in transnational criminal proceedings. It can already be advanced that, even if this legal instrument represents a significant step forward in the protection of fundamental rights in criminal proceedings, to my mind it does not meet the expectations of providing an adequate framework to enhance the protection of the procedural safeguards in criminal proceedings, specifically with regard to transnational proceedings, execution of European Arrest Warrants, or the proceedings that will lie within the competence of the future European Public Prosecutor.[7]

2 The Scope of Application of the Directive on the Right of Access to Lawyer

The scope of application of this Directive is defined in Article 2 DAL. This provision defines to which persons, to which proceedings and from which moment shall the rights to access a lawyer and to communicate with a third person envisaged in the Directive apply.

2.1 Personal Scope of Application

The Directive on Access to Lawyer is intended to ensure the access to lawyer and the communication of the suspect or defendant in criminal proceedings and persons

[5] Note presented by Belgium, France, Ireland, The Netherlands and the United Kingdom, made in Brussels 22.9.2011, DROIPEN 99, COPEN 232. Furthermore, these MS consider that the text of 8.6.2011 does not take into account the existing differences between the national criminal justice systems in establishing minimum standards.

[6] Directive 2013/48/EU of the European Parliament and of the Council of 22 October 2013 on the right of access to a lawyer in criminal proceedings and in European arrest warrant proceedings, and on the right to have a third party informed upon deprivation of liberty and to communicate with third persons and with consular authorities while deprived of liberty.

[7] See Bachmaier (2014), pp 505 ff.

subject to a surrender procedure pursuant to the EAW (Articles 1 and 2 DAL). Expressly, Article 2(3) DAL clarifies that it shall apply also to "persons other than suspects or accused persons who in the questioning by the police or by another law enforcement authority become suspects or accused persons" [Article 2(3) DAL]. It does not apply generally to witnesses, as this provision guarantees that from the moment a witness is considered a suspect, the right to access a lawyer shall be granted.

While no objection can be made to this provision, its practical implementation can be problematic, as there is no precise moment where it can be undoubtedly stated that a witness becomes a suspect. It will depend largely on the authorities interrogating the person summoned as witness to stop the questioning until this person who has become a suspect during the questioning appoints a lawyer. The practice of the different MS may vary greatly regarding the moment when they consider that a person is not anymore a witness and should be treated as a suspect granting him all the defence rights accordingly. In this context, not being possible to define what the elements are to be taken into account to transform the position of the interrogated person from witness to suspect, the Directive could probably have expressed that in case of any doubts as to the need to grant the person interrogated the right to appoint a lawyer, the questioning should be suspended in order to allow the person to be assisted by lawyer.

Furthermore, even if the authorities do not consider the witness as a possible suspect, if the witness expresses his wish to be assisted by lawyer, such possibility should be facilitated promptly. In sum, the moment from which a witness is to be granted the right to access to lawyer should not depend exclusively on the assessment the interrogating officers make, and when they consider that such witness might have participated in the commission of the offense.

To that end, the importance of respecting the exclusionary rule of evidence is essential: no incriminatory statement of the defendant made without respecting the right to legal assistance shall be admitted as evidence. The case law of the ECtHR is very clear on this point[8]; however, if the EU Directive seeks to reinforce the right to access to lawyer and prevent that law enforcement agents keep on interviewing a person as a witness, when they already consider him as a suspect, the exclusionary rule should have been added into the Directive.

[8] The ECtHR has elaborated the so-called Salduz doctrine, following the case of *Salduz v Turkey* of 27 November 2009, Appl. No. 36391/02. The Strasbourg Court has repeatedly underlined that the rights of defence are irretrievably prejudiced when incriminating statements made by the accused during police interrogation without access to lawyer are used for conviction (paragraphs 54 and 55). Among many others, see, for example, *Panovits v Cyprus* of 11 December 2008, Appl. No. 4268/04; *Dayanan v Turkey* of 13.1.2010 Appl. No. 7377/03, *Sebalj v Croatia* of 28 June 2011, Appl. No. 4429/09, *Trymbach v Ukraine* of 12 January 2012, Appl. No. 44385.

2.2 *Objective Scope of Application*

As to the material scope of application, proceedings for imposing sanctions for minor offences by other authorities different from judges of the criminal jurisdiction do not fall within the scope of the Directive on Access to Lawyer [Article 2 (4) DAL]. The initial draft of the Directive did not mention these proceedings when defining the material scope of the Directive and simply stated that the Directive should be applicable to criminal proceedings and EAW procedures.[9] In the text of 25 May 2012, the proceedings for minor offences were excluded from the application of the Directive. This exclusion posed several criticisms: first, because there is no uniform concept of minor offence at the European level, and thus it would be uncertain to which proceedings finally would the Directive be applicable, and, second, because criminal proceedings for minor offences can entail severe economic consequences and therefore excluding the right to legal assistance in such proceedings. Taking into account these considerations, it could be argued if the aim of ensuring minimum standards of the right of defence in criminal proceedings was adequately guaranteed.

These arguments definitely speak in favour of granting the right to legal assistance in all criminal proceedings. The draft of 31 May 2013 amended again the text of the previous Article 2, and the Directive now states that the right to access a lawyer and to communication with a third person is granted in all criminal proceedings and EAW proceedings. The only exception is set out in Article 2(4) DAL: the Directive does not apply to extrajudicial sanctioning procedures for minor offences if deprivation of liberty cannot be imposed as a sanction. Once the sanction is appealed or referred to a court having jurisdiction in criminal matters, the right of access to lawyer would be granted according to the Directive.

The text of the Directive—following the text proposed on 31 May 2013—definitely represents an improvement of the right to defence at this point, clarifying that in all criminal cases before a court with criminal jurisdiction, regardless of the seriousness of the offence or the possibility to deprive the liberty of the suspect or defendant, the Directive shall apply. Furthermore, it also clarifies that, even in administrative proceedings, if a person can be deprived of liberty, the right to legal assistance shall be granted under this Directive [Article 2(4) DAL, last paragraph].

On the other hand, the Directive does not apply to proceedings regarding minor offences that are sanctioned by an authority different from a court with criminal jurisdiction and cannot lead to a deprivation of liberty. The Explanatory Memorandum [point (17) EM] explains this exclusion by stating that it would be disproportionate to require that the competent authority should ensure for minor offences, such as minor traffic offences, all the rights granted under the Directive.[10]

---

[9] See Article 1 PD of 8.6.2011, COM(2011) final.

[10] EM point 17: "In some Member States certain minor offences, in particular minor traffic offences, minor offences in relation to general municipal regulations and minor public order offences, are considered to be criminal offences. In such situations, it would be unreasonable to

This would be the scheme followed in the Directive with regard to minor offences' proceedings:

Criminal offence + court criminal jurisdiction = Directive applies always.
Criminal offence + administrative authority + court criminal jurisdiction = Directive applies only to last stage.
Administrative offence + possible deprivation of liberty = Directive applies always.
Administrative offence + not possible deprivation liberty = Directive does not apply.

At first sight, when reading Article 2(4) DAL, the provision appears to be too complex and lengthy. Article 2(4) DAL states:

> 4. Without prejudice to the right to a fair trial, in respect of minor offences:
>
> (a) where the law of a Member State provides for the imposition of a sanction by an authority other than a court having jurisdiction in criminal matters, and the imposition of such a sanction may be appealed or referred to such a court; or
> (b) where deprivation of liberty cannot be imposed as a sanction;
>
> this Directive shall only apply to the proceedings before a court having jurisdiction in criminal matters.
>
> In any event, this Directive shall fully apply where the suspect or accused person is deprived of liberty, irrespective of the stage of the criminal proceedings.

Was it necessary to draft this article in such a way as to make clear that the right to access to lawyer only applies to proceedings before a criminal court and to any kind of proceedings where a liberty deprivation sanction can be imposed? Probably yes, although this might be the text that better responds to the special features of sanctioning minor criminal offences in certain MS. It has to be borne in mind that the approach of the MS to minor offences is quite different: the same behaviour being treated in one state as administrative offence and sanctioned by administrative authorities, in another state as criminal offence and sanctioned by criminal courts and in others as criminal offence but sanctioned first at the administrative or police level and only upon initiative of the sanctioned person will it be reviewed by a criminal court.

In my opinion, it is positive that Article 2(4)(a) DAL explicitly clarifies that non-judicial sanctioning proceedings for minor offences fall out of the scope of the Directive and only once they are handled before a court with criminal jurisdiction will the right to access to lawyer arise: those cases where minor offences are considered criminal offences but are dealt with by non-judicial authorities will not be considered as "criminal proceedings" for the purpose of granting the right to access to lawyer. This avoids entering into lengthy discussions and divergent interpretations on the question of what is the element that defines the criminal

require that the competent authorities ensure all the rights under this Directive. Where the law of a Member State provides in respect of minor offences that deprivation of liberty cannot be imposed as a sanction, this Directive should apply only to the proceedings before a court having jurisdiction in criminal matters."

nature of a procedure if it is the type of behaviour, the sanction or the authority that imposes the sanction.

In sum, when an offence is contemplated as criminal in a national system but due to its consideration as a minor offence the sanctioning is left at first place to a non-judicial authority (as, for example, the German *Strafbefehl*), the defendant's right to legal assistance will apply only if such proceedings come to the criminal court: the Directive does not apply to minor criminal offences sanctioned by administrative authorities.

And what happens the other way round if a certain behaviour is sanctioned by administrative authorities as an administrative offence in a relevant national legal system, although according to the level of the sanction it could amount to a criminal offence?

The ECtHR has repeatedly stated that the procedural safeguards of defendants in criminal proceedings shall also be applicable to the administrative offence procedures, regardless of the fact that the jurisdiction is within an administrative authority or an administrative court.[11] The Strasbourg Court has tried to avoid that a change of jurisdiction and/or of the denomination of the conduct and the sanction might be used for circumventing the requirements and guarantees set out for criminal proceedings with the aim of lowering those procedural safeguards. There have been some countries, mainly out of EU countries, where detentions have been routinely practised under the administrative offence procedure, and this explains the position of the ECtHR and its case law.

However, in my opinion, the right to have access to a lawyer may be excluded in administrative sanctioning procedures as long as these cannot entail a deprivation of liberty and as long as the right to a fair trial is respected.

Finally, with regard to minor offences against the financial interests of the EU that would fall within the competence of the EPPO, this provision does not pose any problems. The Proposal for a Regulation for an EPPO includes the minor offences within the competence of the EPPO, and thus any kind of criminal offence detrimental to the financial interests of the EU would, according to the Proposal for a Regulation for an EPPO of 17 July 2013, be investigated and prosecuted by the EPPO, although it states that the EPPO can dismiss discretionally such cases [Article 28(2) Proposal Regulation EPPO]. In any event, the Directive on the right to access a lawyer and communicate with a third person would apply to these EPPO criminal procedures in the same way as to all other criminal procedures, as they fall under the jurisdiction of a criminal court.

[11] See, for example, *Galstyan v Armenia* of 15 November 2007 (Appl. No. 26986/03) and *Palaoro v Austria* of 28 June 1994 (Appl. No. 16718/90).

2.3 *Territorial Scope of Application*

With regard to the territorial scope of application of the Directive, it has to be pointed out that the UK, Ireland and Denmark will not be bound by this Directive, following the Protocols in respect to the Area of Freedom, Security and Justice annexed to the TFEU. These countries shall ensure the right to access to lawyer according to their own national rules, in conformity with the EU Charter and the ECHR and the case law of the ECtHR. The position of opting out of some countries may lead to some extent to a certain asymmetrical application of the procedural guarantees of suspects in criminal proceedings at the EU level, which is not desirable, leads to fragmentation of the AFSJ, and does not contribute to enhancing mutual trust. However, this opting out applies also with regard to the establishment of the EPPO, and therefore the issue of the protection of the defence rights in the proceedings led by the EPPO does not have any direct consequence in those countries. From a general point of view and in particular with regard to transnational criminal proceedings and those related to the EAW, it would be highly desirable that all EU countries would adapt their laws to the Directive—regardless of the opting-out position— in order to secure a certain minimum standard, even if they refuse to be subject to the control mechanisms of the ECJ.

2.4 *The Moment from Which the Right of Access to Lawyer Is Granted*

Granting the right of access to a lawyer is a prerequisite to ensure that the person concerned can exercise his right of defence "practically and effectively" [Article 3 (1) DAL]. To this end, the Directive states that the right to access to lawyer and to communicate with a third person shall be granted when the suspects or accused persons "are made aware by the competent authorities of a Member State, by official notification or otherwise, that they are suspected or accused of having committed a criminal offence, irrespective of whether they are deprived of liberty or not" [Article 2(1) DAL]. Apparently, this provision should be enough to ensure that a person is granted the right to legal assistance from the moment he is a suspect. However, pursuant to the wording of this article, the right only applies from the moment the person is informed, either officially or otherwise, of his condition of suspect. Thus, there could be the risk that the authorities could delay the moment from which the fundamental right applies, by simply deferring the moment of notification.

In order to avoid this possible risk, the general provision included in Article 2 (1) DAL is complemented with Article 3 DAL, which defines the moments in time since the suspect or accused person shall be granted the right to access a lawyer in any event: before being questioned [Article 3(1)(a) DAL], upon carrying investigative or evidence gathering acts [Article 3(1)(b) DAL], from the moment of deprivation of liberty [Article 3(1)(c) DAL] and for any court appearance [Article 3 (1)(d) DAL].

In sum, the Directive sets out that the right to access a lawyer shall be granted since the authorities carry out any investigative act against a person because he is being suspected of committing a crime, and this right shall be granted without undue delay if deprived of liberty. Despite the correctness of this rule, controlling the practical implementation of this rule is what may be more difficult, particularly, as mentioned earlier, because during the questioning of a witness it is unclear when the person will start to be considered a suspect and not a witness anymore.[12]

Furthermore, Article 2(1) DAL states that the right to access a lawyer and communicate a third person arises since the "suspect is informed by the competent authorities of the *Member State*". With regard to proceedings carried out by the EPPO, who shall be that competent authority? Pursuant the Proposal for a Regulation for an EPPO, the investigation of offences against the financial interests of the EU shall be conducted either by the European Delegated Prosecutor or by the European Public Prosecutor himself/herself [Article 16(2) Regulation Proposal EPPO]. In my opinion, the notification shall be made either by the European Delegated Prosecutor or by the EPPO directly, even if the EPPO is not an authority *of the Member State* as required by Article 2(1) DAL. But the notification can also be made by any national law enforcement agency that is carrying out investigative acts under the instructions of the EPPO.

In cases of detention in execution of an EAW, the authority executing the EAW shall inform without undue delay about the right to access to lawyer. The execution of a European Arrest Warrant issued within a procedure of the EPPO does not present any differences within the one ordered in another criminal investigation.

3 The Right of Access to Lawyer

The right to access to lawyer is mainly regulated in the long Article 3 of the Directive, complemented with the rules on confidentiality (Article 4 DAL), derogations and waivers (Articles 8 and 9 DAL) and the specific rules on access to lawyer in EAW proceedings (Article 10 DAL). Article 11 mentions the right to legal aid, which is essential for the practical implementation of the right to legal assistance, but Article 11 DAL does not contain a regulation on the right to legal

[12] The Model Rules or Draft EU Model Rules of Criminal Procedure do not mention any precise moment but include a definition of "suspect" in Rule 11, and it should be understood that the person is to be notified from the moment he/she is being investigated in relation to a criminal offence. These Model Rules were drafted within the project "European model rules for the procedure of the future EPPO" financed by the EU and headed by Prof. K. Ligeti and was conducted at the University of Luxembourg. For further information, see www.eppo-project.eu and the final report, published in Ligeti (2013, 2014).

aid,[13] as it only recalls the need to follow the principles set out in the EU Charter and in the European Convention on Human Rights.

Therefore, in this paragraph, we will focus on Articles 3 and 10 of the Directive, trying to analyse these provisions also from the point of view of the protection of the defence rights in transnational criminal procedures.

3.1 Right to Meet and Communicate with a Lawyer

The prerequisite for the exercise of the right of defence is that the person who is suspected of committing a criminal offence can meet and communicate with his or her lawyer. It could be taken for granted that this right is recognised widely in all the procedural codes of all the MS. However, the problem is not a lack of regulation but rather its implementation, and here there are still much more problems that could be thought of. As several research empirical studies show, upon arrest or detention, it takes several hours until the lawyer can appear, and once meeting the suspect, there is often no adequate space to hold a private conversation, and in those cases where it exists, an officer might be present.[14]

The EU legislator, fully aware that the presence of an independent and professional lawyer is one of the most important safeguards to control that the rights of the suspect or accused person are fully respected as well as for preventing cases of ill-treatment and abuses in detention centres, sets out in Article 3(3)(a) of the Directive that the MS shall ensure that the defendant meets with the lawyer, prior to being questioned and that they can converse privately. This right shall be granted without undue delay, upon deprivation of liberty or for the carrying out of certain investigative measures [Article 3(2)(a) to (c) DAL].[15]

[13] The Commission presented on 27.11.2013 the Proposal for a Directive on provisional legal aid for suspects or accused persons deprived of liberty and legal aid in European arrest warrant proceedings, COM(2013)824 final. At the moment of writing this study such Directive has not been adopted yet.

[14] See the empirical data collected in *Pre-trial Emergency Defence*, Schumann et al. (2012), pp. 358–359: 58 % of the officers participating in the research admitted that the supervision or restriction of the pre-trial interview between suspect or defendant and lawyer takes place in Austria. This shows that the mechanisms of the ECHR are not enough to implement this right, which is well established in the case law of the ECtHR. Already in *Brennan v United Kingdom* of 16 October 2001, Appl. No. 39846, the Court recognised that the presence of the police officer within hearing during the applicant's first consultation with his lawyer infringed the right to an effective exercise of his defence rights in violation of the Convention. See also *Öcalan v Turkey* of 12 May 2005, Appl. 46221/99 and *Rybacki v Poland* of 13 January 2009, Appl. No. 52479, this last case dealing with the presence of the prosecutor when the defence counsel met the defendant.

[15] The first draft of the PD of 8 June 2011 recognised the right of the suspect or accused to meet his lawyer. This regulation was criticised, as it did not recognise the right to communicate privately with the lawyer before the questioning. The text presented on 25 May 2012 already improved this provision, laying down the right to communicate "prior to an official interview". Finally, the draft of 31 May 2013 introduces the text that has been finally approved in the Directive.

The exact conditions, time and duration of these communications shall be regulated in the national law "in such a time and manner so as to allow the person concerned to exercise his rights of defence practically and effectively".[16]

3.2 The Content of the Right to Legal Assistance

The Directive recognises the right of the defence lawyer to be present during the questioning and also "to participate effectively" when the suspect or accused is questioned [Article 3(3)(b) DAL]. Legal assistance to the defendant shall also entail the possibility of the lawyer to be present during the investigative acts or evidence-gathering acts the defendant is allowed to attend [Article 3(3)(c) DAL].

Article 3(3)(b) of the Directive has opted for a compromise solution: it does not define the concrete scope of participation of the lawyer during questioning, which shall be regulated by the national law of the MS, but requires that the national rules do not "prejudice the effective exercise and essence of the right concerned" [Article 3(3)(b) PD]. It might be argued that this is not the best approach to harmonising the defence rights and their practical implementation, as the Directive leaves a wide margin to the national legal systems to define what is to be considered "effective participation",[17] and at the end only through an *a posteriori* review by the courts—be it the ECJ or the ECtHR—will it be possible to establish a common approach as to the role of the defence lawyer during the questioning upon arrest.

Despite these criticisms, the fact that the content and application of the Directive will be subject to the mechanisms of control and to the uniform interpretation of the ECJ is undoubtedly a very positive step forward.

As to the participation of the lawyer in investigative acts, Article 3(3)(c) of the Directive only lists three investigative acts where the presence of the lawyer shall as a minimum be permitted and only if these acts are provided in the national law and the defendant would be allowed to be present: (1) identity parades, (2) confrontations, (3) experimental reconstructions of the scene of crime. The initial text of the Proposal of 8.6.2011 was more "generous": the lawyer should be allowed to be present in all those investigative acts the defendant is permitted to attend and if its

[16] The first draft of 6 June 2011 was more precise in this regard, as it required that the duration and frequency of the communication with the lawyer should not be subject to any limitations that could impair the exercise of the right of defence of the suspect or accused. The content of the right to access to lawyer is, however, assessed positively by Arangüena Fanego (2012), p. 1199.

[17] In this sense, the first draft of the Proposal for a Directive on Access to Lawyer of 8 June 2011 was more complete when stating that the lawyer should be allowed, not only to be present but also to put questions, require clarifications and make statements. These acts should be recorded according to the national law. This provision was amended in the process of drafting the PD, and the text as of 25 May 2012 already stated that the MS should ensure the presence of the lawyer and his/her participation during questioning "according to national law". Critical to this change also Blackstock (2012), p. 31.

presence does not prejudice the acquisition of evidence. This provision was redrafted upon the opposition expressed by a group of Member States.[18]

To my mind at this point the Directive should have been more ambitious, including at least a general requirement that the MS shall provide the widest possible participation of the defence lawyer in the investigative stage, as long as this does not prejudice the success of the investigation and establish the exclusionary rule or evidence for not complying with the right of access to a lawyer during those three investigative acts set out under Article 3(3)(c) DAL.

These rights can be derogated "in exceptional circumstances" for following compelling reasons: "urgent need to avert serious adverse consequences for the life, liberty or physical integrity of a person" [Article 3(6)(a) PD] or when "immediate action by the investigating authorities is imperative to prevent a substantial jeopardy to criminal proceedings" [Article 3(6)(b) and Article 8 DAL]. The suspect or accused can also waive the right to be assisted by lawyer at any moment (Article 9 DAL).

3.3 *EAW Proceedings and the Right to Access to Lawyer*

The experience in the execution of EAW has shown the shortcomings of this procedure with regard to the right of defence of the arrested person.[19] The person concerned can, as a rule, only lodge a challenge against the EAW in the executing state, but for this defence to be effective the defendant and his defence lawyer should be made aware of the reasons that led to the issuing of the EAW and the rules for the criminal procedure in the requesting state. In sum, a person subject to a detention under an EAW should be provided with legal assistance not only in the executing state where he or she is kept arrested but also in the issuing state. This has been repeatedly claimed by Bar Associations as well as by scholars.

The Directive aims to address this problem, including a special provision on the right of access to lawyer in European Arrest Warrant proceedings. This provision has been subject to several modifications during the discussions on the Proposal for this Directive, which shows the difficulties in reaching an agreement on the scope of

[18] Note presented by Belgium, France, Ireland, the Netherlands and the United Kingdom, made in Brussels 22 September 2011, DROIPEN 99, COPEN 232, p. 3. To grant access to lawyer to all acts where the suspect's presence is required, for example for taking fingerprints, in their view did not address correctly the balance between the need to protect individual rights and the efficiency of the prosecution and could be against the right to undue delays, apart from increasing the costs. See Bachmaier (2014), pp. 521–526.

[19] See also the Report from the Commission to the European Parliament and the Council on the implementation since 2007 of the Framework Decision on the European Arrest Warrant and the surrender proceedings between the Member States, of 11 April 2011, COM(2011) 175 final. For some very illustrating examples on violations of defence rights in EAW proceedings, see Mansell (2012), pp. 36 ff.

rights in transnational criminal proceedings.[20] Article 10 of the Directive states generally the right to access to a lawyer in the state where the EAW is being executed [Article 10(1) PDAL] and sets out the right of the requested person to appoint a lawyer in the issuing state, whose role will consist in assisting the lawyer appointed in the executing state ("providing him with information and advice") [Article 10(4) PD]. To that aim, the detained person shall be informed of this right, and in case he "does not already have a lawyer" the executing authority shall inform the issuing authority so that it can "provide information to the requested person to facilitate him in appointing a lawyer there" [Article 10(5) PDAL].

This provision represents an important progress towards improving the rights of defence in EAW proceedings. Notwithstanding this positive assessment, it might be considered insufficient to grant an effective protection of the rights of the defendants in cross-border criminal proceedings, especially if the defendant does not have enough economic resources and has to rely on the system of legal aid for exercising his defence rights.[21] Simply stating that the appointment of a second lawyer will be facilitated by providing information to the detainee does not appear to be the right approach in granting this right effectively.

Moreover, the access to a second lawyer is only contemplated with regard to the EAW procedure but not in relation to European cross-border investigative acts that might for example be adopted under the European Investigation Order.

The precise content of the right to access to lawyer in the EAW proceedings in the executing state is listed under Article 10(2) DAL. One could have the idea that this special provision was aimed at enhancing the rights in these transnational cross-border proceedings of arrest or that new formula was introduced to deal with the specificities of such proceedings. However, having a look at the three paragraphs of Article 10(2) DAL, a certain disappointment arises. This provision does not add anything relevant to what has previously been recognised under Article 3 DAL, but rather on the contrary, the wording in Article 10(2) DAL sets lower standards than under Article 3(3)(b) DAL.[22] This inconsistency between these two provisions

---

[20] The first draft of PD of 8 June 2011, the MS should ensure the access to a lawyer in the executing state as well as in the issuing state, but the draft of 25.5.2012 deleted the provision requiring the authorities to facilitate the access to lawyer in both the executing and the issuing state (Article 10 PD of 25 May 2012). The last draft PD of 31 May 2013, which is the text that was finally adopted in the Directive, turns back to the initial text of 2011 and corrects the main drawbacks found in the text of May 2012. On the legal assistance of the person detained under a EAW and its development in the PDAL, see González Cano (2012), p. 1291; Blackstock (2012), p. 33; Mansell (2012), p. 45.

[21] How will the information provided by the issuing authority help him in appointing a lawyer? Shall the issuing authority explain to the detained person and/or his lawyer how to apply for legal aid in the issuing country and what are the requirements? In what language shall this information be transmitted? These might be very practical issues that might not be apt to be dealt with in an EU Directive.

[22] The content is almost the same, but under Article 10(2)(b) only the presence and participation of the lawyer is granted, while under Article 3(3)(b) PD the lawyer shall have the right to participate "effectively" and the national laws shall not "prejudice the effective exercise of the right concerned".

might not have practical consequences, as it can easily be overcome by a systematic interpretation, but could have been avoided.

4 The Right to Communicate and Have a Person Informed of the Deprivation of Liberty

4.1 The Right to Have a Person Informed of the Deprivation of Liberty

Article 5(1) of the Directive regulates the right for detained persons to have "at least one person" informed about the fact of the detention without undue delay. Most persons under arrest or detention will choose that a member of their family or their employer is informed. But the possibility that the detainee desires that another person is informed of his detention cannot be excluded. In this sense, the text of this provision is wider than the initial one proposed in 2004 within the Proposal of a Framework Decision on certain procedural rights: Article 12 of the Proposal FD limited the right to inform of the detention to the family or persons assimilated to the family and the employer, which was clearly too restrictive. This point was criticised already by the MS in 2005, claiming that the suspect should have the right to "have a person of his choice without undue delay informed" of the arrest or detention.[23] We fully agree with the wording of Article 5(1) as it enlarges the scope of the right to communicate and does not limit the communication to one of the persons within certain categories.

Article 5(2) DAL contains a special provision in cases where the detained is a person who has not attained the age of 18 years. In such case, the MS shall ensure that the holder of the parental responsibility is informed without undue delay, unless this information would run counter to the best interests of the child. This provision is consistent with the CoE Guidelines on child-friendly justice of 2010[24] and the Commitment of the EU in strengthening the protection of the children's rights.[25]

The third paragraph of Article 5 DAL provides for the possibility of a temporary derogation of the application of these rights in exceptional and justified cases. It has to be recalled that one of the objections to the first draft of the Proposal for an FD of

[23] See the text of the draft of the working session of 21 November 2005, DROIPEN 54, 21 November 2005.

[24] Guidelines of the Committee of Ministers of the Council of Europe on child-friendly justice, adopted by the Committee of Ministers on 17 November 2010 at the 1098th meeting of the Ministers' Deputies.

[25] Communication from the Commmission to the European Parliament, the Council, the European Economic and Social Committee and the Committee of the Regions "An EU Agenda for the Rights of the Child", COM(2011) 0060, of 15 February 2011.

2004 was that it did not provide for the possibility of delaying or temporarily suspending this communication in certain cases.[26]

The present possibility of restricting or deferring the application of the rights recognised under Article 5(1) and (2) is consistent with a large number of national laws of the MS on criminal procedure that provide for the possibility of delaying the exercise of the right to communicate until certain evidence is secured, other suspects have been detained or adequate measures have been adopted to protect endangered persons. Despite this, it has to be underscored that as any derogation of rights—even if it is only temporarily—the delay in the exercise of right to communication constitutes a limitation on a fundamental right, and thus it is only legitimate when it is sufficiently motivated and limited to the time strictly necessary.

The grounds that allow the derogation are specifically set out in Article 5(3): urgent need to (a) avert very grave consequences "to life, liberty or physical integrity of a person" and (b) prevent that the criminal proceedings are essentially jeopardised. But there is no regulation on the time limit in the Directive; thus, the assessment of the proportionality of this measure will be left to the national laws. In this sense, it might have been appropriate that the Directive had defined a maximum time for the temporarily derogation of the right to have the fact of the detention communicated to a person of their choice: as it stands now, each MS will be able to provide for different time periods and understand the term of "undue delay" in a different sense. The EU legislator has opted here for renouncing to a higher level or harmonisation with the aim of reaching consensus on this Directive.

Finally, the Directive does not establish how to proceed if the authorities, despite their efforts, fail in communicating the fact of the detention to the person the detainee has indicated. It goes without saying that the authorities shall inform the detained person of the difficulties or the impossibility for reaching the person to be informed. But such requirement is missing in the Directive.

The Directive contains a special provision for the case when the detainee is a minor. In such cases, when the MS temporarily derogate the right to inform the parents, the persons who have the parental responsibility or another appropriate adult, the relevant authority for the protection of the welfare of children shall be informed without undue delay. This provision, complemented with the general requirements on derogations listed in Article 8 DAL, is adequate for the protection of the children's rights and interests, but the Directive should have underlined that the derogations pertaining to a minor shall be even more exceptional than in other

[26] In fact, Article 12 of the PFD of 2004 did not mention the possibility of derogating the right to have the detention communicated to a relative or the employer. However, according to the explanation contained in point 15 of the Framework Decision, this suspension was admitted when it could be foreseen that the communication would jeopardise the criminal investigation or affect the security of a particular person. Such approach was definitely not correct, because if derogations are admitted they have to be clearly stated in the text of the legal instrument and not in the Explanatory Memorandum.

cases and that the assessment of the proportionality principle should be subject to higher standards.

4.2 *The Right to Communicate with Third Persons While Deprived of Liberty*

The right to communicate with at least one person they choose without undue delay is envisaged in Article 6 of the Directive. This communication is not only essential for the family to know the whereabouts of the detainee and to confirm directly how he/she is feeling, but it is also essential to adequately organise the legal defence of the detained person. In many cases when a person is detained, it is usually the family who undertakes the arrangements of contacting a reliable lawyer. This is especially true in those MS where the right to legal aid is not granted in an extensive way. In practice, in many cases, it would not be mistaken to state that the access to lawyer of own choice will depend largely on the possibility of communicating with a relative or a person who is close to the detainee. The text of the Directive does not mention the conditions, frequency and manner of exercising this right to communicate with a third person.

The precise regulation on how, when and how often a detained person can communicate with a third person is left to the national laws of the MS, as it is explicitly stated in the Explanatory Memorandum (point 36): they may make practical arrangements "taking account of the need to maintain good order, safety and security in the place where the person is being deprived of liberty". This is fully acceptable, as the right of the detainees to communicate has to be organised in a rational way, providing for adequate security conditions and adapted to the material possibilities of the prison or the detention centre. However, it would have been appropriate to state that the MS should endeavour to ensure that this right to communicate is exercised with an adequate frequency and under minimum conditions. It might be argued that these provisions rather affect the penitentiary regime and the right of inmates and are out of place in this legal instrument, which aims primarily to safeguard the defence rights of the defendant in criminal proceedings and, in particular, the right to access to lawyer. There is no doubt that this Directive shall not enter into details regarding the penitentiary system and the detention conditions. However, when regulating the right to communicate with a third person, it could have already highlighted the need that the exercise of this right is not subject to unjustified conditions by the MS.

As with the right to have a third person informed, Article 6 DAL also admits the possibility of temporarily derogating the right of the detainee to communicate with a third person "in view of imperative requirements or proportionate requirements" [Article 6(2) DAL]. In this case, the grounds to derogate this right are more widely drafted than under Article 5(3) DAL, which is understandable. What is surprising is that Article 8 does not make any express reference to the derogation foreseen under

6(2) DAL, as it does with regard to the derogations of other rights. Does this mean that the derogation of the right to get in touch with a relative without undue delay is not subject to the conditions of other derogations, that is a case-by-case reasoned decision taken by a judicial authority or by another authority, but only subject to judicial review [Article 8(2) DAL]? To the end of protecting the rights of the defendants, it appears that all the requirements set out under Article 8 DAL for derogating rights should also apply to the rights of Article 6, even if there is no reference to it under Article 8 DAL.

4.3 The Right to Communicate with Consular Authorities

Article 7 of the Directive, following the provisions of the Vienna Convention on Consular relations of 1963,[27] guarantees to all non-national detainees the right to communicate with their respective consular authorities. It could be argued that this right is already recognised by international law, and consequently there is no need to reiterate it in but for the purpose of controlling its compliance and promoting an harmonized application within the EU MS it is unquestionable that the inclusion in the Directive is clearly positive. However, out of the text of the Directive there are certain situations that may remain unclear. What happens if the detainee does state that he does not wish the consular authorities to be informed? Is this waiver of a right binding on the MS, or can the MS in that case choose between communicating and not communicating? The question is how far Article 7 DAL provides for the right to communicate if the detained person so wishes or, on the contrary, if this provision also provides for the right to not communicate the detention? Can the will of the detained person go so far as to prohibit a State to communicate with the consular authorities of another state the fact that one of his national is under detention? The text does not offer an answer; therefore, I am inclined to interpret this provision in the light of the rules on international law: there would not be an obligation to communicate if the detained person does not request it, but the will of the non-national under detention cannot refrain the state from communicating such fact to the relevant consular authorities.

Article 7(1) DAL specifically regulates the case where the detainee has "two or more nationalities". In such case, the suspects or accused persons "may choose which consular authorities, if any, are to be informed of the deprivation of liberty and with whom they wish to communicate". This possibility was not foreseen in the initial text of the Proposal for a Directive of 8 June 2011 but was correctly amended later. Out from the text of Article 5(1) it appears that the detainee can exercise his choice freely: that is, request to communicate with the authorities of one of the states of his nationality or the authorities of all the states he is national, not being obliged to reduce his choice only to one of the states. In this sense has to be

[27] See Article 36(1) of the Vienna Convention 24 April 1963.

interpreted the text of Article 5(1) DAL when it states "may choose"; otherwise, it would have stated "has to choose one". This case will not be frequent in practice as the majority of citizens do only have one nationality, but it is appropriate that it has been specifically recognised.

As to the right to have the detention communicated, it applies to all persons who are detained in a state of the EU, who are non-nationals of that state: the rule applies equally to nationals of other MS, as well as to citizens of non-EU states.

Finally, it has to be noted that the right to have the consular authorities informed of the detention and the right to communicate with them cannot be derogated.

5 Transnational Proceedings and the Right of Defence

The main drawback of this Directive is to be found in not what it regulates and how it regulates it but rather what it does not include. In other words, the advancement in the principle of mutual recognition and the establishment of instruments and institutions to develop the judicial and police cooperation for prosecuting more efficiently crimes across the EU territory requires a parallel effort in guaranteeing at the EU level the rights of the defendants.[28] Until now, the defence rights of defendants were put in the EU agenda, but no relevant progress was made in that direction. This imbalance has been subject to continuous criticism, not only with regard to EAW proceedings but also in relation to any transnational European criminal proceedings: if the cross-border investigation and prosecution are facilitated by the principle of mutual recognition and supported by cooperation units and networks, all these measures should be balanced with a similar coordinated multilevel guarantee of the rights of the defendant.

This need is particularly evident with regard to the transnational procedures that will fall under the competence of the future EPPO[29] but should be granted in all criminal proceedings with a transnational dimension. In transnational inquiries when the gathering of evidence is going to take place in another country, the right to be assisted by lawyer during those investigative acts will not be granted. Most of the national laws of the MS do not provide for the possibility of the defendant to be present in the executing State during the evidence gathering. This means that, for example, if a confrontation between two witnesses is carried out by way of international judicial cooperation, according to Article 3(3)(c) of the DAL, not even the lawyer would be granted the right to be present.

---

[28] See for example, Mitsilegas (2008) pp. 34 ff; Bachmaier Winter(2007) pp.44 ff.

[29] The risk of a possible imbalance between the powers and resources of the defendant and the EPPO in transnational criminal proceedings is clear: while the prosecution will count with a specialised network of prosecutors in all EU MS, the defendant facing a procedure with a transnational dimension will not have any parallel assistance and not even the possibility that the authorities of the foreign country grant him the appointment of a defence lawyer there. See Bachmaier Winter (2014), p.530.

Transnational investigations are becoming increasingly relevant within the EU, and these forms of serious cross-border criminality have sparked, together with the need to combat offences against the financial interests of the EU, the expansion of the principle of mutual recognition in criminal matters and the numerous policies and actions towards more harmonisation of criminal law and criminal procedure.

A parallel action is needed in the field of the protection of the suspect's and defendant's rights in criminal proceedings to respect the principle of equality of arms and the full application of the rights of defence: the defendants in EU transnational proceedings should not be put in a disadvantaged position against the prosecution authorities.[30] This requires paying of special attention to the right of legal assistance in transnational proceedings so that the suspect, detained or accused can effectively exercise his right of defence in the requested state, as well as in the issuing state. In other words, the defendant or suspect should be guaranteed the right to a transnational defence.[31]

This need was to be addressed, among other legal measures already in place, by the present Directive on access to lawyer. However, the Directive does not include any special provisions to ensure the defendant's rights in transnational inquiries[32] and therefore does not meet the needs and standards of protection of procedural rights in these types of criminal proceedings. The Directive only includes a special provision to proceedings regarding the execution of European Arrest Warrants (EAW), which as has been seen above does not provide for an adequate solution, as it does not grant the right to be assisted by lawyer in the executing and in the issuing states: it only foresees providing information on the possibility to appoint a lawyer in the issuing state.

6 Conclusions

After analysing the content of the provisions of this Directive, it has become clear that the Directive is to be welcome, because it represents a significant step forward in the strengthening of the defence rights in criminal proceedings in the EU. However, as it has been explained above, there are several shortcomings in the drafting that could have been avoided and other issues that could have been better clarified. Moreover, to my opinion, the Directive fails to address the

---

[30] On the need to establish general principles for transnational criminal proceedings, see Gless and Vervaele (2013), pp. 1 ff. As points out Gless (2013), pp. 90 ff. See also Bachmaier Winter (2013), pp. 126 ff.

[31] The converging of rules of different legal systems in one single proceeding should not result in a lowering of the procedural rights of the parties, and especially the right of defence of the accused. See Krüssmann (2009), p. 134.

[32] On the problems related to transnational inquiries and the protection of human rights, see Vogler (2013), pp. 27 ff. In the same volume, see also Ruggeri (2013), pp. 533 ff.

challenges and additional complexities that transnational criminal proceedings represent for the defence rights.

Even if the Directive refers to the definition and scope of application of many of the rights to the national rules, and even if it does not add essential guarantees to the ones already recognised by the ECtHR in its case law, the Directive undoubtedly offers clear advantages in comparison with the present situation: precisely the common interpretation of its rules by the ECJ and the possibility of resorting to the EU instruments and institutions to enforce compliance with this EU rules. If one can be disappointed for the lack of ambition in improving the defence rights and for the meagre results on the protection of fundamental rights after more than a decade of discussions at the EU level, the added value of this Directive cannot be denied. However, until the right to legal aid is not safeguarded adequately and in an equivalent manner in all Member States, the right to access to lawyer remains in practice far from being a reality, despite all the efforts in providing a new EU legal instrument on the right to access to lawyer. This is especially true in criminal proceedings, where the vast majority of defendants have no economic resources (exception made of economic criminality). One can only wish that it will not take another ten years to come to an agreement on the right of defendants who lack economic means to be provided with adequate legal aid in all EU Member States.

References

Arangüena Fanego C (2012) El derecho a la asistencia letrada y nuevos pasos para su garantía en la Unión Europea. In: Gómez Colomer JL, Barona Vilar S, Calderón Cuadrado P (eds) El derecho procesal español del siglo XX a golpe de tango. Libro homenaje a Juan Montero Aroca. Tirant lo blanch, Valencia, pp 1187–1202

Bachmaier Winter L (2007) Proceso Penal y protección de los derechos fundamentales del imputado en Europa. La Propuesta de Decisión Marco sobre determinados derechos procesales en los procesos penales celebrados en la Unión Europea. In: Garantías fundamentales del proceso penal en el espacio judicial europeo. Colex, Madrid, pp 41–69

Bachmaier Winter L (2013) Transnational criminal proceedings, witness evidence and confrontation: lessons from the ECtHR's case law. Utrecht Law Rev 9:126–148

Bachmaier Winter L (2014) The establishment of a European Public Prosecution's Office and the right to defence: critical approach to the EU proposal for a Directive of access to a lawyer. In: Grasso G, Illuminati G, Sicurella R, Alegrezza S (eds) Le sfide dell'attuazione di una procura europea: definizione di regole comuni e loro impatto sugli ordinamenti interni. Giuffrè Editore, Milano, pp 505–531

Blackstock J (2012) Procedural safeguards in the European Union: a road well travelled? Eur Crim Law Rev 2(1):20–35

Gless S (2013) Transnational cooperation in criminal matters and the guarantee of a fair trial: approaches to a general principle, in the same volume, the problem of safeguarding the rights of defendant in transnational proceedings is not adequately addressed by the ECtHR. Utrecht Law Rev 9(4):90–108

Gless S, Vervaele JAE (2013) Law should govern: aspiring general principles for transnational criminal justice. Utrecht Law Rev 9:1–10

González Cano MI (2012) La armonización de las garantías procesales penales en la Unión Europea. In: Gómez Colomer JL, Barona Vilar S, Calderón Cuadrado P (eds) El derecho procesal español a golpe de tango. Libro homenaje a Juan Montero Aroca. Tirant lo blanch, Valencia, pp 1273–1296

Jimeno-Bulnes M (2009) The EU roadmap for strengthening procedural rights of suspected or accused persons. In: Criminal proceedings, Eucrim, pp 157–161

Krüssmann MT (ed) (2009) Transnationales Strafprozessrecht. Nomos, Baden-Baden

Mansell D (2012) The European arrest warrant and defence rights. Eur Crim Law Rev 1:36–46

Ligeti K (ed) (2013) Toward a prosecutor for the European Union, vol 1. A comparative analysis. Hart Publishing, Oxford

Ligeti K (ed) (2014) Toward a prosecutor for the European Union, vol 2. Draft rules of procedure. Hart Publishing, Oxford

Mitsilegas V (2008) Legitimacy, accountability and fundamental rights in the area of freedom, security and justice. In: Martin M (ed) Crime, rights and the EU justice, pp 34–44

Morgan C (2012) The EU procedural rights roadmap. Background, importance, overview and state of affairs. In: Vermeulen G (ed) Defence rights. International and European Developments, Antwerpen, pp 73–80

Ruggeri S (2013) Transnational inquiries and the protection of fundamental rights in comparative law. Models of gathering overseas evidence in criminal matters. In: Ruggeri S (ed) Transnational inquiries and the protection of fundamental rights in criminal proceedings. Springer, Heidelberg, pp 533–573

Schumann S, Bruckmüller K, Soyer R (eds) (2012) Pre-trial emergency defence. Intersentia, Anwerp

Spronken T (2011) EU policy to guarantee procedural rights in criminal proceedings: an analysis of the first steps and a plea for a holistic approach. Eur Crim Law Rev 1(3):213–233

Vogler R (2005) A world view of criminal justice. Ashgate, London

Part III
Mutual Recognition and Fundamental Rights: The Protection of the Right to Freedom and the Collection of Overseas Evidence

Human Rights Violations and Mutual Trust: Recent Case Law on the European Arrest Warrant

Martin Böse

Contents

Abstract The principle of mutual recognition [Art. 67(3), Art. 82 TFEU] has become a "cornerstone" of the European criminal justice system. It is based upon the idea that a judicial decision that has been delivered in one Member State can be recognized and executed by the authorities of another Member State. But despite the Member States' commitment to common legal values, there are still a lot of differences in the national criminal justice systems and—as a consequence—different standards as well. The article analyzes recent case law on the European Arrest Warrant and addresses the question how to balance mutual trust and judicial control in the executing (requested) Member State, i.e., the efficiency of transnational cooperation on one hand and the protection of human rights on the other.

Keywords European Arrest Warrant • Human rights • Mutual recognition • Mutual trust • Ordre public • Proportionality principle • Trials *in absentia*

M. Böse (✉)
Strafrechtliches Institut, Rheinische Friedrich-Wilhelms-Universität Bonn, Adenauerallee 24-42, 53113 Bonn, Germany
e-mail: boese@jura.uni-bonn.de

S. Ruggeri (ed.), *Human Rights in European Criminal Law*,
DOI 10.1007/978-3-319-12042-3_8

1 Introduction

In the last decade, mutual trust and mutual recognition have become a "cornerstone" of the European criminal justice system. The principle of mutual recognition [Art. 67(3), Art. 82 TFEU] is based upon the idea that a judicial decision that has been delivered in one Member State can be recognized and executed by the authorities of another Member State. But do Member States (courts and law enforcement agencies) really trust one another? Or do we still need control mechanisms in order to ensure respect for fundamental rights?

Despite the Member States' commitment to common legal values, we are still facing a lot of differences in the national criminal justice systems and—as a consequence—different standards as well. The implementation of the principle of mutual recognition reveals that the Member States' obligation to execute a European Arrest Warrant is riddled with a lot of reservations.[1] So the main question still is how to balance mutual trust and judicial control in the executing (requested) Member State, i.e., the efficiency of transnational cooperation on one hand and the rights of the accused person on the other.

2 Human Rights and Mutual Recognition

The principle of mutual recognition is based upon the presumption that each Member State lives up to the common standards and complies with its obligations under the ECHR. However, there are reasons to believe that this presumption is rebuttable and that a violation of human rights may suspend a Member State's obligation to recognize and execute a European Arrest Warrant in individual cases as well. The Framework Decision explicitly states:

> Nothing in this Framework Decision may be interpreted as prohibiting refusal to surrender a person [. . .] when there are reasons to believe [. . .] that the said arrest warrant has been issued for the purpose of prosecuting or punishing a person on the grounds of his or her sex, race, religion, ethnic origin, nationality, language, political opinions or sexual orientation [. . .].[2]

Furthermore, Article 1(3) of the Framework Decision recalls the Member States' obligation to respect fundamental rights and fundamental principles of the Union.[3]

Under the regime on mutual recognition of decisions imposing financial penalties, the corresponding Framework Decision is more clear on that point and explicitly provides for a refusal ground based upon the "European ordre public."

---

[1] See Articles 3–5 of the Framework Decision of 13 June 2002 on the European Arrest Warrant and the surrender procedures between Member States (O.J. L 190 of 18 July 2002, p. 1).

[2] Recital (12) of the Framework Decision on the European Arrest Warrant (supra note 1).

[3] See also recital (13) of the Framework Decision on the European Arrest Warrant (supra note 1).

Article 20(3) of the Framework Decision on the application of the principle of mutual recognition to financial penalties[4] states:

> Each Member State may, where the certificate referred to in Article 4 gives rise to an issue that fundamental rights or fundamental legal principles as enshrined in Article 6 of the Treaty may have been infringed, oppose the recognition and the execution of decisions.

The tension between the obligation to respect human rights and mutual recognition has recently been addressed by the Court of Justice in the area of common asylum policy. Like cooperation in criminal matters, the Common European Asylum System is based upon the principle of mutual recognition and the assumption that each Member State abides by fundamental rights as enshrined in Article 6 TEU.[5] Therefore, the Court held that it can be assumed that the treatment of asylum seekers in all Member States complies with the requirements of the EU FRCh and the ECHR (presumption of compliance). In the eyes of the Court, even a violation of these rights by the Member State responsible will not as such affect the obligations of the other Member States under the Common European Asylum System because otherwise these obligations would be deprived of their substance.[6]

However, the presumption that Member States comply with their obligations under the EU FRCh and the ECHR is not conclusive but allows for evidence to the contrary.[7] The Court concluded that the Member States may not transfer an asylum seeker to another Member State in which systemic deficiencies amount to substantial grounds for believing that the asylum seeker would face a real risk of being subjected to inhuman or degrading treatment (Art. 4 EU FRCh).[8]

3 The European Arrest Warrant and Human Rights

The reasoning of the Court's judgment reaches beyond common asylum policy. Its impact on cooperation in criminal matters, the EAW in particular, has recently been addressed in the *Radu* case.[9]

Mr. Radu was suspected of aggravated robbery and was arrested in Romania on the basis of four European Arrest Warrants issued by Germany. In the surrender proceedings, Mr. Radu raised several objections against the execution of the European Arrest Warrants. In particular, he claimed that the executing state had

---

[4] Framework Decision 2005/214/JHA of 24 February 2005 on the application of the principle of mutual recognition to financial penalties (O.J. L 76 of 22 March 2005, p. 16).

[5] ECJ (Grand Chamber), judgment of 21 December 2011, joined cases C-411/10 and C-493/10, *N. S. and others*, para 14 and 15, with further references.

[6] *Ibid.*, para 80 et seq.

[7] *Ibid.*, para 99 et seq.

[8] *Ibid.*, para 106.

[9] ECJ, judgment of 29 January 2013, case C-396/11, *Radu*.

to ascertain that the issuing state observes the fundamental rights guaranteed by the ECHR and the Charter of Fundamental Rights. If that was not the case, the executing authority would be entitled to refuse to execute the European Arrest Warrant.[10]

However, Mr. Radu referred rather generally to the right to a fair trial but did not specify the alleged violation of this right. In fact, he only raised one point, stating that he had not been given the opportunity to hire a lawyer and to present his defense before the German authorities had issued the European Arrest Warrants.[11]

Not surprisingly, the Court rejected this argument. It can be inferred from the national criminal justice systems that a person wanted for arrest need not be heard before an arrest warrant is issued. Otherwise, it would be impossible to issue an arrest warrant against persons absconding from justice. The Court rightly pointed out that an arrest warrant requires an element of surprise, in particular in order to stop the suspect from taking flight.[12]

On the other hand, the right to be heard is fully respected at a later stage of the proceedings. The Framework Decision on the EAW explicitly states that the arrested person is entitled to be heard by the executing authority (Art. 14), and he will fully enjoy his defense rights after being surrendered to the issuing state. Therefore, the Court concluded that the executing authority cannot refuse to execute a European Arrest Warrant on the ground that the requested person was not heard by the issuing authority.[13] In focusing its reasoning on the right to be heard, the Court carefully avoided to address the general question on how to deal with human rights violations in the issuing Member State.

By contrast, Advocate General *Sharpston* further elaborated on that issue. In her opinion on the *Radu* case, she came to conclusions quite similar to the Court's reasoning in the asylum case. Referring to Article 1(3) of the Framework Decision and to the case law of the European Court of Human Rights in extradition cases,[14] she stated:

> the competent judicial authority [. . .] can refuse the request for surrender [. . .] where it is shown that the human rights of the person [. . .] have been infringed, or will be infringed, as part of or following the surrender process. However, such a refusal will be competent only in exceptional circumstances. In cases involving Articles 5 and 6 of the Convention and/or Articles 6, 47 and 48 of the Charter, the infringement in question must be such as fundamentally to destroy the fairness of the process. The person alleging infringement must persuade the decision-maker that his objections are substantially well founded [. . .].[15]

[10] *Ibid.*, para 16–19.

[11] *Ibid.*, para 26.

[12] ECJ, ibid., para 40.

[13] ECJ, ibid., para 43.

[14] Advocate General *Eleanor Sharpston*, opinion of 18 October 2012, case C-396/11, Radu, para 70 et seq., 74 et seq.

[15] Ibid., para 97.

Although the Advocate General referred to the Court's judgment in the asylum case,[16] she did not subject the exception to mutual trust subject to "systemic deficiencies" in the issuing Member State. Moreover, she explicitly rejected the minimum (evidential) standards of the European Court of Human Rights ("flagrant" violation of human rights "beyond reasonable doubt") but emphasized that the criteria must be defined in such a manner that it is not practically impossible for the arrested person to challenge the legality of surrender ("fundamental" violation, "substantially well founded objections").[17]

Thus, the conclusions of Advocate General *Sharpston* can be considered to create an additional refusal ground that can be derived from primary EU law (the Charter) and that goes beyond the grounds provided for in Articles 3–5 of the Framework Decision. This line of reasoning is valid for any fundamental right enshrined in Art. 6 TEU. In her opinion, the Advocate General explicitly referred to the proportionality of criminal sanctions [Art. 49(3) EU FRCh] but did not examine whether a disproportionate sanction could give rise to a refusal of surrender (see infra Sect. 5).[18]

4 The European Arrest Warrant and Trials *In Absentia*

The implicit refusal ground as construed by Advocate General *Sharpston* will be based upon EU law only. It is rooted in the priority of the Treaties and the Charter over EU legislation. This reasoning does not apply to human rights standards that can be derived from the Member States' constitutions. So the question is whether, if the execution of a European Arrest Warrant does not violate the Charter of Fundamental Rights, a Member State can still refer to constitutional principles in order to refuse surrender. In another most recent judgment, the *Melloni* case, the European Court of Justice has addressed the impact of constitutional principles on the decision on whether to execute a European Arrest.[19]

Mr. Melloni was tried *in absentia* by an Italian court and was sentenced to 10 years' imprisonment for bankruptcy fraud. The Italian authorities issued a European Arrest Warrant for execution of the sentence. After his arrest by the Spanish Police, Mr. Melloni opposed surrender to the Italian authorities, contending that under Italian law, an appeal against the judgment *in absentia* is inadmissible if the convicted person had been defended by a counsel who he or she had appointed.[20]

---

[16] Ibid., para 76.

[17] Ibid., para 82 et seq.

[18] *Ibid.*, para 103.

[19] ECJ, judgment of 26 February 2013, case C-399/11, Melloni.

[20] *Ibid.*, para 14–18.

Due to its relevance in extradition practice, the Framework Decision on the European Arrest Warrant[21] already provided for legal guarantees relating to trials *in absentia* (former Art. 5 No. 1). In 2009, this provision was replaced by the Framework Decision on trials *in absentia* (the new Art. 4a of the Framework Decision on the EAW).[22]

The Framework Decision is closely orientated to the case law of the European Court of Human Rights[23] but provides for more detailed rules on the conditions under which a conviction *in absentia* can be considered to be compatible with the right to a fair trial. In short, the Framework Decision is based on the principle that trials *in absentia* can solely be recognized on the ground that the accused has unequivocally waived his right to be present at the trial.[24]

In particular, the execution of a European Arrest Warrant may not be refused if the requested person "had given a mandate to a legal counselor who was ... accounted by the person concerned [...] to defend him at the trial, and was indeed defended by that counselor at the trial."[25]

In the proceedings against Mr. Melloni before the Italian court, these conditions were met.[26] Since Article 4a of the Framework Decision is an exhaustive provision on the nonexecution of European Arrest Warrants that are based upon judgments *in absentia*, the Court concluded that the Spanish authorities were precluded to make surrender conditional upon a review of the judgment rendered *in absentia*.[27]

In a second step, the Court assesses that the requirements set out in Article 4a of the Framework Decision comply with Article 6 ECHR and the case law of the European Court of Human Rights on trials *in absentia*. The European Court of Human Rights stated in several judgments that the accused may waive his right to be present at trial of his own free will, provided that the waiver is established in an unequivocal manner and is attended by minimum safeguards commensurate to its importance.[28] In the eyes of the Court of Justice, these conditions were also met

[21] Supra note 1.

[22] Framework Decision 2009/299/JHA of 26 February 2009 amending Framework Decisions 2002/584/JHA, 2005/214/JHA, 2006/783/JHA, 2008/909/JHA and 2008/947/JHA, thereby enhancing the procedural rights of persons and fostering the application of the principle of mutual recognition to decisions rendered in the absence of the person concerned at the trial (Official Journal, L 81 of 27 March 2009, p. 24).

[23] See Recital (8) of the Framework Decision.

[24] ECJ (supra note 19), para 52; see also Recital (12) of the Framework Decision: if a person who absconds and makes himself unavailable to be informed of the trial is convicted in absentia, the conviction will not have to be recognized by another Member State, i.e., extradition may be refused because there is no waiver of the right to be present at the trial.

[25] Art. 4a (1) lit. b of the Framework Decision on the European Arrest Warrant.

[26] See in that regard ECJ (supra note 19), para 42–46.

[27] *Ibid.*, para 46.

[28] European Court of Human Rights, judgment of 23 November 1993, Application No 14032/88 (Poitrimol v. France), para 31; for a more detailed analysis of the case law of the European Court of Human Rights, see Böse (2011), p. 489.

because Mr. Melloni had deliberately chosen to be represented by a defense lawyer instead of appearing in person.[29]

Since there has been no breach of "European" human rights, the question arises whether Mr. Melloni can invoke constitutional guarantees that provide for a higher standard on trials *in absentia*. In that respect, the Spanish constitutional court refers to Article 53 EU FRCh stating that

> Nothing in this Charter shall be interpreted as restricting or adversely affecting human rights and fundamental freedoms as recognized ... by Union and international law ... and by the Member States' constitutions.

According to the interpretation suggested by the constitutional court of Spain, this provision of the Charter gives constitutional human rights standards priority over the application of EU law.[30] The European Court of Justice rejected this interpretation because it would undermine the primacy of EU law and thereby seriously affect the unity and effectiveness of EU law.[31] Thus, reference to Article 53 EU FRCh and constitutional human rights standards cannot serve as a basis for an additional refusal ground under the regime of the European Arrest Warrant.

As far as the European Arrest Warrant is concerned, this result is not self-evident. In several Member States, the implementation legislation has been challenged before the constitutional courts.[32] These concerns are also mirrored in the Framework Decision. In recital (12) of the preamble, the Framework Decision on the European Arrest Warrant stresses that it "does not prevent a Member State from applying its constitutional rules relating to due process, freedom of association, freedom of the press and freedom of expression in other media."[33]

Furthermore, in judicial cooperation in civil matters, a corresponding refusal ground based upon the national ordre public is well established.[34] It seems odd that in the area of criminal law, which provides for far more intrusive measures, reference to constitutional standards should be barred.[35]

On the other hand, the primacy of EU law is a strong argument. The concept of mutual recognition would be seriously affected by additional refusal grounds derived from the constitutions of 28 Member States. Although the reasoning of the Court on the priority of EU law over national constitutional law is rather

---

[29] ECJ (supra note 19), para 52.

[30] *Ibid.*, para 56.

[31] *Ibid.*, para 57–60.

[32] See in particular the judgment of the German Constitutional Court of 18 July 2005, official court reports (BVerfGE) vo. 113, p. 273 et seq.; for an overview of the situations in the Member States, see the national reports in Guild (2006).

[33] Supra note 1.

[34] Art. 34 (1) Regulation (EC) No 44/2001 of 22 December 2000 on jurisdiction and the recognition and enforcement of judgments in civil and commercial matters (O.J. L 12 of 16 January 2001, p. 1): "A judgment shall not be recognized 1. If such recognition is manifestly contrary to public policy in the Member State in which recognition is sought ...."

[35] See Herrnfeld (2012), para 25.

convincing, the judgment leaves some doubts on whether the "European" standards on trials *in absentia* are sufficient. In that regard, there are two major shortcomings.

Firstly, the Framework Decision is based upon the concept of a waiver of the right to be present at trial. In particular, the Court of Justice has emphasized that the waiver must be based on the free will of the accused.[36] But what does "free will" mean if an accused is driven by fear of being arrested and held in custody? Is the decision not to give himself up in prison a voluntary waiver of the right to be present at the trial? I have my doubts. The guarantees set out in Art. 6 ECHR may not be used as a whip to make the accused appear in court. Thus, the relevant provision should expressly state that the accused's absence during the trial must not be due to constraint (the fear of being arrested and held in custody). In particular, the presence of the accused should be mandatory in proceedings on serious charges where imprisonment for several years is at stake.[37]

Furthermore, the waiver should be made subject to additional safeguards (legal advice, formal requirement of an express waiver before a judge). Such safeguards are explicitly foreseen for the consent to simplified surrender.[38] In particular, the Directive on the right to interpretation and translation in criminal proceedings makes the waiver subject to several requirements such as prior legal advice or (otherwise) full knowledge of the consequences of such a waiver and an unequivocal and voluntary waiver.[39]

The second objection to the Framework decision on trials *in absentia* is that it defines merely optional grounds for nonexecution of a European Arrest Warrant.[40] In other words, the Framework Decision does not define a minimum standard but a maximum standard on the conditions for surrender: an executing state may not insist upon a higher standard to be applied, but the Framework Decision leaves it up to the executing state to apply a lower threshold on trials *in absentia*. However, since the standard defined in the Framework Decision is mainly based upon the case law of the European Court of Human Rights, it should not be up to the Member State to decide whether to abide by this standard or not. A violation of the right to be present at the trial ought to be a mandatory, not an optional, ground for refusal.

[36] ECJ (supra note 19), para 49 and 52.

[37] See, for a more detailed critical assessment of the Framework Decision and the case law of the European Court of Human Rights, Böse (2011), pp. 500 et seq. and 505 et seq.

[38] Art. 13 Framework Decision on the European Arrest Warrant (supra note 1).

[39] Art. 3 (3) of the Directive 2010/64/EU of 20 October 2010 on the right to interpretation and translation in criminal proceedings (O.J. L 280 of 26 October 2010, p. 1).

[40] See recital (15) of the Framework Decision (supra note 22); see also ECJ (supra note 19), para 40.

5 The European Arrest Warrant and the Proportionality Principle

Last but not least, this contribution will address the impact of the proportionality principle on the European Arrest Warrant. In court practice, the European Arrest Warrant seems to be a "victim of its own success." Being a rather efficient and "user-friendly" instrument, it has also been used for the prosecution of petty offences, although recourse to less intrusive alternatives might have been possible. On this issue, there is no case law on the European, but only on the national, level. In particular, two decisions of the Higher Regional Court Stuttgart have triggered a discussion on the proportionality principle and its impact on the execution of a European Arrest Warrant.

In the first case, a European Arrest Warrant had been issued by Lithuania for the possession of 1,435 g of methamphetamine. In Lithuania, the (abstract) maximum penalty was 2 years' imprisonment; in Germany, the case would probably have been settled by a fine. The court, therefore, stated that extradition detention would be in breach with the proportionality principle, and the arrested person was released.[41]

In a second decision, the Higher Regional Court further elaborated on the relevance of the proportionality principle in surrender proceedings. Referring to Article 49(3) EU FRCh, it stated that the principle of proportionality is a general principle of EU law that is binding upon national courts when applying EU legislation. When assessing the proportionality of extradition arrest, the national court has to take the wanted person's right to liberty, the significance of the charge, and the severity of the possible penalty into consideration.[42] Furthermore, reasonable alternatives to a trial in the issuing state such as summons, questioning and/or *in absentia* proceedings have to be taken into consideration.[43]

For similar reasons, the Higher Regional Court of Karlsruhe refused to order extradition arrest arguing that the issuing Member State did not undertake any efforts to establish the address of the person sought and to summon him and that there was no reason to believe that he would not appear in court.[44] In another

[41] Higher Regional Court Stuttgart, decision of 18 November 2009—1 Ausl. 1302/09.

[42] Higher Regional Court Stuttgart, decision of 25 February 2010—1 Ausl (24) 1246/09, Neue Juristische Wochenschrift 2010, p. 1617 (1618)—English translation: Criminal Law Review 2010, p. 474 (479); see also Higher Regional Court Karlsruhe, decision of 15 March 2007—1 AK 15/07 (no extradition arrest of a person suspect of criminal damage of a car (amount of damage: 730 Euro).

[43] *Ibid.*; see also Schomburg and Lagodny (2012), p. 351; see also Boehm and Rosenthal (2008), mn. 779; Boehm KM In: Grützner et al. (2008), § 15 IRG, mn. 11.

[44] Higher Regional Court Karlsruhe, decision of 15 March 2007—1 AK 15/07, and decision of 5 April 2007—1 AK 17/07.

decision, the Court argued that the person sought might be given the opportunity to surrender to the police of the issuing state by himself.[45]

In the aftermath of these decisions, the proportionality principle has been subject to controversial discussions, in particular in the framework of the fourth round of mutual evaluation that addressed the practical implementation of the European Arrest Warrant.[46] As a consequence, the Council adopted an amendment to the European handbook on how to issue a European Arrest Warrant. In the new version of this handbook, the issuing authority is required to assess whether the use of a European Arrest Warrant complies with the principle of proportionality, in particular if less intrusive means are available.[47]

The question still is what happens if the issuing authority fails to fulfill its obligation. The handbook is silent on this, but it follows from the case law cited above that the executing authority may not execute an EAW if this would amount to a flagrant breach of the proportionality principle.[48]

6 Conclusion

The EAW is a well-established instrument of transnational cooperation in criminal matters in the Union and the "flagship" of mutual recognition. It significantly facilitates and speeds up surrender procedures between the Member States.

Nevertheless, the efficiency of the new instrument also harbors the risk of human rights violations, due to a lack of judicial control and an excessive reliance on mutual trust. Mutual trust cannot be achieved by mere decision but needs a reliable basis that has to rely upon practical experiences in transnational cooperation between the Member States. These experiences are the "core" of mutual trust; "good" experiences can strengthen, and "bad" experiences can undermine mutual trust.

Thus, human rights violations cannot be ignored when deciding upon the execution of a European Arrest Warrant. The case law mentioned above clearly shows that the principle of mutual recognition does not relieve the executing state from its obligation to respect fundamental rights (Art. 1(3) FD EAW). In the framework of this "European ordre public" (Art. 1(3) FD EAW), however, the executing state shall be competent to refuse the execution of an EAW (only) if it reveals to be manifest violations of human rights. The discussion on the principle of

---

[45] Higher Regional Court Karlsruhe, decision of 26 June 2007—1 AK 16/06, Strafverteidiger-Forum 2007, p. 477.

[46] See the final report of the fourth round of mutual evaluations, concerning the European Arrest Warrant, Council-Document 7361/10, pp. 4–7.

[47] See Council-Document No. 17195/1/10, pp. 14 and 15.

[48] This issue has most recently been addressed in a study on the evaluation of the European Arrest Warrant and the implementation of the proportionality principle in France, the Netherlands and Germany; see Albers et al. (2013), pp. 79 et seq.

proportionality illustrates the need for judicial control by the executing state and for trust in the assessment of proportionality by the court of the issuing state.

Criminal law enforcement in Europe is increasingly based upon cooperation and the division of tasks and competences, and this requires both trust and control. So, trust and control are not alternatives but two sides of the same coin.

References

Albers P, Beauvais P, Böse M, Bohnert JF, Langbroek P, Renier A, Wahl T (2013) Towards a common evaluation framework to assess mutual trust in the field of EU judicial cooperation in criminal matters. The Hague 2013. http://www.jura.uni-bonn.de/fileadmin/Fachbereich_Rechtswissenschaft/Einrichtungen/Lehrstuehle/Strafrecht1/Aushaenge/J-18664_WEB_Rapport_Rechtsstaatmonitor__EN_.pdf. Accessed 24 Sept 2013

Boehm KM, Rosenthal M (2008) Das Rechtshilfeverfahren. In: Ahlbrecht H, Böhm KM, Esser R, Hugger H, Kirsch S, Rosenthal M (eds) Internationales Strafrecht in der Praxis. C.F. Müller, Heidelberg

Böse M (2011) Harmonizing procedural rights indirectly: the framework decision on trials in Absentia. N C J Int Law Commer Regul 37:489–509

Grützner H, Pötz PG, Kreß C (eds) (2008) Internationaler Rechtshilfeverkehr in Strafsachen, 3rd edn. C.F. Müller, Heidelberg

Guild E (ed) (2006) Constitutional challenges to the European Arrest Warrant. Wolf Legal Publishers, Nijmegen

Herrnfeld HH (2012) In: Schwarze J (ed) EU-Kommentar, 3rd edn. Nomos, Baden-Baden, Art. 67 AEUV

Schomburg W, Lagodny O (2012) Verteidigung im international-arbeitsteiligen Strafverfahren. Neue Juristische Wochenschrift 65:348–354

Transnational Prosecutions, Methods of Obtaining Overseas Evidence, Human Rights Protection in Europe

Stefano Ruggeri

Contents

Abstract This study analyses the collection of evidence in transnational inquiries in Europe and its consequences on the sphere of fundamental rights of the individuals involved. It stresses that this issue cannot be properly analysed without a broader viewpoint that requires ascertaining which countries are called upon to international cooperation and what substantial link the addressees of the

---

S. Ruggeri (✉)
Department of Law, University of Messina, Piazza Pugliatti No. 1, Messina, Italy
e-mail: steruggeri@unime.it

S. Ruggeri (ed.), *Human Rights in European Criminal Law*,
DOI 10.1007/978-3-319-12042-3_9

transnational prosecution have with the law of these countries. This approach leads to extending the focus to how prosecutorial power should be distributed among several countries claiming the activation of their jurisdiction for the same case and, in a deeper sense, to which qualitative requirements a modern criminal law must have to grant offenders a fair adjudication while facing the challenges of an increasingly multicultural Europe. This study proposes the adoption of a common methodology in the analysis of both problems of the choice of the forum and the decision of the modes of investigation—a methodology that, starting with a strongly human-rights-oriented perspective, pursues the achievement of a delicate balance between individual rights protection and the need for efficient transnational prosecution.

Keywords Choice of the forum • Criminal evidence • Human rights • Transnational inquiries

1 Introductory Remarks

In the last two decades, the significant rise of new types of crimes committed across borders has strengthened the need to enhance transnational prosecution, and we have witnessed significant developments in the field of international cooperation in criminal matters.

To begin with, new modes of cooperation have emerged from the traditional MLA worldwide. In Europe, the CISA posed the basis for a cultural change of extraterritorial investigations, which led to the introduction, by means of the 2000 EUCMACM, of "a new generation of extra-territorial investigations", fully unrelated to the requirement of urgency.[1] From this emerged an unprecedented mode of *transnational* collection of evidence by the joint investigation teams.[2] A further development of this new model, which has allowed for direct cooperation especially among police forces, has been the beginning of the practice of conducting joint investigations, a practice significantly continued even by countries lacking the legislative basis for setting up investigative teams.[3] Outside Europe, it is noteworthy that US case law engages in analysing whether investigations have been

[1] Klip (2012), p. 361.

[2] On the characteristics of the transnational collection of evidence cf., among others, Gleß (2006), pp. 121 ff.

[3] This was the case of the task force set by *Italy* and *Germany* following the Duisburg massacre of 2007. See Scella (2012), p. 215. For an analysis of the functioning of joint investigations in practice, with a particular focus on the Swiss context, see recently Zurkinden (2013), pp. 291 ff.

carried out abroad in a "joint venture" with US officials and therefore whether US officials have played a substantial role in the overseas inquiries, which requires the application of US (constitutional) rules to the extent possible.[4]

But at the EU level, another important change occurred at the end of the 1990s in the way of dealing with judicial cooperation. A close examination of the evolution of EU cooperation in criminal matters shows that the improved MLA system has rapidly developed into the order model by means of the general enshrinement by EU legislation of the principle of mutual recognition as the cornerstone of almost the entire area of judicial cooperation, regardless of the very different nature of the judicial products concerned. The outcome was the mainstream replacement of the traditional request model through a new order model. A close look at its development over the last decade shows, however, a sort of parabolic trend, which has led to such a progressive evolution of the mutual recognition principle over recent years that some of the main features of the MLA system have been re-introduced and mixed with the pure forms of the order model.

Alongside these developments, new investigative tools and ways of speeding up the exchange of data, information and evidence among prosecuting authorities in force of the "principle of availability" have emerged, due to rapid technological and scientific advances.[5] This has certainly contributed to the enhancement of international cooperation, entailing a significant growth in the use of investigative measures impinging in unprecedented fashions on the sphere of the rights of the individuals involved in transnational procedures (suspects, victims, witnesses, etc.). Upon close examination, technological developments have contributed to this phenomenon at least in two ways, i.e., by providing new forms of intrusive investigation (*e.g.*, online search) and by allowing for "direct, reciprocal access to national databases using the full range of new technologies",[6] making national systems of telecommunications services accessible to foreign authorities by means of service providers and others. There is little doubt that such means can touch upon individual rights and in such a hidden way that the notion of "coercion" in its traditional sense has in a great part become perhaps more inappropriate in the field of transnational inquiries than in domestic procedures.

Despite these developments, however, legislative regulations of interferences with fundamental rights in the field of transborder procedures have surprisingly remained scant and uncoordinated. And whereas in cases, such as those on the setting up of joint investigation teams, procedural rules do not distinguish among the types of investigative activities that the team may carry out, the general provisions on the exchange of evidence and information laid down in several international instruments allow for national authorities to obtain the results of intrusive

[4] For an in-depth analysis of US case law, see Thaman (2013a), pp. 519 ff.

[5] See, among others, Böse (2007), *passim*.

[6] In these terms, Vogler (2013), p. 34.

inquiries conducted out overseas through bypassing the limits inherent in the procedures on rogatory letters.[7] In the area of mutual recognition, moreover, it is noteworthy that—despite the explicit reference in the FD EEW to the discretion of the executing authority in choosing whether to use coercive means in the collection of evidence—in recent years we have witnessed a clear legislative tendency to allow for greater application of coercive means in transnational inquiries. However, this tendency, which is proportional to the aim of widening of the order model to any kind of investigative and evidential activity by means of the EIO proposal, still lacks a coherent project of regulation of intrusive investigations.

Viewed from a human rights perspective, the failure to regulate interferences with individual rights in transnational inquiries in a coherent and comprehensive manner is in line with the lack of coordinated protection of fundamental (especially defence) rights in transborder investigations by international texts. Upon close examination, in the field of evidence gathering, EU legislation launched pursuant to the order model reveals even more deficiencies than what was achieved in the field of the request model. Thus, no participation of the defence is foreseen in the investigations conducted in other member states, whereas the combination of *lex loci* with specific formalities of *lex fori*, as we will see, is primarily aimed at fulfilling the need to ensure the movement of evidence and its admissibility in the relevant proceedings rather than the need to find a proper balance of state-related interests, the defendant's rights and the rights of the addressee of the overseas investigation.

To be sure, an unbalanced tension between the need for efficiency of transnational prosecution and the protection of individual rights emerges from the Lisbon Treaty. Certainly, article 82(2)(b) TFEU, by legitimising legislative intervention of the EU institutions with the purpose of protecting the rights of individuals in criminal procedures, relates also to the rights of the individuals involved in *transnational* criminal procedures. Furthermore, the defendant's rights in the field of transborder investigations appear to be only indirectly protected through legislative intervention in the field of admissibility of transnational evidence [art. 82(2)(a) TFEU]. Moreover, whereas the TFEU has, in different fashions, strengthened police and judicial cooperation in criminal matters (*e.g.*, by providing a legislative basis for the future EPPO at a primary law level, by enhancing the role and tasks of Eurojust, etc.), article 82(2)(b) does not allow for the harmonisation of individual rights exceeding the establishment of minimum standards. Whatever the meaning of this provision is, therefore, the introduction of minimum rules to the extent strictly necessary to facilitate mutual recognition calls for a minimalist approach.

Against this background, this paper aims at questioning the properness of this approach, which is not in line with the "unique vulnerability of defendants" and, in

[7] A worrying example is the Italian case, due to the lack of both the instruments of improved MLA and the tools of the order model. Cf. Caprioli (2013), pp. 451 ff.

general terms, of the individuals "facing international investigations", a condition that requires standards of protection "surely exceed[ing] those currently available in domestic proceedings".[8] In light of this, the analysis will focus, by means of comparative method, on what human rights protection transnational procedures must ensure where intrusive investigations are required to obtain overseas evidence in transnational criminal inquiries. In this regard, this paper argues that the modes of conducting investigations and taking evidence *abroad* cannot be chosen independently from the determination of the competent forum and that a common methodological approach should unify—from a human rights perspective—the choice of the power to prosecute and the way of investigating transnational crimes.

2 Transborder Investigations and Interferences with Fundamental Rights: Problems and Human Rights Challenges

2.1 The National Level

Starting with these premises, I shall first analyse which methods guide the collection of transnational evidence in national countries and what human rights protection they provide where interferences with fundamental rights are required. To this end, I have selected four European countries, i.e., *Germany*, *Italy*, *Spain* and *Switzerland*, that will be analysed first separately and then comparatively.

2.1.1 Analysis of National Countries

Analysis of the selected legal systems has been conducted at two levels, which relate to the legislation and the developments of domestic jurisprudences. The need to analyse both levels is particularly evident in the field of transnational inquiries, where case law gains even more relevant roles than in domestic procedures by defining the formalities that must be applied for investigative and evidential activities and by laying down the limits within which overseas evidence may be used. Moreover, as we will see, national jurisprudence often follows common courses despite the different orientation of its respective legal systems.

[8] Vogler (2013), p. 30.

Germany

In Germany, despite the existence of a comprehensive national Law on legal assistance in criminal matters (IRG), the main rules on the collection of overseas evidence can be traced back to international legislation, which, as a general rule, take precedence before the provisions of the IRG "to the extent that they have become directly applicable national law" [art. 1(3) IRG-Germany]. Within Europe, German police and judicial cooperation in criminal matters is mainly based on the ECMLACM, the CISA and the EUCMACM. Thus, pursuant to the most advanced forms of MLA, as we will see, assistance is provided following combination methods of obtaining evidence, whereas extraterritorial investigation powers can be exercised abroad by German officials, as a rule, with respect to the formalities of *lex loci*. A different solution applies to incoming requests for assistance not based on international regulations. Here, as a general rule, assistance must be provided in a manner compatible with relevant principles of national law (§ 73 IRG-Germany), which, in light of efficient international cooperation, mainly relates to *constitutional* law[9]—a general requirement of fundamental importance where intrusive means are at stake.

This limit does not, instead, apply to outcoming requests for assistance, which must follow all the requirements of German criminal law,[10] although it is noteworthy that German case law adopts a rather flexible approach as to the use at trial of the results of overseas inquiries. Also here, the failure to meet the procedural principles of the requesting country, especially where the general standards of the rule of law are at stake, can lead to the inadmissibility of overseas evidence.[11] But apart from these cases, German case law faces the problem of the use of overseas evidence in a very pragmatic way[12]: in principle, foreign evidence is deemed admissible even where it has been taken following procedures other than those laid down by German procedural law, but then, "as a compensation, the judge shall consider this fact when assessing the evidence and, where necessary, give lesser credit to such 'tainted' evidence".[13]

Italy

Among other European countries, Italy shows considerable backwardness in the field of international cooperation in criminal matters.[14] Because of the failure to

[9] Lagodny (2012), para. 3.

[10] Vogel (2012b), paras. 18–20.

[11] See, among others, BGH NStZ 1983, 181. Cf. recently Sinn (2013), p. 413.

[12] Gleß (2003), p. 134.

[13] In these terms, Schünemann (2014), pp. 162 f.

[14] For a detailed analysis of Italian perspective, see Caprioli (2013), pp. 439 ff.

ratify the EUCMACM and to implement most EU instruments, the main international instruments that govern Italian legal assistance with other European countries are still the ECMLACM and the CISA. Moreover, since SAP ECMLACM has not been ratified, cooperation based on the ECMLACM cannot profit the most advanced forms of legal assistance. But a certain backwardness of the Italian legal system in the field of international criminal cooperation also relates to the national rules on judicial assistance in criminal matters, enacted into the 1988 CCP. Despite the title of Book XI (Jurisdictional *relationships with foreign authorities*), not only has the CCP failed to fully jurisdictionalise the forms of legal assistance, but furthermore it has not enacted any provision specifically related to the use of coercive means in the context of transnational inquiries. This lacuna probably derives from the lack of a comprehensive doctrine of interferences with fundamental rights also in the field of domestic procedures, where the rules on "coercive measures" relate to remand detention and other forms of restriction of *personal freedom*.

Against this background, cooperation with other European countries remains, in the absence of specific bilateral agreements, based upon old international instruments that, concerning the forms of obtaining evidence, follow, as a rule, application of the *lex loci* alone. Also here, furthermore, case law has elaborated a compensating mechanism to limit the use at trial of overseas evidence, thus requiring the compatibility of the evidence gathered pursuant to foreign procedures "with fundamental principles of the domestic legal system".[15] This solution, however, entails the serious risk that the standards of protection of individual rights might be lowered beyond that allowed in relation to domestic procedures.[16] On the other hand, where the CCP regulation is applied, article 725(2) CCP-Italy, following the approach of most instruments of the improved MLA system, requires assistance to be provided pursuant to Italian law, but national authorities will be bound to implement foreign requests for the application of special procedures unless they infringe the fundamental principles of national law. Act 367/2001 enacted a similar solution in the field of active rogatory letters [art. 727(5-*bis*) CCP-Italy], but the possibility of requesting the application of Italian procedures in the collection of evidence abroad applies only where an international agreement provides for it and can lead to the inadmissibility of any evidence gathered without respecting the requested formalities [art. 729(1-*bis*) CCP-Italy]. To avoid this risk, Italian authorities often request the transmission of evidence already taken abroad. As a result of the frequent use of the model of (spontaneous) exchange of evidence, often gathered on the basis of informal requests by Italian authorities, not only are the limits inherent in the system of letters rogatory eluded, but the defendant is deprived of any possibility of taking part in overseas investigations.[17]

---

[15] Constitutional Court, dec. 379/1995; Court of Cassation, 8 March 2002, Pozzi, in *CED Cass.* 222025.

[16] In these terms, Caprioli (2013), pp. 445 ff.

[17] *Ibid.*, pp. 451 ff.

Spain

Unlike other European countries, Spain neither has an autonomous Law on judicial assistance in criminal matters nor regulates its international cooperation within the CCP, and only a few generic rules on international cooperation (not only in criminal matters) are contained in the 1985 LOPJ.[18] Judicial assistance is therefore mainly based upon international agreements, and, within Europe, the main instruments remain the ECMLACM, the CISA and the EUCMACM. Interestingly, despite the availability of most tools of improved legal assistance, in Spanish case law the *Tribunal Supremo* is often satisfied with the fact that investigations are carried out in compliance with *lex loci* to admit the use at trial of foreign evidence even where the procedures followed abroad considerably differ from Spanish rules and the investigative activities have interfered with fundamental rights abroad.[19]

Switzerland

Switzerland has a highly developed system of international cooperation, and the Swiss legal system attaches great importance to the collection of evidence by means of intrusive investigations. At an international level, where no more specific agreement applies, the ECMLACM traditionally governs Swiss international cooperation with European countries. Moreover, the association to the Schengen *acquis*, which entered into force in Switzerland in December 2008, within the framework of the 2004 Bilateral Agreements II between Switzerland and the European Union, has brought several changes and simplified several fields of judicial assistance, such as the transfer of evidence.[20] Administrative assistance is regulated separately in the different areas of law, such as prevention of money laundering, terrorism financing, etc.[21]

Within its scope of application, the Swiss IRG attaches great attention to the respect of fundamental rights in transborder inquiries. Thus, as a general rule, providing legal assistance must not infringe the procedural guarantees of both the ECHR and the ICCPR [art. 1(a) IRG-Switzerland], international instruments that "constitute the core of the constitutional fundamental rights" and therefore in Switzerland "prevail over any other international agreement or national law".[22]

Both inside and outside the Schengen area, several investigative activities can interfere with fundamental rights, such as seizure of assets, exchange of evidence

---

[18] For an overview of legal sources for conducting transnational investigations in *Spain,* cf. Gascón Inchausti (2013), pp. 477 ff.

[19] See, among others, STS 13 October 2010 (ROJ 6139/2009). For a detailed analysis of the developments of Spanish case law, see Gascón Inchausti (2013), pp. 480 ff.

[20] Heine and Zürcher-Rentsch (2013), pp. 500 and 504.

[21] *Ibid.*, p. 499.

[22] *Ibid.*, p. 499.

and information, etc. Some of them are regulated by the IRG, which, moreover, contains a general provision concerned with compulsory means that imposes, as a general rule, the respect for the requirement of dual criminality (art. 64 - IRG-Switzerland). Further rules of great importance in light of fundamental rights in the field of transborder inquiries concern the methods of obtaining evidence and defence rights. Concerning the first issue, Switzerland has enacted a very strict rule, which requires perfect compliance of the forms explicitly requested by foreign authorities to obtain evidence with domestic procedural rules (rather than with the relevant principles of domestic law) [art. 65(2) IRG-Switzerland]. In cases of coercive means, this requires, therefore, compatibility with the general rules laid down in CCP-Switzerland (arts. 196 et seq.), and it is noteworthy that, to avoid discriminations with domestic cases, article 65(c) IRG-Switzerland provides that "no essential disadvantage may result [from the procedures requested] to the persons involved".[23] Concerning the defence rights, Federal Act of 4 October 1996 introduced into the IRG a new article 65a, which allows for parties in foreign proceedings to take part in the acts of judicial assistance and to have access to the files, whenever requested by foreign authorities or to facilitate foreign inquiries.

2.1.2 Comparative Conclusions

From these elements we may draw the following conclusions:

(a) National countries have generally failed to enact general rules governing the use of investigative powers relevant to fundamental rights in cross-border cases. Whereas *Italy* does not directly address the issue of letters rogatory entailing restrictions of individual rights, *Germany's* and *Switzerland's* Acts of international cooperation in criminal matters regulate a certain number of investigative powers affecting fundamental rights. The IRG-Switzerland even lays down a general provision on the use of coercive means, which, however, limits itself to requiring the dual punishability of the act that gives rise to legal assistance.

(b) National regulations show the general preference for the application of combined methods of taking evidence aimed at foreign investigations, methods that, in light of the need for efficient international cooperation, are generally based on the clause of compliance of the foreign procedures with the fundamental or relevant principles of domestic law. Significantly in *Italy*, whereas the possibility of requesting the respect for domestic formalities in foreign investigations applies only where an international instrument in force in Italy allows it [art. 727(5-*bis*) CCP-Italy],[24] Italian authorities are generally committed to applying foreign procedures whenever requested abroad pursuant to

[23] Gleß (2011a), p. 89.

[24] See Caprioli (2013), pp. 449 f.

article 725(2) CCP-Italy. The IRG-Germany follows, within its scope of application, a similar approach. These solutions entail, however, considerable risks from a human rights perspective. Especially, the lack of clear rules as to which measures can be requested leaves great uncertainty both to the defendant in the relevant proceedings and the addressee of the measure concerning the procedure that will be followed in regard to the specific investigative activity. Moreover, this rather imperfect combination between procedural rules can lead to due process guarantees being reduced in comparison with domestic cases. Such risks are considerably reduced in *Switzerland*, which, by requiring perfect compatibility of the foreign procedures with Swiss law, does not, however, provide certainty as to the procedural law that will apply to the investigation in question.

(c) Combined methods are generally used at a domestic level to admit overseas evidence in domestic proceedings, and also here the goal of fulfilling the need for efficient international cooperation has led to the widespread preference for the limit of compliance with the relevant principles of national law. Among the analysed countries, *Spain* remains unique by generally adopting a rather pragmatic and humble attitude to overseas evidence, which is often admitted even if gathered with the sole respect of *lex loci* and without the "due process safeguards that would be required if the same investigation took place in Spain".[25] Instead, *Italy* contains—even if only within the scope of the application of article 727(5-*bis*) CCP-Italy, i.e., where an international agreement allows it—a very strict regulation aimed at excluding the use of any piece of evidence taken abroad pursuant to procedures different from those indicated in the request [art. 729(1-*bis*) CCP-Italy]. But despite the wording of this provision, it should be interpreted reasonably, and therefore use should be permitted whenever the failure to fulfil the formalities laid down in the request would not jeopardise the ability of the procedural activity to realise its effects in *Italy*.[26]

The model based on the compliance of the formalities followed overseas only with the fundamental principles of the law of the country where the process takes place has given rise to various criticisms in criminal law scholarship.[27] From a formal viewpoint, this approach certainly produces a significant "de-formalisation of evidential procedures".[28] But the main concern is perhaps that such combined methods of obtaining evidence, as has been noted, aim at responding more to the need for efficient international cooperation than to the human rights challenges that are inherent in transborder inquiries. This of course heightens the risk of discrimination, since with a view to facilitating the use at trial of overseas evidence the

[25] Gascón Inchausti (2013), p. 482.

[26] Caprioli (2013), p. 450.

[27] See, for a different approach, Caprioli (2013), pp. 449 f., who defines the combined method as a "virtuous model".

[28] In these terms, see Gleß (2003), p. 134.

defence rights of the accused might be considerably weakened compared to those that would be granted in domestic procedures.[29]

2.2 *The International and Supranational Levels*

2.2.1 Developments in the Request Model

The traditional MLA system did not provide comprehensive rules on the use of investigative means touching upon fundamental rights, nor did it establish specific methods for the collection of overseas evidence. In its original text, the ECMACM contained no general clause specifically aimed at regulating the adoption even of measures implying the use of coercion in the context of procedures of legal assistance. Nor were there specific rules concerning the methods of taking evidence abroad in cases of intrusive investigations. Concerning the modes of gathering evidence, the strong sovereignist approach posed *lex loci* as the general rule applying to *any* letters rogatory. As a consequence, the protection of the rights of the individuals involved in the proceedings in the home state depended entirely on the standards of the host state. This rendered the participation of the defence of private parties—provided for by several international texts, such as the ECMACM (art. 4)—a rather formal guarantee, since the defence could not help in any way in the proper application of foreign law.

To be sure, certain rules concerned with the use of some intrusive investigative means had already been laid down in the ECMACM with the purpose of enhancing the protection both of the national sovereignty and individual rights. But these rules still lacked a general framework of principles establishing the general conditions for exercising intrusive investigations and therefore limited themselves to laying down only basic requirements (even if not generally applied in the field of letters rogatory).[30] On the other hand, the traditional MLA was clearly characterised by a classical understanding of intrusive investigations as referring to measures restricting fundamental rights (*e.g.*, property) *by means of coercion.*

This system lasted up to the 1980s. But many things progressively changed in the MLA model by means of bilateral agreements. And at the beginning of the 1990s, significant developments were enacted into multilateral instruments. Within the

---

[29] For instance, in Italy, witness evidence taken abroad by means of direct questioning of a judge has been admitted and considered in line with the adversarial principle and the defendant's right to confrontation pursuant to article 111 of the Italian Constitution, although similar evidence would not, as a rule, be admitted at trial if gathered in a domestic procedure. See Court of Cassation, 28 April 2009, Russo, in *CED Cass.* 243938; Caprioli (2013), p. 446.

[30] The main example offered by this Convention related to search and the seizure of property, whose use was allowed to the requested State under the condition that it made its assistance dependent on the respect of the dual criminality requirement [art. 5(1)(a)], although this did not constitute a general requirement of letters rogatory.

Schengen area, the CISA introduced into the European MLA system the possibility of direct contacts between the domestic judicial authorities while sending and receiving requests for assistance [art. 53(1) CISA]. This provided the general framework for a methodological change of approach in the collection of evidence overseas, since the requesting State was allowed to require the fulfilment of specific formalities of its own law, which entailed the duty of the requested authority to apply partially (under certain conditions) foreign law. This change introduced an unprecedented combination of procedural laws to take place, an approach that gave new significance to old mechanisms but raised new legal problems for both the cooperating authorities. Thus, the possibility of the attendance of officials and private parties of the relevant proceedings at the execution of letters rogatory undoubtedly gained an important role by helping the requested authority to fulfil the difficult task of applying foreign law.[31] To reduce the difficulties arising from the application of foreign law, furthermore, some of the international instruments that first adopted this approach required a test of full compliance of the requested procedures with the law and even with the practices of the requested country.[32]

This new approach marked another significant cultural change in the field of judicial assistance. Under the traditional MLA system, the strict application of *lex loci* allowed both parties to ignore foreign law, and it is no surprise that even those countries that continue to use the old MLA system waive their right to verify whether *lex loci* has been respected, thus acknowledging a presumption of compliance with *lex loci*.[33] By contrast, the combination of procedural laws required an additional effort by both sides: the requesting authority had to learn the law and practice while choosing the formalities to be followed in the gathering of evidence overseas, whereas the requested authority had to familiarise itself with *lex fori* to apply it properly.

This cultural change brought about the introduction into international texts of general clauses concerned with the use of coercive measures in the field of transborder inquiries. And even if this did not lead to a substantial change in the way of conceiving coercive means as investigative measures implying the use of coercion, the enactment of general provisions entailed positive effects. Among the main examples, we might quote article 4(1)(e) of the UN MTMACM, which provided for the refusal of assistance if granting it would require the requested State to carry out compulsory measures that would be inconsistent with its law and

[31] It is noteworthy that, outside Europe, the IACMACM strengthened this possibility by allowing officials and private parties of the requesting State not only to be present but furthermore to take part in the execution of letters rogatory (art. 16).

[32] In this sense, article 6 UN MTMACM made legal assistance dependent on the demanding condition of consistency with the law and practice of the host country. Similarly, article 10 IACMACM stated that the procedures specified in the request for assistance ought to be "fulfilled in the manner indicated by the requesting state insofar as the law of the requested state is not violated".

[33] See, in Spain, Supreme Tribunal, judgement of 5 May 2003 (ROJ 3023/2003). On this topic, cf. Gascón Inchausti (2013), p. 484.

practice, if the offence had been the subject of investigation or prosecution under its own jurisdiction. Consequently, only those coercive measures that would have been admissible in a similar domestic case in the host country could be executed. This assured the individuals subject to restrictions through coercive means the same standards of protection as laid down by *lex loci*, though this guarantee did not rule out that—in light of the principle of the most favourable treatment—a *higher* level of protection might be afforded through the formalities of *lex fori* required by the requesting authority.[34]

A further development occurred in the MLA system at the end of the 1990s, concerned with the methods of obtaining evidence abroad, brought about several changes. Thus, the combination of procedural laws was maintained but—in light of the increasing need for more efficient international cooperation—submitted to a test of consistency of the requested formalities of *lex fori* not with the entire law of the requested country but only with its fundamental principles.[35] Surprisingly, moreover, neither the EUCMACM nor the SAP ECMLACM enacted a general clause allowing for a test of consistency of the requested compulsory investigations with *lex loci*, nor is there any general rule on the use of intrusive measures, notwithstanding such rules would have certainly been necessary due to the introduction of international standards on the use of investigative means interfering with fundamental rights in a hidden way, such as undercover inquiries, wiretaps, etc.

2.2.2 Developments in the Order Model

In the field of transborder investigations and obtaining evidence abroad, the application of the principle of mutual recognition showed, since its very beginning, a clear tendency of EU institutions to facilitate international cooperation regardless of whether this might lower the standards of individual rights protection—a tendency perhaps even more accentuated than what happened to the right to freedom by means of the EAW.

In its early years, the order model, despite dealing with securing rather than with taking evidence, drastically reduced the grounds for refusal of assistance. As a consequence, not only did some of the classic sovereignty-based clauses (*e.g.*, the prejudice of essential national security interests) disappear, but some of the surviving grounds for refusal were construed in a way that weakened them and constituted

[34] On the principle of the most favoured treatment of individuals in European criminal law, see Ruggeri A, in this book. Criticism against the application of the clause of the most favoured treatment in transnational procedures has been raised by Böse (2002), pp. 152 ff.; Böse (2003), pp. 238 ff.

[35] See respectively arts. 4 EUCMACM and 8 SAP ECMLACM.

a dangerous backward step in human rights protection.[36] A clear example of this approach is the FD OFPE, which, concerning the modes of securing evidence, inherited the combination of *lex loci* and *lex fori* that characterised the last phase of the MLA system, including the requirement that requests should conform to the fundamental principles of the legal system of the executing country. Compared to this model, however, the degree of integration with foreign law was remarkably reduced, in that the possibility for the issuing authority to require the fulfilment of procedural formalities of its own law was allowed only to the extent necessary to ensure the validity of evidence in the relevant proceedings [art. 5(2)]. Moreover, unlike the MLA instruments, it failed to provide for any form of joint participation of officials and mostly private parties in the execution of the freezing procedure.

But the principle of mutual recognition itself has undergone significant developments over the last decade. A look at the FD EEW of 5 years later shows that the rigorous logic of the order model was remarkably smoothened by the re-introduction of some classic sovereignty-based clauses (*e.g.*, the prejudice of essential national security interests) and, in general terms, by the re-expansion of the list of the grounds for refusal. Even more significantly, the FD EEW has introduced a general clause giving, as a rule,[37] the executing authority full responsibility for choosing whether and which coercive means could be used in the execution of the evidence warrant [art. 11(2)]. This clause has been supported by a further provision, according to which the fulfilment of the formalities and procedures of *lex fori* in the execution of the evidence warrant cannot entail any obligation for the executing State to adopt coercive measures.[38]

[36] Among the most significant examples, we can mention the infringement of the *ne bis in idem* rule, which, unlike what provided for by the FD EAW, became a facultative ground for refusal in the FD OFPE [art. 7(1)(c) FD OFPE].

[37] The only exception relates to the use of measures, including search and seizure, in the case of the offences listed under article 14(2), to which the dual criminality requirement does not apply [art. 11(3)(ii)]. This provision raises many human rights concerns. What is the nature of the measures that must be (always) available in case of those offences? If *any* measure, even of coercive nature, must be available, what is the relationship between the type of the offence (and the severity of its punishment) and the duty to fulfil an evidence order imposing upon the use of coercion? The consequence of this approach is that the issuing authority, while determining the threshold of punishment of the offence under prosecution within the list of article 14(2), also establishes the necessity of using a means of coercion in the concrete case. This result proves unsatisfactory, taking also into account that also the FD EEW has failed to provide for any possibility of joint participation in the execution of the evidence warrant in the host country.

[38] The proposal of 2003 for the adoption of a European evidence warrant provided for some fundamental procedural guarantees to be followed in the collection of evidence, to ensure full respect especially for the subsidiarity and the *nemo tenetur* principles [art. 12(1)(a) and (c) PFD EEW, COM(2003) 688 final]. See Gleß (2011b), p. 606.

3 Solution Models for Setting Fair Procedures of Obtaining Transnational Evidence After the Lisbon Treaty

The entry into force of the Lisbon Treaty constituted the starting point for new debates and the launching of new proposals in the field of transnational evidence. The main aim of these proposals has been the creation of a comprehensive system of conduction of overseas investigations and taking evidence in other member states. But another significant cultural change has inevitably accompanied these initiatives, as their wide scope has shifted the focus to how investigations may be carried out overseas where they impinge on the sphere of individual rights.

With a view to setting up a fair model of gathering transnational evidence pursuant to the new challenges posed by Lisbon, furthermore, I shall analyse three solution models, which respectively emerge from (*a*) a further development of the order model by means of legislative proposals launched after the Lisbon Treaty and two modes of conducting transnational investigations in a strict sense, respectively by means of (*b*) joint investigations and (*c*) a Europe-wide conception of territoriality. The critical analysis of these models will allow us to observe three fundamental requirements for the construction of a fair model of transnational criminal inquiries, i.e., legal multiculturalism, cooperation and coherence in the investigations.

3.1 From the European Commission's Proposals to the Directive on a European Investigation Order: On the Path Towards a New Form of Mutual Recognition?

After the Lisbon Treaty, EU institutions immediately announced important innovations in the field of transnational investigations and taking evidence abroad. Shortly before the entry into force of the Lisbon Treaty, the European Commission had already launched an ambitious challenge for overcoming the limits of the FD EEW. In its Communication "An area of freedom, security, and justice serving the citizens",[39] it proposed the setting up of a comprehensive means of collecting evidence and envisaged the establishment of minimum principles to facilitate the mutual admissibility of evidence between countries, including scientific evidence. This approach was confirmed by the Green Paper of 11 November 2009, in which the Commission launched an ambitious proposal, aimed at covering a much more complex area than that covered by the legal instruments existing at that time, i.e., both the obtaining of evidence in criminal matters by one Member State from

[39] COM (2009) 262 final.

another and the securing of its admissibility in the criminal process that makes use of the evidence. The Commission drafted a distinction between two types of dynamic evidence, i.e., (a) evidence that, although directly available, can be obtained only through procedural activities (interviews of witnesses or suspects, wiretapping, bank accounts, etc.) and (b) evidence that, though it exists, requires further investigation or examination (analysis of existing objects, documents or data or obtaining of bodily material, such as samples or fingerprints). Although this distinction clearly relates to intrusive investigative means, however, the Commission's approach in dealing with these measures remained unclear and the focus seemed to be addressed to investigative non-coercive means only to exclude the application of some grounds for refusal of assistance.

After the entry into force of the Lisbon Treaty, the Stockholm Programme of 11 December 2009 re-affirmed the need to bring order to the fragmentary regime of the existing instruments.[40] And along these lines, the Commission proposed, in its Action Plan Implementing the Stockholm Programme, two legislative initiatives planned for 2011. These initiatives have, however, never been launched, since they were anticipated by eight member states, which in April 2010 presented the ambitious legislative proposal of setting up a comprehensive tool of overseas investigations aimed at gathering almost any type of evidence, including non-documentary and dynamic evidence, i.e., the proposal for a Directive on a new European investigation order (EIO).[41] The genesis of this text has been slow and turbulent, however. Starting in April 2010, examination by the Council lasted more than 1 year; a general agreement on the proposal was not reached until December 2011.[42] After the orientation vote of May 2012 by the European Parliament, furthermore, the Conference of Presidents decided in June 2012 that the European Parliament would suspend its cooperation with the Council, *inter alia*, on the EIO dossier until a satisfactory outcome was achieved on Schengen governance.[43] Cooperation re-commenced in 2012, but the negotiations among the Council, the Parliament and the European Commission lasted up to November 2013, thus ending up in a compromise text.[44] After its confirmation by the Permanent Representatives Committee on 3 December, the EP Committee on Civil Liberties, Justice and Home Affairs voted on the text on 5 December 2013 and on 7 March 2014, after almost 4 years of long examinations, the Directive was finally issued.[45]

[40] The Stockholm Programme—An open and secure Europe serving and protecting citizens (2010/C 115/01), point 3.1.1.

[41] Interinstitutional File: 2010/0817 (COD), COPEN 115 EJN 12 CODEC 363 EUROJUST 47.

[42] See doc. 18918/11, COPEN 369 EJN 185 CODEC 2509 EUROJUST 217.

[43] See http://www.europarl.europa.eu/news/en/pressroom/content/20120614IPR46824/html/EP-suspends-cooperation-with-Council-on-five-justice-and-home-affairs-dossiers.

[44] See doc. 15196/13, COPEN 165 EUROJUST 95 EJN 67 CODEC 2348.

[45] PE-CONS 122/13.

A short look at this long path clearly shows that the text has been largely amended. To be sure, the original draft was not entirely consistent with its ambitious goal of launching a new form of mutual recognition resulting from the combination of the order model with the flexibility of the traditional MLA system—a goal that, moreover, encompassed the achievement of a high level of protection both of state-related interests and individual rights. Despite these aims, the original proposal had drastically reduced the grounds for refusal, which significantly restricted the margins of discretion of the executing authority while threatening both national sovereignty and the sphere of human rights.[46] As has been observed, furthermore, the original proposal had already dropped the emergency brake, introduced by the FD EEW, concerned with the use of coercive means: the executing authority was not left free to decide whether to enforce compulsory measures and, even worse, the choice of which investigative means, including intrusive means, to apply was left, in line with the approach of the proposed instrument, to the issuing authority. Nor did the original draft reproduce the clause, introduced by the FD EEW, banning the issuing authority from compelling the executing authority, by requesting the fulfilment of procedures of its own law in the collection of evidence, to apply coercive methods.

To be sure, the intrusiveness of the investigation abroad clearly emerged from several provisions, and it is therefore no surprise that in the course of the Council examination not only were new grounds for refusal re-introduced (*e.g.*, the principle of *ne bis in idem*), but furthermore article 10(1) was re-structured, and a two-tier list of grounds for refusal was set up just on the basis of the distinction between coercive and non-coercive measures.[47] Although the final text has not reproduced this solution in the same terms, it has maintained a two-track system, based on a distinction between "normal" investigative measures and (among others) non-coercive measures, which "always have to be available under the law of the executing State" [art. 10(2)] and to which two of the normal grounds for refusal do not apply, i.e., the dual criminality requirement (unless the EIO has been issued in relation to one of the serious crimes listed in Annex D) and the respect for the limitations provided for by the law of the executing state and concerned with certain punishment thresholds or types of crimes [art. 11(2)].

This approach still displays a complicated construction, which gives rise to many human rights concerns. The fact that the measures of article 10(2) are provided for in an exhaustive list and that the grounds for refusal have been re-unified in a comprehensive list clearly demonstrates that the new investigative tool—unlike the old EEW—can *normally* impinge on fundamental rights.

[46] Peers (2010), pp. 1 ff. Among the main lacunas, the original text gave no relevance to the principle of *ne bis in idem*, whereas it surprisingly reproduced a typical sovereignist ground for refusal, i.e., the prejudice to essential national security interests [art. 10(1)(b) PD EIO].

[47] See doc. 10749/11 REV 2, COPEN 130 EJN 70 CODEC 914 EUROJUST 85, p. 3.

However, the very different regulation applicable to cross-border investigations and especially the heterogeneous nature of the measures listed in article 10(2) still do not make it possible to clearly understand what is to be meant respectively by "coercive measures" and "non-coercive means" in modern transnational procedures and which principles must govern their use.[48] For instance, hearings of witnesses or experts, despite not being included among "non-coercive measures", are subject to the same regulations: as a consequence, they can be conducted irrespective of whether the act constitutes a criminal offence also under the law of the executing state and therefore without the guarantees that this law provides for in cases of criminal investigations.[49] On the contrary, investigative orders concerned with hearings by videoconference or other forms of audio-visual transmission may seem to be subject to the conditions set out for normal investigative means: thus, they may be refused in (*all*) the cases provided for in article 11, and witnesses and experts must be granted, among others, the right not to testify, which they would have under the law of either the executing or the issuing State.

This example shows in very clear terms how outdated the notion of "coercion" is, since both in domestic and transnational procedures it is no longer able to display the multiple forms of *interference* with the sphere of individual rights, forms not necessarily concerned with the *intrusion* in, or *restriction* of, fundamental rights. In this light, the new instrument still lacks a coherent, comprehensive vision of investigative interferences with fundamental rights. Upon close examination, the topic of fundamental rights protection still appears in a negative manner as a limit to efficient transnational prosecutions[50] rather than as a balancing element and condition for the achievement of fair transnational prosecutions.

As has been noted, the insertion of non-coercive investigative measures into the provision allowing the recourse to another measure, i.e. as a limit to this power, leads to the result that these must *always* be available under the law of the executing state, even if they entail an interference with individual rights, albeit without the use of coercion in a strict sense. In this regard, a particularly worrying issue is the importance attached by the new legislative tool to the collection of evidence already available for the issuing authority. Since the Council general agreement of December 2011, this mode of gathering evidence has appeared among the main aims of the new instrument [art. 1(1)], which will therefore encompass the scope of application of the old EEW. It is noteworthy, moreover, that in the final text obtaining available information appears at the top of the list of the (non-intrusive) investigative activities that must always be available in the executing country. This approach means underestimating the repercussions of this way of collecting

---

[48] For a critical assessment, see Ruggeri (2014a), pp. 18 ff.; Bachmaier Winter (2014), pp. 77 ff.

[49] For instance, Italian CCP requires the authority hearing, in the context either of a criminal inquiry or a criminal process, any person other than the suspect or the defendant to stop them where they declare against themselves, while informing them that a criminal enquiry be initiated against them and that they are entitled to appoint a lawyer of their choice [art. 63(1)].

[50] For a similar criticism to previous versions of the draft proposal, cf. Vogler (2014), p. 48.

evidence on the individual rights sphere. The decision of the issuing authority to request the transfer of evidentiary information already obtained in the executing state excludes any form of control of the overseas investigation by the defence. The general acknowledgement of this mode of obtaining evidence, furthermore, entails the risk of leaving enormous leeway to the issuing authority in choosing whether to order foreign authorities to conduct overseas investigations by means of an EIO or to order them to transfer the information obtained there, often in response to an informal request to do so. However, the modes of obtaining evidence abroad clearly cannot depend upon the discretion of the competent authority, nor can they be chosen irrespective of the link of the involved countries with the alleged offence.

On a deeper level, furthermore, the choice to exclude, in relation to this mode of obtaining evidence, the assessment of dual criminality and the respect for the criminal law requirements established by the law of the executing state shows that the incorrect application of the logic of division of labour, typical of the mutual recognition era, can give rise to serious lacunas in the protection of fundamental rights. This is principally because here the order is concerned with the taking of evidence rather than with the conduction of an investigative measure, which consists in the simple movement of evidence from one state to another—evidence, moreover, collected prior to, and independently from, the EIO procedure and possibly in the context of proceedings with a different subject and often of a different nature. Although evidence was taken in the executing state by means of an investigative measure (*e.g.*, interception of telecommunications) in compliance with the legal requirements provided for by its procedural law in the proceedings for offence A, the free transfer of this evidence to another state by means of the EIO procedure, initiated in the proceedings for offence B, which does not even constitute a criminal offence in the executing state, exposes defendants to the risk of a criminal liability that they would not have run if the prosecuting authority had required the same measure to be conducted abroad. The same applies where the act in respect of which the EIO has been issued, albeit constituting a criminal offence under both legal systems, allows the investigative measure under the law of the issuing state but not under that of the executing state. In both cases, the failure to give relevance to these fundamental requirements will allow for the national authority receiving investigative orders to ignore the repercussions that the simple transfer of evidence can entail upon the sphere of individual rights in the criminal proceedings carried out in another member state.

To this end, it can be doubted that respect for individual rights can be ensured by the general provision allowing for the executing authority to refuse the execution of the EIO that would be incompatible with the executing state's obligations under article 6 TEU and the EU FRCh [art. 10(1)(g)]. The introduction of fundamental rights clauses seems to be a rather programmatic way of acknowledging their value, which does not entirely correspond to specific regulations, especially on the methods of obtaining transnational evidence.

Upon close examination, the general duty to refuse assistance in the event of a breach of a fundamental right (or defence rights) may seem to be subject to the discretion that inspires *all* the situations listed in article 11(1), some of which, moreover, entail clear risks for individual rights. As a consequence, the executing authority is entitled to carry out the sought investigation, thus eventually impinging upon the fundamental rights either of the defendant or of third parties, *notwithstanding* the accused has been finally judged in the issuing state or in another country of the EU area. Even the fact that the act in respect of which the EIO has been issued was committed outside the issuing state and wholly in the executing country does not ban the executing authority from carrying out a (coercive) measure against the defendant, who may be a citizen of, or permanently resident in, the executing country and have legitimately trusted the lack of criminal relevance of their action—a conclusion that endangers both the requirement of legal certainty and EU principle of non-discrimination.

Furthermore, although the final text has dropped the proposed recital 12aaa, according to which member states "should ensure cooperation without endeavouring themselves to assess the respect of Union law and fundamental rights by the other Member States", the commitment required from the cooperating authorities in ensuring respect for individual rights in transborder inquiries still appears to be generic. Starting with "a presumption of compliance by other Member States with Union law and, in particular, with fundamental rights", a presumption rebuttable only where there are substantial grounds for believing that the execution of the EIO would entail the breach of a fundamental right *as established in the EU FRCh*,[51] the Directive shows that EU institutions are still far from the idea of shared responsibility in ensuring full respect for individual rights in transnational investigations.[52] This is probably because they are far from conceiving international cooperation as part of a comprehensive transnational prosecution, which therefore entails an *overall* protection of the defendants and all individuals involved.[53] In order not to abandon the requirements of the mutual recognition system, this way of realising a division of labour—far from granting individuals a level protection of their rights similar to that they enjoy in national cases[54]—is still conceived as a means for offloading onto the cooperating authorities the burden of ensuring respect for individual rights within their own sphere of competence.[55]

These conclusions also apply to the methods of conducting the investigation and taking evidence in another member state. In this regard, the EIO Directive, by reproducing the typical combined mode of obtaining evidence, demonstrates the need for a multicultural approach in the application of criminal *procedural* law in the field of transnational inquiries. What EU legislation still lacks, however, is a

---

[51] Recital no. 19.

[52] On this topic, see especially Vogel (2012a), paras. 40 ff.

[53] For this idea of transnational prosecution, see especially Schomburg et al. (2012), para. 112.

[54] In this sense, instead, the international division of labour should go according to Schomburg et al. (2012), para. 113.

[55] A worrying example relates to the case in which the executing authority opts for a different measure than that requested, since the proposal fails to require a new test of proportionality, necessity and availability by the issuing authority of the different measure.

virtuous *interaction* between the national systems of human rights protection involved in the transnational procedure—a deficiency that the order model has surely inherited from the last phase of the MLA system. As we will see, the solution of combining *lex loci* and *lex fori* upon the condition of consistency with the fundamental principles of the executing country cannot ensure a harmonised complementation of the two procedural laws, since it can seriously alter the balances of interests pursued by the domestic laws. This applies firstly to *lex loci* due to the obligation of the executing authority to comply with foreign requirements that might even be "unfamiliar"[56] with its own law. Nor does this solution, which is clearly aimed at fulfilling the needs of *lex fori* to facilitate the admissibility at trial of evidence in the relevant proceedings,[57] ensure a proper application of *lex fori*. Despite the fact that suspected or accused persons (as well as their lawyers on their behalf) are entitled to request the execution of an investigation order (moreover within the limits and where provided for by national procedural law) [art. 1(3)] and despite the explicit reference to the need to respect the right to defence among the states' obligations that the new instrument cannot modify [art. 1(4)], there is still no trace of any possibility for private parties to take part in investigative activities in a manner remotely comparable to participation allowed to (prosecution) authorities of the executing country. Thus, departing from the approach of the old MLA instruments, the Directive has failed to provide for any form of participation of private parties of the relevant proceedings in the execution of the requested measure—a lacuna that does not only impinge on defence rights but also shows the underestimation of the defence's contribution to securing the correct application of its own law.

3.2 *The Cooperation Model of Joint Inquiries*

There is little doubt that a clear acknowledgement of the new mode of transnational evidence gathering has derived from the enactment of legal regulations for setting up joint investigation teams and obtaining evidence by means of them. It has been observed that this model has not developed in the context of the order model, surprising as it might be that the free movement of judgements and judicial products has not led to establishing a free flow of law enforcement officials from one member state to another.[58] As we have seen, joint inquiries clearly developed from the

[56] This eventuality was explicitly provided for by article 8 SAP ECMACM.

[57] Compared with the international instruments of the third phase of MLA and the FD OFPE, the EIO Directive, like the FD EEW, does not limit the duty of compliance with the formalities of *lex fori* to the sole requirements that are necessary under this law.

[58] See Klip (2012), p. 361. Significantly, the 2002 FD JIT, dating back to the very beginning of the mutual recognition era, did not even mention the principle of mutual recognition as basis for its own regulation.

model of extraterritorial inquiries,[59] and it is noteworthy that the first international instrument that provided a general legal framework for joint investigation teams in Europe was the EUCMACM, which, moreover, marked a significant cultural change in the way extraterritorial investigations can be carried out. As a consequence of this approach, albeit still based on the request model rather than on the order model,[60] the authorities of more than one member state could *ordinarily* carry out joint investigative activities clearly affecting fundamental rights.[61]

Concerning the modes of taking evidence, all the international and supranational legislation that has regulated the conduction of joint investigations over the last two decades,[62] while reproducing the approach of the EUCMACM, has returned to a rather strict application of the (procedural) law of the State in whose territory the team operates.[63] This has marked a highly territorial conception of procedural law—a conception only mitigated in the first instruments that governed the conduction of joint investigations, such as the EUCMACM and the FD JIT, by providing for the possibility that members of the team other than its leader can, when carrying out their tasks, take into account the conditions set by their own authorities in the agreement on setting up the team.[64]

This approach, which entrusts the establishment of investigative methods to case-by-case agreements, entails many risks both for the efficiency of cross-border prosecution and for the rights of the individuals involved in transnational inquiries. Thus, provisions such as those of the EUCMACM and the FD JIT manifestly leave great uncertainty as to the procedures that must be followed and the limits to the investigative powers, since they neither allow for the addressees of the investigative activities to know exactly what conditions may be required nor clarify how these can be made compatible with *lex loci*.

To avoid these shortcomings, a second generation of international instruments, while decoupling the joint inquiries from the mode of legal assistance, has tightened the application of *lex loci*, thus requiring the application of the same standards of obtaining evidence to domestic procedures.[65] At a national level, some domestic

---

[59] Gleß (2006), pp. 122 ff.

[60] All extraterritorial powers may, under the EUCMACM, be activated only upon request. For instance, under article 12, "Each Member State shall undertake to ensure that, *at the request of another Member State*, controlled deliveries may be permitted on its territory in the framework of criminal investigations into extraditable offences".

[61] Both controlled deliveries and covert investigations constitute clear interferences with fundamental rights.

[62] Among international agreements, cf. the 2000 UN CTOC (art. 19), the Agreement on mutual legal assistance between the European Union and the USA (art. 5). At supranational level, see the 2002 FD JIT.

[63] See respectively art. 13(3)(b) EUCMACM and Art. 20(3)(b) SAP ECMACM.

[64] See respectively art. 13(3)(b) EUCMACM and Art. 1(3)(b) FD JIT.

[65] See art. 5(4) of the 2003 Agreement on mutual legal assistance between the European Union and the USA.

legislation has adopted a similar solution,[66] while other regulations have posed legal limits on the power to agree conditions on evidence gathering in the context of joint investigations, in the sense that the national law of the member of the team in a secondary position provides a limit to the tasks that can be required of them.[67] Nevertheless, the application of *lex loci* as basis for any activity conducted by the team can give rise to a plethora of evidential laws in all cases in which the team operates in the territory of more than one Member State.[68] This solution constitutes neither an efficient nor a proper solution in a common area of freedom, *security* and *justice*, since it not only multiplies the risk of incompatibility of the evidence collected with *lex fori* and therefore the risk of its inadmissibility in one or more national procedures,[69] but it can also expose individuals to similar investigative powers interfering with their rights in a possibly different manner according to the State in whose territory the team operates, thus undermining the individuals' trust in legal certainty.

In sum, both these approaches (free agreements on the forms of taking evidence and the application of the sole *lex loci*) give rise to serious concerns from a human rights perspective. Not only does the mode of joint inquiries not satisfy the need for legal certainty as to the evidentiary procedure, but it likewise returns to an even more territorial conception of transnational procedures than that of both the request and the order models, even where the investigations require a coordinated action spread over the territory of many member states—a solution that does not take into due account the trust both of the defendant and the addressee of the investigation in criminal procedural law. And one might argue that this approach has defeated one of the main challenges of joint inquiries, i.e., the creation of an integrated procedure that, by achieving a new balance among competing values, can properly fulfil the (individual rights) needs of the legal (constitutional) systems of the cooperating authorities.

---

[66] In this sense see, for instance, article 7(2) of the Spanish Organic Law 11/2003.

[67] For instance, article 695-3 of the French CCP, inserted by Law 204/2004, provides that "French judicial police officers and agents attached to a joint investigation team may carry out operations ordered by the head of the team, over the whole of the territory of the State in which they are operating, *within the limit of the powers conferred on them by the present Code*" (English translation of the French CCP with the participation of Prof. J. Spencer).

[68] Along the same lines, see Klip (2012), p. 392.

[69] It is noteworthy that the greatest resistance in Italy to the implementation of the FD JIT, which has not yet been transposed in national law, has been mainly due to concerns relating to the use at trial of the results of overseas investigations carried out by the team. On the Italian situation, see Caprioli (2013), p. 453.

3.3 The Federalist Approach

Another model provides an alternative to both of the request and order systems. This model shows a highly original approach, which, starting with the assignment of the prosecutorial competence, also entails, moreover, the power of the competent authority of a single State to investigate directly abroad pursuant to the sole *lex fori*.

Historically, this approach has developed in some federalist contexts, providing an interesting way of obtaining evidence in other provincial states. In Europe, Switzerland adopted this model up to the new StPO of the Helvetic Confederation,[70] thus overcoming the multitude of cantonal procedural legal systems by allowing the competent authority to carry out direct investigations over the whole Helvetic territory under its own law. This approach constituted the core idea of the 2006 project on the transnational procedural unity led by *Bernd Schünemann*—a project that, even after the entry into force of the Lisbon, has not lost its relevance, providing a useful alternative to the model of mutual recognition on the basis of the assumption that European transnational inquiries require a single, coherent set of procedural rules that cannot be ensured through the combined application of two or more (possibly different) procedural laws.[71] Also here, the proposed model is based on the concentration both of prosecutorial and investigative powers in one single member state. This result would be achieved though a prompt assignment of jurisdiction, which in cases of multiple competences of more than one State should follow a two-step approach consisting of the combination of a fixed, hierarchised order of criteria with a flexible procedural solution based upon the focal point of the alleged offence. One of the most significant innovations of this model consists of the introduction of a new institution, i.e., Eurodefensor, whose tasks would include representing the defendant's rights in the assignment of jurisdiction. This is a very delicate phase, since the assignment of jurisdiction would imply the attribution to the competent authority of the power to investigate throughout the EU. Moreover, the fact that investigations and the collection of evidence follow the sentencing state's law would also make the admissibility of evidence a strictly national issue.[72]

Certainly, the main merit of such a federalist model lies in the coherence sought not only by the assignment of the prosecutorial and investigative power to a single state but also by the application of a single procedural law to transnational investigations. These characteristics mark, however, the limits of this approach. Thus, it can be doubted that the choice to link prosecution, adjudication and investigation to a single authority and a single (both substantive and procedural) law can ensure coherence to *any* cross-border investigation, while properly satisfying the need for pluralism that is inherent in the most complex transnational inquiries. Especially in the most complex criminal actions, characterised by a multitude of single crimes committed by several people with different citizenships (and often resident in

[70] Schünemann (2014), pp. 173 ff.

[71] *Ibid.*

[72] *Ibid.*, p. 176.

different countries), concentrating the prosecution in single jurisdictions for single offences, as we will see, seems to satisfy neither the need for procedural economy nor the defendant's interest in avoiding multiple prosecution.[73] In addition to the difficulty of establishing the competent jurisdiction in relation to acts spread over the territory of several states, the solution of assigning the prosecutorial power to a single territorial jurisdiction can hinder the efficient prosecution of the entire criminal phenomenon.

Also, the criteria proposed for the assignment of the power to prosecute and adjudicate the case give rise to some concerns in the federalist approach. If the main criterion for the choice of the jurisdiction remains the territoriality principle, it must be acknowledged that neither the substantive law of the country in which the conduct takes place nor the law of the country in which the consequence of the criminal action occurs is always available to potential offenders, who might be objectively unable to know it in advance. As we will see, there is little doubt that without these essential preconditions the prosecution of human acts under a law that remains extraneous to their perpetrators gives priority to a repressive mindset rather than satisfying the need to grant them a judgment of personal criminal liability.

The risk that the fundamental requirements of availability of criminal law remain unfulfilled is accentuated, especially in cases of complex crimes with several accomplices from different countries, by the adoption of international links other than the territoriality principle, particularly where these criteria do not directly relate to the criminal offence. This can happen, for example, by assigning the prosecutorial power to the country where most items of evidence are located[74]: thus, following this criterion—significantly adopted by models inspired either by a great flexibility or, by contrast, a rigid classification of international links[75]—the assignment of jurisdiction would in a great part depend on how charges are construed and preferred, a decision that can strategically vary to attract the prosecutorial power to one country rather than to another. Moreover, if the adjudication of the case should follow solely the substantive law of the jurisdiction chosen on the basis of the location of important evidence, this law might even be linguistically inaccessible to the offender. But the implications of the federalist approach are perhaps even more dangerous from a procedural viewpoint: if the competent authority were also entitled to investigate under its own procedural law in the

[73] In a different sense, see Schünemann (2006a), p. 100.

[74] See article 2(2) of the Proposal for the Regulation of Trans-national Criminal Proceedings in the European Union containing the model of transnational procedural unity. See Schünemann (2006b), p. 6.

[75] This criterion has been invoked by both the "agreed jurisdiction model" and the "statutory determination model", elaborated within the EAK+/ZEIS research project on cross-border conflicts of jurisdiction. Cf. respectively article 13 of the 2009 Framework Decision on prevention and settlement of jurisdictional conflicts in criminal proceedings, as amended by the proposal of Directive elaborated pursuant to the agreed jurisdiction model, and article 1(5) of the proposal of Directive on the avoidance of jurisdictional conflicts in criminal proceedings conducted pursuant to the statutory determination model. See Sinn (2012b), respectively pp. 603 f., 610 f.

territory of any EU member state, its law might be unknown to the addressees of the inquiry. And why should these bear investigative activities that can touch upon their fundamental rights, such as property or private life, pursuant to procedures laid down by foreign law and over the limits established by their law? As we will see, this does not of course mean that the fundamental requirement of legal certainty could only be fulfilled by applying the territorial law of the country state in which the investigations take place,[76] a law that both the defendant and third parties may also be unfamiliar with.

Interferences with fundamental rights show therefore the natural limit of federalist models, whose coherent application, furthermore, presupposes a uniform fundamental rights framework. Significantly, the former Swiss model worked on the basis of a common Constitution. But despite the great potential of the EU FRCh, the European Union is still far from achieving this goal, especially in the field of procedural criminal law.[77]

4 Multicultural Criminal Offences and Fairness of Transborder Investigative Procedures

4.1 Premise: The Individual at the Centre of Cross-Border Cooperation

In light of the results of the analysis of the aforementioned approaches, two basic premises must be considered for a fair model of transnational investigations being proposed in the current European scenario. First, transborder investigations and the collection of overseas evidence are parts of a much more complex phenomenon and therefore cannot be properly dealt with without a global consideration of transnational criminal justice. This requires starting with determining which criminal laws can legitimately be applied to the transnational case at stake, which jurisdictions can legitimately concur to prosecute it and, finally, whether the country with which the investigations need to be carried out has substantial links with the offence under prosecution and whether the addressee of the concrete investigative means has a substantial link with this country. Second, the European continent, especially within the EU area, is increasingly characterised by two quite opposite phenomena, i.e., (a) the growth of work activities constantly carried out in several countries or in a country other than the one of habitual residence and (b) the increasing flow of people throughout Europe for short periods. These phenomena mark the high level of Europe's multiculturalism and suggest in-depth reflection on the foundations

[76] This was, instead, the proposal of Bitzilekis et al. (2006), p. 251, in cases of coercive means.

[77] Along the same lines, see Bitzilekis et al. (2006), pp. 250 f.

both of the application of substantive criminal law and the conduction of investigations involving people from more than one country.

Both the decision on what jurisdiction may be empowered to prosecute and adjudicate the case and the choice of the most proper mode of collecting evidence in transnational cases have been among the most debated topics over recent years, and several academic solution models have been proposed after the entry into force of the Lisbon Treaty.[78] Certainly, the growth of interest in these areas is a consequence of the fact that the Lisbon Treaty has empowered EU institutions to adopt legislative measures to prevent and solve such conflicts, as well as to harmonise, by means of directives, the field of mutual admissibility of transnational evidence. However, the separate attention paid to these areas by EU primary law has probably determined the development of approaches that surprisingly remain different and independent from each other despite the clear mutual connections between them. This also applies to the EU legislation launched in both fields shortly before the entry into force of the Lisbon Treaty, i.e., the 2008 FD EEW and the 2009 Framework Decision on prevention and settlement of jurisdictional conflicts in criminal matters. Despite their limits and incompleteness, however, these legislative instruments share a common methodological approach that—in light of the mutual recognition principle—consists in leaving the choice of the forum and the modes of taking evidence respectively to a free agreement of the cooperating authorities and the decision of the issuing authority.

After the entry into force of the Lisbon Treaty, consensual solutions have undergone different developments at both a legislative level and an academic level. In the field of transnational inquiries, the EIO Directive, while leaving to the issuing authority the decision of which formalities of its own law should be applied in the collection of evidence in another member state, entrusts the cooperating authorities with a mutual consultation with a view to facilitating (it would seem, also) the most proper definition of the whole procedure for the overseas investigation [(Art. 8(4)]. In relation to jurisdictional conflicts, instead, a recent proposal—launched in Germany by *Bernd Hecker*[79] and joined, as we have seen, by the EAK+/ZEIS research project—aims at restricting the leeway of the cooperating authorities by establishing an exhaustive list of criteria for the definition of the competent forum, even if the choice among them would be anyway left to an *ad hoc* agreement pursuant to the needs of the concrete case.

Despite their high level of flexibility, however, consensual approaches give rise to serious human rights concerns from at least two viewpoints. Firstly, they do not properly satisfy the need for legal certainty, a need of fundamental importance from the perspective both of the criminal justice systems and all the people involved in (transnational) criminal inquiries. Again, there is little doubt that in a common area

---

[78] On the topic of transnational jurisdictional conflicts, see, among others, Sinn (2012c) and Böse et al. (2013). On the topic of transnational evidence, cf., *inter alia*, Ruggeri (2013b), Ruggeri (2014c).

[79] Hecker (2011), pp. 60 ff.

of freedom, security and justice the choice of the competent forum cannot be left to a free agreement between the cooperating authorities.[80] And uncertainty remains even if statutory law lays down the criteria, since the results of any agreement will vary according to what in the concrete case is considered the most proper balance among conflicting interests. For the same reasons, as we have seen, the establishment of the procedure for the investigation at stake cannot depend on the discretion of one national authority choosing which formalities of its own law must be applied abroad.[81] But equally worrying is—secondly—that these solutions reflect decisions in which the defence, either of the accused or of third parties, is not entitled to be involved at all. As has been noted, this deficiency not only impinges upon the sphere of defence rights but also jeopardises the quality of the decision both on the assignment of jurisdiction and on the most appropriate mode of conducting an investigation in cross-border cases. This result is perhaps more unsatisfactory in the field of evidence gathering than in the choice of the forum: thus, while in the choice of the forum the achievement of a proper balance between state-related interests and individual rights is only left to the dialogue between the cooperating authorities, the authority charged with the task of carrying out the required investigation is deprived of a fundamental contribution to apply adequately the requested foreign procedures—a result that also entails risks for the admissibility of the evidence taken in the issuing state.[82]

These observations suggest changing the way we look at this topic by putting the individual at the centre of international cooperation.[83] This should allow for a significant shift of the traditional approach both to the choice of jurisdiction and to decision on the mode of obtaining overseas evidence. To this end, it will be helpful to start with what, following the well-known distinction of the Third Restatement of Foreign Relations Law of the American Law Institute from 1988,[84] is known as "jurisdiction to prescribe".[85] On one hand, the prosecutorial power may only be assigned to a country having a legitimate right to punish transborder offences. On the other, as we have seen, the determination of the best criminal law system to *adjudicate* the concrete offence and the choice of the most proper jurisdiction to *prosecute* transborder cases are logical preconditions to deal with transnational *investigations* and the gathering of overseas evidence in a proper way. For the sake of clarity, therefore, I shall distinguish among three stages, which

---

[80] It is, therefore, quite surprising that some part of criminal law scholarship still overlooks the role of the principle of the legally pre-established judge, which has traditionally been interpreted as concerning the distribution of competence among national jurisdictions (see Dominioni and Pisani (1987), p. 177), as a fundamental right individuals must be granted also in the *common* EU area. See De Amicis (2012), p. 305.

[81] Similarly Schünemann (2014), p. 172.

[82] Ruggeri (2014a), p. 17.

[83] On the role of the individual subject of international cooperation, see the fundamental comparative research coordinated by Eser et al. (2002), *passim*.

[84] American Law Institute (1988)

[85] For a similar methodological approach, see especially Böse (2013), pp. 75 ff.

relate to (a) the identification of the qualitative requirements for criminal law being fairly applied to transborder cases, (b) the elaboration of qualitative criteria to assign (or to distribute) the power to prosecute transborder cases and, finally, (c) the establishment of qualitative methods of investigating and obtaining evidence in a member state other than the prosecuting country.

4.2 *Qualitative Requirements for a Fair Application of Criminal Law to Transborder Cases: The Substantial Link Between the Perpetrator and the Criminal Law System*

In the complex tangle web of international relationships among national countries, it is widely recognised that these no longer have unlimited power to extend to transborder cases their own criminal law, whose application is, instead, subject to strict limits deriving from international, constitutional and European laws.[86] At an international level, however, the principle of non-intervention in foreign affairs cannot hinder the overlapping of several jurisdictions claiming the power to prosecute the same transborder act, as long as a meaningful, internationally recognised link exists.[87] Both constitutional and European laws, instead, impose strict limitations on the extraterritorial extension of the application of domestic criminal law. These limitations directly relate to some of the main principles both of criminal and European laws, especially the principles *nullum crimen sine lege* and *nulla pena sine culpa*, as well as the prohibition of discrimination with regard to fundamental rights of EU citizens such as the right to free movement.[88]

In light of the approach of study, I shall focus on the *nullum crimen sine lege* principle, not only due to its explicit enshrinement in both the ECHR and the EU FRCh but also because it poses the fundamental basis for a judgment of criminal liability to be passed on the accused. From the viewpoint of procedural criminal law, furthermore, the respect for the *nullum crimen sine lege* principle may also be seen as a necessary precondition for the conduction of transnational prosecutions pursuant to the requirements of due process.[89]

To this end, the *nullum crimen sine lege* principle entails unquestionable qualitative requirements, starting with the foreseeability and accessibility of the relevant criminal law provision.[90] Both these requirements pose important human rights

[86] This assumption is the starting point of the DFG project. See Böse and Meyer (2011), pp. 337 ff. Along the same lines, cf. more recently Wörner (2013), p. 481.

[87] Böse and Meyer (2011, p. 338.

[88] A clear analysis of these limits has been conducted by Böse and Meyer (2011), pp. 338 ff.

[89] This approach is usual in US case law. See US v. Shi, 525 F.3d 709, 722 (9th Cir. 2008). Cf. Thaman (2013b), p. 449.

[90] Along these lines, explicitly, see Böse (2013), p. 79.

challenges in the context of transnational prosecutions. Precisely in light of a qualitative extension of the *nullum crimen sine lege* principle to transborder cases, the drastic reduction of the dual criminality requirement introduced by the FD EAW had already raised serious concerns in the middle of the last decade.[91] Especially German criminal law scholarship underlined the repercussion of this approach, which would have exposed defendants to the risk of being surrendered for an act that might not constitute a criminal offence under the law of the executing State.[92] The German *Bundesverfassungsgericht* partially shared this approach in the Decision on the first Act implementing the FD EAW, thus overruling its previous positions, based on the sufficiency of the guarantee of national (German) legal certainty,[93] and stressing the importance of the *nullum crimen sine lege* principle in a country based upon the rule of law.[94] Indeed, the orientation role of criminal law towards the most sensitive values of the society logically requires that the relevant provisions may be reasonably perceived by people to prevent the legal provision of criminal law from becoming a mere fiction.[95] Surprisingly, however, this fundamental requirement, which of course cannot be restricted to the sphere of surrender procedures, has not adequately been taken into consideration in subsequent EU legislation, which has reproduced, albeit with some variations, the strong limitation to the dual criminality requirement.[96] But beyond the sphere of transborder cases in a strict sense, a modern conception of criminal law, characterised by increasing localism,[97] poses—especially in the current multilinguistic European context—unprecedented challenges to the maintenance of its most traditional principles. Thus, in all cases characterised by elements of transnationality, a fair application of criminal law requires the possibility for the offender to *understand* the criminal law provisions and therefore the need that criminal law be *linguistically* "accessible".

These conclusions principally call for in-depth reflection on the extraterritorial application of criminal law on the basis of criteria that do not allow for the proper respect of such fundamental requirements.[98] This mainly applies to the passive personality principle and partially to the protective principle, which cannot always ensure respect for the requirement of foreseeability of the relevant criminal law

[91] To be sure, despite its wide recognition, the dual criminality requirement has over recent decades raised some criticism. See already Jescheck (1954), pp. 531 f.

[92] See particularly Schünemann (2003), p. 188.

[93] BVerfGE 92, pp. 325 ff.

[94] BVerfGE 113, pp. 308 f. See Böse (2012), para. 47.

[95] See Böse and Meyer (2011), p. 339.

[96] Recently, moreover, the Framework Decision 2009/829/JHA on the application, between member states of the European Union, of the principle of mutual recognition to decisions on supervision measures as an alternative to provisional detention has allowed for member states to declare, for constitutional reasons, that they will not apply the waiver of double criminality in respect of some or all of the offences referred to in article 14 [art. 14(4)].

[97] On this topic, see Basile (2009), pp. 206 ff.

[98] See especially Böse and Meyer (2011), pp. 341 ff.

provisions, as offenders often know neither the citizenship nor the identity of the victims, nor have they a proper knowledge of the criminal law of the victims' legal system.[99] Such concerns do not of course relate to the universality principle, since the *nullum crimen sine lege* principle cannot protect the individuals' trust in behaviours entailing internationally recognised human rights violations.[100]

Upon close examination, instead, serious concerns can arise in relation to the main international link, i.e., the territoriality principle, despite its wide acknowledgement by criminal law scholarship.[101] This is especially due to the mainstream tendency, mainly in continental Europe, to expand the scope of application of domestic criminal law to acts committed overseas on the basis of an increasingly widened notion of territoriality either because of the number of accomplices or the complex objective structure of the offence, spread over the territory of several countries, in terms of the place where either the conduct or its consequence occurred.[102] This also demonstrates the inadequacy of the ubiquity theory, which in several transnational cases does not fit the requirement of legal certainty, especially where the place of the consequence is "the result of sheer chance".[103] And the difficulties to tackle these problems grow in the field of transnational *organised* crimes. Here, the failure of many legislation to define the "part" of the conduct committed in the national territory, which allows for national jurisdiction to be applied for the whole criminal action, has led to case law often extending the application of national criminal law for a criminal organisation in relation to all the alleged members even if their main activities take part overseas.[104] However, the overlapping of jurisdictions claiming the power to prosecute the same act upon (partially) territorial basis strengthens the risk of mistakes of law among possibly different regulations, which is difficult to avoid.[105]

To tackle these problems, the traditional tools of criminal law do not always suffice. Thus, even a drastic reduction of the extraterritorial expansion of national jurisdiction will lead to unsatisfactory results as long as national countries demand, as a rule, to *territorially* impose the application of their own criminal law to all acts

[99] For a detailed analysis of this issue, see Böse and Meyer (2011), pp. 341 ff.; Böse (2013), pp. 82 ff.

[100] In these terms Ambos (2011), pp. 6 f.

[101] Along with the EAK+/ZEIS project and the DFG project, see also Biehler et al. (2003), pp. 7 f.; Schünemann (2006b); Ambos (2003), § 4, para. 10 et sqq.

[102] For a comparative analysis of this tendency, see Sinn (2012a), pp. 544 f.; Ruggeri (2013a), pp. 505 f.

[103] Schünemann (2014), p. 174.

[104] See the Italian Court of Cassation, 2nd Section, Decision of 7 April 1999, Cohau, Massimario Cassazione penale 1999, nr. 212974.

[105] See similarly Böse and Meyer (2011), p. 339.

committed within their territory conceived in such a broad view and to all those who are in the national territory,[106] irrespective of whether the aims pursued by the relevant criminal law provision could realistically be perceived by people acting in a specific territorial context. We have noted that the current European scenario is characterised both by the rise in cases of people contemporaneously acting in a country other than that of their domicile and the increasing, provisional flow of people throughout Europe for very short periods. This raises significant challenges especially at EU level, governed now by 28 official languages.

Against this background, it appears that the primacy of territorial jurisdiction can no longer be justified on the basis of the state's pretension to extend unconditionally its sovereignty over all acts committed within its territorial borders,[107] but it can be maintained *as far as* it allows for the offender to be judged as criminally liable according to the human rights requirements of a modern criminal law. From this it follows that the *prosecutio transnationalis*, whichever its features are in the concrete case, must follow the requirement of the *nullum crimen sine lege* principle[108] in respect both to extraterritorial criteria and the territoriality principle. Nor can this conclusion run counter to the traditional principle *ignorantia legis non excusat*. Historically, the strict inexcusability of *ignorantia legis* (as well as the primacy of territorial criminal law) was justified on the assumption that most people regularly lived within the State's territorial borders, within which the criminal law system could thus fulfil its orientation task. And also nowadays the rigid approach to the ignorance and mistakes of the law, albeit attenuated by different clauses of exculpation, still maintain its value starting from the assumption that people have the duty to keep themselves informed on the criminal law system, as well as on its developments. However, in the current multicultural era, this duty can realistically concern only those who can be deemed as substantial members of a relevant country[109]—a condition that should be restricted to those who either are citizens of a country or substantially reside in a specific cultural context, irrespective of whether legally or illegally.[110]

---

[106] Thus, many criminal law systems link the duty of respect for national criminal law by all those who are on national territory to the application of criminal law to any offence (wholly or partially) committed on national territory. In this sense, see Manzini (1948), p. 416, according to whom the rationale of article 5 CP-Italy would not consist in the ubiquity theory but in an extremely broad concept of territoriality, extended both to all the acts committed and the people who were within the national boundaries. For a similar territorial conception, see, in relation to Spanish criminal law, Muñoz Conde and García Arán (2007), p. 151.

[107] For in-depth analysis of the role of national territory with a view of the application of criminal law, see Di Martino (2006), *passim*.

[108] In this regard, see Gropp (2012), pp. 41 ff.

[109] See, among others, Padovani (2012), pp. 242 f.

[110] In this regard, it is noteworthy that in *Denmark* the link between the offender and the national territory is not ruled out by the illegal condition of the former. See Cornils and Greve (2012), p. 194.

This substantial approach shows the limits within which the criminal law can be legitimately applied in transborder cases. If we wish to maintain a territorial approach, the territorial borders of criminal law should be re-defined in a manner that takes into account not the state's territorial boundaries but the capability of national criminal law to reach, by playing its orientation role, those who regularly and substantially belong to the state's cultural context. This requirement gains importance especially in the field of legal crimes, as well as in relation to those offences that contain elements presupposing that the offender is familiar with a specific cultural context (*e.g.*, the *common* sense of decency). The need to guarantee that criminal law can only be applied to those who substantially belong to the context limiting its territorial reach, in the sense proposed here, is even more pressing where the relevant criminal law provision contains legal elements implying technical knowledge of other branches of the national legal system (*e.g.*, administrative law).[111]

Far from being the expression of the anachronistic state's pretension to extend its jurisdiction to acts committed abroad by its own citizens, such as the active personality principle,[112] the choice of such a substantial criterion does not coincide with the law of domicile or residence, which *as such* can give rise to abuses (*e.g.*, in case of domicile chosen abroad for fiscal grounds). Furthermore, the adoption of this perspective not only ensures a qualitative tie between the perpetrator and the substantive criminal law but also provides practical advantages: especially, it allows for offenders to be adjudicated (and eventually punished) on the basis of a criminal law provision they could realistically know also from a linguistic viewpoint. Of course, the requirement of legal certainty entails the need to define clear parameters to identify such a criterion. In this regard, consideration should be given to criteria such as the time spent by the offender in a specific context, his concrete cultural level, viewed in connection with the specific type of crime, etc.

4.3 Qualitative Criteria to Assign and Manage the Power to Prosecute Transborder Cases

This approach must now be verified from the viewpoint of procedural criminal law. Here, the unconditional application of territorial law gives rise to even more concerns than in the field of substantive criminal law and can cause insurmountable difficulties for the defendant to exercise his defence rights effectively. Certainly, the assignment of the prosecutorial power upon territorial basis, especially if the process is conducted in the country where the result of the criminal act took place, can fulfil the need to respect the victim's interest in a local judgement. However,

[111] For an in-depth analysis of the normative elements of criminal law provisions, see Risicato (2004), *passim*.

[112] See Böse and Meyer (2011), p. 342.

this requirement, whose importance cannot be overlooked from a human rights perspective, cannot be satisfied to the extent that it would offload onto the defendant the burden of facing the proceedings in a context with which he might be unfamiliar.[113] This approach would have negative repercussions on the effectiveness of the right to a defence: difficulties might arise as to the choice of, and communication with, the lawyer, and the linguistic barriers to fully understanding procedural activities could jeopardise the choice of the best solution in the concrete case.[114] Furthermore, the proceedings could lead to the adoption of measures touching upon the defendant's rights, starting with his personal freedom, which would thus contribute to accentuating the defendant's sense of isolation from his environment.

To reduce the negative impact on the individuals involved in transnational procedures of the choice to leave the assignment of the prosecutorial power preferably to the territorial jurisdiction, the European Union's legislature has, once again, invoked the mutual recognition principle, *e.g.*, by extending its scope to supervision measures alternative to remand detention, thus allowing defendants who are resident in a country other than that of the proceedings to be provisionally returned to their own country.[115] However, this legislative instrument does not wholly prevent the defendants' isolation from their environment. Paradoxically, it cannot be ruled out that this result may even be enhanced by the adoption of supervision means because of the more extensive possibility for the issuing authority than in ordinary cases to obtain the defendant's surrender by means of a European arrest warrant even beyond the sentencing limits laid down by article 2(1) FD EAW.[116]

In general terms, therefore, the Union follows an approach that starts with the premise that people can *legitimately* be prosecuted in a country they might be fully extraneous to. In a certain sense, it even seems to promote this situation, since, while legitimising free agreements on the jurisdiction, it at best makes the crucial decision of the assignment of the prosecutorial power a matter of pure chance. This has in turn required the adoption of further legislative measures to enhance the effectiveness of the defence rights of the accused called upon to face proceedings in a foreign environment, such as the Directive 2010/64/EU on the right to translation and interpretation in criminal proceedings and the recent Directive 2013/48/EU on the right of access to a lawyer in criminal proceedings and in European arrest warrant proceedings. Nevertheless, these measures only aim at introducing minimum rules and cannot therefore ensure a high level of effectiveness of the right to a defence in criminal proceedings as long as they may be conducted in a country other than that to which defendants substantially belong to.

---

[113] *Ibid.*, p. 341.

[114] For an in-depth study of the linguistic problems in EU cooperation in criminal matters, see, among others, Ruggieri (2013), *passim*.

[115] Framework Decision 2009/829/JHA. See, among others, Rafaraci (2012), pp. 67 ff.

[116] See article 21(2) Framework Decision 2009/829/JHA. See critically on this point Ruggeri (2012), pp. 66 f.

Instead, the solution of choosing the forum of the defendant's substantially own country appears to provide considerable advantages. Especially, it would allow the defendant to face the criminal process in his own cultural context, thus enjoying the best conditions to properly understand procedural activities and effectively exercise defence rights. Furthermore, in cases of coercive means, it would not isolate defendants from their own environment, thus making it unnecessary to invoke mutual recognition to render them to their own country.

From a procedural viewpoint, however, it must be considered that in the dynamic perspective of criminal proceedings, the defendants' identity and their substantial belonging to a specific context are often unknown in the initial stage of the enquiry and need thus to be ascertained. In the pre-trial phase, coordination will inevitably involve territorial jurisdiction as long as the defendants' identity and their relationship with a country have not been clarified. This demonstrates that even a substantial approach cannot entail abandoning the traditional territorial view of jurisdiction at all.

The adoption of a procedural perspective requires further issues to be addressed to solve the practical problems concerned with the assignment of jurisdiction.

4.3.1 Concurrence Among Legitimate Claims of Jurisdiction and Interaction Among Substantial Criminal Laws

The first issue relates to establishing criteria for solutions to deal with possible cases of concurrence among jurisdictions. This may arise when the criterion of substantial and regular belonging does not lead to an unequivocal assignment of jurisdiction. This can happen where the alleged offender may be deemed as belonging to more than one country—a rather realistic situation in an increasingly globalised world, where, as has been noted, many people, although formally residing in one country, live in two or work outside their country of residence (*e.g.*, a surgeon operating regularly in clinics or hospitals in different countries). Here, the question arises as to choice of the country with the *most intensive* substantive connection with the offender.

Yet concurrence can also arise from jurisdictions claiming prosecutorial power on the basis of different international links and irrespective of the ascertainment of the offender's substantial belonging to a specific country. In this regard, it must be borne in mind that any solution must reflect a fair balance among conflicting interests. Even the criterion of the offender's own country, albeit reflecting a clear individual requirement, cannot be satisfied in absolute terms and to the extent that it would frustrate further claims of jurisdiction. This does not lead, in my view, to concluding that the forum may be chosen flexibly among jurisdictions claiming the prosecutorial power on the basis of *any* criterion[117]: as has been observed,

[117] For a flexible solution concerning the choice of the jurisdiction to enforce, see, instead, Böse (2013), pp. 85 f., who, moreover, requires respect for the dual criminality requirement in the event of the choice of derivative jurisdiction.

concurrence may only arise among jurisdictions claiming the power to prosecute on a legitimate basis, thus ensuring respect for the requirements of a human-rights-oriented criminal law. This does not mean, however, that any legitimate claim of jurisdiction can prevail over the other. If so, the cases falling within the universality principle would be insolvable, since the universally recognised character of these crimes would in principle justify the assignment to *any* jurisdiction, including the territorial one.

Such cases show, therefore, the need to achieve a proper balance among conflicting interests. In some cases, the recourse to the main links can help tilt the balance towards one solution or another. Thus, in the field of universally recognised crimes, it would not be superfluous to ascertain to which country the offender is proved to substantially belong[118]: prosecuting the offender in his own country would probably satisfy at best his right to a fair trial in his cultural context, while ensuring his effective defence. Outside the area of universal crimes, furthermore, in controversial cases in which the offender is proved to belong substantially to more than one country, preference might be given to territorial law when the conduct was committed in one of the two states involved. In this light, therefore, territoriality would play a subsidiary role, thus supporting the jurisdiction of the country the offender belongs to, not *vice versa*.[119]

Again, moreover, the perspective proposed here leads us to conclude that the assignment of the prosecutorial power to a jurisdiction other than that of the offender's own country, rather than the extraterritorial exercise jurisdiction, needs be justified. In my view, the sole justification for a state other than the offender's own country to claim its jurisdiction can lie in the need to protect its essential interests, i.e., those values that are essential to ensure its existence and survival.[120] It has been observed that these values do not always reflect state-related interests, such as in cases of offences against the state's personality, but they can also express

---

[118] From a similar viewpoint, *Brazil* provides an extremely interesting model as to the assignment of jurisdiction to fight international crimes such as genocide. In these cases, notwithstanding these are universally recognised crimes, the Brazilian claim of jurisdiction is only apparently unconditioned, since it is mitigated by the recourse to the principle of active personality in terms of either Brazilian citizenship or the offender's domicile in Brazil. See D'Avila (2013), p. 467.

[119] In the "statutory determination model", proposed within the EAK+/ZEIS project, the law of residence plays instead a subsidiary role in cases in which criminal conduct spans multiple member states, but none of the conduct took place in a jurisdiction where the consequences of the conduct were also felt. See Article 1(3) of the proposed Directive on the avoidance of jurisdictional conflicts in criminal proceedings. In: Sinn (2012b), pp. 609 f.

[120] Apparently, where the affected country is not the state in whose territory the conduct took place, also the territorial criminal law should be applied as *lex mitior* to avoid discrimination among EU citizens. Upon closer examination, however, this solution is excessive and unnecessary: where neither the offender substantially belongs to the State in which the conduct took place nor this state's essential interests have been touched upon, nothing seems to justify intervention of the territorial criminal law.

individual interests, *e.g.*, in terms of the protection of victims' rights.[121] Also from this perspective, however, jurisdictional power may be assigned to the state affected in its essential interests on two conditions: (*a*) that the offender was put in the position to realistically know the relevant provision of a criminal law system other than the one of his own context and (*b*) that the offender's own state does not properly protect the essential values of the other country.

The combination of these conditions may, however, give rise to delicate practical problems. In particular, if the properness test requires an inadequate or less adequate protection of the other state's own interests, it should be clarified what this should exactly mean. If this means that the offender's own country does not provide any criminal law protection of the affected country's legal interests at all, the prosecution by another state, even if touched upon in its essential interests, would entail a clear infringement of the *nullum crimen sine lege* principle. It would be extremely difficult to punish, on the basis of the affected country's criminal law provisions, offenders who have legitimately trusted their own law by engaging in what is considered licit conduct under their own legal system.[122] Neither could the affected state's criminal law be applied without this fundamental condition by demonstrating that the offender was in the position to know it, since this would give rise to a violation of the ban on discrimination among EU citizens.

In the light of this, it seems that the prosecutorial power may be assigned to a state other than the offender's own country on the strict condition that this provides criminal law solutions similar to those of the state to which the offender substantially belongs.[123] Moreover, not only would the identity of the relevant criminal law provision ensure the fulfilment by the affected state of the human rights requirements of legal certainty, but it would also reduce the risk of inadequacy of the protection provided by the offender's own country. There is no doubt that, as long as the country with primary jurisdiction protects other states' interests, there is no need for them to intervene.[124] This result could certainly be achieved by extending the principle of assimilation, aimed at protecting EU legal interests, to the protection of the national interests of other EU member states.[125] And it can be expected that in a common area of freedom, security and justice the need to assign

---

[121] In *Hungary*, the new criminal code (Btk.), which came into force in July 2013, has strengthened the role of the passive personality principle in light of a conception of criminal law aimed at protecting either natural or legal persons if they have links with Hungary. See Karsai (2013), p. 490.

[122] On the role of the *nullum crimen sine lege* principle as individual guarantee reflecting the trust in (non)-punishability of a certain behaviour, see the German BVerfGE 73, pp. 234 ff.

[123] As seen above (fn. 111), also models based on the primacy of territorial jurisdiction, such as that elaborated by the DFG project, require an identical criminal law provision in *lex loci* for the exercise of derivative jurisdiction. Significantly, moreover, in *Germany*, the extraterritorial prosecution of crimes on the basis of the passive personality principle requires, as a general rule, that the conduct should constitute a criminal offence under *lex loci*.

[124] Böse and Meyer (2011), p. 342.

[125] *Ibid*., pp. 342 f.

prosecutorial powers to a jurisdiction other than the one of the offender's own country should progressively decrease.

Yet, assuming that the act constitutes a criminal offence under the law of the state having primary jurisdiction, when could another country affected in its own interests legitimately prosecute a transnational crime? In my view, the answer is to be found in the field of procedural law, i.e., where the perpetrator's own country either cannot or does not intend to prosecute the offence: the first situation occurs where the criminal law of the offender's own country makes punishment dependent on a procedural condition the affected state does not provide for,[126] whereas the second can occur in those countries in which the prosecuting authorities can discretionarily decide not to charge. In the latter case, the claim of jurisdiction of the state affected in its essential interests could be construed following the requirements of the principle of representative prosecution.

At any rate, the assignment of jurisdiction to a state other than the offender's own country would not imply overlooking the needs pursued by his own substantial criminal law. These needs can, however, gain relevance only with a view to strengthening the guarantees provided for adjudication by the offender's own law. From a human rights perspective, it would be difficult to accept that the offender could be subject to a more severe punishment or to further measures than those provided by his own law. Here, furthermore, there emerges a first great difference in the way we deal with transnational and national conflicts of jurisdiction, since at a domestic level the settlement of jurisdictional conflicts leads to assigning the prosecutorial power to a jurisdiction, which will act under the *same* procedural and substantive regulation. But at a transnational level, one might doubt that the complex needs of transborder crimes can be properly dealt with by allowing for *one* single jurisdiction to apply only *one* (i.e., only its own) criminal law. In this regard, comparative law clearly shows that this perfect one-to-one-correspondence has widely been broken[127] and that national criminal law may be applied by a country exercising derivative jurisdiction in the strict respect of the mitigating limits established by the law of the country having primary jurisdiction.[128]

Although these examples usually do not entail the application in itself of foreign law[129] and, moreover, establish the limits of exercise of extraterritorial jurisdiction

---

[126] I therefore no longer share the opinion expressed in Ruggeri (2014b), p. 216. It is noteworthy, however, that in *Germany* the dual criminality requirement, provided for the activation of national jurisdiction on the basis of the active personality principle, has been recently deemed as requiring also the respect of procedural *lex loci*. See Wörner (2013), p. 477. Cf. also more extensively Scholten (1995), *passim*.

[127] Di Martino (2006), pp. 29 ff.

[128] Thus, in *Switzerland*, the IRG provides, while establishing the conditions under which Switzerland may claim its right to representative prosecution, that Swiss criminal law must be applied within the mitigating limits laid down by foreign law. Thus, foreign law will be applied whenever it is more lenient than the Swiss system and provided that Swiss authorities may not apply foreign sanctions that are not envisaged under national law [art. 86(2)]. See Gleß (2011a, b), p. 59.

[129] On the application of foreign criminal law, see Cornils (1978), *passim*.

in relation to the primary (territorial) jurisdiction, this approach might, in my view, be adapted to the perspective shared here. This would of course offload to the state claiming derivative jurisdiction a very laborious task, which consists in a global consideration of the offender's position in the concrete case,[130] a consideration that should also encompass the hypothetical assessment of how, following the case law of the offender's own state, he would be dealt with in a similar case by applying foreign law.[131] Whichever the practical difficulties are, however, such solutions provide suggestions of great interest in light of the creation of a model of fair multicultural criminal justice. Nor should this proposal give rise to human rights concerns as to the hybridisation of criminal law systems.[132] Transnational cases naturally require integrated solutions that, moreover, do not appear to infringe the fundamental requirement of legal certainty: since the state affected in its essential interests should intervene in representation not of the territorial jurisdiction but of the jurisdiction of the country the offender substantially belongs to, the sentence will be established within the limits set by the criminal law of *this* country, i.e., by a criminal law system that the offender could know and legitimately trust.[133]

4.3.2 Cooperation Among Jurisdictions in Cases of Complex Crimes and Coordination of Parallel Proceedings

Whereas in general terms transnational crimes counteract the idea that they must be adjudicated only on the basis of a single legal reference system, thus showing the need to partially integrate different criminal law systems, offences of a complex nature suggest that we should reflect on whether transnational cases can be properly prosecuted by only *one* jurisdiction.[134] Here again, the comparison with national conflicts of jurisdiction appears to be misleading, and therefore the solution to

---

[130] In this direction, see what in *Austria* is provided for by the StGB, which in cases of extraterritorial jurisdiction offloads to the Austrian judge the difficult task of ascertaining, while defining the defendant's punishment, that, considering his overall position (*Gesamtauswirkung*), he will not be dealt with less favourably than he would be by applying the territorial law (§ 65). See Höpfel and Kathrein (2011), paras. 6–7.

[131] In this regard, Denmark requires national authorities, by applying Danish law to extraterritorial cases, to respect the foreign *lex mitior* in relation not only to the maximum penalty established by the territorial law [art. 10(2) of the Criminal Law] but also to the foreign case law for sentencing purposes. See Greve (2005), pp. 753 ff.

[132] Alongside *Bernd Schünemann*, several scholars look at the application of foreign law with concern. See, in German literature, Ambos (2011), pp. 128 f.

[133] To be sure, where the affected country is not the state in whose territory the conduct took place, also the territorial criminal law should be applied as *lex mitior* to avoid discriminations among EU citizens. Upon closer examination, this solution is excessive and unnecessary: where neither the offender substantially belongs to the State in which the conduct took place nor this state's essential interests have been touched upon, nothing seems to justify intervention of the territorial criminal law.

[134] Lagodny (2002), p. 263.

submit to one national jurisdiction, by means of the territoriality principle, the acts or omissions of secondary participants irrespective of whether they were in a position to know the relevant foreign criminal law appears to be unsatisfactory. From a procedural viewpoint, one should also consider the repercussions of the concentration of the proceedings on the defence rights of these people, who would thus be obliged to face a criminal process in a country they are unfamiliar with.[135] It has been observed that the consequences of this approach are further aggravated in the field of organised crimes, due to the fact that national case law tends to extend its own jurisdiction over the whole criminal organisation in relation to all the alleged members of the organisation, even if its main activities took part overseas and irrespective of whether all the people charged were in the position to know and understand the law of the prosecuting country and even whether the law of their country criminalises the specific criminal organisation charged at all.

To be sure, even the proposed approach—while providing a proper solution in relation to forms of transborder crimes with a fairly simple structure—does not fit those cases characterised by complex cross-border criminal affairs (or even criminal phenomena) consisting of several offences committed in the territories of several countries and committed by several accomplices residing in different countries and often with different citizenship.[136] Here, the recourse to the law of the country to which the *single* offender substantially and regularly belongs can give rise to a plethora of competing jurisdictions claiming their right to prosecute the *entire* criminal affair. This does not mean, however, that procedural concentration is the most adequate solution.

Apparently, the *Gesamtlösung*, especially if rooted on territorial basis, has the benefit of satisfying, by means of a unified action, the prosecutorial need to grasp the complexity of the most serious and, from a criminological viewpoint, the most relevant forms of transborder crimes. However, this need, which reflects a clear state-related interest, cannot be fulfilled to the extent that it would sacrifice the claim of a fair jurisdiction by all the alleged offenders. In cases of multiple participations, concentrating the proceedings in the main offender's own country would not guarantee to all the alleged participants the application of a criminal law they were in any way familiar with. Furthermore, serious problems emerge in the field of medical responsibility, since an extensive interpretation of the criminal liability for criminal participation by means of omission entails the risk of excessively widening the duty of any specialist doctor to control the conducts of all his colleagues who intervene *abroad* in subsequent moments of the patient's treatment.[137]

---

[135] The model of transnational procedural unity also has a similar shortcoming. See Satzger (2006), p. 148.

[136] For a similar conclusion in relation to the solution provided by the law of residence, cf. Wörner (2013), p. 482.

[137] De Francesco (2013), pp. 137 f.

But the main shortcoming of this approach perhaps lies in the way of dealing with the most complex criminal affairs, which precisely because of the multiplicity of crimes they encompass, as has been noted, cannot be treated properly by a single jurisdiction in the same way as happens for single offences. In a deeper sense and from the perspective of substantive criminal law, most complex (transnational) criminal affairs demonstrate that the notion of "offence" in itself appears to be insufficient, both from an objective and a subjective viewpoint, to grasp the complexity of such criminal phenomena. Here, instead, the concurrence of several criminal powers reveals the need for a pluralist approach, which is, in my view, a value to be preserved rather than a danger to be prevented as long as it allows a proper balance among the (human rights) needs of the states involved to be achieved. Significantly, a part of criminal law scholarship over recent decades has raised many criticisms against the procedural concentration solution, thus underlying the advantages of the so-called "separate solution" (*Einzellösung*).[138] But the solution of adjudicating separately single offenders in relation to the offences of which complex criminal actions are comprised should not be viewed as necessarily entailing a fragmentation of the criminal prosecution, nor does this result necessarily imply a differentiated application of *substantive* criminal laws. In the common European area, criminal law systems can no longer be seen as parts of unconnected legal systems, and an efficient prosecution of complex criminal phenomena cannot be realised through separate legal responses.

This does not, however, mean that countries could be entitled to prosecute *any* form of participation irrespective of the relevance of the accessorial contribution and even of whether the main action can be prosecuted abroad or constitutes a criminal offence.[139] Moreover, even adopting a restrictive interpretation of the accessorial action[140] would not be a proper solution in those countries, such as *Italy*, where the law does not distinguish among the different roles of the accomplices. Neither would it help in those cases in which the criminal action consisted in several acts of equal seriousness, committed in the territories of several countries and by several accomplices.

In a nutshell, precisely the complex features of these criminal affairs reveal the need for a *transcultural multiple prosecution*. Nor would this solution run counter to the human rights requirement of a modern criminal law. Thus, the distribution of

---

[138] Along these lines, meanwhile, see Oehler (1983), para 361. More recently, see also Böse and Meyer (2011), p. 343. Criticism against the *Einzellösung* has been raised, with regard to criminal complicity, by many scholars, however. See, among others, Satzger (2011), p. 51.

[139] In this sense, instead, in *Germany* the StGB, departing from the *Gesamtlösung*, provides for the application of German law to the accomplice's contribution, which took place in German territory, to a criminal action mainly committed abroad even if it does not constitute a criminal offence abroad [§ 9(2)]. It must, however, be borne in mind that the StPO considerably attenuates the severity of this regulation, in that it empowers the Public Prosecutor to waive prosecution where the accomplice's conduct in Germany has contributed to a criminal action that mainly took place overseas [§ 153c(1)(1)].

[140] Along these lines, see Böse and Meyer (2011), p. 343.

powers would take place not among territorial jurisdictions but among the jurisdictions of the countries the accused substantially belong to or among those that can legitimately claim jurisdiction along the lines exposed above. Further, this solution would clearly not jeopardise the defendant's right not to be prosecuted twice, since the national proceedings would be conducted against different defendants.

Against this background, the question here does not concern how jurisdictional conflicts should be solved but the way a proper cooperation can be achieved among different jurisdictions to adequately deal with the same complex transnational affair. Certainly, as long as a concerted action of the national authorities is ensured at the pre-trial stage, coordination will play a fundamental role in preventing the occurrence of jurisdictional conflicts through a proper distribution of resources (and crimes) among the cooperating authorities.

4.4 Multicultural Prosecutions and Differentiated Methods of Taking Transnational Evidence

These observations show that establishing clear rules on the assignment of jurisdiction and on the way several jurisdictions can cooperate in cases of complex crimes does not only constitute a precondition to know who will prosecute and who will cooperate in investigative activities but also helps address the question of how to properly investigate and gather evidence in other countries. The starting point of this analysis is the adoption of the same human rights methodology proposed in the choice of jurisdiction and must lead to construing transnational criminal inquiries in such a way that the requirements of a fair procedure can be respected.

Among the solution models set forth above, the model of transnational procedural unity is unique in its linking of the conduction of transborder investigations to the assignment of the prosecutorial power. This link is, however, not found in either the order or request model or the model of joint investigations—all models that treat the conduction of transborder investigations as a matter of purely evidence law. As far as concerns the methods of obtaining evidence in transborder cases, it is worth observing that all the solution models set forth in this study reveal, albeit in different fashions, a clear territorial conception. Of course, the notion of territoriality varies considerably and can even lead to diametrically opposed solutions, as happens in the traditional MLA model and in the model of transnational procedural unity, which focus on the territorial application, respectively, of the sole *lex loci* and the sole *lex fori*. But a strong territorial conception still inspires both the most advanced MLA instruments as well as the EU tools, not to mention the recent EIO proposal, which, albeit admitting the possible application of specific procedures of *lex fori*, confirm the need to respect the entire *lex loci*.

However, a significant difference can be observed in the way the (territorial) *lex fori* is required in the collection of evidence in a country other than the prosecuting one. It has been noted that both in the most advanced versions of the request model and in the order model (as well as in the model of joint investigations, whenever established in the concrete case), the partial application of *lex fori* is mainly functional to facilitating the admissibility of evidence in the relevant proceedings and thus the needs of prosecution. To be sure, the respect for procedural *lex fori* has great potential for strengthening the guarantees of the defence either of the accused or the addressee of the investigation. Yet the fact that most instruments do not acknowledge, unlike the previous MLA system, the right of private parties to take part in the transnational investigations clearly shows the scarce consideration paid to defence rights. A human rights perspective inspires, instead, the transnational procedural unity both in the choice of the forum (through the contribution of *Eurodefensor*) and in the application of one coherent set of procedural rules in the transborder inquiry, a solution aimed at solving the practical problem of ensuring that the enquiry be conducted on a harmonised basis.

Despite these merits, the model of transnational procedural unity does not necessarily guarantee the activation of the jurisdiction closest to the defendant, nor does it grant *any* addressee of the investigation the procedural guarantees of his own law. On one hand, also the model of transnational procedural unity, like the statutory determination model,[141] provides for a cut-off rule allowing the assignment of prosecutorial power, in cases of several defendants with different citizenships, to the country where the greatest amount of important evidence or simply most of the evidence is located[142]—a solution clearly aimed at facilitating the investigation of the facts rather than at preserving the defendant's right to be adjudicated by a jurisdiction he is familiar with. On the other side, the application of *lex fori* does not guarantee that transnational evidence can be obtained in compliance and within the limits established by the law of the country of the addressees of the investigation, especially in cases of suspicionless third parties.

As noted above, the methodological approach to both these issues will be the same if we put the individual at the centre of international cooperation, and there is no doubt that the need for legal certainty does not constitute a fundamental human rights requirement only in relation to the choice of the most adequate substantive criminal law and the best jurisdiction. Thus, precisely where transnational investigations require measures touching upon fundamental rights, certainty about the applicable procedural law means ensuring the addressee of the investigative measure transparency and clarity about the limits within which the investigation may be carried out and his rights may be restricted—a requirement that, as we have seen, is generally overlooked in the combination methods of taking evidence overseas.

Furthermore, legal certainty does not mean that *any* procedural law may be applied. Also here, the very delicate position of the addressee of the investigation, especially in cases of third parties, suggests reflecting on the properness of solutions inspired by rigid models, such as those based on the application of the sole *lex loci* or the sole *lex fori* in *any* transnational case irrespective of whether the addressee of

[141] Art. 2. See Sinn (2012b), p. 611.

[142] Art. 2(2). See Schünemann (2006a), pp. 5 f.

the concrete investigation is familiar with one or the other law. Both solutions can lead to unsatisfactory results: the defendant, whenever targeted by the investigation, might ignore the *lex loci*, while third parties might be fully unfamiliar with *lex fori*—results that will clearly impinge on the effectiveness of their defence strategies. If this were the case, people might, for instance, have to submit to wiretapping in respect of an offence for which under their own law no interception would be allowed or a search during the night whereas their law establishes precise time limits for such measure.

That said, it must be acknowledged that neither the mode of the transnational enquiry nor the methods of obtaining evidence can be left to the discretional decision of the prosecuting authority or to a free agreement between this authority and a foreign one. This happened in the former Swiss model, which did not lay down clear rules on the choice of the form of the enquiry, which could manifestly give rise to solutions detrimental to the accused and third parties.[143] However, current EU legislation also gives national authorities too much leeway in choosing whether to collect evidence pursuant to the request model or require the beginning of joint investigations. Nor are these shortcomings expected to be overcome by future legislation, since the EIO proposal does not clarify how and to what extent national authorities may have recourse to the new instrument or require the activation of a joint enquiry.

In my view, the main deficiency of this approach is that the choice among the existing modes of gathering transnational evidence and consequently the procedure for conducting the transborder investigation cannot take place without considering two main issues, i.e., (a) which countries are involved in the transnational enquiry, and (b) what link exists between the applicable law and the addressee of the investigation. To this end, however, a distinction can be drawn between the type of international cooperation and the procedures to be followed.

Concerning the choice of the most suitable mode of assistance according to the needs of the concrete case, the most reasonable solution would be to make the decision dependent on whether the country with which cooperation is sought has a substantial link with the alleged offence. State-related interests will, therefore, mainly guide this decision. Thus, where the state in which the sought evidence is located can legitimately compete for prosecution, *e.g.* because more than one State has primary jurisdiction or evidence is placed in a State that needs to defend its own essential interests, the model of joint investigation seems to provide the most adequate form of conducting an enquiry of common interest. Recourse to assistance models should, therefore, be restricted to those cases in which the state in which the sought evidence is located does not have a substantial link with the offence under prosecution.

This distinction does not, however, mean that—as concerns the applicable procedural law—a combination between *lex fori* and *lex loci* should again guide the gathering of evidence in the former case, whereas a pure assistance model in

[143] Schünemann (2014), p. 168.

favour of a foreign affair should (exclusively or to a great extent) legitimise the application of *lex fori* in the latter. We have seen that neither of the two solutions appears to be convincing from a human rights perspective and that to establish the applicable procedural law the focus must be driven to the viewpoint of the addressee and his legitimate claim for the application of a law he could realistically know in advance. Also here, therefore, the choice of the most adequate procedural law should start with considering what country the addressee of the transborder enquiry substantially belongs to and consequently what law establishes the limits within which the investigation may legitimately be carried out. Nor can the need here for a human rights perspective be overlooked because of the different nature of procedural law and the fact that it generally follows the *tempus regit actum* rule.[144] The rigid distinction between substantive law and procedural law has for decades been in great part overcome. In Italy, procedural scholarship has since the 1980s questioned the different regulation on the temporal application of criminal substantive and procedural laws,[145] whereas German literature has focused on the particular nature of those procedural provisions, which contain a sort of procedural projection of substantive law rules for the purposes of the prosecution investigation. These requirements, known in Germany as *Sachgestaltungsvoraussetzungen*,[146] make it possible to draw a distinction between purely procedural rules and procedural rules that are to be deemed as structurally similar to substantive law provisions.[147] This phenomenon is of particular importance in the field of interferences with fundamental rights that, whether by means of coercion or not, are always based on a suspicion of guilt, which implies (albeit differently construed) a clear projection of substantive criminal law and thus requires respect for similar guarantees.

This does not, however, imply that the need for efficient transnational prosecution should not be taken into account: also here, a proper balance between state-related interests and defence rights must be sought with a view to ensuring a fair transnational evidential procedure. In this light, merit should be given to the model of transnational procedural unity for raising criticism of the risk of hybridisation resulting from combined methods of obtaining overseas evidence and for underlining that coherence must constitute a fundamental requirement also in the field of transnational inquiries. Also here, precisely the transcultural character of transnational inquiries requires a complex integrated approach, which in no case seems to be achieved by means of combined methods.[148] One of the main shortcomings of this approach is that they are aimed at combining single procedures of both laws of the cooperating countries, as if they could be dealt with outside the legal context they belong to. However, any procedure reflects specific balances between often-conflicting interests against a constitutional framework. A mixture

[144] See Böse (2013), p. 80, with extensive reference to ECtHR case law.

[145] Nobili (1982), p. 2138.

[146] See, among others, Volk (1978), pp. 147 f.

[147] Along these lines, see Negri (2004), pp. 51 ff.

[148] I therefore no longer share the opinion expressed in Ruggeri (2014b), p. 224.

of single procedural forms can thus alter this scheme and lead to different constitutional balances colliding with each other.

A fruitful alternative to these solutions might therefore consist in the mutual integration of procedural laws according to the needs of the concrete case.[149] The ways this integration can be achieved might vary according to the needs of the different modes of conducting a transnational enquiry and especially depending on the substantial involvement of the cooperating state in the criminal offence under prosecution and on the substantial link between the addressee of the investigation and the law of this state. To this extent, the success of any integration approach methodologically requires a constructive dialogue among the cooperating authorities, as well as, whenever possible, among them and the defence counsels of the people involved, with the aim of setting up an *ad hoc* investigative procedure that reflects a new balance among colliding interests according to the human rights needs of the concrete case. In this light, each of the domestic laws will cease to be part of its own legal system and will not therefore be applied as such.[150] To this end, dialogue must start detecting the constitutional requirements of the countries concerned with the investigation at stake, which will allow for establishing the essential human rights requirements to define the features and limits of the investigation. In this regard, the recourse to the "principle of quality" (*Qualitätsprinzip*) could be of more help in the field of evidence gathering than in that of jurisdictional conflicts,[151] since here the point at stake is not an "out-out-choice" among one or another jurisdiction but the establishment of the most appropriate balance among colliding interests to ensure the highest protection to the individuals involved in transborder inquiries while satisfying the need for a fair transnational investigative procedure.

5 Conclusion

The collection of evidence in transnational inquiries, while interfering with individual rights, cannot be properly dealt with without considering which countries are called upon to participate in international cooperation and what substantial link the addressees of the transnational prosecution have with the law of these countries. This focus requires a complex approach that, with a view to ensuring that the rights of the individuals involved in the transnational inquiry and state-related interests find a fair balance, presupposes the ascertainment of what jurisdiction has the most

[149] Significantly, constitutional scholarship has for the most part superseded the idea of closed Constitutions in favour of the more modern conception of inter-constitutional legal systems, which open towards other charters of human rights at either a supranational or a national level. See Ruggeri A, in this book, § 5.

[150] From a similar perspective, Klip (2012), p. 393, points out that domestic judicial products are no longer products once they go across the border, where different requirements apply.

[151] Lagodny (2002), pp. 264 ff.

appropriate link to prosecute the criminal offence at stake. While analyzing the shortcomings both of an uncontrolled expansion of extraterritorial jurisdictions and an unconditional territorial prosecution, this study has proposed the law of the offender's substantially own country as the preferable solution to ensure a transnational prosecution in line with the requirements of a modern, human-rights-oriented criminal law with a particular focus on the *nullum crimen sine lege* principle. Starting from this premise, the choice of the forum should, however, balance the offender's legitimate claim to be adjudicated pursuant to a criminal law with which he is familiar with the (equally legitimate) claim of jurisdiction by countries affected in their essential interests. Thus, in the current European scenario, characterised by an increasingly transcultural context, the choice of the forum and of the applicable criminal law cannot be left to free bargaining among the competing authorities on the basis of uncoordinated national laws.

The assignment of jurisdiction on this basis can be of great help to choose, where the enquiry transcends national borders, the most appropriate mode of gathering evidence in other countries and the most suitable procedure. Also here, the best starting point seems to be to detect the most suitable procedural law by shifting the viewpoint towards the right of the addressee of the investigation to know in advance the applicable procedural law. This approach appears to be of great importance where the transnational enquiry requires the use of means touching upon fundamental rights, which, because of their intrusive character, are rooted on a suspicion of guilt and thus require the respect for the same human rights requirements acknowledged in relation to the choice of the forum. The addressee of an intrusive investigation, especially if carried out by means of coercion, must therefore be granted legal certainty of the limits within which the enquiry can impinge upon, or even deprive him of, his rights.

Again, furthermore, this fundamental individual claim must be balanced with the sovereign interests of the countries involved in the international cooperation. To this end, an essential requirement to identify the most proper mode of carrying out the investigation is to ascertain whether the cooperating country has a legitimate claim for jurisdiction in relation to the characteristics of the concrete offence under prosecution. Depending on the results of this ascertainment, a proper balance must be sought in the choice of the procedure to be followed among the conflicting interests at stake. To this end, neither the combination between single national procedures nor the exclusive application of a single set of national procedural rules appear to fit the multicultural challenges of a fair transnational criminal law, which seem, instead, to be properly fulfilled by seeking integrated methods of obtaining evidence, aimed at achieving a new balance among different values starting from the constitutional requirements of the countries involved. The ways this integration can take place are of course different, depending on the characteristics of the concrete case, and impose a very difficult task both on the cooperating authorities and the defences of the people involved in the transnational prosecution. To avoid the risk of partial solutions, this task should reasonably be inspired by the pursuit of the globally higher protection of the concrete interests at stake, following the requirements of the principle of quality.

References

Ambos K (2003) §§ 3–4 StGB. In: von Heintschel-Heinegg B, Joecks W, Miebach K (eds) Münchner Kommentar zum Strafgesetzbuch, vol I. C.F. Beck, München

Ambos K (2011) Internationales Strafrecht, 3rd edn. C.F. Beck, München

American Law Institute (ed) (1988) Third restatement of the law—the Foreign relations of the United States, vol 1. St. Paul, West

Bachmaier Winter L (2014) The proposal for a Directive on the European Investigation Order and the grounds for refusal. A critical assessment. In: Ruggeri S (ed) Transnational evidence and multicultural inquiries in Europe. Developments in EU legislation and new challenges for human rights-oriented criminal investigations in cross-border cases. Springer, Heidelberg, pp 71–90

Basile F (2009) Localismo e non-neutralità culturale del giudice penale "sotto tensione" per effetto dell'immigrazione. In: Risicato L, La Rosa E (eds) Laicità e multiculturalismo. Profili penali ed extrapenali. Giappichelli, Torino, pp 206 ff

Biehler A, Kniebühler R, Lelieur-Fischer J, Stein S (2003) Freiburg Proposal on Concurrent Jurisdictions and the Prohibition of Multiple Prosecutions in the European Union. Max-Planck-Institut für ausländisches und internationales Strafrecht. Freiburg i. Br

Bitzilekis N, Kaiafa-Gbandi M, Symeonidou-Kastanidou E (2006) Alternativüberlegungen zur Regelung transnationaler Strafverfahren in der EU. In: Schünemann B (ed) Ein Gesamtkonzept für die europäische Strafrechtspflege/A Programme for European Criminal Justice. Carl Heymanns, Köln, pp 250–253

Böse M (2002) Die Verwertung im Ausland gewonnener Beweismittel im deutschen Strafverfahren. Zeitschrift für die gesamte Strafrechtswissenschaft 114:148–182

Böse M (2003) Das Prinzip der gegenseitigen Anerkennung in der transnationalen Strafrechtspflege der EU – Die "Verkehrsfähigkeit" strafgerichtlicher Entscheidungen. In: Momsen C, Bloy R, Rackow P (eds) Fragmentarisches Strafrecht. Beiträge zum Strafrecht, Strafprozeßrecht und zur Strafrechtsvergleichung. Für Manfred Maiwald aus Anlaß seiner Emeritierung, verfaßt von seinen Schülern, Mitarbeitern und Freunden, 1st edn. Peter Lang, Frankfurt a.M., pp 233–250

Böse M (2007) Der Grundsatz der Verfügbarkeit von Informationen in der strafrechtlichen Zusammenarbeit der Europäischen Union. V&R Unipress, Göttingen

Böse M (2012) Vor § 3. In: Kindhäuser U, Neumann U, Paeffgen H-U (eds) Nomos Kommentar – Strafgesetzbuch, vol I, 3rd edn. Nomos, Baden-Baden

Böse M (2013) Choice of the forum and jurisdiction. In: Luchtman M (ed) Choice of the forum in cooperation against EU financial crime. Freedom, security and justice and the protection of specific EU-interests. Eleven International Publishing, pp 73–87

Böse M, Meyer F (2011) Die Beschränkung nationaler Strafgewalten als Möglichkeit zur Vermeidung von Jurisdiktionskonflikten in der Europäischen Union. Zeitschrift für internationale Strafrechtsdogmatik, pp 336–344

Böse M, Meyer F, Schneider A (eds) (2013) Conflicts of jurisdiction in criminal matters in the European Union, vol I. National reports and comparative analysis. Nomos, Baden-Baden

Caprioli F (2013) Report on Italy. In: Ruggeri S (ed) Transnational inquiries and the protection of fundamental rights in criminal proceedings. A study in memory of Vittorio Grevi and Giovanni Tranchina. Springer, Heidelberg, pp 439–455

Cornils K (1978) Die Fremdrechtsanwendung im Strafrecht. De Gruyter, Berlin

Cornils K, Greve V (2012) Dänemark. In: Sinn A (ed) Jurisdiktionskonflikte bei grenzüberschreitend organisierter Kriminalität. Ein Rechtsvergleich zum internationalen Strafrecht/Conflicts of jurisdiction in cross-border crime situations. A comparative law study of international criminal law. V&R Unipress, Osnabrück, pp 181 ff

D'Avila FR (2013) Normativa e giurisprudenze brasiliane in tema di conflitti transnazionali di giurisdizione in materia penale. La legislazione penale, pp 463–471

De Amicis G (2012) La prevenyione dei conflitti tra giurisdizioni e il trafserimento del processo. In: Kalb L (ed) "Spazio europeo di giustizia" e procedimento penale italiano. Giappichelli, Torino, pp 277–309

De Francesco G (2013) Diritto penale. vol II. Forme del reato. Giappichelli, Torino

Di Martino A (2006) La frontiera e il diritto penale. Natura e contesto delle norme di "diritto penale transnazionale". Giappichelli, Torino

Dominioni O, Pisani M (1987) Sulla compatibilità del trasferimento dei processi penali con i principi dell'ordinamento interno. Indice penale, pp 176 ff

Eser A, Lagodny O, Blakesley C (2002) The individual as subject of international cooperation in criminal matters. Nomos, Baden-Baden

Gascón Inchausti F (2013) Report on Spain. In: Ruggeri S (ed) Transnational inquiries and the protection of fundamental rights in criminal proceedings. A study in memory of Vittorio Grevi and Giovanni Tranchina. Springer, Heidelberg, pp 475–495

Gleß S (2003) Die "Verkehrsfähigkeit von Beweisen" im Strafverfahren. Zeitschrift für die gesamte Strafrechtswissenschaft 115:131–150

Gleß S (2006) Beweisrechtsgrundsätze einer grenzüberschreitenden Strafverfolgung. Nomos, Baden-Baden

Gleß S (2011a) Internationales Strafrecht, Grundriss für Studium und Praxis. Helbing & Lichtenhahn, Basel

Gleß S (2011b) Europäische Beweisanordnung. In: Sieber U, Brüner F H, Satzger H von Heintschell-Heinegg B (eds) Europäisches Strafrecht. Nomos, Baden-Baden, pp 596–610

Greve V (2005) Strafzumessung im internationalen Strafrecht. In: Arnold J, Burkhardt B, Gropp W, Heine G, Koch H-G, Lagodny O, Perron W, Walther S (eds) Menschengerechtes Strafrecht. Festschrift für Albin Eser zum 70. Geburtstag. C.F. Beck, München, pp 751 ff

Gropp W (2012) Kollision nationaler Strafgewalten – nulla prosecutio transnationalis sine lege. In: Sinn A (ed) Jurisdiktionskonflikte bei grenzüberschreitend organisierter Kriminalität. V&R Unipress, Osnabrück, pp 41–63

Hecker B (2011) Statement: Jurisdiktionskonflikte in der EU. Zeitschrift für die internationale Strafrechtsdogmatik 2:60–63

Heine G, Zürcher-Rentsch M (2013) Report on Switzerland. In: Ruggeri S (ed) Transnational inquiries and the protection of fundamental rights in criminal proceedings. A study in memory of Vittorio Grevi and Giovanni Tranchina. Springer, Heidelberg, pp 497–507

Höpfel F, Kathrein U (2011) § 65 StGB. In: Höpfel F, Ratz E (eds) Wiener Kommentar zum Strafgesetzbuch. 21. Lieferung, Austauschheft April 2011 (§§ 61–67). Manzsche Verlags- und Universitätsbuchhandlung, Wien, pp 67–74

Jescheck H-H (1954) Die internationale Rechtshilfe in Strafsachen in Europa. Zeitschrift für die gesamte Strafrechtswissenschaft, pp 518–544

Karsai K (2013) La via ungherese alla risoluzione dei conflitti: più paternalismo, meno flessibilità. La legislazione penale, pp 485–491

Klip A (2012) European criminal law, 2nd edn. Intersentia, Anwerp-Oxford

Lagodny O (2002) Viele Strafgewalten und nur ein transnationales ne-bis-in-idem? In: Donatsch A, Forster M, Schwarzenegger C (eds) Strafrecht, Strafprozessrecht und Menschenrechte. Festschrift für Stefan Trechsel zum 65. Geburtstag. Schulthess, Zürich, pp 253–267

Lagodny O (2012) Vor § 73. In: Schomburg W, Lagodny O, Gleß S, Hackner T (eds) Internationale Rechtshilfe in Strafsachen, 5th edn. C.H. Beck, München, pp 409–444

Manzini V (1948) Trattato di diritto penale italiano. I. Utet, Torino

Muñoz Conde F, García Arán M (2007) Derecho Penal. Parte general, 2nd edn. Valencia, Tirant Lo Blanch

Negri D (2004) Fumus commissi delicti. La prova per le fattispecie cautelari. Giappichelli, Torino

Nobili M (1982) Successione nel tempo di norme sui termini massimi della custodia preventiva e principi costituzionali. Foro italiano I: ...

Oehler D (1983) Internationales Strafrecht, 2nd edn. Carl Heymanns, Köln

Padovani T (2012) Diritto penale, 10th edn. Giuffrè, Milano

Peers S (2010) The proposed European Investigation Order. Assault on human rights and national sovereignty. www.statewatch.org. Accessed 22 Aug 2011

Rafaraci T (2012) The application of the principle of mutual recognition to decisions on supervision measures as an alternative to provisional detention. In: Ruggeri S (ed) Liberty and Security in Europe. A comparative analysis of pre-trial precautionary measures in criminal proceedings. V&R Unipress, Göttingen, pp 67–83

Risicato L (2004) Gli elementi normativi della fattispecie penale. Profili generali e problemi applicative. Giuffrè, Milano

Ruggeri S (2012) Libertà personale e procedimento penale nel diritto comparato: tutela del processo e tutela della persona in Europa. Revista de Estudos Criminais, pp 9–69

Ruggeri S (2013a) Concorrenza tra potestà punitive, conflitti transnationali di giurisdizione e tutela dei diritti della persona: il contributo della comparazione giuridica. La legislazione penale, pp 501–540

Ruggeri S (ed) (2013b) Transnational inquiries and the protection of fundamental rights in criminal proceedings. A study in memory of Vittorio Grevi and Giovanni Tranchina. Springer, Heidelberg

Ruggeri S (2014a) Introduction to the proposal of a European Investigation Order: Due process concerns and open issues. In: Ruggeri S (ed) Transnational evidence and multicultural inquiries in Europe. Developments in EU legislation and new challenges for human rights-oriented criminal investigations in cross-border cases. Springer, Heidelberg, pp 3–25

Ruggeri S (2014b) Transnational investigations and prosecution of cross-border cases in Europe: Guidelines for a model of fair multicultural criminal justice. In: Ruggeri S (ed) Transnational evidence and multicultural inquiries in Europe. Developments in EU legislation and new challenges for human rights-oriented criminal investigations in cross-border cases. Springer, Heidelberg, pp 193–228

Ruggeri S (ed) (2014c) Transnational evidence and multicultural inquiries in Europe. Developments in EU legislation and new challenges for human rights-oriented criminal investigations in cross-border cases. Springer, Heidelberg

Ruggieri F (ed) (2013) Criminal proceedings, language and the European union. Linguistic and legal issues. Springer, Heidelberg

Satzger H (2006) Die europäische Vollstreckungsübernahme. In: Schünemann B (ed) Ein Gesamtkonzept für die europäische Strafrechtspflege/A Programme for European Criminal Justice. Carl Heymanns, Köln, pp 146–159

Satzger H (2011) Internationales und Europäisches Strafrecht, 5th edn. Nomos, Baden-Baden

Scella A (2012) Verso le squadre investigative comuni: lo scenario italiano. In: Rafaraci T (ed) La cooperazione di polizia e giudiziaria in materia penale nell'Unione europea dopo il Trattato di Lisbona. Giuffrè, Milano, pp 215–230

Scholten H-J (1995) Das Erfordernis der Tatortstrafbarkeit in § 7 StGB. Ein Beitrag zur identischen Norm im transnationalen Strafrecht. Iuscrim, Freiburg i.Br

Schomburg W, Lagodny O, Gleß S, Hackner T (2012) Einleitung. In: Schomburg W, Lagodny O, Gleß S, Hackner T (eds) Internationale Rechtshilfe in Strafsachen, 5th edn. C.H. Beck, München, pp 2–50

Schünemann B (2003) Europäischer Haftbefehl und EU-Verfassungsentwurf auf schiefer Ebene – Die Schranken des Grundgesetztes. Zeitschrift für Rechtspolitik, pp 185–480

Schünemann B (2006a) Die Grundlagen eines transnationalen Strafverfahrens. In: Schünemann B (ed) Ein Gesamtkonzept für die europäische Strafrechtspflege/A Programme for European Criminal Justice. Carl Heymanns, Köln, pp 93–111

Schünemann B (ed) (2006b) Ein Gesamtkonzept für die europäische Strafrechtspflege/A Programme for European Criminal Justice. Carl Heymanns, Köln

Schünemann B (2014) Solution models and principles governing the transnational evidence-gathering in the EU. In: Ruggeri S (ed) Transnational evidence and multicultural inquiries in Europe. Developments in EU legislation and new challenges for human rights-oriented criminal investigations in cross-border cases. Springer, Heidelberg, pp 161–180

Sinn A (2012a) Jurisdictional law as the key to solving conflicts: comparative law observations. In: Sinn A (ed) Jurisdiktionskonflikte bei grenzüberschreitend organisierter Kriminalität. Ein Rechtsvergleich zum internationalen Strafrecht/Conflicts of jurisdiction in cross-border crime situations. A comparative law study of international criminal law. V&R Unipress, Osnabrück, pp 531–554

Sinn A (2012b) Draft models of a regulatory mechanism for the avoidance of jurisdictional conflicts. In: Sinn A (ed) Jurisdiktionskonflikte bei grenzüberschreitend organisierter Kriminalität. Ein Rechtsvergleich zum internationalen Strafrecht/Conflicts of jurisdiction in cross-border crime situations. A comparative law study of international criminal law. V&R Unipress, Osnabrück, pp 597–615

Sinn A (ed) (2012c) Jurisdiktionskonflikte bei grenzüberschreitend organisierter Kriminalität. Ein Rechtsvergleich zum internationalen Strafrecht/Conflicts of jurisdiction in cross-border crime situations. A comparative law study of international criminal law. V&R Unipress, Osnabrück

Sinn A (2013) Report on Germany. In: Ruggeri S (ed) Transnational inquiries and the protection of fundamental rights in criminal proceedings. A study in memory of Vittorio Grevi and Giovanni Tranchina. Springer, Heidelberg, pp 409–417

Thaman SC (2013a) Report on USA. In: Ruggeri S (ed) Transnational inquiries and the protection of fundamental rights in criminal proceedings. A study in memory of Vittorio Grevi and Giovanni Tranchina. Springer, Heidelberg, pp 509–529

Thaman SC (2013b) Conflitti transnazionali di giurisdizione in materia penale: il sistema statunitense. La legislazione penale, pp 449–459

Vogel J (2012a) Vor § 1. In: Grützner G, Pötz P-G, Kreß C (eds) Internationaler Rechtshilfeverkehr in Strafsachen, 4th edn. C.F. Müller, Heidelberg, pp 1–196

Vogel J (2012b) Vor § 73. In: Grützner G, Pötz P-G, Kreß C (eds) Internationaler Rechtshilfeverkehr in Strafsachen, 4th edn. C.F. Müller, Heidelberg, pp 1–94

Vogler R (2013) Transnational inquiries and the protection of human rights in the case-law of the European court of human rights. In: Ruggeri S (ed) Transnational inquiries and the protection of fundamental rights in criminal proceedings. Springer, Heidelberg, pp 27–40

Vogler R (2014) The European investigation order: fundamental rights at risk? In: Ruggeri S (ed) Transnational evidence and multicultural inquiries in Europe. Developments in EU legislation and new challenges for human rights-oriented criminal investigations in cross-border cases. Springer, Heidelberg, pp 45–49

Volk K (1978) Prozeßvoraussetzungen im Strafrecht. Zum Verhältnis von materiellem Recht und Prozessrecht. Gremer, Ebelsbach am Main

Wörner L (2013) Conflitti transnazionali di giurisdizione in materia penale. La prospettiva del diritto tedesco. La legislazione penale, pp 473–484

Zurkinden N (2013) Joint investigation teams. Chancen und Grenzen von gemeinsamen Ermittlungsgruppen in der Schweiz, Europa und den USA. Duncker & Humblot, Berlin

Part IV
Transnational Organised Crime and the Protection of Victims' Rights in Criminal Proceedings

Transnational Organized Crime and European Union: Aspects and Problems

Vincenzo Militello

Contents

Abstract The fight against criminal organizations and their ability to carry out illegal activities beyond the national borders has represented a "bridge head" in the European path towards the harmonization of criminal laws in the member states. After considering the role played by the harmonization of criminal law in the European Union treaties, the study underlines how the difficulty in defining the concept of transnational organized crime could result in an excessive European intervention. In order to avoid such a risk, it is useful to refer to other relevant international sources, like the 2000 Palermo UN Convention, and also to recent European documents on the matter (in particular, a Resolution by the European Parliament of the 25th October 2011). The final part of the paper is dedicated to the

---

Revised version of a contribution published in Böll Stiftung H, Schoenenberg R (eds), Transnational Organized Crime. Bielefeld, 2013, pp. 255–266. Reproduced by permission of Transcript Verlag.

V. Militello (✉)
Dipartimento Scienze Giuridiche, della Società e dello Sport, University of Palermo,
Via Maqueda, no. 172, 90134 Palermo, Italy
e-mail: vincenzo.militello@unipa.it

S. Ruggeri (ed.), *Human Rights in European Criminal Law*,
DOI 10.1007/978-3-319-12042-3_10

necessity to reconsider the traditional guarantees in the new European dimension, especially in the light of the European Court of Human Rights and the European Charter of Fundamental Rights and their counterweight activity to prevent an unbalanced European intervention against organized crime.

Keywords European Union • Harmonization of criminal law • Transnational organized crime

1 Introductory Remarks

The fight against criminal organizations and their ability to carry out illegal activities that reach beyond national boundaries has long since signaled the need to go beyond a type of European integration that is confined to merely economic aspects. Among the objectives of the European Union—implicitly dealt with in the 1992 Maastricht Treaty and then expressly in the 1999 Amsterdam version—there is the intent to create a shared space not only for goods and citizens but also for "justice, freedom and security" (today art. 3 in the TEU post-Lisbon).

The fight against organized crime in particular represents a "bridgehead" in the European harmonization of national criminal law systems of the member states. The peculiar ability of criminal organizations to expand beyond national borders, facilitated by the abolition of the barriers once restricting the movement of people and goods within the EU, has gradually affected the traditional national autonomy in the field of criminal law. Formerly, such national sovereign authority had prevented any European intervention in this area, and, even when the need for greater European cooperation in the fight against transnational crime had been acknowledged, it still influenced the guidelines developed by the European Union.

The reason was to be found not only in the reservation of the member states to wide their sovereign criminal powers but also in the need to reconsider the consequences of such a new transnational dimension on the traditional guarantees given under national systems of criminal law.

After examining what role the harmonization of criminal law plays in the current European Union treaties (Sect. 2), we will consider how the difficulty of defining the concept of transnational organized crime may lead to European interventions that go beyond the limits of "reasonableness" (Sect. 3). In order to avoid such a risk, it is useful to refer to other relevant international sources, such as the 2000 Palermo UN Convention (Sect. 4). Nevertheless, the more recent European decisions on the matter (in particular, a resolution by the European Parliament of October 25, 2011) seem to have paid significant to the main problems involved (Sect. 5).

On a general level, the effectiveness of normative instruments against organized crime highlights a more general problem. The European Union's action in the criminal law also shows the need to rethink the traditional guarantees and fundamental principles developed within the political context of nation states: In order to maintain the criminal law system as a means to protect all citizens, it is necessary to reconsider traditional guarantees within the framework of the new European dimension. This difficult topic will be addressed in the final sections of this essay—with reference to the European Court of Human Rights (Sect. 6) and the European Charter of Fundamental Rights and their counterweight activity to prevent unbalanced European action against organized crime (Sect. 7).

2 The Role played by the Harmonization of Criminal Law in the European Union Treaties

Over the last decade, the competencies of the European Union in matters of criminal law have progressively grown. The Lisbon Treaty extended the rules regarding harmonization of criminal offenses and their penalties to up to ten areas of "particularly serious crime with a cross-border dimension" [art. 83(1)(1) TFEU].[1]

An EU intervention is also granted in cases where "the approximation of criminal laws and regulations of the member states proves essential to ensure the effective implementation of a Union Policy in an area which has been subject to harmonization measures" [art. 83(2)].[2] Lastly, a special area is defined regarding offenses against the Union's financial interests [art. 325 and art. 86(2)].[3]

The tendency to expand the EU's competencies in the field of criminal justice and to diversify the areas of intervention reflects the ever-greater role played by the European Union and its institutions. Moreover, the EU's citizens have supported European action in the fight against crime, perceived as one of the EU's main objectives, as shown by *Eurobarometer* data.

In this respect, it seems curious that, in article 83(1)(2) TFEU, organized crime is listed last among the sectors that can be subject to harmonization, as this seems to neglect the fact that organized crime, as a clear example of transnational crime,[4] has very much accentuated the need for member states to coordinate their national criminal policies both within the EU and within the wider context of the United Nations.[5]

---

[1] For a different view, see Satzger (2010), p. 117, who holds that the Lisbon Treaty has narrowed the scope to harmonize questions of criminal law. However, the Treaty does not seem to limit but rather enhance possibilities for harmonization, as it specifies areas that may be integrated (see below).

[2] See Bernardi (2011); Grasso (2011), p. 2326; Sicurella (2011b), p. 2626; Siracusa (2010), p. 796; Heger (2009), p. 410.

[3] The autonomy of this specific area is claimed by Sieber (2011), p. 175; Sicurella (2011a), p. 42. See also Grandi (2010), p. 125. The three different juridical grounds for European intervention in criminal matters are also highlighted by the European Commission in a recent communication [COM(2011) 573 of 20.11.2011] "Towards a European Union's Criminal Policy: Ensuring the Effective Implementation of EU Policies Through Criminal Law", 5–6. On this aspect, see Klip (2012), p. 6.

[4] Along with terrorism, especially after the 9/11 attacks, see Marauhn and Meljnik (2006), p. 479; Kress and Gazeas (2011b), p. 349.

[5] On this matter, see Herlin-Karnell (2008), p. 331; Zöller (2009), p. 340; Bernardi (2011), p. 2 at fn. 7; Centonze (2008), p. 25. For a critical assessment, see Elholm (2009), p. 219. For United

Since 1997, organized crime, along with terrorism and drug trafficking, has been named in European treaties as a possible subject for the harmonization of criminal law [art. 31(1)(e) EUT Amsterdam version, already referred to by article 61(1)(a) ECT].[6] Harmonization of criminal law is aimed at "developing a close cooperation in the fields of Justice and Home Affairs," as a new goal of the EU that goes beyond the original intent of the European Economic Community (art. B EUT, Maastricht version of 1992). In the 1990s, the importance of cooperation against cross-border crime, including its organized forms, led to a twofold intervention strategy: the mutual recognition of judicial decisions and the approximation of criminal law.

These two approaches will have to be integrated in order to overcome differences between the criminal justice systems of individual member states [a link highlighted in arts. 67(3) and 82(1) TFEU].[7]

Within this general framework, the European Union has adopted many regulations to fight criminal organizations. Even before the Amsterdam Treaty came into effect (1 May 1999), this was regarded as one of the first "European duties of criminalization"[8]: at the end of 1998, the Council passed a "joint action" relating to the participation in criminal organizations in the EU's member states.[9] This innovative point was also included in the 1997 Action Plan against Organised Crime,[10] which has long represented a European policy programme on criminal matters.[11]

Nations documents, see A compilation of UN Document 1975–1998. See also Fijnaut (2000), p. 124; Mueller (2001), p. 13 s; Michelini and Polimeni (2007), p. 6.

[6] For the link between these sectors, see, for instance, Zeder (2008), p. 211, and also Militello (2000), p. 34.

[7] For recent studies on mutual recognition, see Harms and Knauss (2011), p. 1479; Suominen (2011), p. 56.

The lack of consideration for the here highlighted connection between mutual recognition and harmonization characterizes the radical criticism of the principle of mutual recognition made by Schünemann (2009), p. 119. A contrary opinion is held by Klip (2012), who points out that the European arrest warrant was successful in a context that lacked the harmonization of domestic legislations. Actually, this proves quite the contrary: the differences between national criminal law systems are the basis for the resistance against the European arrest warrant in several countries (*e.g.*, Germany and Italy).

[8] Even if, originally, the concept had a weaker meaning as there was no judicial control in case of nonfulfillment by the member states. For an in-depth examination of such a delicate issue, see Paonessa (2009), p. 14.

[9] Joint Action of 12 December 1998, in OJEC L 351 of 29 December 1998, which accompanies the other two joint actions dealing with illicit proceeds and corruption in the private sector of respectively 3 December 1998, in OJEC L 333 of 9 December 1998, and 22 December 1998, in OJEC L 357 of 31 December 1998.

[10] The Plan was published in OJEC C 251 of 15 August 1997. An updated list of other European actions and documents relating to organized crime can be found in Kress and Gazeas (2011a), p. 327.

[11] The first Action Plan on the topic was followed by a similar document "Prevention and Control of Organized Crime at the Beginning of the Millennium" (in OJEC C124/1 of 3 May 2000). References to organized crime are also contained in the wider "The Hague Programme:

However, the outstanding importance thus accorded to the topic of organized crime is not reflected in article 83(1)(2) of the Treaty, where, as pointed out earlier, the reference to organized crime is only to be found at the end of a long list of criminal activities requiring harmonization—a list on which terrorism is named first [unlike art. 31(1)(e) of the Amsterdam version of the TEU, where terrorism was only mentioned after organized crime].[12] Such a marginal placement of organized crime, together with the traditional vagueness of the concept, carries the risk that the scope of the legal provisions of article 83(1)(2) will be widened excessively, so as to (ideally) include any form of crime among the fields of possible European harmonization.[13]

This risk has to be avoided in order to prevent a definition of organized crime so wide that, although endorsed by article 83(1)(2) TFEU, will be nothing but a worthless duplicate concerning many of the criminal activities named in the same article. In particular, trafficking in human beings, drugs, and arms, and also money laundering and corruption, are all activities that share characteristics that they are "normally" carried out in organized forms, especially when performed transnationally.[14] In order not to lose sight of the real meaning of organized crime, it is necessary to identify its typical characteristics. A definition of organized crime is even more important if we consider that, even before the Lisbon Treaty came into effect, many criminal activities now enumerated in article 83(1)(2) had already been the object of European decisions. These measures established minimum standards

strengthening Freedom, Security and Justice in the European Union" (in OJEC C 53/1 of 3 March 2005), especially paras. 2(3), 2(6), 2(7).

[12] This impression is strengthened by the lack of reference to organized crime among the priorities identified by the European Council in relation to matters referred to by article 83(1); see The Stockholm Programme, an Open and Secure Europe Serving the Citizen, adopted by the EU Council on 3 March 2010, in OJEC C 115 of 4 May 2010, para. 3(3) (where the priorities are as follows: trafficking in human beings, terrorism, drug trafficking, sexual exploitation of children and child pornography, cyber-crime). Appropriately, the European Parliament has nevertheless pointed out the nonexhaustive character of "these objectives... and that the order of priorities could have been better structured," and, at the same time, it also accurately highlighted how "the fight against terrorism and organized crime is and must remain a key priority within the framework of internal security strategy": Committee on Civil Liberties, Justice and Home Affairs, Report on the European Union's Internal Security Strategy [2010/2308 (INI)] rep. on 24 April 2012 (Rapporteur Rita Borsellino).

[13] See, e.g., Grandi (2010), p. 120 at fn. 25. On the spaces of uncertainty of the concept of organized crime in the previous 2008 Framework Decision of the Council on the fight against organized crime (see below Sect. 4), see, *e.g.*, Calderoni (2008), p. 2700.

[14] See Sánchez García de Paz (2004), p. 641. See also the Europol Reports on the phenomenon, compiled annually since 2000, Europol (ed), 2000 European Union Organised Crime Situation Report, Luxembourg 2001, in specie 10; on this topic, see Sinn (2006), p. 503. Lastly, a confirmation of the connection pointed out in this article can be found in the Internal Security Strategy for the EU, approved by the Council of Europe on 25 and 26 March 2010 (Internal Security Strategy for the European Union—Towards a European Security Model, Luxembourg 2010, p. 14).

concerning both illicit conducts and corresponding penalties.[15] Therefore, the fact that the Amsterdam Treaty only referred to organized crime, terrorism, and drug trafficking did not hamper the further inclusion of several of the sectors, now expressly contained in the list referred to by article 83(1) as areas of European harmonization.[16] Besides, the current Treaty on the Functioning of the European Union envisages the possibility to extend harmonization measures to forms of crime that are not explicitly listed in article 83(1)(2). This will happen with regard to the evolution of crime, for example, when new criminal activities surface that are similar to those that are already the object of a possible harmonization of criminal law [art. 83 (1)(3)]. Nevertheless, two characteristic elements are required: a particular "seriousness" and a "cross-border dimension" of the crime. Therefore, future efforts to harmonize criminal law may not exploit the vague definition of organized crime.

Furthermore, formal procedures (unanimity of the Council and consent of the Parliament) may not be taken as the sole basis to extend areas that are subject to harmonization. On the contrary, it will be necessary to verify that each new form of crime that is to be the subject of harmonization meets the two above-mentioned conditions ("seriousness" and "cross-border dimension") referred to in the Treaty.

3 The Concept of Transnational Crime and the Boundaries of the European Harmonization

The reference to the transnational dimension of a specific crime may turn out to be rather useless when it comes to determining which new criminal phenomena should be subject to a harmonized legal reaction by the European Union. In fact, in the Lisbon Treaty system, the transnational dimension is derived from the "nature" and "impacts" of the offenses discussed, that is, the objective fact that criminal

[15] The following framework decisions go in the same direction: the decision of the Council of 29 May 2000 on protecting the euro against counterfeiting (2000/383/JHA); Framework Decision of 28 May 2001 combating fraud and counterfeiting of non-cash means of payment (2001/413/JHA); Framework Decision of 26 June 2001 on money-laundering and confiscation of crime-related proceeds (2001/500/JHA); Framework Decision of 13 June 2002 on combating terrorism (2002/475/JHA); Framework Decision of 19 July 2002 on preventing and combating trafficking in human beings (2002/629/JHA); Framework Decision of 28 November 2002 on the strengthening of the legal framework to prevent the facilitation of unauthorized entry, transit and residence (2003/568/JHA); Framework Decision of 27 January 2003, on the protection of the environment through Criminal Law (2003/80/JHA) (annulled by the Court of Justice–Great Chamber, 13 September 2005, case C-176/03); Framework Decision of 12 July 2005 against ship-source pollution (annulled by the Court of Justice–Great Chamber, 23 October 2007, case C-440/05); Framework Decision of 22 December 2003 on combating the sexual exploitation of children and child pornography (2004/68/JHA); Framework Decision of 24 February 2005 again on confiscation (2005/212/JHA); Framework Decision of 28 November 2008 amending the framework decision 2002/475/JHA on combating terrorism (2008/919/JHA).

[16] See arts. 29 and 31(e) TEU, Amsterdam version, according to which all areas of "organized and non-organized" crime may be the object of criminal harmonization measures. See Satzger (2008), pp. 114 f.

activities affect different states. But there is also reference to the "need to combat" particular types of crime "on a common basis." Such a perspective is no longer objective, as it expresses the wish to harmonize criminal law across a number of states—and such a definition will not be able to limit an (over)extension of legal harmonization.

In order to avoid this risk, the above-mentioned indications included in article 83 (1)(3) should not be considered the only elements that define the transnational dimension of European harmonization in criminal law. Here, it is useful to refer to the concept mentioned in article 3(2) of the 2000 UN Convention of Palermo that was also signed by the EU. This document refers to criminal offenses occurring in more than one state and involving organized criminal groups and views the involvement of a criminal organization as a particularly serious offense because it makes it more difficult to ascertain the liability of individual participants.

Provided that European harmonization follows the standards set for its extension to new forms of crime and respects the principle of subsidiarity, this will legitimate further European interventions, especially as action by individual states will not produce results (art. 5 TEU). It is precisely this difficulty to fight transnational criminal groups that establishes a "special need to combat them on a common basis," as referred to by article 83(1)(3); otherwise, such a requisite would appear empty or dangerously vague.[17]

4 The Reference to the International Legal Frameworks on Organized Crime

The reference to organized crime in the above-mentioned European treaties is not to be interpreted as a merely criminological concept, with an inevitably uncertain definition.[18] Rather, the concept of organized crime as object of action by the Union has to be derived from supranational measures with defined legal characteristics, at least on the international level.

There are three different international legal frameworks: the above-mentioned European Joint Action of 1998, the Palermo UN Convention of 2000 on transnational organized crime, and the more recent Framework Decision of the Council on the fight against organized crime (2008/841/JHA of 24 October 2008).

In all of these texts, the notion of criminal organization is described using naturalistic and normative elements, both of which require further definition. Among the naturalistic elements, the most recent formulation in the 2008 Framework Decision stresses the participation of more than two people in a crime and its persistence over a period of time. The requisites concerning the "seriousness" of the

[17] The wording appeared problematic in the decision of 20 June 2009 on the Lisbon Treaty of the German Bundesverfassungsgericht (Neue Juristische Wochenschrift 2009, 2288 n. 359).

[18] This opinion is maintained by Ambos and Rackow (2009), p. 402.

offense and the existence of a "structured association," on the other hand, are normative and need to be evaluated. Generally, the normative references here are too narrow in one case and too vague in the other.

The "seriousness" of the relevant "offenses" is defined as follows: the crimes in question must be punishable by at least 4 years imprisonment [art. 1(1)]. In this way, however, the law ends up including criminal activities that are viewed very differently by individual criminal law systems. Thus, the reference to a specific penalty neglects to address the still very considerable differences between criminal law systems in different EU countries.[19]

On the other hand, the definition of "structured association" does seem to appear vague: Excluded from this are only groups "randomly formed for the immediate commission of an offence." Subsequently, however, it is specified that "the group does not need to have formally defined roles for its members, continuity of its membership, or a developed structure" [art. 1(2) FD 2008].

The wording of this provision is overly general, and it fails to draw a distinction between organized crime and other cases in which a number of people commit a single offense. In order to define such a difference, elements of criminal organizations, such as a division of tasks involving at least three people and with the intent of committing multiple offenses, will have to be included.

The unclear approach adopted by the Framework Decision was probably caused by the need to find a compromise with criminal justice systems based on common law. Within these systems, the offense of "conspiracy" encompasses both the simple agreement to commit an offense and the commission of one or more offenses by an organized group. This same model is to be found in international documents [art. 2(1)(a)(b) FD 2008].[20]

The first such definition of "conspiracy" describes the subjective and objective factors that justify prosecution for the participation in a criminal organization. On the subjective level, it is stressed that the perpetrator must have had knowledge of the criminal group's illegal activities or at least of its illegal aims; on the objective level, it is pointed out that he/she will have to have actively participated in the group's criminal activity. This is followed by a long list of examples [art. 2(a)].

The second definition of "conspiracy" describes the agreement, even with just one other person, to commit a serious offense with the aim of directly or indirectly obtaining a financial or other material benefit. Here, the derivation from the Anglo-Saxon concept of conspiracy is very clear and includes precisely the agreement between two or more persons to engage jointly in an unlawful act or a lawful act carried out by illegal means. The specific dangerousness of criminal organizations—as differentiated from the simple complicity in a crime—is thus lost.

This problem cannot be solved by reference "to aims of benefit" agreed upon before the crime was perpetrated. The intent to illegally acquire material benefits is

[19] For an example, see Militello (2003), pp. 188 f.

[20] On this dual model, see Maljević (2011), p. 123.

typical for a great number of offenses—it is a necessary condition–but it is not sufficient to justify prosecution for participating in an organized criminal group.

The criminalization of the (mere) agreement to carry out a particular offense conflicts with the traditions of criminal systems that punish only criminal acts that have been perpetrated. In this regard, the European Framework Decision recognizes the possibility that state parties agree that an act of furtherance of the unlawful agreement is needed in order to justify prosecution for the participation in a criminal organization. Such an approach, although it may jeopardize the process of harmonization, would be in line with the "harm principle."

A whole system of rules defines liability for the participation in a criminal organization. The 2008 Framework Decision mentions terms of imprisonment (art. 3), the possibility to consider the commission of a serious offense within the framework of a criminal organization as an aggravating factor [art. 3(2)], the possibility that crown witnesses may receive reduced sentences or none at all (art. 4), and the liability of legal persons for offenses established in articles 1 and 2, with corresponding penalties (arts. 5 e 6).

5 The New Position of the European Parliament on the Matter

The European Parliament, in an important resolution on organized crime, recently adopted by a large majority, seems to have become aware of the problematic nature of some of the European regulations above mentioned.[21] The Parliament calls for greater harmonization and demands clearer definitions of the offenses. Moreover, it points to the need to go beyond the current dual approach regarding liability (membership/conspiracy) (para. 7).

Particular attention is given to the fight against the proceeds of crime. The Parliament stresses that, besides the "extended confiscation" and the seizure of assets registered in the name of third parties, there is a need for legislation allowing the use of confiscated assets for social purposes (paras. 8 e 9). Specific attention is also given to the protection of witnesses and informers (para. 12) and to the creation of a special Committee of the European Parliament (para. 15). This Special Committee on Organized Crime was set up on March 2012 with the task of analyzing and assessing the implementation of the Union's legislation on organized crime, corruption, and money laundering. The resolution also calls for the extension of the remit of the European Public Prosecutor's Office to include cross-border organized crime and corruption, and it stresses the importance of strengthening agencies such as Eurojust, Europol, and OLAF (paras. 18–23).

[21] Resolution of EU-Parliament P7_TA(2011)0459 (Rapporteur S. Alfano) approved by the Plenary Assembly on 25 October 2011.

Beyond the individual measures tackled in the resolution, it is worth highlighting the scope and organic structure of the document. It expresses an integrated approach to the phenomenon similar to that to be found in theoretical analyses of organized crime.[22] The European Parliament has adopted other similar documents on this topic: for example, the Action Plan of 1997,[23] the Joint Action of 1998 on the participation in a criminal organization,[24] and the proposal for a Framework Decision on the same matter.[25]

The added value of the more recent resolution lies in that it is not bound to a specific precedent. The resolution was adopted by the Parliament in its autonomy, and it may encourage further initiatives by the Parliament and the Council.

The document, however, also has some weak points. To begin with, it does not devote adequate attention to prevention, which is indispensable in the fight against organized crime. In order to tackle the phenomenon effectively, it will be necessary to develop social prevention measures and to heighten the regard for legality in our societies. Such an integrated approach has been highlighted, for example, in the Memorandum on the Prevention and Control of Organised Crime (2000).[26]

An additional weakness of the 2011 Resolution is its inadequate focus on the harmonization of penalties. This aspect is especially pertinent, as there still are considerable discrepancies between the legal systems of the member states.[27]

Lastly, the mechanisms to combat organized crime are not balanced by references to a need to harmonize legal guarantees, something that is needed to translate them into the different legal systems. In this respect, the rather general reference to basic rights and fundamental freedoms, included in the opening remarks of the Framework Decision of 2008, is just a "style clause," that is, something that cannot be translated consistently into the different national constitutional traditions.

What is really needed is a supranational framework of guarantees.

---

[22] Recently, *e.g.*, see Spapens (2010), p. 185.

[23] EU-Parliament, Comm. On Civil Liberties and Internal Affairs, Report on the Action Plan against organised Crime, doc it\RR\331\338487—PE 223.427/def., n. 17 (Rapporteur *Cederschöld*).

[24] EU-Parliament, Report on the 1998 Joint Action against Organised Crime (Eapporteur *Orlando*).

[25] EU-Parliament, Comm. LIBE Resolution 28 September 2005 (Rapporteur *Dunn*).

[26] Prevention and Control of Organized Crime at the Beginning of the Millennium (fn. 11).

[27] See, *e.g.*, Bernardi (2008), p. 381.

6 Illicit Proceeds as Crucial Field of the Fight Against Organized Crime

The fight against illicit proceeds, particularly through confiscations and penalties, is a crucial field. This aspect of organized crime is not explicitly discussed in the 2008 Framework Decision, yet it is the object of many harmonization measures laid out in previous Framework Decisions, and it is forcefully addressed in the above-mentioned resolution of the European Parliament.[28] Here, especially for Italian scholars, the most problematic point regarding the protection of the rights of individuals concerns confiscation undertaken as a preventive measure.

On this topic, the ECHR has stressed the need for guarantees (in particular, *Sud Fondi s.r.l. vs. Italy*, 20 January 2009). However, the overall validity of the seizure of proceeds of crime was not denied, something that has become crucial in Italy's fight against organized crime (recently, see *Bongiorno et al. vs. Italy*, 5 January 2010). Nevertheless, although Italy has recently improved its compliance with the rulings of the ECHR, the actual impact of the relevant case law is still limited to a few areas, areas that are undoubtedly important, yet this is not sufficient to overhaul a whole legal system as needed in the fight against organized crime.[29]

7 The Reference to the European Charter of Fundamental Rights

A firmer basis to achieve such a goal may be found in the European Charter of Fundamental Rights, which is now legally binding and has the same status as the EU Treaty. The Charter contains a long list of rights that aim to expand and harmonize the overall level of justice in Europe, and it thus runs counter to an uncritical increase of the use of repression at a national level.[30]

The expansion of EU action into the area of criminal law has long been criticized, and even the end of the rule of law has been predicted should this continue.[31] However, there are also various attempts to explore new directions: from *Corpus juris* to Euro crimes, from the European project for combating

[28] See the Framework Decision of 26 June 2001 on money laundering and confiscation (2001/500/JHA) and the Framework Decision of 24 February 2005 on confiscation of crime-related proceeds (2005/212/JHA). In the European Parliament Resolution (as fn. 21), see, especially, D and points 8–10.

[29] On this aspect, see the recent collection of essays edited by Manes and Zagrebelsky (2011), and also Militello (2008), p. 1421.

[30] Militello (2004), p. 139. On the importance of the Charter, see the recent and precise analysis by Manacorda (2011), p. 147; see also Maugeri (2007), p. 8; Cortens and Limborgh (2011), p. 41.

[31] See, *e.g.*, Albrecht and Braum (1998), p. 465; Braum (2000), p. 493; Moccia (2001), p. 54; Hassemer (2003), p. 14, Kaiafa-Gbandi (2004), p. 290.

organized crime to the Alternative Project for a European Criminal law and Procedure and to the recent Manifesto on the European Criminal Policy.[32]

Today, the framework offered by the Treaty of Lisbon seems to have largely overcome many of the disadvantages produced by the lack of democratic legitimation for a European intervention in matters of criminal law. The Treaty provides legislative procedures, including the coparticipation of the European Council and Parliament, in order to safeguard democratic values. Nevertheless, the EU may still get involved in areas to do with criminal law without intervening too much in areas of national sovereignty. The principles of proportionality and subsidiarity that have to guide interventions in criminal law can draw important lessons from the values enshrined in the European Charter of Fundamental Rights, which constitutes, at the same time, the limit and the foundation of a new Criminal Law of the European Union.

References

Albrecht A, Braum S (1998) Defizite europäischer Strafrechtsentwicklung. Kritische Vierteljahresschrift für Gesetzgebung und Rechtswissenschaft, 460–481

Ambos K, Rackow P (2009) Erste Überlegungen zu den Konsequenzen des Lissabon-Urteils des BVG für das Europäisches Strafrecht. Zeitschrift für die internationale Strafrechtsdogmatik, 397–405

Bernardi A (2008) L'armonizzazione delle sanzioni in Europa: linee ricostruttive. In: Grasso G e Sicurella R (eds) Per un rilancio del progetto europeo. Giuffrè, Milano, pp 381–454

Bernardi A (2011) La competenza penale accessoria dell'Unione Europea: problemi e prospettive. www.penalecontemporaneo.it

Braum S (2000) Das "corpus iuris" – Legitimität, Erforderlichkeit und Machbarkeit. Juristenzeitung, 493–500

Calderoni R (2008) A definition that could not work: the EU framework decision on the fight against organized crime. Eur J Crime Crim Law Crim Justice 16:265–282

Centonze A (2008) Criminalità organizzata e reati transnazionali. Giuffrè, Milano

Cortens G, Limborgh W (2011) Grondrechtenbescherming na het Verdrag van Lissabon. In: Spapens A, Groenhuijsen M, Kooijmans T (eds) Universalis: liber amicorum Cyrille Fijnaut. Intersentia, Antwerp, pp 39–47

Delmas-Marty M, Vervaele JAE (eds) (2000) The implementation of the Corpus Juris in the Member States. Intersentia, Antwerp

Elholm J (2009) Does EU criminal cooperation necessary mean increased repression? Eur J Crime Crim Law Crim Justice 17:191–226

European Criminal Policy Initiative (2009) A manifesto on European criminal policy. Zeitschrift für die internationale Strafrechtsdogmatik, 707–716

Fijnaut C (2000) Transnational crime and the role of UN in its containment through international cooperation: a challenge for the 21st century. Eur J Crime Crim Law Crim Justice 8:119–127

Grandi C (2010) Riserva di legge e legalità penale europea. Giuffrè, Milano

Grasso G (2011) Il Trattato di Lisbona e le nuove competenze dell'Unione, Studi in onore di Mario Romano. Jovene, Napoli, pp 2307–2350

[32] Cf. Delmas-Marty and Vervaele (2000); Militello and Huber (2001); Tiedemann (2002); Schünemann (2006); Schünemann (2008), p. 119; European Criminal Policy Initiative (2009).

Harms M, Knauss P (2011) Das Prinzip der gegenseitigen Anerkennung in der strafrechtlichen Regelung der EU. In: Heinrich M et al (eds) Festschrift für Claus Roxin zum 80. Geburtstag am 15. Mai 2011. Walter de Gruyter, Berlin, pp 1479–1496

Hassemer W (2003) Ein Strafrecht für Europa. In: Zieschang F et al (eds) Strafrecht und Kriminalität in Europa. Nomos, Baden-Baden, pp 3–25

Heger M (2009) Perspektiven des Europäischen Strafrechts nach dem Vertrag von Lissabon. Eine Durchsicht des (wohl) kommenden EU-Primärrechts vor dem Hintergrund des Lissabon-Urteils des BVerfG vom 30.6.2009. Zeitschrift für die internationale Strafrechtsdogmatik, 406–417

Herlin-Karnell E (2008) The Treaty of Lisbon and the criminal law: anything new under the sun? Eur J Law Reform 10:321–337

Kaiafa-Gbandi M (2004) Europäisches Strafrecht – Die Perspektive des Grndrechtsschutzes nach dem Verfassungsentwurf für Europa. Kritische Vierteljahresschrift für Gesetzgebung und Rechtswissenschaft, 3–23

Klip A (2012) European criminal policy. Eur J Crime Crim Law Crim Justice 15:3–12

Kress C, Gazeas N (2011a) Organisierte Kriminalitat. In: Sieber U, Brüner FH, Satzger H, von Heintschell-Heinegg B (eds) Europäisches Strafrecht. Nomos, Baden-Baden, pp 324–333

Kress C, Gazeas N (2011b) Terrorismus. In: Sieber U, Brüner FH, Satzger H, von Heintschell-Heinegg B (eds) Europäisches Strafrecht. Nomos, Baden-Baden, pp 334–350

Maljević A (2011) “Participation in a Criminal Organisation” and “Conspiracy”. Different legal models against criminal collectives. Duncker & Humblot, Berlin

Manacorda S (2011) Carta dei diritti e CEDU: una nuova topografia delle garanzie penalistiche in Europa. In: Manes V, Zagrebelsky V (eds) La convenzione europea dei diritti dell’uomo. Giuffrè, Milano, pp 147–190

Manes V, Zagrebelsky V (eds) (2011) La convenzione europea dei diritti dell’uomo nell’ordinamento penale italiano. Giuffrè, Milano

Marauhn T, Meljnik K (2006) Völkerrechtliche Maßnahmen zur Bekämpfung von organisierter Kriminälitat und Terrorismus. In: Gropp W, Sinn A (eds) Organisierte Kriminalität und kriminelle Organisationen. Nomos, Baden-Baden, pp 479–502

Maugeri P (2007) I principi fondamentali del sistema punitivo comunitario: la giurisprudenza della Corte di giustizia e della Corte Europea dei diritti dell’uomo. In: Grasso G e Sicurella R (eds) Per un rilancio del progetto europeo. Giuffrè, Milano, pp 83–162

Michelini M, Polimeni G (2007) Il fenomeno del crimine transnazionale e la Convenzione delle N.U. contro il crimine organizzato transnazionale. In: Rosi E (ed) Criminalità organizzata transnazionale e sistema penale italiano. La convenzione ONU di Palermo. Ipsoa, Milano, pp 1–31

Militello V (2000) Agli albori di un diritto penale comune in Europa: il contrasto al crimine organizzato (The dawn of a common criminal law in Europe: the fight against organized crime). In: Militello V, Paoli L, Arnold J (eds) Il crimine organizzato come fenomeno transnazionale. Forme di manifestazione, prevenzione e repressione in Italia, Germania e Spagna. Giuffrè, Milano, pp 3 ff

Militello V (2003) Partecipazione all’organizzazione criminale e standard internazionali di incriminazione. Rivista italiana di diritto e procedura penale, 184–223

Militello V (2004) I diritti fondamentali fra limite e legittimazione di una tutela penale europea. Ragion pratica, 139–160

Militello V (2008) Der Einfluss der Entscheidungen des Europäischen Gerichtshofes für Menschenrechte auf die italienische Strafrechtsordnung In: Sieber U et al (eds) Strafrecht und Wirtschaftsstrafrecht. Dogmatik, Rechtsvergleich, Rechtstatsachen. Festschrift für Klaus Tiedemann zum 70. Geburtstag. Carl Heymanns, Köln, Berlin, München, pp 1421–1434

Militello V, Huber B (eds) (2001) Towards a European criminal law against organised crime. Proposals and summaries of the Joint European Project to counter organised crime. Edition iuscrim, Freiburg i.Br

Moccia S (2001) L’involuzione del diritto penale in materia economica e le fattispecie incriminatrici del corpus juris. In: Bartone N (ed) Diritto penale europeo. Padova, pp 33–56

Mueller G (2001) Transnational crime: definitions and concepts. In: Williams P e Vlassis D (eds) Combating transnational crime. Concepts, activities and responses. Frank Cass Publishers, London, pp 13–21

Paonessa C (2009) Gli obblighi di tutela penale. Ed. ETS, Pisa
Sánchez García de Paz I (2004) Perfil criminológico de la delincuencia transnacional organizada. In: Pérez Álvarez F (ed) Serta in memoriam Alexandri Baratta. Ed. Universidad de Salamanca, Salamanca, pp 621 ff
Satzger H (2008) Internationales und Europäisches Strafrecht, 2nd edn. Nomos, Baden-Baden
Satzger H (2010) Internationales und Europäisches Strafrecht, 4th edn. Nomos, Baden-Baden
Schünemann B (ed) (2006) Ein Gesamtkonzept für die europäische Strafrechtspflege/A programme for European criminal justice. Carl Heymanns, Köln
Schünemann B (2008) Alternative project for a European criminal law and procedure. In: Bassiouni M, Militello V, Satzger H (eds) European cooperation in penal matters: issues and perspectives. Cedam, Padova, pp 119–135
Schünemann B (2009) Ein Kampf ums europäische Strafrecht – Rückblick und Ausblick. In: Joerden JC et al (eds) Vergleichende Strafrechtswissenschaft.: Frankfurter Festschrift für Andrzej J. Szwarc zum 70. Geburtstag. Duncker & Humblot, Berlin, pp 109 ff
Sicurella R (2011a) "Prove tecniche" per una metodologia dell'esercizio delle nuove competenze concorrenti dell'UE in materia penale. In: Grasso G, Picotti L, Sicurella R (eds) L'evoluzione del diritto penale nei settori di interesse europeo alla luce del Trattato di Lisbona. Giuffrè, Milano, pp 3–66
Sicurella R (2011b) Questioni di metodo nella costruzione di una teoria delle competenze dell'Unione Europea in materia penale. In: Studi in onore di Mario Romano. Jovene, Napoli, pp 2569–2644
Sieber U (2011) Einführung. In: Sieber U, Brüner FH, Satzger H, von Heintschell-Heinegg B (eds) Europäisches Strafrecht. Nomos, Baden-Baden, pp 25–93
Sinn A (2006) Das Lagebild der organisierten Kriminalität in der EU. Tendenzen, rechtliche Initiativen und Perspektiven einer wirksamen OK-Bekämpfung. Organisierte Kriminalität und kriminelle Organisationen, Gropp W, Sinn A (Hrsg.), Nomos, Baden-Baden, pp 503–524
Siracusa L (2010) Il transito del diritto penale di fonte europea dalla 'vecchia' alla 'nuova' Unione post-Lisbona. Rivista trimestrale di diritto penale dell'economia, 779–841
Spapens T (2010) Macro networks, collectives, and business process: an integrated approach to organized crime. Eur J Crime Crim Law Crim Justice 18:185–216
Suominen A (2011) The principle of mutual recognition in cooperation in criminal matters. Intersentia, Antwerp
Tiedemann K (2002) Wirtschaftstrafrecht in der Europäischen Union. Duncker & Humblot, Berlin
Zeder F (2008) Mindestvorschriften der EU in materiellen Strafrecht: Was bringt der Vertrag von Lissabon Neues? Era Forum, 209–227
Zöller M (2009) Europäische Strafgesetzgebung. Zeitschrift für die internationale Strafrechtsdogmatik, 340–349

New Perspectives for the Protection of the Victims in the EU

Tommaso Rafaraci

Contents

Abstract This paper deals with protection of victims of crime in criminal proceedings and is focused on Directive 2012/29/EU establishing minimum standards on the rights, support and protection of victims of crime, also in consideration of former FD 2001/220/JHA on the standing of victims in criminal proceedings.

Keywords Child victims • Criminal proceedings • Individual assessment • Measures of protection • Special measures • Victims of crime

---

T. Rafaraci (✉)
Department "Seminario giuridico", University of Catania, Via Gallo no. 24, Catania, Italy
e-mail: trafaraci@lex.unict.it

S. Ruggeri (ed.), *Human Rights in European Criminal Law*,
DOI 10.1007/978-3-319-12042-3_11

1 The Victim in the AFSJ

The legal basis of the EU action for the protection of victims of crime lies in Article 82(2)(c) TFEU. This provision grants the EU the competence to legislate, by means of directives, for the establishment of minimum rules concerning the rights of victims while taking into account the differences between the legal traditions and systems of the Member States.[1]

However, already much time before the adoption of the Treaty of Lisbon, FD 2001/220/JHA on the standing of victims in criminal proceedings was adopted under the former third pillar. In fact, this FD—the very first piece of "hard law" about victims under international law[2]—has given the Court of Justice the chance to deal with the issue concerning the influence of third-pillar measures on domestic law, in the well-known Pupino ruling[3] on harmonious interpretation of EU law.[4]

Although the FD was not far-reaching, it was not intended to deal with "cross-border victims" only (i.e., nonnational and nonresident in the Member State where the crime has been committed). In any case, the FD represented the first move to initiate a debate on the general issue concerning the central role of victims in criminal justice systems.[5]

2 Directive 2012/29/EU

Following the Stockholm Programme[6] and the Resolution of the Council of 10 June 2010 on a *Roadmap for strengthening the rights and protection of victims, in particular in criminal proceedings*, the debate on the role of victims in criminal

[1] The objective, common to all the provisions under Article 82 TFEU, is the approximation of the laws and regulations of the Member States, to the extent necessary to facilitate mutual recognition of judgments and judicial decisions and police and judicial cooperation in criminal matters having a cross-border dimension.

[2] For an overview concerning victims both under the "big" Europe of the European Council and the "small" Europe of the European Union, see Venturoli (2012), pp. 88 f.; Gialuz (2012), pp. 59 f.; Allegrezza (2012), pp. 55 f.; Amalfitano (2011), pp. 643 f.

[3] C-105/03, 16 June 2005, Pupino. For a comment on the Pupino case, see Luparia (2005), p. 3541.

[4] Manes (2006), p. 1150; Manes and Sgubbi (2007), pp. 1–180.

[5] In the absence of a definition of the concept of "victim," the European Court of Justice has affirmed that only natural persons are victims within the meaning of FD 2001/220/JHA on the standing of victims in criminal proceedings (C-467/05, Dell'Orto, 28 June 2007). See Balsamo (2008), p. 778. The Court of Justice has also made clear that Art. 9(1) of FD 2001/220/JHA must be interpreted as meaning that, under a system governing the liability of legal persons, the provision does not preclude a situation in which the victim of a criminal act is not entitled to seek compensation for the harm directly caused by that act in the course of criminal proceedings from the legal person who committed an administrative offense (C-79/11, Giovanardi, 12 July 2012).

[6] The Stockholm Programme—An open and secure Europe serving and protecting citizens, OJ C 115 of 4 May 2010.

proceedings resulted in Directive 2012/29/EU establishing minimum standards on the rights, support and protection of victims of crime and replacing Council Framework Decision 2001/220/JHA.[7]

This Directive is a wide-ranging measure, which aims at establishing a general statute for victims of crime under the EU while addressing the specific issue of the protection of vulnerable victims.[8]

Although the Directive reproduces provisions already foreseen in the old FD, it has the merit to organize other specific provisions about victims foreseen in legal acts concerning the repression of particularly serious crimes. In this regard, we believe that it is appropriate to draw a clear-cut distinction between the protection of victims of crime (already committed) and preventive protection, the last one ruled by substantive criminal law that is lately increasingly oriented to put the victim at the center of the choices of incrimination.[9] A blurring distinction between the protection from the risk of primary victimization (i.e., the risk to become a victim of crime) and the protection from the risk of secondary and repeat victimization (before and during criminal proceedings) may result in unbalanced choices in social-preventive terms.

The central role of the victims of crime needs also to be balanced with the protection of the rights of the accused, on which the EU is legislating in parallel, following the Resolution of the Council of 30 November 2009 on a *Roadmap for strengthening procedural rights of suspected or accused persons in criminal proceedings* (currently at its third stage).[10]

3 Right to Participation, Information and Support in Criminal Proceedings

Right to participation of victims in criminal proceedings and their protection against harm that may derive from the same proceedings represent the core issue of the Directive, whereas information and support provide the necessary instruments for the effectiveness of participation and protection.

---

[7] Civello Conigliaro (2012), p. 1 ff.

[8] Canzio et al. (2010), pp. 255 ff.

[9] Venturoli (2012), p. 112. See also Eusebi (2013), p. 527, who underlines the trend of substantive criminal law to favor preventive protection.

[10] The first step has been reached with the adoption of Directive 2010/64/EU on the right to interpretation and translation in criminal proceedings, OJ L-280, p. 1, of 26 October 2010. For a comment on this Directive, see Rafaraci (2011), p. 124; Gialuz (2013), p. 227. The other step has been reached with Directive 2012/13/EU on the right to information in criminal proceedings, OJ L-142, p. 1, of 1 June 2012. The third step has been reached with the Directive 2013/48/EU on the right of access to a lawyer in criminal proceedings and on the right to communicate upon arrest, OJ L-294, p. 1, of 6 November 2013.

Participation implies various rights that rely on national legislation. The key provision on participation is Article 10, which reproduces Article 3(1) of the FD: the victim is granted the right to be heard during criminal proceedings and to provide evidence. However, it is made clear in the Directive that the applicable procedural rights are the national ones. This is a reserve in favor of national legislation in line with the interpretation of the FD given by the Court of Justice in the *Katz* case. During criminal proceedings initiated by the victim in Hungary, the judge denied the victim the possibility to be heard as a witness since the prohibition that inhibits the public prosecutor from testifying must be applied to the private prosecutor too. The Court of Justice affirmed that the FD is to be interpreted as not obliging a national court to permit the victim to be heard as a witness in criminal proceedings instituted by a substitute private prosecution. However, in the absence of such a possibility, it must be possible for the victim to be permitted to give testimony, which can be taken into account as evidence.[11] Thus, the right of the victim to be heard—the core of the guarantee of participation—is of procedural nature.

In another case concerning the interpretation of the FD, the Court of Justice stated that the FD must be interpreted as not precluding the mandatory imposition of an injunction to stay away for a minimum period, provided for as an ancillary penalty by the criminal law of a Member State, on persons who commit crimes of violence within the family, even when the victims of those crimes oppose the application of such a penalty. This implies that the right to be heard does not grant the victim any power to influence the assessment of the penalty and its *quantum*. In the same case, the Court specified that Member States, having regard to the particular category of offenses committed within the family, can exclude recourse to mediation in all criminal proceedings relating to such offenses. Thus, the victim does not derive from the EU measure (the then FD and the current Directive) any prerogative affecting substantive criminal law.[12]

Anyway, private prosecution is a possibility that can be granted only according to national legislation. Domestic law is also relevant in relation to the right of the victim to ask for a review of the decision not to prosecute: the procedural rules for such a review shall be determined by national law (Art. 11). Also, the right to obtain a decision on compensation by the offender in the course of criminal proceedings, within a reasonable time, is granted except where, in certain cases, national law provides for such a decision to be made in other legal proceedings (Art. 16).

Under the Directive, participation is rightly considered as to include also the access to restorative justice services. On this issue, Art. 12 is more detailed than the corresponding provision under the FD (Art. 10): relevance is given to the measures that Member States shall take to safeguard the victim from secondary and repeat victimization, from intimidation and from retaliation. It is also required to verify the

---

[11] C-404/07, Katz, 9 September 2008.

[12] C-483/09 and C-1/110, Gueye and Sànchez, 15 September 2011. See Luparia (2012), pp. 50–51; and Vozza (2011), p. 1.

interest of the victim to restorative justice services and that the victim is provided with full and unbiased information about the relevant process and the potential outcomes, as well as information about the procedures for supervising the implementation of any agreement.

The right to understand and to be understood (Art. 3), the right to receive information from the first contact with a competent authority (Art. 4), the right to receive (or not) information about the case (Art. 6), the right to interpretation and translation (Art. 7) are some of the most important safeguards for participation to criminal proceedings.

On the other hand, the right to access victim support services (Art. 8) and support from victim support services (Art. 9), to be granted before, during and after criminal proceedings, are meant to protect the victim regardless of the proceedings, on the basis of elementary obligations of social solidarity.[13]

4 Right to Protection in the Proceedings

Right to protection is provided under Chapter 4 of the Directive. Under Art. 18, Member States shall ensure that measures are available to protect victims and their family members from secondary and repeat victimization, from intimidation and from retaliation, including against the risk of emotional or psychological harm, and to protect the dignity of victims during questioning and when testifying. When necessary, such measures shall also include procedures established under national law for the physical protection of victims and their family members. This kind of measures may have a criminal or noncriminal nature and may be applied both during the pretrial phase and after the sentence. Directive 2011/99/EU on the European protection order[14] deals with measures of criminal nature: mutual recognition applies to protection measures adopted by national judges in favor of victims, or potential victims, of crimes.[15]

As far as protection against secondary victimization is concerned, the key provisions of the Directive are those regarding protection of victims that have specific protection needs. The FD already outlined this category of victims, also dealt with by Council of Europe Recommendation Rec(2006)8 of the Committee of Ministers on assistance to crime victims and by other specific measures adopted at EU and international levels relating to repression of very serious crimes, in particular

[13] See Recommendation Rec(2006) of the Committee of Ministers to Member States. See also Gialuz (2012), p. 75.

[14] Camaldo (2012), p. 16.

[15] The application of the principle of mutual recognition to protection orders of noncriminal nature is the objective of a proposal for a Regulation on mutual recognition of protection measures in civil matters [COM(2011) 276 final], according to measure C of the *Roadmap for strengthening the rights and protection of victims, in particular in criminal proceedings*, annexed to Resolution of the Council of 10 June 2011.

Directive 2011/36/EU on preventing and combating trafficking in human beings and protecting its victims (replacing the FD 2002/629/JHA)[16] and Directive 2011/93/EU on combating the sexual abuse and sexual exploitation of children and child pornography (replacing the FD 2004/68/JHA).[17]

It is debated which requirements must be satisfied in order to establish the vulnerability of a victim; in particular, what is debated is whether this *status* must be connected to the personal conditions of the victim (minor age, mental illness, disability) or to the type of crime committed against the victim or to both of these factors, occurring together or separately. Council of Europe Recommendation Re (2006)8 of the Committee of Ministers seems to be oriented towards this last approach. On the other hand, the first version of the Directive (May 2011)[18] adopted a different approach. First of all, two couples of categories of victims were *a priori* singled out, on the basis of personal conditions and objective factors (child victims and disable people and victims of sexual abuse and trafficking of human beings). Second, an individual assessment was foreseen, in consideration that the reaction of victims to crime can markedly vary according to specific conditions and the circumstances of crime so that victims not included in the given categories may have been considered vulnerable. In the final text of the Directive, presented on 21 June 2012, this approach has been changed and the individual assessment on a case-by-case basis has become more relevant, so as to avoid the risk of discrimination against those people with particular personal conditions.

Currently, the only *a priori* category of victims subjected to special protection is that of child victims, whereas the heading "vulnerable victims" is no longer used in favor of the heading "victims with specific protection needs." In relation to this ample category of victims, Chapter 4 of the Directive establishes a procedure for the recognition of specific protection needs, which relies on an individual assessment in order to verify the *an* and the *quantum* of specific protection measures, additional to the general protection measures provided to any victim of crime.

Under the framework of the general protection measures, Article 19 establishes the right to avoid contact between victims and their family members, where necessary, and the offender within premises where criminal proceedings are conducted, unless the criminal proceedings require such contact [Art. 8(3) of the FD provided the same]. Article 20 requires that, without prejudice to the rights of the defense and in accordance with rules of judicial discretion, Member States shall ensure that during criminal investigations victims do not incur in the risk of secondary victimization and that their dignity is safeguarded. To these ends, interviews of victims must be conducted without unjustified delay after the

---

[16] For an analysis of the Directive, see Spiezia and Simonato (2011), p. 3197.

[17] Cfr. Verri (2012), p. 1; Camaldo (2012), p. 16. In the institutional framework of the Council of Europe, for the protection of children against sexual crimes, it has been adopted the Convention on the Protection of Children against Sexual Exploitation and Sexual Abuse (signed in Lanzarote, 25 October 2007). In Italy, this Convention has been ratified by Law 172/2012. For a comment on this Law, see Peccioli (2013), pp. 140 f.; and Tribisonna (2013), pp. 270 f.

[18] COM(2011) 275 final. See De Amicis (2011).

complaint with regard to a criminal offense has been made to the competent authority; the number of interviews of victims must be kept to a minimum, and interviews must be carried out only where strictly necessary for the purposes of the criminal investigation; victims may be accompanied by their legal representative and a person of their choice, unless a reasoned decision has been made to the contrary; medical examinations must be kept to a minimum and must be carried out only where strictly necessary for the purposes of the criminal proceedings.

Under the framework of the general protection measures, Article 21(1) guarantees the right to protection of privacy, including personal characteristics of the victim taken into account in the individual assessment and images of victims and of their family members. Where the victim is a child, Member States ensure that competent authorities may take all lawful measures to prevent public dissemination of any information that could lead to the identification of the child victim.[19]

5 Victims with Specific Protection Needs: Individual Assessment and Special Measures

The list of protection rights granted to victims is short and flexible. However, the individual assessment—potentially applicable to any victim—is directed to identify, in the single case, specific protection needs.

This procedure is ruled under Article 22. Paragraph 1 affirms that Member States shall ensure that victims receive a timely and individual assessment, in accordance with national procedures, to identify specific protection needs and to determine whether and to what extent they would benefit from special measures in the course of criminal proceedings, due to their particular vulnerability to secondary and repeat victimization, to intimidation and to retaliation. Paragraph 2 affirms that the individual assessment shall, in particular, take into account (a) the personal characteristics of the victim, (b) the type or nature of the crime and (c) the circumstances of the crime. This implies that the assessment stems from a reversed representation of the committed crime, where the point of view is the one of the victim rather than the one of the author of the crime.

The need to take into consideration both objective and personal conditions is confirmed by paragraph 3 of Article 22, where it is made clear that, in the context of the individual assessment, particular attention shall be paid to victims who have suffered considerable harm due to the severity of the crime; victims who have suffered a crime committed with a bias or discriminatory motive that could, in particular, be related to their personal characteristics; victims whose relationship to and dependence on the offender make them particularly vulnerable. In this regard,

[19] Art. 21(2) provides that in order to protect the privacy, personal integrity and personal data of victims, Member States shall, with respect for freedom of expression and information and freedom and pluralism of the media, encourage the media to take self-regulatory measures.

victims of terrorism, organized crime, human trafficking, gender-based violence, violence in a close relationship, sexual violence, exploitation or hate crime and victims with disabilities shall be duly considered. The list of the crimes taken into consideration is far from being a closed list and does not affect the *ad hoc* assessment, which is not precluded for different types of crime. This approach is to be welcomed because it allows flexibility to its maximum extent, and therefore it guarantees the best possible protection while preventing from abstract discrimination relating to personal conditions of victims. This approach is opportune even if it risks raising some doubts concerning uncertainty of protection when the assessment is particularly strict.[20] Only where victims are children does this risk not exist, since a presumption of existence of specific needs of protection concerning child victims is given, even though the evaluation of the actual specific needs is left to the individual assessment anyway.

The victim is not a passive object of the assessment: according to Article 22(6), individual assessments shall be carried out with the close involvement of the victims and shall take into account their wishes, including where they do not wish to benefit from the special measures provided. This leads to a system where the victim can waive his right to special protection measures even where he has been found to be vulnerable, on the basis of the recognition of the right to self-determination.[21]

Special measures are listed under Article 23, which draws a distinction between different stages of criminal proceedings. During criminal investigations, the available special measures are (a) interviews with the victim being carried out in premises designed or adapted for that purpose, (b) interviews with the victim being carried out by or through professionals trained for that purpose,[22] (c) all interviews with the victim being conducted by the same persons unless this is contrary to the good administration of justice, (d) all interviews with victims of sexual violence, gender-based violence or violence in close relationships, unless conducted by a prosecutor or a judge, being conducted by a person of the same sex as the victim, if the victim so wishes, provided that the course of the criminal proceedings will not be prejudiced. During court proceedings, the available special measures are (a) measures to avoid visual contact between victims and offenders, including during the giving of evidence, by appropriate means, including the use of communication technology; (b) measures to ensure that the victim may be heard in the courtroom without being present, in particular through the use of appropriate

[20] Gialuz (2012), pp. 71–73.

[21] Gialuz (2012), p. 78.

[22] Art. 25 of the Directive specifically addresses the need of training of practitioners. Also, Art. 5 of the Council of Europe Convention on the Protection of Children against Sexual Exploitation and Sexual Abuse (see *sub* note nr. 17) addresses the need of recruitment, training and awareness raising of persons working in contact with children. In line with this provision, the Italian law implementing the Convention emended the Italian Code of Criminal Procedure so as to require that psychologists and psychiatrics take part in interviews of children also during investigations. See Tribisonna (2013), p. 273.

communication technology; (c) measures to avoid unnecessary questioning concerning the victim's private life not related to the criminal offense; and (d) measures allowing a hearing to take place without the presence of the public.

These measures are not new to national judicial systems, which already provide for these types of measures, in certain cases in a more fragmented way (this is the case of the Italian criminal procedure). Nonetheless, the merit of the Directive lies in the possibility to apply these measures to any victim with specific needs of protection.

6 Additional Measures for Child Victims: Video Recording of Interviews

The list of additional measures for child victims, as provided by Article 24, is quite short in consideration that these victims can already benefit from the measures provided for any other victims with specific needs of protection. However, one measure in the list is of great importance: in criminal investigations, all interviews with the child victim may be audiovisually recorded, and such recorded interviews may be used as evidence in criminal proceedings [Art. 24(1)(a)]. This measure is particularly relevant because video recording of interviews helps in preventing misuse of audition of children, especially when the crime at issue is sexual abuse. This is a useful instrument both for the protection of the victim that must be interviewed according to specific protocols and for the cognizance in the proceedings, where reliability and completeness in the documentation of evidence is of utmost important.

The most sensitive issue concerns the possibility to use such interviews as evidence. It remains, however, that the procedural rules for the audiovisual recordings and—most importantly—their use as evidence are determined by national law [Art. 24(1)]. It must be borne in mind that, while video recording may guarantee more transparency, it does not eliminate the limit of interviews carried out without the person being cross-examined by the defense. Under the Italian criminal procedure, according to Article 111(4) and (5) of the Constitution, this is a limit that results in negative consequences for the use of interviews as evidence.

However, the European Court of Human Rights has emphasized the importance of audiovisual recording for the protection of the victim: starting from the *Doorson* ruling,[23] the Court has constantly affirmed that, where necessary, fair trial is the balance between the rights of the defendant and the rights of the victim. Nonetheless, the same Court has stated that the showing of audiovisual recordings is not enough for the fairness of the trial. What is necessary is that the defense has had the chance to address questions to the interviewed person either directly or through a

[23] ECHR, 26 March 1996, Doorson v. Netherlands. More recently, see ECHR, GC, 15 December 2001, Al-Khawaja and Tahery v. United Kingdom.

third person or via the use of appropriate communication technology.[24] Indeed, the Court applies the well-established rule according to which fair trial demands that during the proceedings, at any stage, the defense must have had at least one chance to cross-examine the person earlier interviewed *inaudita altera parte*.[25] This is a sort of deferred cross-examination, less strict than the cross-examination during court proceedings, as expressly required under the Italian criminal procedure.

7 Final Remarks

The Directive does not go beyond these limits. The provision concerning audiovisual recordings and their use as evidence is embedded in a context where the adoption of protection measures, both general and special, expressly preserves defense rights (Arts. 18, 20, 23). As already underlined above, Article 24(1) is clear when making a reservation in favor of the application of national law, a reservation that can be found in other provisions of the Directive, granting Member States a certain margin of discretion.

Of course, this margin of discretion is given in consideration of the diversity between legal tradition and national criminal procedural systems. It is given also to allow the Court of Justice to better mediate in the interpretation of the Directive. Indeed, it is worth recalling what we have already mentioned[26]: especially in the most recent case law, the Court of Justice has avoided supporting interpretations that cannot be definitely grounded in the relevant EU measure.[27]

[24] ECHR, 28 September 2010, A.S. v. Finland; ECHR, 27 April 2009, A.L. v. Finland; ECHR, 24 September 2007, W.S. v. Poland; ECHR, 10 February 2006, Bocos-Cuesta c. Netherlands.

[25] On the issue of anonymous or vulnerable witnesses, see Balsamo and Recchione (2008), pp. 319 f. and 323 f.

[26] See above Sect. 3.

[27] C-507/10, Bernardi, 21 December 2011. Following a stricter approach than the one followed under the Pupino case, and emphasizing the margin of discretion left to national legislation, the Court of Justice has affirmed that Arts. 2, 3 and 8(4) of FD 2001/220/JHA on the standing of victims in criminal proceedings must be interpreted as not precluding provisions of national law, such as Articles 392(1a), 398(5a) and 394 of the Italian Code of Criminal Procedure, which, first, do not impose on the Public Prosecutor any obligation to apply to the competent court so that a victim who is particularly vulnerable may be heard and give evidence under the arrangements of the *incidente probatorio* during the investigation phase of criminal proceedings and, second, do not give to that victim the right to bring an appeal before a court against that decision of the Public Prosecutor rejecting his or her request to be heard and to give evidence under those arrangements.

References

Allegrezza S (2012) La riscoperta della vittima nella giustizia penale europea. In: Allegrezza S, Belluta H, Gialuz M, Luparia L (eds) Lo scudo e la spada. Giappichelli, Torino

Amalfitano C (2011) L'azione dell'Unione europea per la tutela delle vittime di reato. Diritto dell'Unione europea 3:643–682

Balsamo A (2008) La persona giuridica non riveste la qualità di vittima. Cassazione penale 2:778–783

Balsamo A, Recchione S (2008) La protezione della persona offesa tra Corte europea, Corte di Giustizia delle Comunità europee e carenze del nostro ordinamento. In: Balsamo A, Kostoris R (eds) Giurisprudenza europea e processo penale italiano. Giappichelli, Torino

Camaldo L (2012) Novità sovranazionali. Processo penale e giustizia 2:16–20

Canzio G, Rafaraci T, Recchione S (2010) La tutela della vittima nel sistema penale della giustizia. Opinioni a confronto. Criminalia 1:255–299

Civello Conigliaro S (2012) La nuova normativa europea a tutela delle vittima da reato. Una prima lettura della direttiva 2012/29/UE del Parlamento europeo e del Consiglio. Diritto penale contemporaneo. www.penalecontemporaneo.it. Accessed 22 Nov 2012

De Amicis G (2011) Proposta di direttiva del Parlamento europeo e del Consiglio che istituisce norme minime relative alle vittime di reato (COM (2011) 275 final del 18 maggio 2001) e proposta di regolamento del Parlamento europeo e del consiglio relativo al riconoscimento. Diritto penale contemporaneo. www.penalecontemporaneo.it. Accessed 14 June 2011

Eusebi L (2013) La risposta al reato e il ruolo della vittima. Diritto penale e processo 5:527–531

Gialuz M (2012) Lo statuto europeo delle vittime vulnerabili. In: Allegrezza S, Belluta H, Gialuz M, Luparia L (eds) Lo scudo e la spada. Giappichelli, Torino

Gialuz M (2013) La lingua come diritto: il diritto alla interpretazione e traduzione nel processo penale. In: Ruggieri F, Rafaraci T, Di Paolo G, Marcolini S, Belfiore R (eds) Processo penale, lingua e Unione europea. Cedam, Padova

Luparia L (2005) Una recente decisione della Corte di giustizia sull'allargamento delle ipotesi di audizione del minore in incidente probatorio. Cassazione penale 11:3541–3545

Luparia L (2012) Quale posizione per la vittima nel modello processuale italiano? In: Allegrezza S, Belluta H, Gialuz M, Luparia L (eds) Lo scudo e la spada. Giappichelli, Torino

Manes V (2006) L'incidenza delle "decisioni-quadro" sull'interpretazione in materia penale: profili di diritto sostanziale. Cassazione penale 3:1150–1164

Manes V, Sgubbi F (eds) (2007) L'interpretazione conforme al diritto comunitario in materia penale. Bononia University Press, Bologna

Peccioli A (2013) La riforma dei reati di prostituzione minorile e pedopornografia. Diritto penale e processo 2:140–150

Rafaraci T (2011) Il diritto di difesa nelle procedure di cooperazione giudiziaria nel contesto dell'Unione europea. In: Rafaraci T (ed) La cooperazione di polizia e giudiziaria nell'Unione europea dopo il Trattato di Lisbona. Giuffrè, Milano

Spiezia F, Simonato M (2011) La prima direttiva Ue di diritto penale sulla tratta degli esseri umani. Cassazione penale 9:3197–3215

Tribisonna F (2013) Le modifiche al codice di procedura penale: regole processuali più severe per l'imputato e maggiore tutela del minore. Diritto penale e processo 3:269–278

Venturoli M (2012) La tutela della vittima nelle fonti europee. Diritto penale contemporaneo 3–4:86–113

Verri A (2012) Contenuto ed effetti (attuali e futuri) della direttiva 2011/93/UE. Diritto penale contemporaneo. www.penalecontemporaneo.it. 28 Mar 2012

Vozza D (2011) La "saga" della giurisprudenza europea sulla tutela della vittima nel processo penale continua con la sentenza Guye. Diritto penale contemporaneo. www.penalecontemporaneo.it. 8 Nov 2011

Part V
Developments in European Criminal Procedure Law and Their Influence on Domestic Legal Systems: The Italian Perspective

The Influence of the Directive 2012/13/EU on the Italian System of Protection of the Right to Information in Criminal Procedures

Giuseppina Laura Candito

Contents

Abstract After a brief analysis of the scope of Directive 2012/13/EU, this paper addresses its impact on the Italian system in order to examine the effectiveness and adequacy of the guarantees provided for the accused by Italian procedural law compared to EU legislation and Strasbourg case law. The study reveals the difficulties of the Italian procedural system, which despite its accusatorial approach is still searching for an effective balance between investigative needs and rights of the suspect.

Keywords Completeness of the investigation • Right of defense • Right to information

G.L. Candito (✉)
Department of Law, University of Messina, Piazza Pugliatti No. 1, 98100 Messina, Italy
e-mail: giusylaura.candito@libero.it

S. Ruggeri (ed.), *Human Rights in European Criminal Law*,
DOI 10.1007/978-3-319-12042-3_12

Abbreviations

CCP-Italy	Italian Code of Criminal Procedure
Const.-Italy	Italian Constitution
CP-Italy	Italian Penal Code
D.l.	Decree-Law
D.lgs.	Legislative Decree
ECHR	European Convention on Human Rights
ECtHR	European Court of Human rights
EU FRCh	Charter of Fundamental Rights of the European Union
ICCPR	International Covenant on Civil and Political Rights
OJEU	Official Journal of the European Union

1 Introduction

The Directive 2012/13/EU[1] on the right to information in criminal proceedings is measure B of the Roadmap[2] adopted by the Council on 30 November 2009, aimed at strengthening the rights of suspects and defendants.

The provision of common minimum standards in the field has been advocated[3] by all the European institutions, especially the Commission, which, in fact, highlighted that

> It is not always the case that suspects, and even sometimes the law enforcement officers questioning them, have full knowledge of the relevant rights. If suspects were properly aware of their rights on arrest there would be fewer allegations of miscarriage of justice and violations of the ECHR. [. . .] A simple and inexpensive way to ensure an adequate level of knowledge is to require Member States to produce a short, standard written statement of basic rights: the Letter of Rights.

In light of this, there was first published a Green Paper on the "Procedural safeguards for suspects and defendants in criminal proceedings throughout the European Union,"[4] and the adoption of a Framework Decision was later proposed,[5]

---

[1] Directive 2012/13/EU of the European Parliament and of the Council of 22 May 2012 on the right to information in criminal proceedings published on 1 June 2012, L-142. One of the first comments on the Directive: Ciampi (2012, 2013), p. 21.

[2] Taking a step-by-step approach, the Roadmap called for the adoption of Measures regarding the right to translation and interpretation (measure A); the right to information on rights and information about the charges (measure B); the right to legal advice and legal aid (measure C); the right to communication with relatives, employers, and consular authorities (measure D); and special safeguards for suspects or accused persons who are vulnerable (measure E). The Roadmap emphasizes that the order of the rights is only indicative and thus implies that it may be changed in accordance with priorities.

[3] Cape et al. (2007), p. 3.

[4] COM (2003) 75 def., of 19 February 2003.

[5] COM (2004) 328 def., of 28 April 2004. Dedola (2006), p. 168; Nascimbene (2009), p. 522; Piattoli (2007), p. 549; Rafaraci (2013), p. 331.

which would require all Member States to prepare a Letter of Rights for the suspect, containing a statement of fundamental rights. Despite the interest expressed in this initiative, the text was not approved because of disagreement within the Council. In fact, the laws of the Member States differ from each other, not only on "whether" to recognize those rights but also on "how" to grant such guarantees to the suspect or accused.[6]

However, this setback has not led to a state of definitive paralysis: the protection of the defense rights in criminal proceedings has found new life in the conclusions of the Stockholm Programme.[7] Precisely within this program, the Commission's initiative became concrete, with the issue of the Directive in question, whose deadline for transposition was set for 2 June 2014.

2 The Three Aspects of the Right to Information in Directive 2012/13/EU

In order to properly examine the impact of Directive 2012/13/EU on the Italian system, we need to start by looking at the right to information as outlined in this Directive, emphasizing above all the intrinsic connection with the system of guarantees provided both by the EU FRCH and the ECHR.[8] Pursuant to recital no. 14, the Directive is based on Articles 6, 47, and 48 EU FRCh, as well as on Articles 5 and 6 ECHR as interpreted by the European Court of Human Rights. This is confirmed in the nonregression clause established in Article 10:

> Common minimum rules should lead to increased confidence in the criminal justice systems of all Member States, which, in turn, should lead to more efficient judicial cooperation in a climate of mutual trust. Such common minimum rules should be established in the field of information in criminal proceedings.

Regarding the scope of application, the references in Article 2 to the person under investigation and to the proceedings shows that the European legislature is concerned with the most sensitive aspect of the right to information, that concerning the pretrial phase.[9]

[6] COM (2010) MEMO/10/351 of 20/07/2010: "the way suspects are informed of various fair trial rights depends on what country they are in: a suspect will be told of their right to interpretation orally in Belgium, in writing in Hungary and through a Letter of Rights in Germany." Moreover, not all the states "tell suspects about their right to remain silent."

[7] Programme approved on 10–11 December 2009 and published in the OJEU, 4 May 2010, C-115, p. 1. Confalonieri (2010), p. 75.

[8] Chiavario (2001), p. 195.

[9] Article 2(1) provides that "This Directive applies from the time persons are made aware by the competent authorities of a Member State that they are suspected or accused of having committed a criminal offence until the conclusion of the proceedings, which is understood to mean the final determination of the question whether the suspect or accused person has committed the criminal offence, including, where applicable, sentencing and the resolution of any appeal."

The right to information is then given three different meanings: the right to information on rights, the right to information on the accusation and the right to access materials of the case.

2.1 *The Letter of Rights*

As regards the first aspect, Article 3 states that

> Member States shall ensure that suspects or accused persons are provided promptly with information concerning at least the following procedural rights, as they apply under national law, in order to allow for those rights to be exercised effectively:
>
> (a) the right of access to a lawyer;
> (b) any entitlement to free legal advice and the conditions for obtaining such advice;
> (c) the right to be informed of the accusation, in accordance with article 6;
> (d) the right to interpretation and translation;
> (e) the right to remain silent.

The provision, although it recognizes a core of rights open to subsequent supplementation, as evidenced by the phrase "at least," lends itself to two criticisms. Foremost, the use of the adverb "promptly" could cause differences regarding the timing of providing information, such as to suggest the provision of a mandatory term. In this regard, an important indication comes from recital no. 19, which sets the first formal interview as the deadline for providing such information. A further obstacle to the effectiveness of such rights may come from the reserve of national law: it is clear that by granting the right to information on rights in the manner and within the time limits of domestic law, the impact of harmonization would be greatly weakened.

Having made this premise, we need to dwell on the extent of the rights granted to suspects and accused persons. Among these, the first to be raised is the right of access to a lawyer. The indispensability of qualified defense in a criminal trial has been repeatedly reaffirmed by the European Court of Human Rights,[10] which deems it necessary for the suspect to be given the possibility to defend himself and to benefit from technical assistance. For example, the Court has stated that

> a person charged with a criminal offence who does not wish to defend himself in person must be able to have a recourse to legal assistance of his own choosing; if he does not have sufficient means to pay for such assistance, he is entitled under the Convention to be given it free when the interests of justice so require.[11]

[10] Marzaduri (1997), p. 272.

[11] ECtHR, 25 April 1983, Pakelli v. Federal Republic of Germany, Application no. 8398/78. Mowbray (2004), p. 117.

The guarantee of technical assistance has recently been codified in Directive 2013/48/EU,[12] whose scope, in following that of Directive 2012/13/EU, ranges from the time that one is informed he is under investigation until the conclusion of the proceedings, including, if applicable, sentencing and any appeals. Member States ensure access to defense counsel as soon as possible and in any event prior to the start of any questioning, when procedural actions are performed relating to the collection of evidence, which require the presence of the suspect or accused person, and in any case as soon as the suspect is deprived of his liberty. Any departures from these rules may be justified only if they are supported by the need to avert serious adverse consequences for the life or physical integrity of a person, may not be based on the type or severity of the offense, must not go beyond what is necessary, should be limited as far as possible in time, and, finally, must not affect the fairness of the proceedings.

If the suspect or the accused person has made any self-incriminating statements without being guaranteed the right of access to counsel, the Directive, in line with the consistent case law of the Strasbourg Court,[13] lays down that such statements are unusable. Without prejudice to the provisions of domestic law, it is of particular importance that the suspect or accused may waive the assistance of counsel, provided that he has received prior legal advice on the consequences of such a waiver and that this is clear and unambiguous.

The protection of foreign-language speakers is provided under Directive 2010/64/EU,[14] with which the European legislature implemented measure A of the Roadmap.

This minimum core is supplemented by the additional guarantees provided for under Art. 4(2) if the person is subject to arrest or detention within the meaning of Framework Decision 2002/584/JHA. The distinguishing feature of this provision is the way it enables the lawfulness of an arrest to be challenged, a detention order to be reviewed or an application for bail to be made.

2.2 The Right to Information About the Accusation

Regarding the second aspect, article 6 establishes the right to information about the accusation, a term that, as specified in recital no. 14, is used to describe the same concept expressed in Article 6(1) ECHR. Member States must ensure that suspects or accused persons are provided with all the information about the nature and legal

[12] Directive 2013/48/EU of 22 November 2013 on the right of access to a lawyer in criminal proceedings and in European arrest warrant proceedings, and on the right to have a third party informed upon deprivation of personal liberty and to communicate with third persons and with consular authorities while deprived of liberty. See Bachmaier Winter, in this book. As for the impact of the Directive on the Italian system, see Arasi, in this book.

[13] ECtHR, 14 October 2010, Brusco v. France, Application no. 1466/07.

[14] Morgan (2011), p. 11.

classification of the offense that they are suspected or accused of having committed. These guarantees must be ready no later than the time when the merits of the charge are submitted for examination by the judicial authorities, in order to ensure fair proceedings and the effective exercise of defense rights.

If, in the course of the investigation, there occur changes in the terms of the accusation such as to substantially affect the position of the suspects or accused persons, this must be communicated in due course.[15] This specification reflects the most recent Strasbourg case law, whereby

> any differences in the legal classification of the offence, if not the subject of an adversarial procedure, constitutes a violation of Article 6(3)(a) of the Convention.[16]

As noted with reference to the Letter of Rights, the failure to establish a deadline by which to provide information about the accusation means the risk of an illusory protection, a risk even more exacerbated, in this context, by the suspect's inability to exercise a defensive strategy that actually affects the decisions of the prosecution. In fact, only by having a reasonable time could the suspect and his lawyer have access to the file, submit documents, carry out defense investigations, and offer a different reconstruction of the alleged facts. As clarified by the European Court:

> the right to an adversarial process, as required by Article 6 of the Convention, means that both the prosecution and the defence must be given the opportunity to have knowledge of and comment on the observations made and evidence presented by the other.[17]

In this perspective, the wording of Article 6 of the Directive could undermine the primary objective of the harmonizing provision, namely to ensure the fairness of the proceedings.

2.3 *The Right of Access to the Materials of the Case*

Finally, as regards the right of access to the materials of the case, this extends to all the evidence in the possession of the competent authorities, both that supporting innocence and that supporting guilt.[18] For the purposes of the effective exercise of the right to defense, this must be granted in due time, at the latest when the merits of the accusation are submitted to the judgement of a court.

---

[15] Thus reads the recital no. 29, taken up in Article 6(4).

[16] ECtHR, 11 December 2007, Drassich v. Italy, Application no. 25575/04. In this respect, see Quattrocolo (2009), p. 343 and Zacchè (2009), p. 781. Along the same lines, see also ECtHR, 19 December 2006, Mattei v. France, Application no. 34043/02; ECtHR, 20 April 2006, I.H. v. Austria, Application no. 42780/98; in this regard, see De Matteis (2008), p. 224.

[17] ECtHR, 1 June 2006, Fodale v. Italy, Application no. 70148/01.

[18] Cf. recital no. 30, which states that "Documents and, where appropriate, photographs, audio and video recordings, which are essential to challenging effectively the lawfulness of an arrest or detention of suspects or accused persons in accordance with national law, should be made available to suspects or accused persons or to their lawyers [. . .]."

Denials or restrictions on the exhibition of a document must be duly justified and weighed in relation to the rights of defense of the suspected or accused person, taking into account the various stages of criminal proceedings. Article 7(4) provides that access may be refused if this

> may lead to a serious threat to the life or the fundamental rights of another person or if such refusal is strictly necessary to safeguard an important public interest, such as in cases where access could prejudice an ongoing investigation or seriously harm the national security of the Member State in which the criminal proceedings are instituted.

Against a decision to deny the right of access, Article 7 expressly provides that Member States should grant remedies under domestic law. However, the efficiency and effectiveness of such a provision should be reconsidered in the light of recital no. 36, under which such a right does not entail the obligation to provide for a specific or separate appeal procedure or mechanism with which to challenge a failure or refusal to allow access. Beyond the limits established by recital no. 36, the provisions governing access are sketchy even where they do not provide any remedy in the event of inaction by the competent authority.

3 The Right to Information and Defense Guarantees: The System of Italian Procedural Law and the Possible Impact of the EU Directive

The obligation to transpose the Directive at the national level now leads us to question the status of national legislation and to suggest interpretative approaches that can ensure conformation with European Union law without undermining the roots of the procedural system. The analysis then follows the lines of the tripartite division of the right to information resulting from the Directive, namely the right to information about rights, the right to information about the accusation, and finally the right to access the evidence, also acknowledging the changes contained in the draft legislative decree implementing the Directive currently under examination.[19] Through this scheme, which consists of four articles, the Government aims to amend some provisions of the Code of Criminal Procedure and Law 69/2005, concerning the implementation of the Framework Decision on the EAW (2002/584/JHA), without envisaging express or implied repeals. To summarize the scope of the new directive, it can be said that the national legislature has tried to guarantee the right to information in three ways, respectively, relative to the preliminary investigation, to interim measures, and to arrest and holding for questioning.

[19] Assigned on 1 April 2014 with a deadline of 11 May 2014 to the 2nd Justice Committee, to the 14th Policies Committee of the European Union and to the 5th Budget Committee.

3.1 *Information About Rights (with Specific Reference to the Right of Defense)*

Starting with the letter of rights, Italian procedural regulations are such that they cannot fully conform with what is required by the recent supranational regulation.

In Italy, the main regulatory reference is contained in Article 369-bis of CCP-Italy, introduced by Law 60/2001. Entitled "Informing the person subject to investigation on the right to defence," this provision is intended to ensure the accused—starting with the completion of the first procedural action that the defense counsel is entitled to attend and, in any case, before the request to appear for questioning—information on the compulsory assistance by professional counsel in a criminal trial, the name of the court-appointed counsel and the obligation of his remuneration, the right to appoint his own defense lawyer, and the warning that failure to appoint his own counsel will lead to him being assisted by counsel appointed by the court, as well as on the conditions that may entitle him to legal aid. The rule is based on the assumption, which is a core principle of Italian law, of the essential need for a professional defense, based on the premise that (only) qualified counsel is able to engage in effective debate with the public prosecutor and other parties to the proceedings.[20]

Article 369-bis of CCP-Italy does not however envisage the right to translation and interpretation or the right to silence.[21]

On the first point, the protection of foreign-language speakers is provided for by the rules on the translation of documents, and in particular Article 143 CCP-Italy, in conjunction with Article 111(3) Const.-Italy. Although the Supreme Court had initially supported a more rigid and literal interpretation than that proposed by the Constitutional Court,[22] the principle whereby the suspect's participation in the proceedings should be effective and not purely random has now been well

[20] The Constitutional Court, since the early 1970s, has based its rulings on the premise that qualified counsel must participate in the proceedings. Thus, Constitutional Court decision no. 100/70 declared that the part of Article 304-*bis*(1) 1930 CCP-Italy that excludes the right of the accused to be assisted by counsel during questioning was illegitimate. Cf. Chiavario, (1970), p. 2180; Tonini (1971), p. 1285; Amodio (1972), p. 740. On the issue of self-defense, this possibility is ruled out a priori, not only in cases where the defendant has expressly stated that he does not want to benefit from it (see Constitutional Court, decision no. 125/1979) but even when the person concerned is qualified to practice law. See Court of Cassation, Division II, 16 July 2013, Stara, n. 1890, in www.europeanrights.eu.

[21] ECtHR, 8 February 1996, Murray v. United Kingdom, Application no. Series A-300, in which the European Court stated that the silence of the accused cannot have such adverse consequences that the burden of proof is shifted to the defense, since this would violate the principle of the presumption of innocence.

[22] For a reconstruction of the approach, cf. Court of Cassation, Division I, 3 June 2010, Hassan, in *CED Cass.* no. 247760; Court of Cassation, Division I, 21 October 2009, Yang, in *CED Cass.* no. 245564; Court of Cassation, Division VI, 1 October 2008, Darvina, in *CED Cass.* no. 242227; Court of Cassation, Division I, 20 December 2004, Owusu, in *CED Cass.* no. 230142.

established.[23] This, on the other hand, does not oblige authorities to make copies of every kind of document but rather the need to identify those documents that specifically raise issues crucial to the defense and that as such must be translated.[24] The scope of application thus depends on a functional and not merely formal criterion, so that, as stated by the Supreme Court, the failure to provide translation could result in the invalidity of a judgment only where ignorance of the language prevents the full exercise of the right of defense.

The choice of a functional criterion is in line with the ECtHR, according to which

> Article 6(3(e) does not go so far as to require a written translation of all items of written evidence or official documents in the procedure. The assistance should be such as to enable the defendant to have knowledge of the case against him and to defend himself, notably being able to put before the court his version of the events.[25]

Precisely regarding the provision of Article 143 CCP-Italy,[26] Legislative Decree 32/2014 has implemented[27] the Directive, thus significantly reformulating it. In fact, from the very first paragraph, we may discern the legislature's attempt to implement the "linguistic guarantee" in function of the effective exercise of the right of defense, as can be seen in particular from the interpolation whereby an accused person who does not know the Italian language has

> also the right to free assistance from an interpreter to communicate with his counsel before being questioned, or in order to submit a request or written statement in the course of the proceedings.

Again, the same goal is pursued in the second paragraph, which, in adherence to the principle that the translation is required of all those documents that may affect the position of the accused, provides for the written translation, within a period such

---

[23] Gialuz (2012), p. 433.

[24] Constitutional Court, decision 10/1993, with a note by Lupo (1993), p. 52.

[25] ECtHR, 19 December 1989, Kamasinsky v. Austria, Application Series A no. 168.

[26] The previous wording of Article 143 CCP-Italy was as follows: "1. A defendant who does not know the Italian language has the right to be assisted free of charge by an interpreter in order to understand the charges against him and to take an active role in the proceedings. For Italian citizens, knowledge of the Italian language is presumed unless proven otherwise.

2. In addition to the case referred to in paragraph 1 and Article 119, the investigating authority shall appoint an interpreter when a text in a foreign language or a dialect not easily intelligible needs to be translated, or when a person who wants or is obliged to make a statement does not know Italian. The statement may also be made in writing and in this case is included in the case file together with the interpreter's translation.

3. The interpreter is appointed even when the judge, the prosecutor or the police officer has personal knowledge of the language or dialect requiring interpretation.

4. The performance of interpreting services is mandatory."

[27] The costs involved in translating the proceedings in a criminal trial, however, will be subject, in the 3 years from 2014 to 2016, to a substantial provision of funds, amounting to €6,084,833.36 per annum, from the Revolving Fund provided for under Article 5 of Law 183/1987, which will ensure the availability of additional resources for the purposes of providing information in criminal proceedings involving use of the measure in question.

as to enable the exercise of rights and the right to defense, of documents regarding information on civil rights and defense rights, of precautionary measures, of the notice of the conclusion of the preliminary investigation, of court orders that establish dates for the preliminary hearing, of committal documents, and of documents regarding conviction and sentencing.

The breakdown of this list is not to be considered exhaustive, since the third paragraph acknowledges the right time regarding both the initiative of a party and the order of the court to grant free translation of other documents or even solely of parts of them, considered essential for enabling the defendant to know the charges against him. The acknowledgment of this possibility moreover seems to be confirmed by the fact that refusal to do so can be appealed against, together with the judgment.

Directly related to the reform of Article 143 CCP-Italy is also the introduction in Article 104 CCP-Italy[28] of an additional paragraph, 4-*bis*, which establishes that

> A defendant in custody, a person arrested or held for questioning, who does not speak Italian, has the right to the free assistance of an interpreter in order to confer with his lawyer in accordance with the preceding paragraphs.

Critically, however, we may see that the urgent nature of these procedural situations makes the problem of ascertaining the lack of knowledge of Italian by the person deprived of personal freedom particularly complex. The new regulation does not specify, in fact, whether the notion of "lack of knowledge," for the purpose of acknowledging the right to a translator or interpreter, should also include a level of knowledge sufficient to allow the defendant to follow the proceedings or understand, but not the ability to express himself except for with great difficulty.[29]

As to the right to remain silent,[30] there is no doubt that the principle of not being obliged to incriminate oneself comes into play from the investigation stage onwards. Significantly, Article 64 CCP-Italy in outlining the basic rules of questioning,[31] provides that the accused person should be expressly warned of his right not to answer any questions; otherwise, any statements he makes may be considered unusable.

---

[28] The wording of Article 104 CCP-Italy is as follows: "1. The accused person in custody has the right to meet with his lawyer from the moment of enforcement of the measure.

2. The person arrested *in flagrante delicto* or detained in accordance with Article 384 has the right to meet with his lawyer immediately after arrest or detention.

3. In the course of the preliminary investigation, when there are specific and exceptional reasons for caution, the court at the request of the public prosecutor may, by means of a motivated order, defer, for a period not exceeding five days, the exercise of the right to meet with the lawyer.

4. In the event of arrest or detention, the power provided for in paragraph 3 may be exercised by the prosecutor up to the time when the arrested or detained person appears in court."

[29] See the Report of the Office of the Maxims Archive of the Court of Cassation on Legislative Decree 32/2014, concerning the right to interpretation and translation in criminal proceedings. Cf. Gialuz (2014).

[30] Grevi (1972) and Patanè (2006).

[31] Mazza (2004), p. 42.

However, precisely in terms of chronology, the reference in Article 369-*bis* of CCP-Italy to the "completion of the first procedural action which the defence counsel has the right to attend" poses delicate problems in terms of balancing conflicting interests. From the wording of the provision, it clearly emerges that the requirements of confidentiality give way to the benefit of information to the suspect, to an "assisted act," and therefore to a discretionary choice of the prosecution. Thus, it could well happen that the public prosecutor does not intend to complete the procedure and that the subject learns he has been under investigation only at the conclusion of the investigation. As we shall see, the notice of conclusion of the investigation, a link between the investigation phase and that of judgment, contains not only a summary of the laws that have allegedly been broken but also notice of submission of the relative documentation and of the right to examine it, as well as specifying the right within 20 days to submit documents and memoranda and ask to be interviewed. And, regarding the relationship between the two institutions, the case law of the Court of Cassation has clarified that information on defense rights must necessarily precede, under penalty of nullity, the notice of completion of investigations where, during the investigation, no activity which the lawyer should have attended has been carried out.[32]

That said, it is questionable whether the Directive is able to prevent such an eventuality and ensure information during the investigation phase such as to allow the suspect to prepare an adequate defense in view of the contributions that he can make in the final phase of the investigation. In this sense, as noted above, the scope of Article 3 is rather vague, since, by merely requiring that the communication must be provided promptly, it does not establish a deadline, leaving this to be decided by domestic legislation. The failure to provide a term establishing the adoption of a so-called concept of relation reflects the desire to balance the various values involved in the proceedings. Even the European legislature, although viewing defense guarantees as unalienable, prefers "flexible" information requirements, modulated according to the various stages of the proceedings and specificities of each case.

From the point of view of implementation, we can see that the draft Legislative Decree aims to affect the guarantee provided for under Art. 369-*bis*(1)(c) in two respects: with regard to the timing of information, establishing the sending of the notice of the conclusion of the preliminary investigation as the deadline for informing the suspect, and in terms of content, implementing the wording of paragraph d-*bis* of the provision on informing the accused person of his right to an interpreter and to the translation of fundamental documents.

Along the same lines are the amendments made to Article 386 CCP-Italy,[33] which establishes that the police officers who performed the arrest or detention or had the arrested person delivered into their custody must submit to the arrested or

---

[32] Court of Cassation, Division IV, 4 May 2007, no. 22528; Court of Cassation, Division I, 6 February 2008, no. 19174.

[33] Article 386(1) provides in its current wording: "The officers and police officers who made the arrest, enforced detention or had the arrested person delivered into their custody, shall immediately inform the public prosecutor of the place where the arrest or detention was effected. They shall also warn the arrested or detained person of his right to appoint a defence lawyer."

detained person, under penalty of the nullity of subsequent procedural actions, a written communication prepared in a clear and precise form (and for a person who does not speak Italian, this also involves translating it into a language he understands), informing him of all his rights.[34]

Still, there was felt the need to bring the implementing law in line with Framework Decision 2002/584/JHA on the European arrest warrant and the rendition procedures between Member States while also envisaging as part of this the delivery of a written notice, in a clear and precise form, informing the subject of the ad hoc guarantees provided under Article 12.[35]

3.2 *Information About the Accusation*

3.2.1 Foreword: Information on the Accusation and Protection of Procedural Needs

As far as regards information on the accusation, on a methodological level, the transposition of Directive 2012/13/EU is an important opportunity to examine the effectiveness and adequacy of the guarantees provided for the suspect and the accused person by Italian procedural law, compared to EU legislation and Strasbourg case law.

In terms of domestic law, the declaration of the right of defense as "inviolable at every stage and level of the proceedings" in Article 24(2) Const.-Italy is counterbalanced by a codified system that betrays to a large extent its merely civil rights scope. With specific regard to the information in question, however, the constitutional reform of 1999 included in Article 111(3) Const.-Italy a provision that grants all individuals charged with a criminal offense the statutory right to be

---

[34] Namely:

(a) the right to appoint a defence lawyer and to be granted legal aid at state expense when envisaged by law;
(b) the right to receive information on the charge;
(c) the right to an interpreter and to the translation of fundamental documents;
(d) the right to remain silent;
(e) the right to access documents which underpin the arrest or detention;
(f) the right to inform the consular authorities and family members;
(g) the right to emergency medical care;
(h) the right to be brought before judicial authorities for confirmation of the arrest within 96 h of being arrested or detained;
(i) the right to appear before the court to be examined and to appeal to the Supreme Court against the order confirming arrest or detention.

[35] The police officer who carried out the arrest shall inform the person in a language he can understand of the warrant and of its contents, of the possibility of consenting to being handed over to the judicial authority issuing the warrant, of his right to appoint a lawyer of his own choice, and of the right to be assisted by an interpreter.

notified promptly and confidentially of the nature and cause of the charges made against them.

A strictly literal interpretation of the situation resulting from such constitutional provisions might lead us to believe that the suspect must be informed immediately of any investigation against him, in order that he may exercise promptly and at the same time as the investigating body the power to search for and collect evidence. Such a reading appears to be almost obligatory if we are to give a complete meaning, in particular, to the provision contained in Article 111(3). On close examination, we can see that it is bound to protect also the suspect during the investigation prior to the beginning of a trial: on one hand, the person accused is usually informed of the indictment once committal proceedings have begun, while, on the other hand, the requirement of confidentiality arises routinely in the investigation phase but not in the trial.[36] However, this interpretation does not take into adequate account the origin of such a provision, inserted in the Constitution in order to give recognition and constitutional value to a fundamental guarantee contained in the ECHR. It may be useful to point out that, of all the guarantees acknowledged to the person "charged with a criminal offence" in Article 6(3) ECHR, the one in question imposes a burden of detail in terms of the information, extending to the nature of and reasons for the charge, which seems to presuppose the formulation of a formal accusation at a more advanced stage of the proceedings.[37]

On the other hand a model obliging the investigative bodies to inform the suspect only if they establish a precise investigative line, albeit strictly adhering to the charge,[38] does not take into account the antagonistic forces inherent in criminal proceedings.[39] Completeness and authenticity of the investigation, on one hand, and defense prerogatives, on the other, dictate that the process involves a negotiated solution. [40]

As highlighted by the Constitutional Court[41]:

> the principle of the equality of arms does not necessarily imply identity between the procedural powers of the public prosecutor and the accused. In fact, a difference in treatment may be justified, within reason, by the peculiar institutional position of the prosecutor, by his function, and by requirements related to the proper administration of justice.

Thus, the investigative requirement of confidentiality will prevail over the right to defense to the point that it suppresses it,[42] whenever the needs of the

[36] Marzaduri (2002), pp. 164 ff.

[37] Trechsel (2005), p. 722.

[38] Nobili (1998), p. 20.

[39] Ciampi (2010), p. 84.

[40] Caprioli (2007a), p. 250; De Caro (2007), p. 618; Frigo (2007), p. 87.

[41] Constitutional Court, decision no. 432/92; Constitutional Court, decision no. 98/1994; Constitutional Court, decision no. 421/2001; Constitutional Court, decision no. 347/02. In particular, Constitutional Court, decision no. 26/07. For a complete discussion of the principles of criminal procedure illustrated by the Constitutional Court, see Gaeta (2011), p. 48.

[42] Molinari (2009), p. 541.

investigation become dominant. However, precisely the principle of reasonableness requires extension of the right to defense whenever there is an action that will affect the trial stage. The strength of the system thus depends on a diachronic reconstruction of the process, where the individual positions can only be appreciated in terms of the whole.

Precisely in this regard, it is interesting to note the contribution of Strasbourg case law to the abandonment of excessive formalism. In particular, it was responsible for establishing the autonomous notion of accused person,[43] whereby what is important is not the making of the charge but any "official notification given to an individual by the competent authority of an allegation that he has committed a criminal offence."[44]

This can also take place at a time prior to the submission of a formal accusation to the judicial authority: relief measures such as the confirmation of a seizure, a request to come in for questioning, or a request for authorization to proceed thus become significant. It is not necessary for the indictment to be precise and definitive but rather that the document produced or to be produced is in practice such as to possibly affect the position of the subject on the basis of a charge related to a crime.[45] The presumption of innocence also leads to this conclusion, as acknowledged in Italy by Article 27(2) Const.-Italy. There is no doubt that its scope can be appreciated not only in the decision-making moment but also in research activity and the gathering of evidence. Therefore, the defendant must have the opportunity to actively contribute to the reconstruction of the fact with similar powers to those of the prosecution.[46] Nor can this reconstruction be denied by the fact that information should be given "as soon as possible." Also in this case, it is necessary to see the legislation in terms of the dynamics of the proceedings, so that information need not be given immediately, but compatibly with the need for investigative effectiveness.[47]

Ultimately, it can be concluded that the right to information on the charge should be understood not as an inflexible right anchored to a specific stage of the proceedings but rather as a form of protection whose degree of detail varies according to the phase of the investigation and the degree to which the action from time to time in question affects the individual rights of the person subject to criminal proceedings. That said, it must be ascertained whether and to what extent procedural legislation allows such information and in what terms the Directive in question may have an effect. In this regard, domestic legislation proves to be strongly lacking in at least three respects, due to the following factors: (a) the

[43] De Salvia and Zagrebelsky (2006); Letsas (2007), p. 37.

[44] ECtHR, 27 February 1980, Deweer v. Belgium, Application no. series A-35, ECtHR, 19 December 1982, Foti et al. v. Italia, Application no. series A-69, commented in Cassazione Penale 1983, p. 520.

[45] van Dijk and Viering (2006), p. 539; Harris et al. (2009), p. 208.

[46] Illuminati (1979), p. 181.

[47] Tonini (2001), p. 11.

absence of tools aimed at ensuring adequate knowledge of the charge at the preliminary stage, (b) the existence of presumptions that hinder the effective provision of information, (c) the establishment of mechanisms for indirect knowledge of the charge.

3.2.2 Criminal Proceedings and Information Tools Used by the Prosecution

Preliminary Inquiries and Tools for Providing Information on the Charge

The inadequacy of the instruments aimed at allowing the provision of information on the accusation can be seen right from the preliminary investigation stage.

In fact, the Code of Criminal Procedure provides for the possibility of access to the register in which the state prosecutor immediately records every crime report he receives or has acquired of his own initiative and, at the same time or by the time the information is viewable, records the name of the person to whom the crime is attributed (Art. 335 CCP-Italy). This right, however, in addition to being dependent on the impulse of the person who suspects he is being investigated,[48] brings somewhat uncertain results.[49] Indeed, not only is there the risk that the person will apply to an office other than the one that may have started investigations but also that his request remains unanswered. As to the first possibility, applying to the wrong public prosecutor's office is not remedied by automatic transmission of the request to the competent office, a failing that seems somewhat anachronistic. In terms of the latter aspect, the regulation does not provide for any period within which a reply must be given, nor can the 15-day period provided for under Article 121(2) CCP-Italy be deemed to apply.

In addition to these limitations, Article 335 CCP-Italy shows a number of exceptions to disclosure to the interested party of any investigations regarding him. It is thus, mainly, possible that the prosecutor may deny access to the register by making the investigations subject to official confidentiality, due to "needs pertinent to the investigation," a purely formalistic reasoning that makes the limitation of the suspect's rights even more obvious. Even more problematic is the situation in which the registration relates to an offense under Article 407(2)(a) CPP-Italy, for which the possibility of communication is ruled out *a priori* on the basis of the absolute presumption that informing suspects in such cases always puts the needs of the investigation in jeopardy. Moreover, the list of these crimes

[48] Ciampi (2010), p. 238, highlights the alarming situation of an inverse relationship between innocence and opportunities for access.

[49] Giostra (1996), p. 194, talks about this in terms of a "judicial slot machine."

over the years has been applied extensively,[50] since it covers various offenses not so much based on the same legal concept but resulting from the same sense of emergency characterizing recent legislation. A particularly sensitive issue occurs when the request for access is made by a person subjected to investigation for a series of crimes, only for some of which the above prohibition on communication applies, or by a subject accused of a common crime in the context of a procedure in which others happen to be investigated for acts of organized crime.[51]

Finally, one of the most significant problems posed by this provision concerns the absence of any check on the timing of registration, a significant issue given that this is the moment from which the time limit for conclusion of the investigation runs. By leaving the task of registering the crime to the investigating body, there is the risk that this monopoly may become abuse: the prosecutor, violating his duty of fairness and procedural correctness, may temporarily register the notice of crime in the so-called modello 45, a form used to record events that do not constitute criminal offenses, then conduct the investigation and only in the final phase transfer the registration to the so-called modello 21, the form used to record actual crime reports, with the result that the time limit for completion of the investigation will only start to run from that moment.[52]

The injury resulting from any procrastinations *sine die* is exacerbated by the reluctance of the case law of the Court of Cassation, which, in a now consolidated approach, has argued that

> the failure to register does not determine the unusability of the investigative actions performed, since the time limit for completion of the investigation has yet to start running [...] the appreciation of the timeliness of registration in fact falls within the exclusive discretion of the prosecutor and is exempt from review by the court.[53]

The ruling out of any penalty has not affected the positions of the Constitutional Court that, despite the issues of legitimacy raised in Article 335 CCP-Italy, which fails to provide the possibility of backdating the time from which the effects of

---

[50] Having regard to the most recent interventions, we may mention Law Decree 98/2001, converted into Law 196/2001, which included the cases referred to in Articles 270(3) CP-Italy "Subversive associations", 270-*bis*(2) CP-Italy "Associations for the purpose of international terrorism or subversion of the democratic order" and 306(2) CP-Italy "Armed gangs: training and participation" as well as the Law of 11 August 2003, which inserted Articles 600 CP-Italy "Forcing persons to live in a state of slavery or servitude" and 602 CP-Italy "Purchase and sale of slaves."

[51] According to one approach, the prohibition of communication should only apply to the person against whom proceedings have been initiated for one of the offenses referred to in Article 407(2)(a) CCP-Italy, thus having a limited subjective extent, which may not be extended to the other codefendants. Cf. Conti (1995), p. 44; Riviezzo (1995), p. 147. Another line of scholarship argues, however, for a markedly objective interpretation of the provision of Article 335(3) CCP-Italy, seeing it as therefore applicable to all parties involved in an offense under Article 407(2)(a) - CCP-Italy. See D'Ambrosio (1995), p. 1157.

[52] Orlandi (1995), p. 261.

[53] Court of Cassation, Joint Divisions, 24 September 2009, Lattanzi, in *CED Cass*. no. 244376.

registration run, in cases of undue delay or omission, has always ruled that such requests are inadmissible "due to the ambiguity of the claim."[54]

However, while in the absence of an ad hoc sanction, one feels bound to disagree—especially because of the emphasis given to the aspect of timing the supply of information in Directive 2012/13/EU—with the rulings of the Supreme Court and the Constitutional Court. Furthermore, it is possible to show how the negative implications of late registration will have repercussions not only on the effectiveness of the right of defense but also on the principle of reasonable duration of the proceedings.

The procedural system of preliminary investigations does not provide any ways of compensating for the failings in the system of access provided for in Article 335 CCP-Italy. Nor does the right to be informed governed by 369 CCP-Italy seem to fulfill this purpose. Even though this instrument aims to ensure the suspect information on the existence of a criminal investigation against him, the information is subject, similar to what was seen for the information provided for under Article 369-bis of CCP-Italy, to the completion "of an assisted act" and, as far as regards the subject matter, is very limited, since the suspect only has to be informed about the laws allegedly violated. Here it is also possible to highlight a further critical aspect whose implications may be mitigated by transposition of the Directive. Indeed, one often sees a discrepancy between the fact and violations alleged in the indictment and the information contained in the notice given to the suspect. Equally open to criticism is the orientation of case law that rules out any obligation to reiterate the information in cases where, in the course of the investigation, the charge is changed or the criminal act is given a different legal classification. Defense needs would require exactly the opposite, so as to ensure the flow of information and keep the suspect informed of every single change in the situation. In this respect, therefore, we may hope that the adaptation to European regulations puts an end to the practice, widespread in prosecutors' offices, of amending the preliminary charge without at the same time promptly informing the suspect of the fact. This need is envisaged in recital no. 29 of the Directive, taken up in Article 6(4), which provides that

> Where, in the course of the criminal proceedings, the details of the accusation change to the extent that the position of suspects or accused persons is substantially affected, this should be communicated to them where necessary to safeguard the fairness of the proceedings and in due time to allow for an effective exercise of the rights of the defence.

However, the draft Legislative Decree seems to contain nothing of this nature and, toeing the line of minimal compliance, omits any reference to continuity of information. Rather, the legislator, in article 369 CCP-Italy, merely introduces paragraph 1-*bis*, under which

> the public prosecutor shall also inform the person under investigation and the victim of their right to communication provided for under Article 335(3).

The reference to the right of access to the register of crime reports, albeit noteworthy, in that it encourages the performance of an action otherwise left to the discretion of one of the parties, does not seem sufficient to make up for the lack

[54] Constitutional Court, decision no. 306/2005 and Constitutional Court, decision no. 400/2006.

of compliance of this legislation with European standards, since the instrument is, as seen, subject to a number of limitations that make access to the register not only difficult but also pointless.

Conclusion of the Investigation and Information Tools of the Prosecution

The deficiencies of procedural rules with regard to information about the accusation are accentuated in the delicate stage of completion of the investigation and preparation of the formal charge. If the case is dropped, regulations envisage the possibility of the suspect not being informed of the fact that—possibly without his knowledge—criminal investigations regarding him have been carried out and completed, the only exception being when, during the investigations, he has been subjected to coercive measures [Art. 409(1) CCP-Italy]. As for the inverse hypothesis, in which the prosecutor considers it necessary to formulate an indictment, Law 479/1999, by bringing forward the moment of providing information, previously deferred to the time when the prosecutor filed the document containing the charge, introduced the requirement to serve notice of completion of the investigation when the prosecutor considers it necessary to begin committal proceedings.

The notice of conclusion of the investigation is a multifaceted instrument that, in responding to the needs to inform the suspect, contains, primarily, a summary statement of the laws that have allegedly been violated. However, the absence of any requirements as to the degree of specificity of the accusation is at the basis of the practice of so-called crypto-charges, namely generic or alternative charges, in which the prosecutor essentially follows the letter of the criminal law, without specifying the concrete elements of the case.

Since this practice clearly affects the possibility of preparing an effective defense, there has been conflicting case law regarding the procedural consequences of these charges. The case law of the Court of Cassation initially considered that a request for indictment containing a generic or indefinite charge displayed generic so-called intermediate nullity.[55] A different view can be seen in another reconstruction whereby, in the absence of an express provision of law, we may not speak of nullity, since a measure declaring the nullity of the request for trial, and the simultaneous return of the documents to the prosecutor, would be abnormal.[56]

[55] Court of Cassation, Division V, 11 July 2001, Di Lorenzo, in *CED Cass*. no. 220208; Court of Cassation, Division I, 24 October 2003, Guida, in *CED Cass*. no. 229513; Court of Cassation, Division V, 20 May 2004, Fraglia, in *CED Cass*. no. 22884. Intermediate invalidities may be reported *ex officio* or at the request of a party by the expiry date prior to the closing of the instance of judgment to which they relate, and are remediable. These are referred to indirectly under Article 180 CPP-Italy, which includes violations of rules concerning (a) the involvement of the PM in the proceeding; (b) the intervention, assistance, and representation of the accused; (c) the summons of the injured person and the complainant.

[56] Court of Cassation, Division V, 12 December 1991, Cavuoto, in *CED Cass*. no. 189547; Court of Cassation, Division VI, 5 May 1992, Nichele, in *CED Cass*. no. 191347; Court of Cassation, Division I, 17 December 1998, Adamo, in *CED Cass*. no. 212454; Court of Cassation, Division I, 4 April 2003, Esposito, in *CED Cass*. no. 28987 and Court of Cassation, Division VI, 7 October 2004, Romanelli, in *CED Cass*. no. 42011.

Recently, the Joint Sections of the Court of Cassation have adopted the latter approach,[57] stating that the amendment of a charge lacking the requirements of specificity should take place through a "remedy within the phase," that is, through a request to the investigating body to supplement the wording using the instruments referred to in Article 423(1) CCP-Italy. Therefore, only in the case of inertia on the part of the prosecution will recourse be made to the "external remedy," i.e., to the return of documents to the prosecutor, resulting in a regression to the investigation stage. In this case, the prosecutor's office may carry out new surveys, provided, however, that the original or extended term has not yet expired.

Comparing the situation in Italy, both in terms of legislation and case law, with the directive in question, we find a clear discrepancy in relation to Article 6, under which "all information is provided promptly with all necessary details." It is clear that the European legislator prefers a more effective guarantee, insofar as the more detailed the charges are, the greater chance the defense has of conducting relevant investigations and of making an informed decision on whether to ask to be heard.

Starting precisely with Article 1 of the Draft Decree, in the implementation of Articles 4 and 8 of the Directive, this provides for the amendment to article 293 (1) (a) and to article 386 (1)(d) CCP-Italy, in order to introduce into domestic law the requirement of timely delivery of a notice, in writing, aimed at informing the person held or arrested of his rights.[58] Moreover, the new paragraph 1-*bis* clearly lays down that these operations must be recorded in the case file.[59]

---

[57] Court of Cassation, Joint Divisions, 20 December 2007, no. 5307 in www.penale.it.

[58] Article 293(1) CCP-Italy, if reformed, will be formulated as follows:

> The officer or agent with the duty of bringing the person into custody delivers to the accused person, under penalty of the nullity of subsequent procedural actions, a written communication prepared in a clear and precise form, and, for a person who does not speak Italian, translated into a language which he understands, which shall inform him of:
>
> a) the right to appoint a defence lawyer and to be granted legal aid at state expense when envisaged by law;
> b) the right to receive information on the charge;
> c) the right to an interpreter and to the translation of fundamental documents;
> d) the right to remain silent;
> e) the right to access documents which underpin the measure;
> f) the right to inform the consular authorities and family members;
> g) the right to emergency medical care;
> h) the right to be brought before the court no later than 5 days after the start of detention, if the measure applied is that of preventive custody in prison, or not more than ten days if the person is subject to a different precautionary measure;
> i) the right to appear before the court to be examined, to appeal against the custody order and to apply for it to be replaced or revoked.

[59] Paragraph 1-*bis* establishes that "the officer or agent responsible for carrying out the order shall immediately inform the defence lawyer who may been appointed by the accused or assigned *ex officio* in accordance with Article 97, and shall draw up a report of all the operations performed, making mention of delivery of the communication referred to in paragraph 1. The report shall be forwarded immediately to the judge who issued the order and to the prosecutor."

Proceedings by decree lead to even greater tensions with the right of defense.[60] This special procedure, figuratively defined as "condemnation without trial,"[61] is characterized by the fact that the conviction is issued solely on the basis of a request by the public prosecutor, on which the court decides without a hearing and thus without any communication being provided to the subject, who nevertheless as a result of this request formally assumes the role of defendant. In other words, there is no form of information about the accusation either before or at the time it is officialized. This procedure is in fact the only example in procedural law of a charge without service. When convicted, the defendant may react with an appeal aimed at being given the opportunity to take advantage of all the defense opportunities missed.

The postponement of adversarial proceedings, according to consistent case law, regarding both legitimacy[62] and constitutionality,[63] has the task of achieving a balance with the guarantees that should guide a criminal investigation. However, on closer inspection, this is a last-ditch effort to save a procedure whose incompatibility with the Constitution is evident from a comparison with Article 111 Const-Italy, which not only recognizes the adversarial method as a characteristic element of *every* proceeding but, as we have seen, also acknowledges that (*every*) person accused of an offense has the right to be promptly informed of the accusation against him. There is no equality of arms in proceedings in which the suspect is not allowed to have any influence on the decisions of the public prosecutor and where the sentence is issued on the basis of evidence collected unilaterally.[64]

This leads to the need to ensure effective knowledge of the criminal sentence. Thus, the Constitutional Court declared the unconstitutionality of the part of Article 460(4) CCP-Italy that fails to provide for revocation of the criminal court order and the return of documents to the prosecutor also when it is not possible to effect service at the address stated pursuant to Article 161 CCP-Italy. In support of the decision, the Court referred to the intention to

> anchor the system of service to effective knowledge of the criminal court order, so that the addressee is placed in a position to effectively choose between appeal and acceptance.[65]

Moreover, the conviction value of the criminal court order has led the legislature to strengthen defensive tools under Law 60/2001, providing for service of the order on the court-appointed defense lawyer. Along the same lines, we find the ruling of the Constitutional Court that removed any doubt as to the possibility of an independent power to appeal on the part of the court-appointed defense lawyer.[66]

---

[60] Ruggeri (2008), p. 25.

[61] Cordero (2006), p. 235.

[62] Court of Cassation, Division III, 7 July 2000, Capretto, in *CED Cass*. 2000.

[63] Constitutional Court, decision no. 292/4 and Constitutional Court, decision no. 132/03.

[64] Nicolucci (2003), p. 1069.

[65] Constitutional Court, decision no. 504/00.

[66] Constitutional Court, decision no. 55/10.

Upon closer inspection, however, the system of service for convictions by court order is unable to ensure the suspect's effective knowledge of the situation. Nor may the fact that the court-appointed defense lawyer may appeal be seen as supplementary to the various options that should be available to a suspect to participate in the proceedings, since it comes at a time when the criminal proceedings have already run their course and thus represents an aspect of defense "*during* the proceedings" but not also "*from* the proceedings."[67]

3.2.3 Presumptions of Knowledge and the Right of Defense

The guarantee of the accused person's right to be informed leads us to reflect on the adequacy of the system of service of procedural documents, which has regrettably been largely based on a series of legal presumptions, and cannot ensure effective knowledge of the accusation, with evident repercussions on the right of defense.

These presumptions are evident in cases in which the procedural document is delivered at one of the addresses provided for under Articles 159,[68] 161(4),[69] and 169[70] CCP-Italy. In fact, the timely completion of the service procedure does not always correspond to the achievement of the objective pursued. Therefore, if presumption can be justified in cases where the defendant participates in the proceedings, on the contrary, in proceedings where the defendant is defaulting, legis-

[67] Ciampi (2010), p. 698.

[68] If it is not possible to perform service in the manner provided for in Article 157, the court arranges for a further attempt to trace the accused person, particularly in the town of his birth, at his last registered address, at his last residence, at the place where he habitually works and at the central prison administration. If the research proves unsuccessful, the court issues a ruling of unavailability with which, after having appointed a lawyer for the defendant if he has not already appointed one himself, orders that service be performed by delivering a copy to the defendant's lawyer. 2. Service performed in this manner is valid to all intents and purposes. The untraceable person is represented by his counsel.

[69] If service at the address determined in accordance with paragraph 2 becomes impossible, service is made by delivery to the defence counsel. The same procedure envisaged for the cases provided for in paragraphs 1 and 3 is applied when the defendant has failed to state or establish an address for service, or when such information is incomplete or unusable. However, when it emerges that, due to unforeseeable circumstances or force majeure, the defendant was not in a position to communicate the change of address for service originally stated or chosen, the provisions of Articles 157 and 159 shall apply.

[70] If the case documents clearly show that the person against whom proceedings are to be made is registered as living or is effectively living at an address outside Italy, the judge or prosecutor sends a registered letter with acknowledgment of receipt, specifying the proceeding authority, the offence and the date and the place where it was committed, together with a request to state or choose to establish an address for service in Italy. If within 30 days of receiving the registered letter the defendant has made no statement or decision to establish address for service as required, or if the statement provides insufficient information or is unsuitable, service shall be performed by means of delivery to the defence counsel.

lation leads to an inevitable discrepancy between legal and effective knowledge.[71]

This was reflected in the original code-based system with the possibility of bringing remedies against sentences issued at the conclusion of proceedings carried out *in absentia*. The original text of Article 175(2) CCP-Italy allowed the time limit for bringing an appeal or opposition to be recalculated, but only for an accused person who demonstrated that he had not effectively been informed of the order, and provided that an appeal had not already been made by his counsel, and that it was not his fault or, in cases of default judgment served on the defense counsel, that the accused person had not voluntarily avoided cognizance of the proceedings. Upon closer examination, therefore, access to the remedy was frustrated by a real *probatio diabolica* for the defendant,[72] in sharp contrast with both Article 24 (2) Const.-Italy and Article 6(1) and (3)(c)(d)(e) ECHR and, finally, Article 14(3) (d) ICCPR—all provisions that establish that only the defendant's conscious and voluntary choice not to participate in the proceedings may permit their performance in his absence.

It is not surprising, therefore, that the European Court of Human Rights has pointed out, in various pilot rulings,[73] the structural weakness of the Italian system, warning of the need to reform the system allowing the recalculation of time limits for appeal, by providing a certain and effective remedy.[74] This is behind the amendment of Article 175(2) CCP-Italy under Law Decree 17/2005, converted into Law 60/2005,[75] whereby

> If a default judgment or conviction has been passed, the defendant shall be re-entitled, at his request, to the time limit for an appeal or objection, unless he effectively knew about the proceedings or the measure and voluntarily decided not to appear or to lodge an appeal or objection. To this end, the judicial authority shall make all necessary checks.

Following amendment of the Law, most case law considers the reentitlement to be a genuine right of the person concerned, since the new law introduced "a kind of presumption *iuris tantum* of lack of knowledge,"[76] with the resulting burden on the proceeding authority to ascertain that the accused knew of the proceedings and decided not to participate in them. Admittedly, this reform provides a stimulus for

---

[71] Quattrocolo (2005), p. 298.

[72] Caprioli (2007b), p. 391.

[73] Starting with the judgment ECtHR, 22 June 2004, Broniowski v. Poland, Application no. 31443/96, the Grand Chamber of the European Court inaugurated a series of rulings that do not just recognize the violation of one of the regulations under the convention but, having highlighted the structural weakness within the legislation of a State, suggest the most appropriate way to comply with the required standards.

[74] ECtHR, 18 May 2004, Somogyi v. Italy, Application no. 67972/01, with note by Tamietti (2004), p. 3797; ECtHR, 11 September 2003, Sejdovic v. Italy, Application no. 56581/00, with note by Tamietti (2005), p. 989.

[75] Chiavario (2005a), p. 253.

[76] Court of Cassation, Division VI, 16 December 2008, in *CED Cass.* no. 242430; Court of Cassation, Division I, 14 October 2008, Guida, in *CED Cass.* no. 229513; Court of Cassation, Division V, 29 May 2006, Fraglia, in *CED Cass.* no. 40734.

prosecuting authorities to adopt mechanisms to ensure effective knowledge of the accusation by the defendant.

The effectiveness of the mechanism, however, has been challenged by some commentators,[77] which emphasizes the fallaciousness of legislation based on the observation that in judicial practice requests for the recalculation of time limits are often rejected with arguments that essentially reintroduce presumptions of knowledge on the part of a person judged *in absentia*. This is the approach taken by the Court of Cassation, which, for the purposes of actual knowledge of the act, equates service on the defense lawyer with that performed on the defendant in person. It argues that

> counsel has a clear responsibility to effectively bring to the attention of his client any document relating to him, and similarly, the defendant has the precise duty to foster his relations with counsel, in order to keep informed on developments in the proceedings.[78]

In the presence of counsel appointed by the defendant himself, it would thus be seen as "entirely reasonable" to assume actual knowledge of the proceedings by the absent party, without prejudice—the same case law specifies—to the possibility of providing appropriate evidence to the contrary. However, it is clear that by accentuating the difference between the evidential value of service performed on counsel appointed by the defendant himself, and service performed on counsel appointed by the court, the end result is the more or less veiled reintroduction of the legal presumption of knowledge. These presumptions are completely unrelated to the system of protection of the ECHR, which, also with regard to the relationship between knowledge of the documents and a relationship of trust with counsel, focuses the effective enjoyment of the procedural guarantees on their formal recognition. Thus, the European Court did not find a violation of Article 6 ECHR when the appointment by the accused of his own legal counsel right from the early stages of proceedings resulted in more insistent demands for information by a person subject to the application of a precautionary measure.[79] In other words, Strasbourg case law, highlighting the factual circumstances underlying the performance of the mandate, acknowledges that the lawyer has the role of transmitting to or consolidating in the accused the knowledge necessary to consciously deal with the proceedings, without however maintaining that there is a general principle of equivalence between service on the defense lawyer and proof of actual knowledge on the part of the defendant.

More formalistic, however, is the position of the case law of the Court of Cassation, which, in postulating a stronger presumption of knowledge of the proceedings by a defaulting party who has appointed his own lawyer, however gives rise to considerable doubts as to the equality of rights compared to the accused

[77] Berni (2007), p. 1258; Buzzelli (2007), p. 3388; Quattrocolo (2005), p. 298.

[78] Court of Cassation, Division VI, 10 November 2011, in *CED Cass.* no. 2634.

[79] ECtHR, 28 February 2008, Demebukov v. Bulgaria, Application no. 68020/01.

person defended by court-appointed counsel.[80] Indeed, according to the case law of the Court of Cassation, only the latter fully enjoys the reversal of the burden of proof envisaged under Article 175(2) CCP-Italy. Moreover, the difference in treatment is also apparent in Article 157(8-*bis*) CCP-Italy, pursuant to which an appointed defense counsel, even if the registered address for service is his, may refuse to be served a document related to the proceedings. We wonder in this case what kind of consequences should derive from the presumption of knowledge of procedural actions; since it has to be regarded as a refusal, it should not need to be motivated or even notified to the client.

With regard to the potential impact of the Directive being analyzed, it is desirable that the assertion of the right to information in its three aspects and the need to ensure the effectiveness and practicality for the procedural prerogatives of the accused may lead to a restructuring of the system of service by means of legislation able to address the issues repeatedly found at the supranational level. It seems that the only way to ensure achievement of the purpose of the notification is to consider "service into the hands of the person concerned" as the necessary form. Although this may entail the risk of burdening procedures, there may be benefits in the use of certified electronic means that prove receipt of the document. As stated by the Court of Cassation,[81] certified mail is a method of service itself aimed at satisfying the need to simplify and speed up communications and service, and it follows that greater importance should be given to the potential of this medium.

3.2.4 Right to Information and Indirect Knowledge of the Accusation

The inadequacy of Italian procedural law to ensure effective knowledge of the charge can lastly be seen in the analysis of hypotheses whereby the information has been given to the accused person indirectly. Examples include service performed at the address of the lawyer, as well as cases in which notices are received by relatives of the interested party, this meaning not only the people who live permanently with the recipient of the document and are registered as members of his family but also those who, for other reasons, are in the home at the moment of service, as long as they show to the court service officer that they are cohabiting with the recipient, albeit purely temporary. In such cases, the service officer will be responsible for assessing the reasonable expectation that the document will be received by the person concerned, which very often, because of the workload, becomes a mere formality and fails to correspond to any certainty as to the likelihood of the accused being informed.

---

[80] Court of Cassation, Division VI, 21 January 2011, no. 5332, Minicozzi, in *CED Cass.* no. 249466 and Court of Cassation, Division VI, 2 December 2009, Condello, in *CED Cass.* no. 245343.

[81] Court of Cassation, Joint Divisions, 20 June 2012, in *CED Cass* no. 10143.

Even more controversial is the legitimacy of the system regarding service on legal persons,[82] considered valid even if performed by delivery to the legal representative charged with the offense on which the administrative offense depends.

In this regard, the Constitutional Court has recently made a ruling,[83] which, however, declared inadmissible the issue of the constitutionality of Article 43(2) of Legislative Decree no. 231/2001, raised in reference to Articles 3, 24, 76, 111, and 117 (1) Const-Italy and, significantly, 6 ECHR. According to the referring court, the contested provision would give rise to a situation of systematic incompatibility due to the fact that the provision ensures the validity of notification made to the legal representative accused of the commission of the alleged offense, at the basis of the legal person's responsibility. The validity of this notification seems to conflict with the provision contained in Article 39(1) of the legislative text, which rules out that a legal person may be represented in criminal proceedings by its own legal representative, if the latter is accused of the crime on which the administrative offense depends. In this case, delivery of the document in the hands of a subject beset by a conflict of interest would prejudice the effectiveness of the legal person's right of defense.

In refuting this reconstruction, the Constitutional Court pointed out above all the fallacy of the assumption whereby the reasons that lead to the incompatibility of the legal representative in criminal proceedings, charged with an offense that the legal person is allegedly guilty of, automatically affect the service system. According to the Court, the reason of incompatibility laid down in Article 39(1) in the event of a conflict of interests, responds to the need to ensure that both parties, the accused and the legal person, develop their own defensive strategy. They may not be considered as one and the same person, but this should not compromise the cognitive purpose of service. In this sense, the Constitutional Court stresses that the validity of service performed on the legal representative is justified by the reasonable presumption that the latter, in the faithful exercise of his duties, informs the other organs of the legal person of the document served and allows them to evaluate the possibility of entering an appearance through a different representative, possibly appointed solely for the purpose of taking part in the proceedings. The opposite hypothesis, based on the disloyal conduct of the legal representative, must instead be regarded as exceptional and pathological.

Although valuable, the distinction between the authority to represent the legal person and the authority to receive documents for it is, however, excessively formal, when what is being questioned is a right to information, which is, for the reasons already presented, intrinsically concrete and effective. A compensatory approach could be provided by those provisions that envisage, in both the intermediate and trial phases, the repeated service of notice of the preliminary hearing, if it is proved or appears likely that the defendant has not effectively been informed of it, provided that this is not due to his fault and falls outside the cases of service on

[82] Moscarini (2011), p. 1268.

[83] Constitutional Court, decision no. 249/11, with note by Varraso (2011), p. 3211.

his counsel.[84] However, we cannot fully agree that the provision in question is suitable to make up for the shortcomings of the system of notifications contained in Legislative Decree 231/2001. In fact, besides the fact that the court has an enormous and unquestionable understanding of these factual situations, the burden of proving ignorance of notice of the hearing bears on the defendant. On closer inspection, this provision is inspired by a vision by now widely disputed, whereby the procedural system is called upon to remedy only (at least) cases when the accused is probably unaware of proceedings, rather than to provide tools to assure effective knowledge of the proceedings and charges against him.

Beyond the provision referred to, the traditional ways of providing information on crimes, with the adjustments provided for in Articles 55 and 57 of Legislative Decree 231/2001, are used for legal persons. However, it should be stressed that in this context we once again see the aforementioned limits of a system that subjects information to the investigative decisions of the prosecutor, made worse by the fact that there is no requirement to register the name of the person investigated for the alleged offense. Therefore, the legal person may not have cognizance of the situation of incompatibility laid down in Article 39(1), nor can we rule out the possibility of a legal representative initially not involved in the matter being investigated at a later time.

In light of the above, the current service system does not yet seem capable of providing effective knowledge of the procedural documents on the part of those who do not really know that they are under investigation or charged and, on the other hand, are unable to tackle the manoeuvres of "the pseudo-untraceable."[85] Once again, it is clear that we need to radically intervene on the system, considering delivery directly to the interested person as the only acceptable form of serving documents. This conclusion is confirmed by the findings of the commission set up to study the reform of the criminal process in 2006, presided over by *Prof. Giuseppe Riccio*. As provided for in the "Draft" of the "Riccio Commission," if personal delivery is not possible, it is necessary to send the person notice of the filing of the document, and if they fail to collect a copy by the deadline, the police will proceed with compulsory notification, being authorized to forcibly enter the premises of a private dwelling, if they maintain that the person to whom the document is addressed is inside, with consequent power to forcibly accompany the person to their offices for the sole purpose of carrying out service directly to the interested party.[86]

The need for urgent and radical intervention appears unavoidable if we are to bring domestic regulations in line with the rapid evolution of EU legislation, which even before the Directive of 2012, with Council Framework Decision 2009/299, subordinated the mutual recognition of decisions rendered *in absentia* to the

---

[84] See, respectively, for the intermediate phase and the trial, Articles 420-*bis* and 484(2-*bis*) CCP-Italy. See Marandola (2011), p. 3207.

[85] Chiavario (2005b), p. 11.

[86] Cf. § 24 of the "Draft".

presence of a number of alternative conditions, namely (a) the fact that the defendant was summoned in person and thereby informed of both the time and place fixed for the hearing and of the issuance of the decision in the case of failure to appear in court or (b) the fact that, after receiving notification of the decision and being informed of the right to retrial, or appeal, the defendant expressly stated that he did not contest the decision or did not request a retrial or had not filed an appeal within the established time.[87]

3.3 Access to the Materials of the Case

Regarding the right to information on the materials of the case, the recent Directive also seems to have a significant influence on Italian procedural law. Article 7 of the Directive provides for this right no later than when submitting the merits of the charge to the court. In this regard, we should remember that one of the functions of the notice of conclusion of the investigation, envisaged under Article 415-*bis* of CCP-Italy, is that of allowing the suspect to view the documentation relating to the whole investigative activity in cases where the prosecutor is preparing to make an accusation against him. However, in its practical application, this mechanism is weakened by case law, which considers that if the prosecutor fails to file some of the documents relating to the investigation, this omission results only in the unusability of the documents but not in the invalidity of a subsequent request for trial.[88]

In this regard, it is significant that the Directive requires Member States to introduce enforceable remedies for the denial to exhibit documents. Such a right of appeal does not seem to be confirmed in the code or in case law. The scope of Article 8 of the Directive is, however, limited not only by the reference to national legislation, slavishly set forth at the beginning of the text, but also by the content of recital no. 36, according to which the guarantee of the right of access does not entail the obligation to provide for a specific appeal procedure, a separate mechanism or claim procedure. The provision therefore seems to be more emphatic than effective. In this regard, the draft Legislative Decree prefers an endoprocedural solution, providing as a penalty the nullity of subsequent actions in the event of a denial or failure to exhibit documents.

4 Conclusions

At the conclusion of this discussion, we can say that the transposition of Directive 2012/13/EU represents a daunting test for the Italian legislature, called to engage in an overall reform of procedural regulations that are largely noncompliant with

[87] Siracusano (2010), p. 115.

[88] Court of Cassation, Division, 8 June 2006, no. 26867; Court of Cassation, Division, 11 January 2007, no. 8049.

supranational legislation. Entrusting the stability of the system to the adversarial nature of the proceedings, as a way of reconciling the conflicting demands of a comprehensive and effective investigation, on one hand, and ensuring that the suspect is actually informed, on the other, is an option that is neither appropriate nor sufficient.

We have seen that the right to information seen as a guarantee that is subject to various restrictions, especially in the trial phase, contrasts with the new supranational instrument, based on the principle of immediate and full disclosure. The central importance given to the timing of the information conflicts with the negative wording of Article 369 CCP-Italy, which makes the "assisted" nature of the procedural action[89] the criterion of access to the right of defense.

A similar conclusion is reached by shifting the focus from the timing to the scope of the information. It was stressed that the need to provide information by way of guarantee is satisfied by providing information on the individual procedural action and not the inquiry as a whole,[90] since it is not intended to inform those concerned of the existence of ongoing investigations but rather to allow them to appoint a defense lawyer to deal with certain procedural activities. The promotional nature of the regulation is also borne out by the fact that further information need not be provided if the charge is modified, it being assumed that the suspect, aware that he is under investigation, has an interest in following the development of investigations.[91] This presumption inevitably clashes with the provisions of Article 6(4) of the Directive, whereby the suspects or accused persons are promptly informed of any changes to information regarding the accusation.

The possibilities of an effective exercise of the right to information are further undermined by case-law practice, according to the orientation whereby a notice should not be sent whenever knowledge was otherwise ensured by means, for example, of a request to appear for questioning or to appoint a defense lawyer.[92]

Nor is a greater degree of guarantee provided by the suspect taking his own initiatives to satisfy his right to information. As already pointed out, not only may the person who wants to view the register of crime reports provided for under Article 335 CCP-Italy be refused access in the event of an offense under Article 407 CCP-Italy, but he may actually be given misleading information, since if he applies to the wrong office, his request is not automatically forwarded to the prosecutor's office actually in charge of the investigation. We should also emphasize the serious harm caused not only to the effectiveness of the right to information but also to the reasonable duration of trials, since the late entry of the offense in the register does not lead to any penalties.

---

[89] This situation occurs mainly in cases of unrepeatable technical investigations, questioning, inspections, show ups, and searches.

[90] Amodio (1996), p. 106.

[91] Court of Cassation, Division VI, 21 February 1995, Iuzzolini, in *Cassazione Penale* n. 456.

[92] Manzionei (1999), p. 261.

These deficiencies are exacerbated at the threshold of criminal prosecution. We have seen that Article 415-bis of CCP-Italy, providing for the formulation of the charge with the "summary statement of the fact being prosecuted," facilitates the practice of so-called crypto-charges. In this respect, the solution consisting of a request to the public prosecutor to provide additional information for the indictment, while supported by growing case law, is not entirely suitable to fill the information gap: obeying the logic "of now for then," this instrument only responds to the needs of the accused to be defended *in* the proceedings, but not *from* them.

It seems that a significant contribution to overcoming the limitations of such a system can be derived from Directive 2012/13/EU, which in recital no. 28 states that information provided to suspects or accused persons should be provided in a timely manner, at the latest before their first questioning by the police or other competent authority, and shall contain a description in sufficient detail of the facts, including, if known, the time and the place and the possible legal classification of the alleged offense, taking into account the stage of the criminal proceedings in which the description is provided, in order to safeguard the fairness of the proceedings and allow for an effective exercise of the rights of defense. Also, importantly, the "summary nature" of the information generally provided to the accused according to accepted judicial practice should be brought in line with the standards required by the EU.

However, the draft Legislative Decree currently being examined by the Parliamentary Commissions does not seem to fully express the need for innovation and to bring the system in line with the standards required by the EU and conventions, being mainly limited to actions aimed at achieving minimum compliance. Therefore, we need to ask whether the scheme outlined is actually able to achieve the desired objectives, namely: (a) in the short term, to give full effect to the right of the person charged with a crime or arrested in execution of a European arrest warrant, to be adequately and promptly informed of the rights and powers granted under the procedural system, in order to fully understand the charge and have the time and conditions necessary to prepare his defense; (b) in the medium and long terms, greater harmonization of domestic legislation with that of EU Member States and, consequently, the strengthening of mutual trust in their justice systems, a prerequisite for the mutual recognition of judgments and judicial cooperation in transnational criminal matters.

In this sense, the indicators allowing us to monitor the achievement of objectives[93] will be the clarity with which information about rights is communicated in writing to the recipients, the timeliness with which they receive written communications, and the correctness with which the communications of the rights are translated into a language understandable to the recipient.

[93] Every 2 years, the Ministry of Justice will carry out the scheduled audit, which will not only check the correctness and timeliness with which information on rights is communicated to and if necessary translated for the recipients but also assess whether there have been procedural exceptions or judgments of appeal, based on proceedings that are invalid due to the failure to provide, or to provide in a clear form, the communication of rights in writing.

References

Amodio E (1972) La presenza del difensore all'interrogatorio istruttorio dell'imputato: epilogo di un conflitto e prospettive per l'effettività della difesa tecnica. Rivista italiana di diritto processuale penale 746 ff

Amodio E (1996) Nuove norme sulle misure cautelari e sul diritto di difesa. Giuffrè, Milano

Berni G (2007) Un po' di luce e molte ombre per l'imputato contumace. Giurisprudenza italiana 3:1258–1262

Buzzelli S (2007) Restituzione nel termine e sentenza contumaciale: dopo una riforma inappagante è necessaria una svolta. Cassazione Penale 9:3386–3395

Cape E et al (2007) Procedural rights at the investigative stage: towards a real commitment to minimum standards. In: Various Authors (eds) Procedural rights at the investigative stage of the criminal process in the European Union. Oxford Law, Oxford

Caprioli F (2007a) Inappellabilità delle sentenze di proscioglimento e parità delle armi nel processo penale. Giurisprudenza costituzionale 52:250 ff

Caprioli F (2007b) Cooperazione giudiziaria e processo in absentia. In Rafaraci T (ed) L'area di libertà, sicurezza e giustizia: alla ricerca di un equilibrio fra priorità repressive ed esigenze di garanzia. Giuffrè, Milano, pp 391 ff

Chiavario M (1970) Un salto qualitativo con cautela della giurisprudenza della Corte Costituzionale: l'interrogatorio istruttorio e la presenza del difensore. Giurisprudenza Costituzionale, 2179 ff

Chiavario M (2001) Sub art. 6 C.E.D.U. In: Bartole S et al (eds) Commentario alla Convenzione Europea dei diritti dell'uomo e delle libertà fondamentali. Cedam, Padova, pp 168 ff

Chiavario M (2005a) Commento articolo per articolo alla L. 22 aprile 2005, n. 60. Legislazione penale 3:253–259

Chiavario M (2005b) Non è tutto oro quel che luccica nel nuovo processo in absentia. Diritto e giustizia 19:10 ff

Ciampi S (2010) L'informazione dell'indagato nel procedimento penale. Giuffrè, Milano

Ciampi S (2012) La direttiva del Parlamento europeo e del Consiglio sul diritto all'informazione nei procedimenti penali. Note a margine della Direttiva 2012/13/UE. www.penalecontemporaneo.it

Ciampi S (2013) *Letter of rights* e *full disclosure* nella direttiva europea sul diritto all'informazione. Diritto penale e processo 1:21–27

Confalonieri A (2010) Europa e giusto processo. Giappichelli, Torino

Conti C (1995) La radiografia della nuova normativa su misure cautelari e diritto di difesa. Guida al diritto 33:94 ff

Cordero F (2006) Procedura penale. Giuffrè, Milano

D'Ambrosio L (1995) Sub art. 18 l. 8 agosto 1995, n. 332. Diritto penale e processo 10:1157 ff

De Caro A (2007) L'illegittimità costituzionale del divieto di appello del pubblico ministero tra parità delle parti e diritto al controllo del merito della decisione. Diritto penale e processo 618 ff

De Matteis L (2008) Diversa qualificazione giuridica dell'accusa e tutela del diritto di difesa. In: Balsamo A, Kostoris RE (eds) Giurisprudenza europea e processo italiano. Giappichelli, Torino, pp 217 ff

De Salvia M, Zagrebelsky V (2006) Diritti dell'uomo e libertà fondamentali. In: Fumagalli Meraviglia M (ed) vol I, II. Giuffrè, Milano

Dedola R (2006) Il difficile itinerario vero una decisione quadro sui diritti e le garanzie procedurali per indagati e imputati. In: Various Authors (eds) Equo processo: normativa italiana ed europea a confronto. Cedam, Padova, pp 159 ff

Frigo G (2007) Una parità che consolida disuguaglianze. Guida al diritto 8:87 ff

Gaeta P (2011) Principi costituzionali in materia penale. Quaderno predisposto in occasione del XII ° incontro trilaterale delle Corti Costituzionali italiana, spagnola e portoghese. Madrid 13–15 ottobre 2011

Gialuz M (2012) L'obbligo di interpretazione conforme al diritto sull'assistenza linguistica. Diritto penale e processo 4:434–440

Gialuz M (2014) Il decreto legislativo di attuazione della direttiva sull'assistenza linguistica (n. 32 del 2014): un'occasione sprecata per modernizzare l'ordinamento italiano. www.penalecontemporaneo.it

Giostra G (1996) Problemi irrisolti e nuove prospettive per il diritto di difesa: dalla registrazione delle notizie di reato alle indagini difensive. In: Grevi V (ed) Misure cautelari e diritto di difesa. Giuffrè, Milano, pp 189 ff

Grevi V (1972) *Nemo tenetur se detegere*. Interrogatorio e diritto al silenzio nel processo penale italiano. Giuffrè, Milano

Harris DJ et al (2009) Law of European convention on human rights. Oxford University Press, New York

Illuminati G (1979) La presunzione d'innocenza. Zanichelli, Bologna

Letsas G (2007) A theory of interpretation of the European convention on human rights. Oxford University Press, New York

Lupo E (1993) Il diritto dell'imputato straniero all'assistenza dell'interprete tra codice e convenzioni internazionali. Giurisprudenza costituzionale 73 ff

Manzionei (1999) L'attività del pubblico ministero. In: Aimonetto MG (ed) Indagini preliminari e instaurazione del processo. Utet, Torino, pp 261 ff

Marandola A (2011) Sulla validità costituzionale del regime delle notificazioni all'ente effettuate al rappresentante legale imputato del medesimo reato. Giurisprudenza Costituzionale 4: 3207–3211

Marzaduri E (1997) L'identificazione del contenuto del diritto di difesa nell'ambito della previsione dell'art. 6 n. 3 lett. c) della Convenzione Europea dei diritti dell'uomo. Cassazione Penale 3/4:178–193

Marzaduri E (2002) Law 1 March 2001 no. 63 – Modifiche al codice penale e al codice di procedura penale in materia di formazione e valutazione della prova in attuazione della legge costituzionale di riforma dell'art. 111 della Costituzione. Legislazione penale 1/2: 164–172

Mazza O (2004) L'interrogatorio e l'esame dell'imputato nel suo procedimento. Giuffrè, Milano

Molinari FM (2009) Il segreto investigativo. Giuffrè, Milano

Morgan C (2011) The new European directive on the rights to interpretation and translation in criminal proceedings. In: Braun S, Taylor J (eds) Videoconference and remote interpreting in criminal proceedings, University of Surrey, Guildford

Moscarini P (2011) I principi generali del procedimento penale de societate. Diritto penale e processo 10:1268–1276

Mowbray AR (2004) The development of positive obbligations under the European convention on human rights by the European court of human rights. Hart, Oxford

Nascimbene B (2009) Le garanzie giurisdizionali nel quadro della cooperazione giudiziaria penale europea. Diritto penale e processo 4:518–524

Nicolucci G (2003) Il decreto penale di condanna tra principio del contraddittorio e diritto di difesa. Diritto penale e processo 1069 ff

Nobili M (1998) Dal garantismo inquisitorio all'accusatorio non garantito? In: Nobili M (ed) Scenari e trasformazioni del processo penale. Cedam, Padova, pp 29 ff

Orlandi R (1995) Commento all'art. 18 legge n. 332 del 1995. In: Various Authors (eds) Modifiche al codice di procedura penale. Nuovi diritti della difesa e riforma della custodia cautelare. Cedam, Padova, pp 254 ff

Patanè V (2006) Il diritto al silenzio dell'imputato. Giappichelli, Torino

Piattoli B (2007) Diritti fondamentali: obiettivi e programmi dell'Unione europea in materia di giustizia penale. Diritto penale e processo 549 ff

Quattrocolo S (2005) Commento all'art. 2 D. l. 18.2.2005 n. 17. Legislazione penale 3:292–304

Quattrocolo S (2009) La corte europea dei diritti dell'uomo e il principio di correlazione tra accusa e sentenza: un invito ad un ripensamento del principio Iuranovit curia? Legislazione penale 1(2):343–366
Rafaraci T (2013) The right of defence in the EU judicial cooperation in criminal matters. In: Ruggeri S (ed) Translation inquires and the protection of fundamental rights in criminal proceedings. Springer, Berlin
Riviezzo C (1995) Custodia cautelare e diritto di difesa. Milano, Giuffrè
Ruggeri S (2008) Il procedimento penale per decreto. Dalla logica dell'accertamento sommario alla dinamica del giudizio. Giappichelli, Torino
Siracusano F (2010) Reciproco riconoscimento delle decisioni giudiziarie, procedure di consegna e processo in absentia. Rivista Italiana di Diritto e Procedura Penale 1:115–144
Tamietti A (2004) Iniquità della procedura contumaciale ed equa riparazione sotto forma di "restitutio in integrum": un passo verso un obbligo giuridico degli Stati Membri. Cassazione Penale 11:3797–3818
Tamietti A (2005) Processo contumaciale e Convenzione europea dei Diritti dell'Uomo: la Corte di Strasburgo sollecita l'Italia ad adottare riforme legislative. Cassazione Penale 3:983–1001
Tonini P (1971) Corte Costituzionale e presenza del difensore all'interrogatorio dell'imputato. Rivista italiana di diritto processuale penale, 19 ff
Tonini P (2001) La prova penale. Cedam, Padova
Trechsel S (2005) Human rights in criminal proceedings. Oxford University Press, Oxford
van Dijk P, Viering M (2006) Right to a fair and public hearing. In: van Dijk P et al (eds) Theory and practice of the European convention on human rights, 4th edn. Intersentia, Oxford
Varraso G (2011) Rappresentante legale "incompatibile" e notificazioni all'ente nel D. lgs. n. 231 del 2001. Giurisprudenza Costituzionale 4:3211–3218
Zacchè F (2009) Cassazione e iura novit curia nel caso Drassich. Diritto penale e processo 6:781–788

New Perspectives for the Protection of Personal Data in Criminal Proceedings in the European Union and Repercussions on the Italian Legal System

Federica Crupi

Contents

Abstract This paper seeks to examine, after a brief overview of current EU legislation on personal data protection in the field of judicial cooperation in criminal matters, the European Commission's proposal for a directive on the protection of individuals with regard to the processing of personal data by competent authorities for the prevention, investigation, detection, and prosecution of criminal offenses or the execution of criminal penalties.

This proposal, if approved, will be the source of Community law governing the use and exchange of information relating to such data between the Member States as well as—and this is a significant change from the past—their use by individual national authorities.

The exchange of information is in fact becoming, more than ever, an indispensable tool in the prevention and suppression of crime.

F. Crupi (✉)
Department of Law, University of Messina, Piazza Pugliatti n. 1, 98100 Messina, Italy
e-mail: federica.crupi@hotmail.it

S. Ruggeri (ed.), *Human Rights in European Criminal Law*,
DOI 10.1007/978-3-319-12042-3_13

The circulation of information, however, must be balanced against the need for privacy, a principle now enshrined in the EU's Treaties and Charters.

Therefore, after having carried out an analysis of the Directive proposal, we highlight its critical aspects.

Finally, we look at the Italian legal system to understand how the new EU regulatory framework may be transposed into the legislation of a Member State and whether or not domestic legislation complies with EU regulations.

Keywords Judicial cooperation • Privacy • Regulatory harmonization • Security

1 Introduction

The implementation of a comprehensive, coherent, modern, and robust framework for data protection in the European Union is an objective that the European Commission aims to achieve through the reform of data protection.[1]

The rapid evolution of the digital world has in fact led EU institutions to promote the creation of a regulatory system that, by transversally affecting all the policies of the union, can strengthen individuals' rights to protect their personal data, also and especially in terms of the prevention, investigation, detection, or prosecution of criminal offenses and related judicial activities.

While the protection of personal data in the field of police and judicial cooperation in criminal matters has so far been governed by Framework Decision 2008/977/JHA, this legislation is destined to undergo a change by virtue of the adoption of the proposal for a directive 2012/0010 (COD),[2] presented by the European Commission to replace existing legislation.

However, before examining the proposal in question, we need to understand whether and how the right to protection of personal data is significant in the EU legal system, above all following the recent approval of the Lisbon Treaty.

If, in fact, one of the objectives identified by the Treaty is the creation of an area of freedom, security, and justice (Art. 3 TEU), it should be noted that the development of solid cooperation in judicial and security matters must take into consideration the safeguard of the right to the protection of personal data.[3] The Nice Charter[4] elevated this right to the rank of a fundamental right of the person, with its own specificity and autonomy, not to be considered merely as an (implicit) aspect of the wider protection of privacy.[5]

---

[1] COM (2012) 9 final, Brussels, 25 January 2012.

[2] Proposal for a Directive 2012/0010 (COD), Brussels, 25/01/2012, COM (2012) 10 final.

[3] Marchetti (2012), p. 3.

[4] Art. 8 EU FRCh.

[5] Rodotà (2000), p. 1.

The protection thus provided applies *erga omnes*, giving rise to a duty to respect it both by public organizations, whether they be EU institutions and bodies or domestic ones, and by individuals whose activity may affect the rights in question.[6]

The Lisbon Treaty itself also introduced in Article 16(2) TFEU a specific legal basis for the adoption of rules on the protection of personal data, also in the context of police and judicial cooperation in criminal matters. Moreover, paragraph 1 of that article already established that every person has the right to the protection of their personal data.

Article 16(2) TFEU establishes, therefore, the Union's effective competence in the field, thus giving EU legislators such a wide margin of maneuver that they are able to establish a mandatory level of protection, even regardless of the need to ensure the movement of personal data.[7]

Precisely because of the regulatory framework set forth above, Declaration no. 21, annexed to the final proceedings of the conference for approval of the treaty, had recognized that in the field of judicial cooperation in criminal matters, specific rules on the protection of personal data could turn out to be necessary. This is because judicial cooperation between Member States is necessarily based on a constant exchange of information and data aimed at suppressing and preventing crimes.

A dual requirement is therefore apparent: to allow the filing and circulation of information necessary for the suppression of criminal behavior and at the same time to ensure an adequate level of protection for privacy.[8]

It will thus be necessary to find a balance between security and privacy.

Moreover, European law has always required that the principles of relevance, nonexcessiveness, and proportionality function as guidelines for the manner of collecting personal data in the context of judicial cooperation so that only the collection of relevant data and those strictly necessary for the investigations is permitted, using means proportionate to the aim pursued by the prosecuting authorities.[9]

Having established our general premises, and before examining the proposed directive, we need briefly to look at the existing regulatory framework.

---

[6] Cortese (2013), p. 2.

[7] Cortese (2013), p. 3.

[8] Belfiore (2013), p. 2.

[9] Court of Justice, 16 December 2008, C-524/06, Huber; Court of Justice, 24 November 2011, C-468/10, C-469/10, Asnef and Fecmd.

2 The Current Regulations: Decision 2008/615/JHA and Decision 2008/977/JHA

In the field of judicial cooperation in criminal matters, particularly in combating terrorism and cross-border crime, Decision 2008/615/JHA highlights the importance and need to exchange information quickly and effectively.

The accuracy, timeliness, and sufficiency of the duration of data storage (Art. 28); the need for measures to prevent intrusion or manipulation of the data (Art. 29); and the right to be informed of the use of one's personal data (Art. 31) are just some of the rights recognized by these regulations.

But it is Decision 2008/977/JHA that has been, until now, the regulatory framework of reference for the protection of personal data processed in the scope of police and judicial cooperation.

Although the decision was aimed at ensuring an adequate level of protection for fundamental human rights, in particular the right to privacy, with a view to balancing the need to protect public security, this balance does not seem to have been achieved, since so far security has always prevailed over privacy.[10]

But the greatest limitation of Decision 2008/977/JHA is probably its highly circumscribed scope, since it is applicable only to cross-border data but not to processing carried out by the police and judicial authorities at a strictly national level.[11]

This has led to further difficulties for authorities operating in the field of judicial cooperation in understanding the exact distinction between strictly national and cross-border processing of data. It is also problematic for those authorities to make a prior assessment as to whether "national" data will subsequently be subject to cross-border exchange.

Moreover, the decision leaves an excessively wide margin of interpretative discretion to Member States in the implementation phase, and no advisory group to promote uniform interpretation of the provisions in question has been envisaged.

In view of the regulatory framework described above, the European Data Protection Supervisor, in an opinion issued in January 2011, expressed the need to strengthen the regulation mentioned above to increase the protection of both private and public interests.[12]

What is needed, clarified the EPDS, is stronger and more effective regulatory intervention, which does not leave much room for the discretion of Member States in the implementation phase, without, however, precluding the possibility of adopting additional rules to provide a higher level of protection.

---

[10] Belfiore (2013), p. 8.

[11] Report on the proposal for a Directive, COM (2012) 10 final.

[12] The EDPS regretted that "the Commission has chosen to regulate this with a separate legal instrument that provides an inadequate level of protection, far less than that of the proposed regulation ... the proposal does not meet the requirement of a consistent and high level of data protection ..."

3 The Proposed Directive

There was an attempt to respond to criticisms of existing legislation in the proposal for a directive of 25 January 2012, on which we need to focus our attention.

This proposal, aimed at replacing the above-mentioned decision 2008/977/JHA, is part of a broader framework of regulatory reform suggested by the Commission, which also includes a proposal for a Regulation to replace the current Directive, 1995/46/EC. The latter is the cornerstone in the system of existing EU legislation on the protection of personal data and is intended to ensure both the protection of the fundamental right to the protection of personal data and the free movement of data between Member States.

It has been observed that the proposal for a Directive in question has its legal basis in Article 16 TFEU and seems to be compatible with the principles of subsidiarity and proportionality that circumscribe the scope of EU action in the matters under consideration.

It is in fact precisely the need for uniform intervention in a sector, such as that of the protection of personal data, in which we find significant fragmentation of the legislation of the Member States, as well as a growing need for rapid data exchange in order to prevent and combat crime, that justifies intervention by the Union. The satisfaction of this requirement of uniformity, among other things, was announced as an objective of the Stockholm Programme in 2009.[13]

On this point, however, there does not seem to be a consensus from the Italian *Camera dei Deputati*, the French Senate, the German *Bundesrat*, the *Chambre des rapresentantys* of Belgium, and the Swedish *Riksdagen*, fearful of an excessive invasion of national prerogatives.[14]

As to proportionality, the Directive appears to be the most appropriate tool for achieving the aims described above, ensuring at the same time the long-awaited harmonization as well as a great deal of flexibility in terms of implementation at a national level.

But it is the scope of the proposed directive that deserves particular attention, since, unlike the provisions of the 2008 decision, it is not limited to cross-border data. The rules in question would in fact be implemented with reference to all data-processing activities carried out by the competent authorities even at a strictly national level (Art. 2) for purposes of an "institutional" nature.[15]

This aspect marks the beginning of a path taken by EU legislation aimed at achieving conformity with supranational law also in the field of domestic procedures.

---

[13] Stockholm Programme, 4 May 2010.

[14] Opinion of the 14th Committee of the Italian Chamber of Deputies, Doc XVIII-bis, no. 73.

[15] Marchetti (2012), p. 27.

3.1 The Main Provisions of the Proposed Directive

Moving on, then, to a more detailed examination of the proposal, we see that it has as its primary objective the balance between security and privacy that the EPDS had defined necessary in the field of judicial cooperation (Art. 1).

The proposed law, like the definitions it contains, reproduces the provisions of Decision 2008/977/JHA but provides new definitions of the concept of "biometric data," "genetic data," and "competent authorities" (Art. 3) on the basis of the provisions of Article 87 TFEU,[16] as well as a definition of "child" taken from the Convention on the Rights of the Child.

As far as regards the criteria of lawfulness of the processing of personal data (Art. 7), the proposed directive restricts them, highlighting that those for lawful processing, as identified in Article 7 of Directive 95/46/EC, cannot be applied in the field of judicial cooperation in criminal matters. Legal use is where the data is necessary for the performance of a task by a competent judicial authority on the basis of national legislation, for the fulfillment of a legal obligation to which the data controller is subject, for the protection of vital interests of the interested party or of a third party, and for the prevention of an immediate and serious threat to public safety.

As far as regards, however, the prohibition on processing certain categories of data, Article 8 of the proposed directive adds to the existing provisions of Directive 95/46 EC the prohibition of processing genetic data in accordance with the provisions of the case law of the European Court.[17] This prohibition, in any case, is not applicable if the processing is authorized by national legislation aimed at establishing appropriate safeguards, functional to the preservation of a vital interest of the person concerned or of a third party, and if the processing relates to data made public by the person concerned himself.

Perfect compatibility with the resolution of Madrid,[18] moreover, can be seen in the provisions (Arts. 10–17) aimed at listing the rights granted to the person concerned. First among these is the right of access, consisting of the right to receive confirmation from the person in charge of the processing data procedure concerning him. This right may however be removed, if necessary and in a proportionate manner, in a democratic state, for the achievement of higher interests such as not compromising investigations and protecting public security.

A new feature in the provisions of Decision 2008/977/JHA is the introduction of specific provisions (Arts. 30–32) on the obligations and responsibilities of data controllers, especially concerning the guarantee of transparency and access.[19]

[16] Report on the proposal for a Directive, COM (2012) 10 final.

[17] ECtHR, 4 December 2008, *S. and Marper v United Kingdom*, Application no. 30562/04 and no. 30566.

[18] Madrid Resolution on international standards and privacy of 5 November 2009.

[19] Marchetti (2012), p. 27.

As far as regards, however, the transfer of personal data to third countries or to international organizations, the proposed Directive permits such a transfer only where necessary for the purposes of prevention, investigation, detection, or prosecution of criminal offenses (Art. 33).

In addition, such transfers may occur only after an assessment of adequacy carried out by the European Commission (Art. 34), and pending this evaluation the flow of data will be possible only if their protection is in any case guaranteed by a legal instrument applicable to the case in point, which could be an international agreement, or if the data supervisor considers that in the case submitted for his opinion there are adequate safeguards for the protection of privacy.

Member States do, however, have a margin of discretion with regard to the legislation mentioned above (Art. 36), but only when this is strictly necessary for the protection of the concerned person or a third party or where the data processing is essential to prevent a threat to public security, to prevent or to punish a crime, or to exercise or defend a right in court.

Compared to the provisions of the JHA decision, moreover, the duties of supervisory authorities should also be extended to ensure that they contribute to the achievement of a consistent application of the law throughout the Union; Member States will have the task of establishing the duties of these authorities (Art. 45), major players in a campaign to raise public awareness on rights relating to the protection of personal data.

If, in addition, Directive 95/46/EC provides for a general obligation of cooperation, Article 48 of the proposal being examined instead lays down a real obligation of mutual assistance between Member States in the field of judicial cooperation.

Finally, it should be noted that the proposed directive provides a mechanism for jurisdictional appeals (Arts. 50–55) that the person concerned may bring against the data supervisor or against the supervisory authority. It will also be possible to submit a preemptive appeal to the latter. The proposal also introduces common rules for court actions and obliges Member States to acknowledge that the person concerned is entitled to compensation for any damage caused to him by the use of his personal data.

Member States will therefore have to introduce into their legal systems penalties applicable to infringements of the Directive and ensure their enforcement (Art. 55).

3.2 Critical Comments on the Proposed Directive

Although the proposed directive is worthy of praise, becoming part of a comprehensive set of rules for the protection of personal data that will be applied across the EU, one cannot avoid also levelling some criticisms at it.

The proposal in fact disappointed the European Data Protection Supervisor, who regretted that

> the Commission has chosen to regulate this matter in a self-standing legal instrument which provides for an inadequate level of protection, by far inferior to the proposed Regulation.[20]

The EDPS made three main criticisms:

1. While it is true that the positive aspect of the proposal is that it covers domestic data processing, the legislative package as a whole proposed by the Commission is weak since it fails to intervene on specific instruments adopted in the field of judicial cooperation in criminal matters, such as the Prum Decision and the provisions relating to Europol and Eurojust.[21]
2. In addition, the proposed Directive departs from the general rules contained in the proposed regulation, departures that should be explicitly justified on the basis of a balance between the public interest and fundamental rights. However, the legislation in question contains no such justifications.
3. Moreover, one cannot fail to observe that the Directive does not contain any obligation for the competent authorities to demonstrate compliance with it. In addition, conditions for cross-border data transfer seem to be insufficient, and the powers of the supervisory authorities are unduly limited.[22]

In light of this, there are many proposals to amend the rules in question made by the EDPS,[23] some of which are worth noting.

It would only be fair to introduce an analysis system based on objective data, to determine whether data processing is indeed a necessary and proportionate measure for the purposes of the prevention, investigation, detection, and prosecution of criminal offenses.

As for the collection of data, governed by Article 4 of the proposal, this may take place for specified, explicit, and legitimate purposes, and subsequently the data may be processed in a way that is incompatible with those purposes; in this regard, a whereas clause should clarify the meaning of "compatible use" so that it may be given a restrictive interpretation.[24]

As regards the lawfulness of the processing (Article 7), also in this case, specification of the considerations of public interest that make such treatment lawful would be appropriate.

The EDPS also highlighted the need for the proposal to include mechanisms that ensure the setting of time limits for the deletion of data, establishing storage periods that vary according to the categories of data concerned, as well as checks on their quality.

It seems appropriate, moreover, to introduce a provision that requires the person responsible for the procedure to inform the person concerned of any rectification,

---

[20] Opinion of the EDPS of 7 March 2012.

[21] *Ibid.*

[22] *Ibid.*

[23] *Ibid.*

[24] *Ibid.*

cancellation, or variation of the data, unless this is impossible or exceedingly difficult.

As far as regards, however, the possibility for Member States to adopt legislative measures aimed at delaying, limiting, or omitting the supply of information to the person concerned and to establish to which categories of data such exceptions may apply to (Art. 11), we would need to ensure a restrictive interpretation of the provision referred to above. Moreover, we would also need a restrictive interpretation of the part of Article 13 that gives states the possibility of establishing the categories of data for which exceptions may be made to the provisions on the right of access.

As for the transfer of data to other countries, as we have noted, Article 35 of the proposed Directive outlines the appropriate safeguards that must be offered for the purposes of an international transfer of data, in the absence of a decision of adequacy from the Commission.

It is then Article 36 of the proposal that defines the exceptions for the transfer of data on the basis of Article 26 of Directive 95/46/EC and of Article 13 of Framework Decision 2008/977/JHA.

Precisely in this regard, according to the opinion of the EDPS, it would be correct to clarify, in a whereas clause, that the exemptions used to justify the transfer should be interpreted very narrowly and, in any case, should not allow the transfer of a whole series of data but only those that are strictly necessary. The requirement of documenting transfers should also be introduced.[25]

A further point of criticism of the proposal regards the part of Article 44 that establishes that the supervisory authorities should not be competent to assess data processing carried out by the courts in the exercise of their functions: a whereas clause should specify what is meant by "jurisdictional functions."

Finally, it would be desirable to align the powers of supervision over the national police authorities with the provisions of Article 53 of the proposed Regulation.

3.3 Impact of the Proposal on the Italian Legal System

At this point in the discussion, it may be interesting to examine the compatibility of the proposed directive with one of the legal systems of the Member States. I have chosen Italy, since its Privacy Code seems to faithfully reflect EU legislation for the protection of personal data.

Under Italian law, the protection of personal data is regulated by Legislative Decree no. 196/2003 (better known as the Privacy Code).

The guiding principle of the whole consolidation law is that any person has the right to protect personal data concerning him (Art. 1), thus making it perfectly compatible with Article 16 TFEU and introducing a fundamental right of the person

[25] *Ibid.*

independently of the more general right to privacy under Article 1 of Law 675/1996.[26]

The analysis of the main provisions of the legislation in question shows that Article 7—regulating the right of access to personal data and other rights and establishing that the person concerned has the "right to obtain confirmation of 'existence or not of personal data concerning him, even if not yet recorded, and their communication in an intelligible form"—seems to be perfectly compatible with the provisions relating to access contained in the proposed directive (Art. 12).

Even the exceptions to access, referred to in Article 8 of the Privacy Code, seem perfectly compatible with the provisions of Article 13 of the proposed Directive, which refer to limitation of the right in question in order not to jeopardize investigations, inquiries, or judicial proceedings or for reasons of public safety or national security.

Article 13 of the Privacy Code—after acknowledging the interested party's right to be informed about the purpose of data processing, the compulsory nature of providing data, etc.—departs from the obligation of prior information if the personal data are to be used to enforce or defend a right in court proceedings, provided that they are used exclusively for such purposes and only for the time strictly necessary.

This provision appears to be in perfect harmony both with the provisions of Article 7 of the proposal (which considers as legitimate any processing of personal data that is functional to protecting the interests also of a third party) and with the exceptions to the obligations to provide prior information under Article 11 of the proposal.

Continuing in this comparative analysis, we should quote Article 26 of the consolidation law on privacy, containing stronger protection of sensitive data in line with Article 8 of the proposed directive.

The use of such sensitive data is only permissible with the consent of the person concerned and authorization from the EDPS, except for use without prior consent in cases where the processing is necessary to enforce or defend a right in court proceedings, provided that such use is exclusively instrumental to the pursuit of the listed aims and only for the time strictly necessary.

The exception described above also passes the test of compatibility with Article 8 of the proposal, which, while laying down the nonusability of sensitive data, establishes that domestic legislation may introduce exceptions to this rule provided it ensures adequate guarantees. Article 26 of the Privacy Code does in fact envisage an exception to the obligation to provide prior information but in any case leaves the supervisory body in control, which, of course, is to be considered an adequate guarantee for the protection of the person concerned.

We should also consider Article 53 of the Privacy Code, which excludes from police control a number of provisions, such as those relating to the means of access

[26] Briganti (2005), p. 2.

by the person concerned, codes of ethics and standards of conduct, and obligations regarding the provision of information to the interested party.

These exceptions, as shown, do not appear to subvert the general protections provided by the Privacy Code,[27] precisely because they are functional to data processing by the police and its institutional aims.

Nevertheless, Article 55, in keeping with the safeguards imposed by European legislation, lays down that

> the processing of personal data which implies greater risks of harm to the person concerned, with particular reference to genetic or biometric databanks . . . is performed in respect of the measures and precautions aimed at safeguarding the interested party laid down under Article 17 on the basis of prior notification pursuant to Article 39.

The rule cited above, therefore, reflects the civil rights rules imposed by Article 8.

Regarding the transfer of data to third countries, Italian legislation governs such transfer under Article 43 et seq. of the Privacy Code; in comparison with Article 33 of the proposed directive, this provision seems to have a wider scope in that it contains a reference to a general concept of the public interest such as to justify the transfer, as well as allowing the transmission, of data for the carrying out of investigations by the defense.

Article 33, however, seems to limit the transfer of data to cases where it is functional to the prevention, investigation, detection, and prosecution of criminal offenses or to the enforcement of criminal penalties. Moreover, Article 34 provides protection for civil rights by envisaging the prior approval of adequacy on the part of the Commission discussed above.

As to the violation of the provisions relating to privacy, Article 11 of the Privacy Code provides for the unusability of any data processed in violation of the rules set out in Decree 196/2003.

As regards, however, the use of data in court proceedings, Article 160(4) of the Privacy Code lays down that

> the validity, effectiveness and usability of records, documents and measures in proceedings based on the processing of personal data that fails to conform to the provisions of law or regulations are governed by the applicable procedural rules in civil and criminal matters.

In this regard, Article 191 CCP-Italy (under which evidence obtained in violation of the provisions of law is deemed to be unlawfully acquired and therefore unusable) will regulate the matter in question, even if this provision merely confirms the nonusability of evidence obtained in violation of the prohibitions established by law.

If this legislation seems to be highly civil-rights oriented, as well as in line with Community provisions, the case law of the Court of Cassation seems less so, since it has ruled that[28]

---

[27] Gennari (2011), p. 1185B.

[28] Corte di cassazione, III Sezione, 29 settembre 2011, Z.S., in www.altalex.it, n. 35296.

> relating to the protection of personal data, their use in the context of court proceedings does not constitute a violation of the relative regulations, since such regulations are not applicable in general, pursuant to Articles 7, 24, 46 and 47 of Legislative Decree. 196/2003, when the data are collected and managed as part of trial proceedings. In this case, in fact, the judicial authority is seen as the data controller, and is responsible for the protection of confidentiality and the proper performance of the trial.

According to the case law cited, therefore, the production of documents concerning personal data would always be allowed during a trial if this is necessary for the exercise of the right of defense, even without the data controller's consent and regardless of how knowledge of such data is acquired.

This exercise of the right of defense, however, must still be in compliance with the EU principles of fairness, relevance, and proportionality as also required under law 675/1996.[29]

Another issue emerging in the Italian legal system, which should be mentioned, is that regarding the more or less legitimate power of the supervisory body to assess the judiciary in the exercise of its functions. This assessment, if admitted, could be in breach of Article 44 of the proposal, which provides that "Member States shall provide that the supervisory authority is not competent to supervise processing operations of courts when acting in their judicial capacity."

There is no doubt that the right to protection of personal data is a fundamental right, but since it must also be applied in the context of (criminal or civil) proceedings, it is necessary to perform the difficult balancing act of the conflicting interests at play.[30]

However, there certainly emerge doubts concerning the constitutionality of the Italian legislation if we accept that an administrative authority such as the supervisory body can carry out an in-depth assessment of the judicial function.

A combined reading of Articles 47 and 160 of the privacy code shows that "the processing of personal data directly correlated to the assessment in court proceedings of matters and disputes is carried out for reasons of justice" and that, in assessing compliance with the provisions of the consolidation law in the judicial sector, "the supervisory body shall adopt an appropriate approach that takes into account mutual responsibilities and the particular institutional position of the court" (Art. 160).

Having completed this audit, if the supervisory body considers the actions of the magistrate noncompliant with the provisions of law, it "sets forth to the data controller or supervisor the necessary modifications and additions and checks that they are implemented."

It has been observed that under Article 160 of the Privacy Code, any illegality found by the supervisory body dealing with judicial activity is governed by the procedural rules regarding the validity, effectiveness, and usability of the relative documents but that it is not clear what the consequences are for the magistrate's

---

[29] See fn. 28.

[30] Sorrentino (2001), p. 2.

failure to comply with the instructions given by the supervisory body regarding any amendments to be made.[31]

The discipline hitherto mentioned brings with it questions of compatibility with the Italian Constitution, since administrative control of judicial activity would not be permissible.

In fact, as clarified by the Italian Court of Cassation,[32] the supervisory body is an administrative authority that cannot be allowed to criticize the work of the judiciary, since such a concession would violate the principle of judicial independence proclaimed by the Constitution and the Italian Constitutional Court.[33]

Article 24 of the Constitution would also be violated, since the assessment made by the supervisory body would not involve the parties in any way.[34]

However, it must be assumed that the observations of the administrative authority may only constitute the basis for evaluations regarding the validity, effectiveness, and usability of documents, assessments that will be, however, made by the competent court. This reading thus seems to be in perfect harmony with the provisions of Article 44 of the proposed directive, avoiding the doubts of incompatibility previously expressed.

Finally, Italian legislation would seem to be incompatible with the proposed Directive, insofar as the interested party has no right to appeal to the supervisory body in the event of data processing carried out for reasons of justice (Art. 47); the proposal for a directive in fact introduces a number of provisions (Chapter VIII) concerning the actions that the applicant may bring to guarantee his rights. This apparent incompatibility would, however, be diminished by virtue of the power given to the supervisory body to independently conduct its own investigations, which we discussed above.

Finally, with regard to the obligation introduced by the directive and addressed to the Member States to give the interested party the right to compensation for damage caused consequent to the use of personal data, the Italian legal system has for some time envisaged that a violation of confidentiality may be seen as an infringement of procedural rules and may give rise to the civil and disciplinary liability of legal practitioners.

4 New Techniques and the Italian Criminal Trial

Having reached this point in the discussion, it is worth examining in detail Italian legal regulations relating to the use and retention of DNA and digital fingerprints, in order to see whether they are compatible with EU law.

[31] Sorrentino (2001), p. 3.

[32] Court of Cassation, 1th Section, 20 May 2002, www.privacy.it, n. 7341.

[33] Constitutional Court, 440/88.

[34] Sorrentino (2001), p. 5.

For some time, the Council of Europe has shown its interest in "genetic data," precisely in order to enable the international exchange of data obtained by means of DNA analysis.

In 2009, Italy joined the Treaty of Prum concerning cooperation between the Member States of the European Union in the fight against terrorism, illegal immigration, and cross-border crime, an aim for whose realization the search and exchange of information contained in the databases of different countries is essential. No less important are the tools used by Europol and Eurojust, such as archives of data in connection with national databases as well as the exchange and processing of personal data, including DNA profiles, of those individuals suspected of crimes falling within the competence of the bodies mentioned.

With reference to Italy, only recently, with Law 85/2009, was a national DNA database set up, also following Italy's famous Zefil Ilir case, during which there emerged the existence of a dense network of databases in the various local offices of the Carabinieri special branch, RIS, despite the lack of any adequate security legislation.

This legislative guarantee was in fact introduced in 2009 in a law whose compatibility with the rules of the European Union should be examined, albeit briefly.

In the first place, precisely in order to guarantee the right to privacy, by limiting its scope to the confines of investigative needs,[35] and the number of persons for whom DNA profiles can be collected, Article 9 of the aforementioned law establishes that for the purposes of preserving associated data in the national bank, samples will be taken only from certain persons. These are those who have been remanded in custody or put under house arrest, those arrested *in flagrante delicto* or apprehended, those who are detained or interned on the basis of a final judgment for an intentional crime, those subject to alternative measures to detention following a final judgment for an intentional crime, or those sentenced to imprisonment, whether the sentence is provisional or final.

A sample may also be taken in proceedings for intentional crimes for which arrest *in flagrante delicto* is envisaged.

The list given, in the opinion of *Oliveri*,[36] is too long, but, in the light of the comparative assessment we are trying to carry out, we can observe that a restriction of the scope of the persons subject to tests is in line with the provisions of Article 8 of the draft directive, which allows genetic data to be processed as long as domestic legislation provides adequate protection for civil rights.

With the same focus on civil rights, Article 11 of Law 85/2009 provides that the tests should be carried out in such a way that no diseases from which the person concerned is suffering may be identified. Pursuant to Article 12, moreover, the type of access is second level,[37] since the investigating authority will first compare data

[35] Rivello (2013), p. 1670B.

[36] Oliveri (2009), p. 241.

[37] Felicioni (2009), p. 9.

and will be able to identify the subject only in the event of possible compatibility. Such identification, therefore, does not take place directly.[38]

The second paragraph of the latter provision also lays down that access to the database is allowed exclusively for identification purposes and for reasons of international police cooperation and is not admitted for any other purposes.

If, so far, the law seems to have required adequate safeguards, also envisaging a significant role for the supervisory authority (Art. 15), many doubts arise regarding the maximum period for which collected data may be held.

What, in fact, raises doubts as to its compatibility with EU law is the fact that genetic data may be cancelled only *ex officio*, while interested parties are not entitled to request their cancellation, to have the "right to be forgotten."[39]

Furthermore, the fact that a DNA profile cannot be preserved for over 40 years after the last circumstance that led to its filing, and that biological data cannot, however, be kept for over 20 years, has raised many doubts as to what seems an excessively broad time frame.[40] A similar situation is found only in France,[41] where, however, the collection of such data is much more circumscribed, being limited to cases of particularly serious crimes.

This is not the only criticism made of Law 85/2009, since we can see that the law does not in any way rule out—since it makes no mention of the issue—the continued existence of other genetic databanks used by individual institutions, thus perpetuating that "genetic jungle" that existed before the legislation in question came into force.[42]

A totally different matter is the collection and retention of fingerprints, which for the ECtHR is tantamount to interference by national authorities in the right to respect for individual privacy.[43]

In the Italian system in particular, the retention of fingerprints is not subject to any objective nor subjective limit,[44] and no time limits for their retention are even envisaged, unlike in the case of DNA profiles.

On this point, the Strasbourg court believes that[45]

> the retention at issue constitutes a disproportionate interference with the applicants' right to respect for private life and cannot be regarded as necessary in a democratic society. This conclusion obviates the need for the Court to consider the applicants' criticism regarding the adequacy of certain particular safeguards, such as too broad an access to the personal data concerned and insufficient protection against the misuse or abuse of such data. Accordingly, there has been a violation of Article 8 of the Convention in the present case.

---

[38] Rivello (2013), p. 1670B.

[39] Fanuele (2011), p. 119.

[40] Busia (2009), p. 77.

[41] Fanuele (2011), p. 117.

[42] Gennari (2011), p. 1195B.

[43] European Court of Human Rights, *M.K. v. France*, Application no. 19522/2009.

[44] Scarcella (2013), p. 2850B.

[45] ECtHR, 4 December 2008, *S. and Marper v United Kingdom*, Application no. 30562/04 and no. 30566.

The Court, in particular, requires that collection and storage comply with the principle of proportionality in relation to the purposes and should be limited in time as, among other things, the legislation examined requires.

Specifically, the Italian Code of Criminal Procedure merely provides the rules for the taking of fingerprints by the police, while Article 57 of the Privacy Code refers to a decree of the President of the Council of Ministers specifying collection and retention methods in accordance with the principles of the consolidation law.[46]

This decree, however, has not yet been adopted, with the consequent risk that the Italian state may be exposed to multiple appeals before the ECtHR.

Finally, the case law of the Italian Constitutional Court has ruled that the comparison of fingerprints taken and those already in the possession of the judicial authorities consists of a mere assessment of objective data pursuant to Article 354 CCP-Italy and that, therefore, the defense guarantees laid down in Article 360 CCP-Italy need not be observed.

It seems clear, therefore, that Italian legislation does not always guarantee the same level of protection for privacy imposed by EU law.

5 Conclusion

What we have seen above shows that the intervention of the Commission in the field of personal data is highly significant today, since it is aimed at creating comprehensive harmonization, if not the actual standardization of current law.[47]

The latter, in fact, seems crucial in a field such as judicial cooperation in criminal matters, although more could perhaps be done precisely in this field.

In fact, despite the fact that the choice of a directive is certainly respectful of the principle of subsidiarity, the fear is that the attempt at harmonization expressed in this type of regulatory action, moreover non-self-executing, will be met by irregular implementation at a state level.

Precisely because it is not self-executing, in fact, the proposed directive does not seem to conflict with the Italian legal system adopted as a model in this paper, since this is a system that, on the whole, guarantees a high level of data protection.

It is certain, however, that by accepting the recommendations of the EDPS, the standard of protection could be raised, bringing it in line with EU law. In this case, Italy, along with other Member States, would have to amend existing legislation.

[46] Scarcella (2013), p. 2851B.

[47] Cortese (2013), p. 317.

References

Belfiore R (2013) The protection of personal data processed within the frame work of police and judicial cooperation in criminal matters. In: Ruggeri S (ed) Transnational inquiries and the protection of fundamental rights in criminal proceedings. Springer, Heidelberg

Briganti G (2005) Il codice della privacy. www.altalex.it

Busia G (2009) Privacy a rischio per la durata della conservazione. Guida al Diritto 30:78

Cortese B (2013) La protezione dei dati di carattere personale nel diritto dell'un ione europea dopo il Trattato di Lisbona. Diritto dell'Unione Europea (II) 2:313–328

Fanuele C (2011) Conservazione di dati genetici e privacy: modelli stranieri e peculiarità italiane. Diritto Penale Processuale 17:117–124

Felicioni P (2009) L'Italia aderisce al trattato di Prum: disciplinata l'acquisizione e l'utilizzazione probatoria dei profili genetici. Diritto Processuale Penale 2(2):6–24

Gennari G (2011) Genetica forense e codice della privacy: riflessioni su vecchie e nuove banche dati. Responsabilità civile e previdenza 5:1184B–1189B

Marchetti G (2012) I recenti passi avanti compiuti dall'Unione europea nella direzione di un'armonizzazione dei sistemi penali. Centro studi sul federalismo

Oliveri O (2009) La legge sul prelievo di materiale biologico e la funzione della difesa. In: Scarcella A (ed) Prelievo del DNA e Banca dati nazionale. Cedam, Padova

Rivello P (2013) Tecniche scientifiche e processo penale. Cassazione penale 4:1691–1719

Rodotà S (2000) Discorso di presentazione della "Relazione per l'anno 2000". www.garanteprivacy.it

Scarcella A (2013) Osservazioni a CEDU, sez. V, 18 aprile 2013, n. 19522. Cassazione Penale 7–8:2848B–2854B

Sorrentino F (2001) La protezione dei dati personali nel processo. Questione giustizia 1:122

The Effects of the Directive 2013/48/EU on the Italian System of Precautionary Measures: Defence Rights in Remand Hearings

Simona Arasi

Contents

S. Arasi (✉)
University of Messina, Piazza Pugliatti n. 1, Messina, Italy

Tor Vergata University of study of Rome, Via Orazio Raimondo 18, Rome, Italy
e-mail: sarasi@unime.it

S. Ruggeri (ed.), *Human Rights in European Criminal Law*,
DOI 10.1007/978-3-319-12042-3_14

Abstract Within the European area of justice, Directive 2013/48/EU aims to establish common minimum standards on the right of access to a lawyer for suspects and defendants in criminal proceedings throughout the European Union. In this paper, we analyse the possibility of extending the guarantees provided for by Italian criminal procedural law in relation to an emblematic activity, the questioning of a person subjected to preventive custody. Many issues remain unresolved, and there seem to be numerous shortcomings in the text of the new Directive, especially if we are to ensure the practicality and effectiveness of the protection it envisages.

Keywords Formal interview under caution • Right of defence due process • Suspect/defendant in vinculis

1 Foreword

Speaking of the effects on the Italian criminal justice system of the EU Directive adopted on 22 October 2013,[1] concerning the right of access to a lawyer,[2] means addressing very wide issues, which lend themselves to various interpretations. This paper analyses the effects of the provisions of this supranational precautionary instrument system, focusing on the interview of the person subject to preventive measures.

This topic of analysis is justified by the fact that within this procedure, there typically coexist, on one side, typically evidence-gathering functions and, on the other, functions of defence, monitoring, and civil rights guarantees. This examination is also useful in consideration of the scope of the recent Directive, extended to proceedings *de libertate*, even if they are aimed at handing over the accused by means of the EAW.

[1] Directive 2013/48/EU of the European Parliament and of the Council of 22 October 2013 on the right of access to a lawyer in criminal proceedings and in European arrest warrant proceedings, and on the right to have a third party informed upon deprivation of liberty and to communicate with third persons and with consular authorities while deprived of liberty.

[2] In accordance with Recital 15, "the term 'lawyer', in this Directive, refers to any person who, in accordance with national law, is qualified and entitled, including by means of accreditation by an authorised body, to provide legal advice and assistance to suspects or accused persons".

2 Brief Notes on the Relationship Between EU and Domestic Law

For a correct understanding of the issues, we must consider the relationship between EU law and national law. When Italy joined the European Union, it accepted and committed itself to the simultaneous application within its own legal system of both domestic and European laws.[3]

With regard to primary sources, Italy has taken steps to introduce the order of execution of each Treaty into the same law with which it authorised their ratification.[4] The validity of the treaties was initially justified by the Italian Constitutional Court in the reference to Article 11-Const Italy, which legitimates limitations of sovereignty without the need to provide for a constitutional amendment.[5] Today, following the amendment of Title V of Const.-Italy,[6] the Italian Constitution contains an explicit reference to the EU legal system in Article 117.[7]

As far as regards the adaptation[8] of the Italian system to secondary sources,[9] this takes place through the adoption by the State of national measures that the very documents of the Union prefigure or require for their implementation.

Considering this, we should assess how the rules of European origin are located within the State, with particular reference to the hierarchy of sources.[10] The Constitutional Court, called on various occasions to assess the relationship between legal systems, particularly between directly applicable European laws and domestic legislation, initially considered laws of European derivation to be of equal rank to domestic legislation.[11]

---

[3] With specific regard to the relationship between Community law and national law, see, among many others, Azzena (1998), pp. 132 ff. See also Carbone (2006), pp. 547 ff.

[4] The implementation of these categories of treaties by ordinary law has given rise to considerable discussion. According to some, the adaptation on the part of Italy to treaties involving limitations of state sovereignty should have taken place by means of a constitutional provision.

[5] Constitutional Court, dec. 14/1964.

[6] The amendment of Title V of Const.-Italy took place through Constitutional Law no. 3 of 18 October 2001.

[7] In fact, the amended version of Article 117 Const.-Italy does not cause any changes of a "procedural" nature to allow limitations of sovereignty but merely to acknowledge the participation of Italy in the EU system.

[8] The term "adaptation" to European law refers to the way in which the sources of law of the European legal system become part of the individual Member States' legislation.

[9] With regard to the distinction, within the sources of EU law, between primary and secondary sources, see Ruggeri (2005), p. 210.

[10] Ruggeri (2006), pp. 432 ff.

[11] Constitutional Court, dec. 14/1964. The Constitutional Court justified this decision on the basis of the fact that the founding treaties were endorsed by the formal instrument of domestic law. Thus, the criterion to be used in case of conflicting rules, according to the Court, was that of the ordinary succession of laws over time.

Around the mid-1970s, the Court established the primacy of "Community law" over domestic law, on the basis of Article 11 Const.-Italy and recognised the illegality of state acts aimed at implementing the regulations. It, however, ruled that a national court called upon to pronounce judgment could automatically waive application of the incompatible domestic provision. If a similar domestic law existed, according to the Court, it could only be eliminated after its repeal or a ruling of unconstitutionality.[12]

The Court of Justice adopted a slightly different position, finding that the primacy of Community laws over internal regulations implied that, by virtue of their direct applicability, they should be immediately applied in national law, prevailing over any incompatible domestic legislation, even if the latter was introduced at a later date.[13]

A significant shift occurred in the mid-1980s, when the Constitutional Court ruled that it was legally possible for the national court to independently disapply any domestic laws incompatible with European law, acknowledging the primacy of the latter over the former.[14] The lack of a requirement for the judge to return a judgment of constitutionality, until then considered necessary, was based on the fact that domestic law and EU law are two separate independent legal systems, although coordinated.[15] According to the Court, the distinction between our system and that of the Union implies that European legislation did not become part of domestic law, nor is it subject to the rules laid down by the laws and acts having the force of state law. This means, according to the Court, that this regulatory action is attributed with the force and value of law, since it is acknowledged as having the effectiveness that it possesses in the system of origin.

In subsequent decisions, the Court of Justice ruled that the non-application of internal rules incompatible with Community law should take place not only when those rules conflict with a European regulation but also when they are in conflict with any European provision that produces direct effects. It also ruled that this obligation applies both to courts and administrative bodies.[16]

---

[12] Constitutional Court, dec. 183/1973.

[13] Court of Justice, dec. Simmenthal, 9 March 1978, case C 106/77. In particular, in the opinion of the Court of Justice, "the national court is called upon, within its jurisdiction, to apply provisions of Community law, and is under a duty to give full effect to those provisions, if necessary not applying, of its initiative, any conflicting provision of national legislation, even if adopted subsequently, without having to request or await for the prior setting aside of such a provision by legislative or other constitutional means".

[14] Constitutional Court, dec. 170/1984.

[15] The Constitutional Court promoted the "dualist" conception of law. This was in contrast with the findings of the Court of Justice under the so-called monistic conception, which recognised the existence of a single legal order, the European one.

[16] See Court of Justice, 22 June 1988, Fratelli Costanzo, case 103/1988. Subsequently, the Court of Justice ruled that not even domestic administrative measures can be applied if they are contrary to the directly applicable rules of European law. On this point, see Court of Justice, 29 April 1999, Ciola, Case 224/1997.

As can be seen from the decisions cited, the result achieved by the Court of Justice and the Constitutional Court, albeit via different routes, is the same: the affirmation of the primacy of European law and the automatic disapplication by national courts of the incompatible domestic law. In the following period, the Constitutional Court, adopting the approach expressed by the Court of Justice, ruled that the court should not apply the internal rules if these are incompatible not only with the regulations but also with laws producing direct effects, i.e., both the provisions of the Treaty[17] and the directives.[18]

Directive 2013/48/EU falls precisely within this legal-institutional context, increasingly inclined to give paramount importance to legislative sources of a European, rather than domestic, origin, also in the field of criminal justice.[19] This applies primarily with reference to the aforementioned duty of the national court to disapply domestic rules incompatible with EU rules that have "direct effect"[20] and, moreover, to interpret Italian provisions in accordance with European legislation that does not have direct effect.[21] But it applies also and above all with reference to the duty of national courts to comply with the interpretation of EU law provided by the Court of Justice of the European Union.[22]

This would seem to determine a change in the relationship between the judge and the law. The criminal judge reconstructs the abstract circumstances of the case, performing an interpretation, so to speak, of the second degree, which can result in the "creation" of a rule of criminal procedure to be applied to the case, rather than that determined by the national legislature.[23] The domestic law is the subject of an

[17] Constitutional Court, dec. 389/1989.

[18] Cf. Constitutional Court, dec. 64/1990 and Constitutional Court, dec. 168/1991.

[19] One cannot fail to point out that over the years the so-called theory of limits and counter-limits has been introduced to limit the advance of Community law within the constitutional structures of the Member States. The term "counter-limits" was perceptively coined by Barile, who in the early 1970s used it to indicate those limitations (the fundamental principles, or rather, as stated by the Constitutional Court, the supreme principles and inalienable rights of the person) to limitations of sovereignty pursuant to Article 11 Const.-Italy. See, by way of example, Cartabia (1995), pp. 102 ff. This theory was an important spur to the affirmation of a genuine European protection of fundamental rights. Along these lines, cf. Cartabia (2007), pp. 13 ff.

This theory has long been debated. In the opinion of other authoritative scholars, counter-limits do not exist on a theoretical level, for the reason that the contradiction between Article 11 Const.-Italy and the remaining fundamental principles may not be resolved under the system to the benefit of either one or the other. This contradiction, however, needs to be composed in accordance with the usual rule of "balancing" values, a rule that may variously lead to the prevalence of one or the other value. Cf. Ruggeri (2006), pp. 289 ff.

[20] Kostoris (2014), p. 36.

[21] Sotis (2007), pp. 33 ff.; Viganò (2010), pp. 617 ff. On the distinction between European legislation with "direct" and that with "indirect" effects, cf. the recent reconstruction by Kostoris (2014), pp. 35 ff.

[22] In this regard, see Manes (2007), pp. 15 ff.

[23] Kostoris (2014), p. 39, talks of "'integrative' effect" produced by a consistent interpretation and stresses that the outcome of the interpretation "will be the result of the combination between the domestic and supranational law".

interpretation whose parameters are legislative (domestic and European) and case law (Court of Justice) principles.[24]

In the range of instruments protecting the fundamental rights of the accused, the legal system of the European Union may act as a strong lever, principally, for reasserting the rule of law, in the face of "deviant" domestic case law.[25] The reference to EU law could moreover help overcome any structural weaknesses in domestic law: when it conflicts with the fundamental rights outlined at a European level and provided that the European framework is capable of producing direct effects, it should be set aside.[26]

In a system of the "multi-level" protection of rights, we need to verify what scope for innovation these acts have in terms of providing procedural guarantees, compared to the levels of protection ensured under Italian law and judicial practice in terms of the application of domestic rules.

In general, criminal courts should be attributed with the duty of interpreting European law "on the basis of the interpretative principles in force in the legal system of origin, and not those established in the Italian system".[27] However, by virtue of the "non-regression clause" usually provided for in the Directives issued in this field,[28] no provision of these texts can be interpreted as limiting the procedural guarantees laid down by domestic legislation (constitutional and ordinary) or by the Charter of Fundamental Rights of the European Union, the ECHR, international law or the law of any other Member State.[29]

---

[24] The Court of Justice may well affirm incompatibility with EU law of a certain interpretation of the internal standard and therefore, ultimately, bind the national court "to give priority in resolving the dispute to the European source of law (as authoritatively interpreted by the Court of Justice)". See Viganò (2011), p. 14. The mechanism mentioned in the text implies the risk that the consistent interpretation of national law in conformity with Union law is conducted on the basis of a binding case law of the Court of Justice based on an inexact reconstruction of national law by the supranational court. With reference to the problem posed by the fact that the Court of Justice, for the purpose of finding the incompatibility of national provisions with EU law, knows the national law through information provided by the referring court, that may however be incorrect or incomplete; see Kostoris (2014), p. 31. With regard to the "Pupino" case, see Lupària (2005), p. 3544. See also Campailla (2012), pp. 99 ff. Some authors point out that "it does not seem correct to have the supranational law with which domestic law is in conflict to play at the same time the role of benchmark against which to measure the conflict and that of a tool to resolve it". See Kostoris (2014), p. 42.

[25] On this phenomenology, from a criminal procedure perspective, see Amodio (2003), p. 8.

[26] With reference to the instrument of non-application, see Gaito (2010), p. 40.

[27] Viganò (2014).

[28] By way of example, see Article 14 of Directive 2013/48/EU. In literature, cf. Bubula (2014).

[29] The result, in this area of the process, is a recovery of the (natural) pre-eminence of domestic law for the criminal court.

3 The Right of Defence in Remand Proceedings in Italian Procedural Law: The Formal Interview Under Caution

3.1 General Characteristics of the Formal Interview Under Caution

In order for a more detailed examination of the issue before us, we should now dwell on the essential characteristics of the interview of a person subject to a personal precautionary measure, since this represents the most significant expression of the delicate relationship between authority and freedom in the field of precautionary measures.[30] Significantly, the Italian Code of Criminal Procedure of 1930 had included the regulation on arrest warrants at the beginning of the book dedicated to the stage of evidence gathering, with the clear objective of defining the status (detention) of the accused person[31] and making it an instrument for the successful collection of evidence in criminal matters.[32]

With a remarkable qualitative leap compared to the previous law, which allowed the accused person in detention to have his first meeting with the lawyer only after the end of questioning,[33] the law containing the delegation for the new Italian Code of Criminal Procedure[34] granted him the right to meet with the lawyer immediately, or no later than 7 days from implementation of the measure limiting his personal freedom.[35] This constituted the first step in the development of the instrument as a means of defence.[36]

The fact that the detention order was issued without involving the accused person and only on the basis of material acquired and selected by the Public Prosecutor led the legislature in 1988 to establish that after execution of the order the person in custody should be questioned.

Article 294 of the Italian Code of Criminal Procedure (hereafter, CCP-Italy) provides that the court "which has decided to apply the measure"[37] must proceed

[30] Mazza (1994), pp. 822 ff.

[31] Marzaduri (1992), pp. 278 ff.

[32] In accordance with an inquisitorial vision, the accused person was considered "the repository of a truth to be squeezed out of him". On this point, see Cordero (1987), pp. 19 ff.

[33] Article 135 of the 1930 CCP-Italy.

[34] Law 81/1987.

[35] Art. 2(6) of the Law 81/1987.

[36] From a "beast of confession" (see Cordero 1987, p. 19) we now have a person with precise rights and guarantees, including the right not to contribute in any way to his own conviction. On this point, see Mazza (2010), p. 714.

[37] In terms of European case law, the concept seems to be highly innovative in scope; in fact, it does not seem to be confined to establishing contact with any judge but includes establishing contact with the judge who decided on the application of the precautionary measure, unlike Article 5(3) ECHR, which only speaks of "a judge".

with questioning at most 5 days after the commencement of preventive custody in prison or at most 10 days for other measures.[38]

According to the Constitutional Court, for the defendant *in vinculis*, questioning is the most effective means of defence regarding solely the custody order issued.[39]

The defence, due to the knowledge of the actions carried out by the Public Prosecutor at the basis of his request, may try to scale down, through the European measure, the weight of the elements in the charge. It is precisely through questioning that the court must assess whether the conditions for enforcement of the measure remain. Therefore, formal interview under caution is indispensable, under penalty of invalidity.

Before the amendment introduced by Law 63/2001, Article 294(4) CCP-Italy envisaged for the prosecution and the defence the "right to intervene" rather than the obligation to do so. Consequently, if the defender had not exercised this option, the court was not obliged to appoint any replacement pursuant to article 97(4) CCP-Italy.[40]

Following Law 63/2001, the possibility of intervention on the part of the prosecutor remains, but the presence of the lawyer at the questioning was established as a necessary condition for its validity. In this way, the formal interview under caution is similar to the other hypotheses envisaged under Article 503(5) CCP-Italy,[41] those referred to in Articles 391[42] and 422 CCP-Italy.[43]

If the relevant conditions are met, Article 97 CCP-Italy applies here: in other words, it will be necessary to appoint a lawyer if the defendant fails to do so, assigning one to him pursuant to article 97(4) CCP-Italy in the event of failure to contact, non-appearance of or abandonment on the part of the lawyer appointed by the defendant or the court.

In terms of penalties, violation of the provision constitutes nullity as provided for under Article 179 (1) CCP-Italy. Acknowledgement of the invalidity of the procedure results in the loss of effectiveness of preventive custody, leading to the need for a valid interview, which must be completed prior to the issuance of a new measure (Art. 302 CCP-Italy). It also means that none of the statements made up to that point may be used as evidence.

[38] Act 332/1995 extended the list of measures that may require the performance of questioning, previously required only for house arrest.

[39] Constitutional Court, dec. 77/1997. In literature, see Santoriello (1999), pp. 1257 ff.

[40] Court of Cassation, Joint Sections 12 October 1993, no. 748, Thomas, in *CED Cass.* 195625.

[41] Article 503 CCP-Italy, inserted among the regulations on the adversarial procedure, governs the examination of private individuals.

[42] Article 391 CCP-Italy governs the hearing for the confirmation of arrest in flagrante delicto and detention for questioning.

[43] Article 422 CCP-Italy provides for the provision of supplementary evidence by the judge in the evidentiary phase of the preliminary hearing in order to issue a ruling not to prosecute.

3.2 *Interview Between the Lawyer with the Accused in Preventive Custody and Its Deferment*

In order to more thoroughly examine the issue before us, it seems only right to analyse the provision contained in Article 104 CCP-Italy, which governs the right, and not merely an option, of the person in custody to speak to his lawyer.

This regulation, on one hand, conforms to the requirements of equal treatment, as well as to the exercise of a defence[44] for defendants (or suspects) held in custody and those at freedom,[45] and, on the other, complies with Article 93 of the European Prison Rules,[46] according to which "the accused has the right, from the moment of imprisonment [...] to receive visits from his lawyer in order to prepare his defence".[47] The Code of Procedure provides that, as a rule, the person remanded in custody, like the person held for questioning or arrested, has the right to meet with his lawyer immediately after being deprived of personal freedom [Art 104 (1) and (2), CCP-Italy].[48]

It was therefore provided that the defender, whether appointed by the defendant himself or by the court, should be immediately notified of the enforcement of restrictive measures [Articles 293(1) and 386(2) CPP-Italy],[49] and the defence lawyer has the right to access the places where the person held for questioning, arrested or subjected to preventive custody is being held (Art. 36 of the Rules Implementing the CCP-Italy).

In order to guarantee the full exercise of the right of defence pursuant to article 24 Const.-Italy, after the execution of such measures, the Constitutional Court has emphasised the need to ensure

> "that the lawyer has the most comprehensive and facilitated understanding of the elements on which the request of the prosecutor is based, in order to provide appropriate and informed assistance during questioning" of the person held in custody, "and to be able to assess with full knowledge of the situation the most appropriate instruments to protect the

---

[44] Arts. 3, 13(1) and 24(2) Const.-Italy.

[45] Conso (1970), pp. 242 ff.

[46] Recommendation No. R (1987) 3 adopted by the Committee of Ministers of the Council of Europe on 12 February 1987, eur-lex.europa.eu. See also the more recent Recommendation R (2006)2, adopted on 11 January 2006, eur-lex.europa.eu.

[47] Kostoris (1995), p. 41. In the interest of completion, moreover, the Constitutional Court has also taken steps, declaring the illegality of Article 18 of Law no. 354 of 26 July 1975, in the part in which it does not require that the detainee convicted by a final judgment should have the right to confer with his lawyer right from the beginning of enforcement of the sentence. Cf. Constitutional Court, dec. 212/1997.

[48] This rule also applies to a prisoner serving a sentence. Cf. Constitutional Court, dec. 212/1997.

[49] Knowledge of the procedures up to that time carried out by the prosecution, which is brought to the defence lawyer by virtue of the provision of Article 293(3) CCP-Italy, represents the fulfilment of a necessary, though not sufficient, condition for a more adequate technical defence and has a direct impact in terms of the suspect's self-defence.

> personal liberty of his client, from a request for review, revocation or replacement of the measure to the filing of an appeal".[50]

The right in question[51] is available from the beginning of the deprivation of liberty, whether as a result of preventive custody or in cases of arrest and holding for questioning. In this regard, it must be made available automatically, without any obstacles for the defence lawyer.

The aim of the instrument is mainly to allow defence strategies to be agreed during questioning. In any case, since the right to interview is absolute in nature, it is not possible to impose any purpose on the meeting between detainee and lawyer, nor may the interview be influenced by the fact that the former is in solitary confinement.[52]

Article 104 CCP-Italy provides, however, a limit to the right to meet with the lawyer in the case of "specific and exceptional reasons for caution". For these reasons, the interview may be deferred for a period not exceeding 5 days.[53]

The Court of Cassation[54] has pointed out, on the line of consolidated maxims, that

> the order adopted by the investigating magistrate to postpone the interview is justified in the event of exceptional precautionary requirements, regarding the danger of pre-establishing defensive strategies aimed at hindering 'the course of justice', going beyond the legitimate exercise of the right of defence, or at delaying or preventing the identification of the other associates who have not yet been identified during the investigation.

This approach displays, however, a theoretical danger, since there is no proof that the delay of the interview is, in practice, essential in order to avoid compromising the proceedings.

Equally theoretical is the assessment made in the field of organised crime. Here, according to the Court of Cassation:

> danger of suppression of evidence is related to the intrinsic seriousness of the alleged offence of mafia association, the plurality of suspects (35 people) and the plurality of alleged criminal offenses and purpose of the criminal association (multiple cases of continued aggravated extortion).[55]

---

[50] Constitutional Court, dec. 192/1997.

[51] It may be legitimately waived by the accused person who refuses to be interviewed, without prejudice to the validity of subsequent procedural actions.

[52] Kostoris (1990), pp. 1391 ff.

[53] Prior to the amendment to article 104(3) CCP-Italy, introduced under Article 1 of law no. 332 of August 8, 1995, the postponement was for a time not exceeding 7 days.

[54] For the reference to "the danger of pre-establishing a common strategy", see Court of Cassation, Division VI, 3 May 2006, no. 15113, Luparini, CED Cass, 21768.

[55] Court of Cassation, Division VI, 22 January 2010, no. 2941 and previously, the Court of Cassation, Division V, 27 September 1993 Zambrotti, Archivio nuova procedura penale, 1993, p. 716: "The measure which, pursuant to article 104 CCP-Italy, postpones the right of the accused remanded in custody to confer with defence counsel may also be based on the seriousness of the facts (regarding a plurality of suspects), together with the need to avoid the possibility of establishing preordained and common defensive arguments of convenience". For criticism of

Insofar as the deferral departs from the general principle, it should be applied only when strictly necessary.[56]

We should note that this limit was not considered contrary either to Articles 3 and 24(2) Const.-Italy or to Article 6 ECHR, which do not preclude a reasonable postponement of the first contact between the accused and lawyer "in the more important interests of the administration of justice".[57]

We should mention from the outset the critical issues that emerge in relation to the parameter indicated in Article 8(1)(c) of the Directive, whereby "any temporary exemption pursuant to article 3 (5) or (6), or of Article 5(3) is not based solely on the type or severity of the alleged offence".

3.3 *Judicial Review on the Justification of Preventive Custody*

Postponing the interview violates the minimum guarantees that inform the rules of due process and should therefore be subjected to close scrutiny.[58]

The limitation of this right is possible from the beginning of detention and, in the event of it being extended for the full period allowed by law, any contact between defence lawyer and prisoner would, in fact, be prevented before the interview under Article 294 CPP-Italy.[59]

Significantly, the prosecutor has the possibility to request that the judge examines the suspect within 48 h following "capture" [Art. 294(1-*ter*) CCP-Italy]. In this

---

this, see Scalfati (2010), pp. 1093 ff. Cf., Court of Cassation, Division IV, 29 October 2007, no. 39827, Cambria, *CED Cass.*, 237 845: "although the ban on conversation between suspect and lawyer could also be based on the alleged severity of facts regarding a number of suspects, there must however be indicated, even in this case, the specific need to avoid the possibility of establishing pre-established and common defensive arguments of convenience, since this need cannot be inferred by way of presumption and/or be considered implicit in the subjective and objective connotations of the alleged offence leading to a custodial measure". According to the Court of Cassation, Division VI, 2 October 2006, no. 32622, Litizzi, *CED Cass.*, 235019, "the danger of compromising evidence that the measure aims to avoid is clear from the seriousness of the facts, the plurality of suspects and the organized context of the activity engaged in".

[56] The legislature did not, therefore, underestimate the risks of possible undesirable relations between the defendant and the lawyer such as to undermine the requirements of the investigation. Grevi (1996), pp. 3 ff.

[57] Court of Cassation, Division I, 20 April 1995, no. 719, Spiro, *CED* 200224.

[58] On this point, see Trevisson Lupacchini (1993), p. 193; Giunchedi (2002), p. 133. Some scholarship, however, believes that the literal meaning should not be overlooked, whereby it seems that the reasons for the postponement, while having to be sought in the context of "reasons of caution" relating to the arrest, must possess a *quid pluris* that justifies their uniqueness and specificity.

In case law, see Court of Cassation, Division VI, 15 July 2003, Vinci, *CED Cass.* 326223.

[59] If the interview continues after the 5th day, it should be suspended, to allow the meeting with the lawyer up to that point denied. Kostoris (1995), p. 41.

case, if the ban on meeting the lawyer is ordered for the maximum period, the prosecutor still has 3 days to question the suspect, resulting in an inevitable risk of making the formal interview under caution an instrument that provides no effective protection.[60]

The prosecutor, where permitted, may independently prevent the suspect from meeting his lawyer and, in the meantime, question the person arrested, held for questioning, or subjected to preventive custody.[61]

From a detailed examination of the regulations in question, the results achieved are far from clear, especially in the preliminary phase, in which problems concerning the limitation of personal freedom normally arise.

The judge for preliminary investigations, when questioning the person detained, while having to provide a reasoned order at the request of the prosecutor, is unlikely, given the limited time, to be able to effectively assess whether or not postponement is necessary. He will largely base his decision on evidence provided by the prosecution, that is, by one of the parties, with a negative impact on the effectiveness of judicial review. Nor is there any point appealing to the obligation of the prosecutor, introduced under Law 332/1995, to attach to the application for a precautionary measure all the information favourable to the suspect, an obligation that cannot be considered satisfied at the time of submission of the request but must also include the new judicial review of the legality of preventive custody during pre-trial questioning. In fact, it is always the prosecutor who determines which factors are favourable to the accused and which should be forwarded to the judge. The exception, therefore, ends up becoming the rule and fully allows the judge for the preliminary investigations and the public prosecutor to question the detained suspect, without the latter having had any contact with his lawyer. The absence of a contact with the lawyer prevents the accused from preparing an adequate defence. Even if the interview is preceded by a prior meeting with the lawyer, it will still be extremely difficult for the latter, due to the strict time requirements governing preventive custody, to carry out a "parallel defensive investigation" with the interview in mind. Moreover, given the unfortunate wording of Articles 335 and 369 CCP-Italy,[62] it may well happen that the suspect becomes aware of criminal proceedings against him only when the precautionary measure is enforced. The very discovery of procedural documents by the prosecutor to the interested party often remains something that should happen in principle but is not supported by practice.

The filing of procedural documents, pursuant to Article 293(3) CPP-Italy, then, is often pointless, since the issue of copies may not interfere with the short, binding

[60] Grevi (1996), pp. 3 ff.

[61] Unlike in the cases of custodial measures, questioning by the prosecutor pursuant to article 388 CCP-Italy is completely independent and may therefore be conducted prior to the examination performed by the judge to immediately check the legitimacy of the restrictive measure. Constitutional Court, dec. 384/1996.

[62] See the chapter by Candito, this volume, Sect. 3.2.2.

time limits laid down for the questioning of an accused person, it being evident that neither may the lawyer demand nor may the judicial authority grant extensions of such terms when it turns out to be infeasible to copy all the documents required within the strict time limits established for questioning. This situation occurs systematically in cases where the prosecutor requests that questioning take place within 48 h.

These drawbacks, in part, do not occur in the less frequent event of application of the precautionary measure and questioning after the charge has been made.[63]

As the lawyer, among other things, is not granted any opportunity to ask direct questions to the accused, he is forced to provide passive support.

Note, also, that the questioning may be conducted by the same judge who ordered the precautionary order, who will clearly seek confirmation of his earlier decision. Nor does the judge have the competence to engage in further investigations, at least not if these are requested by a party in the proceedings, to assess in greater detail the evidence collected during questioning.[64] Once the legality of the measure has been confirmed during questioning and the process has been completed with the subsequent adversarial meeting (even if its adversarial nature is not achieved or is not achieved effectively), the procedural system does envisage any tools for the periodic assessment of the judge's decision to order preventive custody, but merely adheres to standard procedural deadlines.

The right of the lawyer to attend the interview is an obligation in terms of professional ethics, and failure to allow this results in disciplinary liability, but the reality of court-appointed counsel and legal aid is dramatic.

The prevalence of a merely formal guarantee of the right of defence is even more evident when there is the recourse to pre-precautionary measures (a prelude, at least usually, to the issue of an order for a custodial measure), which are applied at the actual time when a crime is allegedly committed.

In this hypothesis, the use of the instruments provided for in Articles 291(1) and 293(3) CPP-Italy is only theoretical: the defence and civil rights aspects of questioning succumb to satisfy investigative needs that, in the event of arrest or holding for questioning, take priority and are easy to implement at a time when the detainee is in a position of severe psychological inferiority, which is not compensated for by the necessary presence of a lawyer, since the latter must remain silent and is kept almost entirely in the dark regarding the details of the case.

[63] In this case, the lawyer and the accused will already have had the opportunity to inspect and take copies of the entire file of the prosecutor, in accordance with the combined provisions of Articles 416(2) CCP-Italy, 419(2) and (3) CCP-Italy and 131 Rules Implementing the CCP-Italy. The conversation between the accused person and his lawyer, after the request for trial, can no longer be postponed; the parties will have had the time necessary to properly prepare their defensive strategies. There in any case remain some intrinsic limits to the ways of carrying out the interview in question.

[64] The Constitutional Court, in judgment no. 384 of 1996, justified and legitimated this discipline. Constitutional Court, dec. 384/1996.

Note that the physical and psychological pressure caused by solitary confinement is such as to greatly diminish, if not cancel, a person's freedom of self-determination. This ends up frustrating the adversarial process during questioning and the effectiveness of judicial review. The perverse mechanism of the deferral of the meeting with the lawyer laid down by Article CPP-104 Italy is strictly linked to the application of caution, to emphasise that the person subjected to the restriction of personal freedom, in his moment of greatest psychological weakness, is a tool with which to obtain statements. At the same time, therefore, the immediate recognition of a qualified defence is seen as compromising the genuineness of the procedural action, and not an indispensable condition for allowing more effective self-defence, also in terms of the guarantee whereby nobody is obliged to incriminate himself.

In light of the above, it is regrettable that investigative needs take priority over the rights of freedom of the detained person.[65] This restriction of liberty must never be enforced merely to avoid contact between the defendant and his lawyer in view of questioning pursuant to article 294 CCP-Italy or a remand hearing. It would be desirable, therefore, for the reasons for the postponement to be made clear right from the moment of arrest.[66] Deferral may not be used to prevent the flow of information between the defendant and his lawyer with the aim of obtaining "unadulterated" information from the suspect during questioning.[67]

4 The Guarantees Provided Under Directive 2013/48/EU

4.1 Minimum Standards on the Right to Appoint a Lawyer: Scope and Content. Principle of Effectiveness and Practicality

Within the framework of reinforcing the procedural rights of suspects or defendants in criminal proceedings,[68] Directive 2013/48/EU[69] establishes minimum

[65] Dalia and Cimadomo (1999), pp. 501 ff.

[66] Spangher (1993), pp. 26 ff.

[67] Case law has found it legitimate to prevent the immediate meeting between the defendant and his lawyer in order to prevent irregularities due to the adoption of common defensive strategies of convenience. Court of Cassation, Division VI, 15 July 2003, Vinci, *CED Cass* 326223.

[68] On 30 November 2009, the Council adopted a Resolution regarding a roadmap for reinforcing the procedural rights of suspects or defendants in criminal proceedings. The "roadmap" calls for the adoption of measures regarding the right to translation and interpretation (measure A); the right to information about rights and the charge (measure B); the right to legal advice and legal aid (measure C); the right to communication with relatives, employers and consular authorities (measure D); and special safeguards for vulnerable suspects and defendants (measure E).

[69] Directive 2013/48/EU, cit. For a more detailed discussion of the Directive, see the chapter by Bachmaier Winter, this volume.

standards[70] concerning the right to avail oneself of a lawyer in criminal proceedings and in execution proceedings for the European arrest warrant.[71]

This Directive should be implemented taking into account the relevant provisions of Directive 2012/13/EU,[72] which establish that suspects and accused persons should be informed immediately of the right to avail themselves of a lawyer and that if they should be subjected to the restriction of personal freedom, they must immediately receive a letter of rights that contains information on this right.[73]

In order to perform a more accurate examination of the effects of the Directive in question on the procedure of the formal interview under caution, especially to see if there is the possibility of increasing guarantees for a detained accused person compared to the provisions contained in the Italian Code of Criminal Procedure, we need to identify, principally, its scope of application and then, subsequently, the scope of the right at issue and, finally, the possibility of derogations and waivers.

Pursuant to article 2(1), the Directive

> applies to suspects or accused persons in criminal proceedings from the time when they are made aware by the competent authorities of a Member State, by official notification or otherwise, that they are suspected or accused of having committed a criminal offence, and irrespective of whether they are deprived of liberty. It applies until the conclusion of the proceedings, which is understood to mean the final determination of the question whether the suspect or accused person has committed the offence, including, where applicable, sentencing and the resolution of any appeal.

The moment when time starts to run is, therefore, identified by the material concept of "charge", in line with that developed by the European Court of Human Rights.[74] As is known, in the context of the ECHR, this term has acquired its own independent meaning, responding to a "material concept" that identifies it with "the official notification, emanating from the competent authority, of the accusation of having committed a criminal offence". Consequently, in this sense, one can be "charged" before being brought before a judicial body, since it is not even necessary to include the "accusation" in a communication to be received by the person concerned. On this basis, the following were therefore considered times when proceedings begin and from which civil rights guarantees come into effect: arrest

[70] Recital 14 and 54 of Directive 2013/48/EU and article 1 of Directive 2013/48/EU. Note that Recital no. 54, then, provides, in addition to the power of Member States to ensure a higher level of protection than that provided for by the Directive itself, the duty to ensure a level of protection no lower than the rules of the EU FRCh and the ECHR, as interpreted by the case law of the Court of Justice and the ECtHR.

[71] Council Framework Decision 2002/584/JHA of 13 June 2002 on the European Arrest Warrant and the surrender procedures between Member States.

[72] Directive 2012/13/EU of the European Parliament and of the Council of 22 May 2012 on the right to information in criminal proceedings. On this issue, see the chapter by Quattrocolo, this book.

[73] Recital 14.

[74] On this point, see Ubertis (2012), pp. 21 ff.; Bartole et al. (2012), pp. 185 ff.

in flagrante delicto, the issuance of a preliminary injunction, the request to present oneself for questioning before the magistrate, the questioning of a person suspected of having committed a criminal offence, formal notification of the accusation.

The "accusation", therefore, may also emerge during questioning [Art. 2(3)]. In this case, i.e. when a person other than a suspect or an accused person, such as a witness, in turn becomes a suspect or accused person during questioning carried out by the police or by another law enforcement authority in the context of criminal proceedings, it is appropriate to immediately suspend questioning.[75]

Having identified the scope of application, we need to identify the scope of the right in question.

Article 3, entitled "The right of access to a lawyer in criminal proceedings" provides that Member States must ensure that suspects and defendants have the right to meet in private and to communicate with the lawyer assisting them [Articles 3(1) and 4].[76] Therefore:

> Member States shall ensure that suspects and accused persons have the right of access to a lawyer in such a time and in such a manner so as to allow the persons concerned to exercise their rights of defence practically and effectively.

One of the key principles of the new Directive is thus clear: the defence must be practical and effective.

Also, the practical arrangements that Member States may establish regarding the duration and frequency of meetings or the safety of the lawyer and of the suspect or accused person[77] or the duration, frequency and methods of communication between suspect-accused persons and the lawyer assisting them[78] should not prejudice the effective exercise or essence of the rights of the suspects or accused persons.

The principle of effectiveness, then, clearly emerges from Article 3(3)(b), where it is stated that

[75] See Recital 21. This provision is in accordance with the principle of the protection against self-incrimination.

[76] In detail, Article 4 lays down the principle of confidentiality of communications between suspects or accused persons and their lawyer in the exercise of their right to avail themselves of a lawyer, including meetings, correspondence, telephone conversations and other forms of communication permitted under national law. In the same vein, Recital 33, after recognising the essential nature of confidentiality in order to ensure a fair trial, however recognises the procedures applicable in the event of circumstances that lead to the objective and concrete suspicion that the lawyer is involved in an offence with the suspect or accused person. This derogation is justified by the fact that the criminal activity of the lawyer should not be considered an example of legitimate assistance. It is also specified that the obligation to respect confidentiality implies for Member States not only the prohibition to interfere in such communications or access them but also the duty to ensure, if the suspects or accused persons are deprived of their liberty or are otherwise in a place under state control, that the provisions relating to communication defend and protect confidentiality.

[77] Recital 22.

[78] Recital 23.

> Member States shall ensure that suspects or accused persons have the right for their lawyer to be present and participate effectively when questioned. Such participation shall be in accordance with procedures under national law, provided that such procedures do not prejudice the effective exercise and essence of the right concerned. Where a lawyer participates during questioning, the fact that such participation has taken place shall be noted using the recording procedure in accordance with the law of the Member State concerned.[79]

This concept (effectiveness) can lead to abuse and leaves plenty of room for manoeuvre in legislation and domestic case law.

Substantial doubts also arise in terms of establishing the time from which the right in question must be guaranteed.

The Directive makes frequent use of the phrase "without undue delay", which is somewhat vague.[80]

Article 3(2) states that this moment occurs when the first of the following events happens:

> a) before they [the suspects or accused persons] are questioned by the police or by other law enforcement or judicial authority;
> b) upon the carrying out by investigating or other competent authorities of an investigative or other evidence-gathering act in accordance with point (c) of paragraph 3;
> c) without undue delay after deprivation of liberty;
> d) where they have been summoned to appear before a court having jurisdiction in criminal matters, in due time before they appear before that court.

Some doubt of interpretation arises when it comes to identifying the time referred to in point a). According to the literal meaning, to speak of "before they are questioned" in an indefinite way would not make much sense, especially seeing the precise mention of the moment when evidence statements are made as a possible time to initially apply the Directive. Recital 20 partially resolves the issue (although strangely is not taken up in the text of Article 3), establishing that

> For the purposes of this Directive, questioning does not include preliminary questioning by the police or by another law enforcement authority the purpose of which is to identify the person concerned, to verify the possession of weapons or other similar safety issues or to determine whether an investigation should be started, for example in the course of road-side check or during regular random checks when a suspect or accused person has not yet been identified.

We should note the heterogeneous nature of the situations illustrated, intended to be extended as an analogical criterion, and the impossibility of attributing a single meaning to the term "questioning".[81]

---

[79] Along the same lines are Recitals 25, 26, 28 and 29.

[80] By way of example, see Article 3(2).

[81] For example, also in terms of summary information, the only case where the lawyer's assistance is obligatory is that provided for under Article 350(5) CCP-Italy ("at the place or in the immediacy of the fact" for "the immediate continuation of the investigation").

This term must be understood not in the formal, but in the substantial, sense, inspired by the civil-rights spirit of the Directive, evident, inter alia, in the emphasis with which it protects, in particular, those who have been deprived of personal freedom.

Partially different are the regulations governing the right of access to a lawyer in the event of the EAW.

Article 10 in fact establishes legal assistance in the executing state and in the issuing state, requiring both to provide information.[82] This rule must be read, even for practical reasons, together with the recitals.

4.2 Exceptions to the Right of Access to a Lawyer and **Deminutio** *of Protection*

The rules regarding exemptions, albeit temporary, raise various doubts.[83] One wonders, in particular, whether they can lead to a *deminutio* of protection and to what extent they can be admitted.

The first hypothesis of a departure from the application of paragraph 2(c) exists when, because of the geographical remoteness of the suspect or accused person, it is impossible to guarantee the right of recourse to a lawyer without undue delay after the deprivation of liberty, provided that there are exceptional circumstances and only in the stage preceding the trial [Art 3 (5)].[84]

It is also possible to waive the right of access to a lawyer in exceptional circumstances and in the period preceding the trial, only if there is the urgent need to avert serious adverse consequences for the life, liberty or physical integrity of a person or there is a need for immediate action of the investigating authorities to avoid seriously compromising criminal proceedings [Art 3 (6)].[85]

Although Article 8 provides the general conditions for the application of these exemptions—such as respect for the principle of proportionality, a strict limitation

---

[82] The lawyer appointed in the issuing State will have the role of assisting the lawyer appointed in the executing state "by providing that lawyer with information and advice" [Art 10 (4)].

[83] Note that in Directive 2012/13/EU, there is a single derogating provision in relation to the right of access to investigative documents.

[84] Recital 30, not fully referred to in Article 3 (5), specifies that during a temporary derogation for this reason, if it is impossible to have immediate access to a lawyer due to the geographical remoteness of the suspect or accused person, the Member States should establish communication via telephone or videoconference, unless this is impossible.

[85] Recitals 31 and 32, not included in their entirety in Article 3(6), provide the competent authorities with the power to question suspects or accused persons without the presence of a lawyer only if they have been informed of their right not to respond and may exercise this right, provided that the interview does not prejudice defence rights, including guarantees against self-incrimination. Questioning can take place only for the purpose and to the extent necessary to obtain information essential to avoid serious negative consequences for the life, liberty or physical integrity of a person.

in time, its not being based solely on the type or severity of the offence, its not affecting the overall fairness of the proceedings and the necessary judicial authorisation—doubts arise about possible abuse, resulting in irreparable harm to the rights of defence. It should be noted, inter alia, that many of these conditions are expressed in somewhat ambiguous and generic terms.

In the light of the analysis, it seems that, in some parts, the regulations for the right of access to a lawyer and, consequently, the right of defence of the person subject to the restriction of personal freedom are incomplete.

5 The Effects of Directive 2013/48/EU on the Italian System: A Comparison of Regulatory Systems

5.1 A New Step Towards the Harmonisation of Defence Rights in Criminal Matters

Directive 2013/48/EU is a significant step forward in strengthening the rights of the defence in criminal proceedings in the European Union: the variegated mosaic originating from European law is enhanced by an additional component of a civil-rights nature. It offers undoubted advantages compared to the current situation, although it does not add essential safeguards to those already recognised by the ECHR and case law.

Within the aim of the European Union for the construction of a European area of freedom, security and justice,[86] the Directive aims to establish common minimum standards on the rights of suspects and defendants in criminal proceedings throughout the European Union to have access to a lawyer.[87]

It is placed in a perspective of progressive and, so to speak, "timid"[88] rebalancing in favour of the protection of the rights of the accused with respect to the "repressive and preventive [perspective] or better [...] efficiency divorced from an interest in uniform legislation ensuring civil rights",[89] seen in the first legislative

[86] Some authors speak of a new step in the "slow" path towards creating a "European statute of defence guarantees". Among others, see Siracusano (2013), p. 77. Others speak of "'European codification' of minimum rules for the protection of the rights of defence". Among others, Vigoni (2014), p. 14.

[87] See also, on this point, Council Framework Decision 2002/584/JHA of 13 June 2002 on the European arrest warrant and the surrender procedures between Member States, http://europa.eu.

[88] Rafaraci (2011), p. 129, speaks of "prudent gradualism", in reference to the EU approach to the issue of procedural rights. More generally, on the "uncertain" path of European integration in the field of criminal procedure, see, among many others, Catalano (2007), p. 522.

[89] The criticisms are levelled by Mazza (2011), p. 34.

acts undertaken by the European Union in the field of police and judicial cooperation in criminal matters.[90]

In other words, there seems to be a historic transition from a conception of the harmonisation of criminal procedure of the Member States as a means to achieve the goal of more effective cooperation in combating transnational crime[91] to a conception of the harmonisation of procedural safeguards set up by the law of the Member States as a value in itself.

In fact, it is true that legislative harmonisation is, in the European system, "aimed at—and consequently also limited to—the need to facilitate mutual recognition"[92]: harmonisation constitutes the basis of mutual recognition[93] and, therefore, of judicial cooperation.[94] It is also true, however, that the purpose enshrined at the highest level of the scale of the sources of European law, to achieve an effective "area of freedom, security and justice",[95] is placed in a dimension concerning the protection of fundamental rights, principally the right of defence of the accused and the suspect, which goes far beyond judicial cooperation.[96]

In the European construction, there is, alongside the security approach, that "liberal approach based on the security of rights (the actual exercise of rights and legal freedoms) also in the face of institutional powers", which authoritative scholarship has recently dealt with.[97]

From a careful examination of the Directive, it however becomes clear that the approach taken by the EU in the field of the protection of "procedural rights" has gaps, also in terms of method. The broad perspective adopted in the "Stockholm Programme", in the selection of procedural safeguards subject to harmonisation, risks "not maintaining any direct connection with the protection of rights according to common minimum standards in cross-border situations, which are the specific

---

[90] For the particular problems of administrative and judicial cooperation in criminal tax law, see Corso (2013), pp. 465 ff.

[91] For an emphasis on the existence of a logical order between cooperation and harmonisation, cf. Galantini (2002), p. 271.

[92] In the sense that the harmonisation of defensive guarantees facilitates "the application of the principle of mutual recognition, given that the existence of a common framework of essential individual guarantees increases the mutual trust on which that principle is based", Rafaraci (2011), p. 120.

[93] In turn, the principle of mutual recognition of judgments and judicial decisions is the cornerstone of judicial cooperation in criminal matters in the Union [Art 82(1) TFEU]. Caprioli (2007), p. 391, talks of an authentic "cornerstone" of judicial cooperation, In addition, see Siracusano (2011), p. 85; Gaito (2010), pp. 33 f.

[94] For the connection between judicial cooperation and harmonisation, see Article 82(2) TFEU. From the point of view of the protection of the rights of defence, see Rafaraci (2011), p. 119; from the point of view of evidence, see Allegrezza (2007), pp. 691 ff.

[95] Art. 3(2) TEU.

[96] Gaito (2010), p. 33, points out that the protection of fundamental rights assumes a "central role" in the functioning of the EU after the Lisbon Treaty.

[97] Pulitanò (2013), p. 1628.

and legitimate field of the Union's competence pursuant to article 82 TFEU".[98] Moreover, the cultural impulse to increase the level of protection of fundamental rights, with respect to cross-border situations, seems to be able to live with an approach of experimentation of the potential of EU law, in terms of the protection of procedural guarantees in "internal" situations.

5.2 The Effects of Directive 2013/48/EU and Unresolved Issues

If we try to assess what actual impact is had on Italian criminal proceedings by the duties deriving from Directive 2013/48/EU, it seems appropriate to distinguish, in terms of the structure of the European provisions, between "rules of conduct" and "programmatic rules".[99] Before the expiry of the deadline for transposition,[100] there will be no chance to instantly apply European standards, although clear, precise and unconditional in nature,[101] or to disapply conflicting domestic rules of procedure.[102] However, at least according to what seems the preferable view, the technique of consistent interpretation must immediately be implemented,[103] and therefore the meaning of the domestic rules must be defined in line with the civil-rights standards established at a European level, where these are higher than those provided by the former. With this in mind, the greater is the precision of the provision of the Directive, the greater will be the degree of its reception in domestic law, through interpretative activity.

As Gaito maintains:

---

[98] See, again, Rafaraci (2011), p. 130, according to whom "an action by the Union that does not restore the connection with the procedural context inherent in cross-border situations probably remains, on one hand, insufficient and, on the other, of dubious legality".

[99] Viganò (2014), p. 10.

[100] Article 15 specifies 27 November 2016 as a deadline for transposition.

[101] In relation to the above requirements for the immediate application of European standards, see recently, Kostoris (2014), p. 22.

[102] Viganò (2014), p. 7, among others, differentiates between non-application, consistent interpretation and direct application.

[103] On the possibility for the rules of a European Directive to produce indirect effects, i.e. related to the duty of consistent interpretation imposed on the domestic judge, from their entry into force, with regard to Directive 2010/64/EU regarding interpretation and translation, see Gialuz (2012), pp. 434 ff., who is critical of the contrary interpretation of the Court of Cassation, Division III, 18 March 2011, no. 26703, www.dirittoegiustizia.it. In this ruling, the Supreme Court relied heavily on the provision of Article 8 of the Directive, under which the Member States have to adopt the internal rules necessary to implement the Directive, until 27 October 2013, to exclude the existence of a duty of translation of the judgment for an accused person who does not understand the Italian language. To overcome this interpretative position, see, however, Court of Cassation, Division III, 12 July 2012, no. 5486, Gallo, *CED Cass.* 2013, 2185. In literature, see Gialuz (2013), pp. 2188 ff.

> Europe does not replace the State in the administration of justice for individual cases, but grants individuals a number of rights and dictates rules of organisation and operation aimed at the Member States.[104]

The rules of the Directive outline requirements for states to devise their domestic law so as to implement the "minimum standards" envisaged at a European level.

It has been observed that according to the new Directive, there should be granted to the accused person or suspect an "effective exercise of the rights of defence". It follows that its concrete application would provide a higher level of assurance than is currently envisaged by Italian legislation, at least in relation to the formal interview under caution. However, in my opinion, even after the adoption of the Directive in question, many issues remain unresolved, and there appear to be numerous gaps in the text: the terms adopted by the European legislator are often ambiguous, and the discretion given to the authorities in terms of "legitimate" exemptions is broad. There is, then, still much to be done.

There are still doubts about establishing the scope of application: talking about "before being questioned" in vague terms does not make much sense. The situations exemplified in the Directive are heterogeneous, destined to extend according to an analogical criterion, and even the meaning to be given to the term "questioning" is not unambiguous.[105]

Since there is such ambiguity in the use of the words used (for example, reference is made to the word "questioning" or the phrase "without undue delay"), it is difficult to find any greater protection than that provided in Italian law.

5.3 *Is There an Extension of Protection Also in the Case of the Exceptions Provided for by the Directive?*

The guarantees provided by the Directive in question in relation to the effectiveness of the right can be circumvented by formally legitimate mechanisms.

One wonders if the provision of exceptions to the general rules precludes a consistent interpretation. The domestic regulations could establish conditions for the exercise of the rights of suspects and accused persons not covered by the Directive or more stringent requirements than those contained within the EU act. For this reason, it must be clarified whether the consistent interpretation may apply to these restrictions or not.

In this regard, it is necessary to distinguish between the level regarding the requirements of the individual guarantees and that concerning the limits within which the exceptions operate. From both points of view, it is possible that "self-

---

[104] Gaito (2010), p. 26.

[105] For example, also in terms of summary information, the only case where the lawyer's assistance is obligatory is that provided for under Article 350(5) CCP-Italy ("at the place or in the immediacy of the fact" for "the immediate continuation of the investigation").

executing" guarantees coexist with purely programmatic exceptions. By way of example, we may consider the rules contained in Article 3, undoubtedly central in the context of the Directive being analysed. As seen earlier, both paragraph 5 and paragraph 6 of this Article grant Member States the power to "temporarily derogate" application, in the phase prior to the trial, from certain guarantees provided for under Article 3, indicating criteria and limits of derogations applicable at the domestic level. In both cases, these are European regulations that are not completely clear, but while paragraph 5 is related to a discipline that is itself programmatic [paragraph 2(c)], concerning the right of recourse to a lawyer ("without undue delay after the deprivation of liberty"), paragraph 6 also relates to rules of "conduct".

Assuming that domestic rules provide for derogations,[106] as mentioned, the domestic system, in cases unrelated to the derogated regulation, should be interpreted solely in accordance with the civil-rights rules of the Directive. Conversely, where there are the conditions for applying the domestic derogation rules, they must be construed in accordance with European regulations establishing derogations. Derogation clauses mitigate the expansive force of European standards but do not cancel out the rules of interpretation. National criminal courts must apply the guarantee arrangements envisaged under national law, in a manner consistent with EU regulations in terms of both aspects mentioned above.

The fact that the derogations provided for by the Directive are not regulated in detail, at least as far as regards the parameters that the judicial authorities must follow, means that any abuse of them would cause, in principle, an irremediable prejudice to the rights of the defence.

5.4 The Exceptions Provided for by the Italian Code of Criminal Procedure and "Compatibility" with the Principles of Directive 2013/48/EU

The exceptions related to the possibility of delaying the talks between an accused person and his lawyer, as governed by the Italian CCP, contrast with the provisions of paragraph 2(a) and paragraph 3(a) of Article 3 of the Directive.

Given that the power to delay the exercise of the right to meet the lawyer is compatible with Directive 2013/48/EU, another issue is whether or not there are points of tension between the criteria set for taking this decision established on a domestic level [Art 104(3) CCP-Italy] and those enshrined at a European level [Art 3(6) and Art 8(1) Directive]. We see, in this regard, that the supranational regulations are more analytical than the Italian ones. Under the latter, the decision limiting the right to talk to one's lawyer is based on establishing "specific and exceptional

[106] It should be stressed that this is a power of the states, not an obligation.

reasons of caution", a somewhat flexible criterion that fails to indicate, moreover, in what direction the precautionary aim of the measure is projected.[107]

Equally flexible, but more precise, is the regulatory framework embodied in Directive 2013/48/EU. In this context, the temporary derogation from the right to meet and communicate (i.e., confer) with the defender, exceptional and limited to the period preceding the trial, presupposes "special circumstances of the case" from which we can deduce the existence of "imperative reasons". These are vague parameters, but more meaningful than the "reasons of caution", albeit "specific and exceptional" provided for by Article 104(3) CCP-Italy.[108]

Such practices prejudicial to the rights of the qualified defence should be abandoned, through the interpretation of Article 104 CCP-Italy in accordance with Directive 2013/48/EU. This could take place both by precluding the use of the instrument in question to tackle the danger (hypothetical or concrete) of the preparation of a defence line of convenience and by asking for an assessment of the "specific and exceptional" reasons, based on factors other than the nature of the offences. In this context, the "reasons of caution" provided for under the Code could not be appealed to in order to prevent the preparation of (self-)defence strategies of whatever kind, since the relationship between an accused person and his lawyer is an inviolable freedom. Instead, the exception to the right to meet in private with the lawyer should be applied only in circumstances that demonstrate both a (concrete) danger such as those laid down by the Directive (serious negative consequences for the life, liberty or physical integrity of a person; substantial impairment of the criminal proceedings)[109] and the need to postpone the interview to avert the danger deemed to exist. In short, an approach inspired by European regulations, aimed at correcting a domestic practice not in line with the fundamental principles of Italian criminal procedure, compensating for a choice embodied in the Code of 1988, in this aspect is open to criticism.[110]

6 Final Remarks

In light of the above, the importance of Directive 2013/48/EU, as a significant step towards an extension of the rights of defence in criminal proceedings, is evident.

---

[107] For the view whereby the assumption of the measure contained in Article 104(3) CCP-Italy "is closely related to [...] the precautionary needs underlying the restrictive measure", see Cass., Division VI, 13 October 2009, no. 39941, Valsena, CED Cass., 244265.

[108] Based on these regulatory lines, Italian case law has developed an interpretation whose misalignment with European regulations should be noted. On this point, see Mazza (2010), pp. 89 f.

[109] With reference to the value of life and personal safety, see Giuliani (2013), p. 154.

[110] According to Marandola (2006), p. 362, "the choice not to encode with sufficient precision the cases when derogation is possible has led to practices which are divergent from the real legislative intention".

The added value of this European measure, even though it does not add essential safeguards to those already recognised by the ECtHR, is especially clear if we consider that, after more than a decade of discussions at the EU level, the results relating to the protection of fundamental rights at a European level were scarce.

From a comparison between supranational and Italian regulations, with particular reference to the formal interview under caution, it emerges that the former is more analytical than the latter, giving the judge less discretionary power. As a corollary, we see that the guarantee of the right of defence is greater in Europe. An interpretation of Italian law in a manner consistent with Directive 2013/48/EU would thus be desirable, also in order to abandon the practice detrimental to the right in question.

In any case, we cannot fail to have some doubts about the meaning of some expressions used in the Directive, and clarification from the European legislature would be welcome on this point.

References

Allegrezza S (2007) Cooperazione giudiziaria, mutuo riconoscimento e circolazione della prova penale nello spazio giudiziario europeo. In: Rafaraci T (ed) L'area di libertà sicurezza e giustizia. Giuffrè, Milano, pp 691–720

Amodio E (2003) Il processo penale tra disgregazione e recupero del sistema. Indice penale 5–18

Azzena L (1998) L'integrazione attraverso i diritti. Dal cittadino italiano al cittadino europeo. Quaderni del dipartimento di diritto pubblico Università di Pisa. Torino, pp 128–149

Bartole S, De Sena P, Zagrebelsky V (2012) Commentario Breve alla Convenzione Europea per i Diritti dell'Uomo. In: Cian G, Trabucchi A (eds) Commentario Breve alla Convenzione Europea per i Diritti dell'Uomo. Cedam, Padova

Bubula F-A (2014) La Direttiva 2013/48/UE sul diritto al difensore e a comunicare con terzi e autorità consolari in caso di privazione della libertà personale. www.penalecontemporaneo.it

Campailla S (2012) L'obbligo di interpretazione conforme tra diritto dell'Unione, Convenzione europea dei diritti dell'uomo e ruolo della Corte di Strasburgo. Processo penale e giustizia 99–108

Caprioli F (2007) Cooperazione giudiziaria e processo in absentia. In: Rafaraci T (ed) L'area di libertà sicurezza e giustizia: alla ricerca di un equilibrio fra priorità repressive ed esigenze di garanzia. Giuffrè, Milano, pp 391–402

Carbone M (2006) Il ruolo della Corte di giustizia nella costruzione del sistema giuridico europeo. Diritto pubblico comparato ed europeo II:537–552

Cartabia M (ed) (1995) Principi inviolabili e integrazione europea. Giuffrè, Milano

Cartabia M (2007) L'ora dei diritti fondamentali nell'Unione Europea. In: Cartabia M (ed) I diritti in azione. Universalità e pluralismo dei diritti fondamentali nelle Corti Europee. Il Mulino, Bologna

Catalano EM (2007) Molte incertezze e piccoli passi nel percorso di europeizzazione del diritto processuale penale. Diritto penale e processo 10:522–538

Conso G (1970) Colloqui con l'imputato detenuto e diritto di difesa. Archivio Penale 1:242–258

Cordero F (1987) Procedura penale. Giuffrè, Milano

Corso P (2013) Scambio di informazioni tra Paesi UE: dalla cooperazione amministrativa a quella giudiziaria? Corriere tributario 465–483

Dalia AA, Cimadomo D (1999) Difensore (diritto processuale penale). Enciclopedia del diritto. Giuffrè, Milano, pp 501–511

Gaito A (2010) L'adattamento del diritto interno alle fonti europee. In: Dominioni O, Corso P, Gaito A, Spangher G, Dean G, Garuti G, Mazza O (eds) Procedura penale. Giappichelli, Torino, pp 25–41

Galantini N (2002) Prime osservazioni sul mandato d'arresto europeo. Foro ambrosiano 5:261–279

Gialuz M (2012) L'obbligo di interpretazione conforme alla Direttiva sul diritto all'assistenza linguistica. Diritto penale e processo 6:434–448

Gialuz M (2013) La Corte di cassazione riconosce l'obbligo di tradurre la sentenza a favore dell'imputato alloglotto. Cassazione penale 3:2188–2194

Giuliani L (ed) (2013) Autodifesa e difesa tecnica nei procedimenti *de libertate*. Cedam, Padova

Giunchedi F (2002) Indagato *in vinculis*, colloquio differito e diritto di difesa. Giurisprudenza Italiana 4:133–148

Grevi V (1996) Più ombre che luci nella l. 8 agosto 1995 n. 332 tra istanze garantistiche ed esigenze del processo. In: Grevi V (ed) Misure cautelari e diritto di difesa. Giuffrè, Milano, pp 3–51

Kostoris RE (1990) L'isolamento del detenuto in custodia cautelare tra sistema penitenziario e nuovo processo penale. Rivista italiana diritto e procedura penale 4:1391–1402

Kostoris RE (1995) *Sub* art. 1 l. 8 agosto 1995 n. 332. In: Giostra G, Grifantini FM, Illuminati G, Marchetti MR, Marzaduri E, Orlandi R, Peroni F, Presutti A, Rafarci T, Rigo F, Scella A, Spangher G, Tonini P, Voena GP, Zappalà E (eds) Modifiche al codice di procedura penale. Nuovi diritti della difesa e riforma della custodia cautelare. Padova, Cedam, pp 145–157

Kostoris RE (2014) Diritto europeo e giustizia penale. In: Kostoris RE (ed) Manuale di procedura penale europea. Giuffrè, Milano, pp 1–87

Lupària L (2005) Una recente decisione della Corte di Giustizia sull'allargamento delle ipotesi di audizione del minore in incidente probatorio. Cassazione penale 4:3544–3565

Manes V (2007) I rapporti tra diritto comunitario e diritto penale nello specchio della giurisprudenza della Corte di Giustizia: approdi recenti e nuovi orizzonti. In: Sgubbi F, Manes V (eds) L'interpretazione conforme al diritto comunitario in materia penale. Bononia University Press, Bologna, pp 1–180

Marandola A (ed) (2006) L'interrogatorio di garanzia, dal contraddittorio posticipato all'anticipazione delle tutele difensive. Cedam, Padova

Marzaduri E (1992) Imputato ed imputazione. Digesto penale, VI, pp 278–298

Mazza O (1994) Interrogatorio ed esame dell'imputato: identità di natura giuridica e di efficacia probatoria. Rivista italiana diritto e procedura penale 4:822–840

Mazza O (2010) Interrogatorio dell'imputato. Enciclopedia del diritto. Annali, III, Milano, pp 712–756

Mazza O (2011) La procedura penale. Diritto Penale e Processo, Speciale Europa e giustizia penale, pp 34–43

Pulitanò D (2013) Diritti umani e diritto penale. Rivista italiana diritto e processo penale 2:1628–1636

Rafaraci T (2011) Il diritto di difesa nelle procedure di cooperazione giudiziaria nel contesto dell'Unione europea. In: Rafaraci T (ed) La cooperazione di polizia e giudiziaria nell'Unione europea dopo il Trattato di Lisbona. Giuffrè, Milano, pp 119–134

Ruggeri A (2005) Fonti, norme, criteri ordinatori. Lezioni. Giappichelli, Torino

Ruggeri A (2006) Le fonti del diritto europeo ed i loro rapporti con le fonti nazionali. In: Costanzo P, Mezzetti L, Ruggeri A (eds) Lineamenti di diritto costituzionale dell'Unione europea. Giappichelli, Torino, pp 210–345

Santoriello C (1999) La nuova disciplina dell'interrogatorio della persona sottoposta a provvedimento cautelare. Una prima lettura dopo alcune sollecitazioni del giudice costituzionale ed un pronto intervento del legislatore. Giurisprudenza italiana 1257–1272

Scalfati A (2010) Sub art. 104. In: Giarda A, Spangher G (eds) Codice di procedura penale commentato, I. Milano, Ipsoa, pp 1093–1104

Siracusano F (2011) Nuove prospettive in materia di processo in absentia e procedure di consegna. In: Rafaraci T (ed) La cooperazione di polizia e giudiziaria in materia penale. Giuffrè, Milano, pp 85–104

Siracusano F (2013) Una lenta progressione verso la costruzione di uno "statuto europeo" delle garanzie difensive. In: Ruggieri F, Rafaraci T, Di Paolo G, Marcolini S, Belfiore R (eds) Processo penale, lingua e Unione Europea. Cedam, Padova, pp 77–94

Sotis C (2007) Il caso "Pupino": profili sostanziali. In: Sgubbi F, Manes V (eds) L'interpretazione conforme al diritto comunitario in materia penale. Bononia University Press, Bologna, pp 33–48

Spangher G (1993) Soggetti. In: Conso P, Grevi V (eds) Profili del nuovo codice di procedura penale, 4th edn. Cedam, Padova, pp 1–64

Trevisson Lupacchini T (1993) Sul diritto dell'imputato in vinculis al colloquio con il difensore. Giurisprudenza italiana 2:193–205

Ubertis G (2012) L'autonomia linguistica della Corte di Strasburgo. Archivio Penale 1:21–28

Viganò F (2010) Il giudice penale e l'interpretazione conforme alle norme sovranazionali. In: Corso P, Zanetti E (eds) Studi in onore di Mario Pisani. La Tribuna, Piacenza, pp 617–631

Viganò F (2011) Fonti europee e ordinamento italiano. In: Viganò F, Mazza O (eds) Europa e diritto penale - Diritto penale e processo, pp 4–21

Viganò F (2014) L'adeguamento del sistema penale italiano al "diritto europeo" tra giurisdizione ordinaria e costituzionale. Diritto penale contemporaneo 1:1–13

Vigoni D (2014) La "codificazione europea" delle regole minime per la tutela dei diritti della difesa. Processo Penale e Giustizia 2:14–19

The Impact of Directive 2012/29/EU on the Italian System for Protecting Victims of Crime in Criminal Proceedings

Giuseppe Alvaro and Alessandro D'Andrea

Contents

Abstract The evolution of organized crime and the serious consequences it has on the social fabric have gradually led both national legislators and the EU institutions to introduce measures aimed not only at repressing this phenomenon but also at protecting the victims of organized crime. This paper analyzes the impact of the recent Directive 2012/29/EU on the Italian legal system. The issues covered relate, in particular, to identification of the victim; the right to information, which needs to be balanced against the confidential nature of investigations; powers allowing victims to see their rights respected; and, finally, the institutions' role in providing direct assistance and support for these vulnerable persons.

Keywords Assistance services • Family • Organized crime • Protection of the victim • Review • Right to information • Role of the victim • Victim

G. Alvaro (✉) • A. D'Andrea
Department of Law, University of Messina, Piazza Pugliatti 1, 98100 Messina, Italy
e-mail: giusealvaro@gmail.com; dndale89@hotmail.it

S. Ruggeri (ed.), *Human Rights in European Criminal Law*,
DOI 10.1007/978-3-319-12042-3_15

1 Introduction

Organized crime is one of the main threats to the internal security of the EU and the fundamental freedoms of its citizens. Traditionally, organized crime means a form of delinquency organized in a stable manner, with a hierarchical framework and a common goal, which is expressed in the commission of various criminal activities.[1] Usually, the ultimate aim of these organizations is financial gain, but they may also be interested in controlling the territory and penetrating the various centers of power of the Member States. Significantly, in 1976, the United Nations, identifying the phenomenon of organized crime, realized its devastating social consequences and highlighted:

> the large-scale and complex criminal activity carried on by groups of persons, however loosely or tightly organized, for the enrichment of those participating and at the expense of the community and its members.

The vastness of this criminal phenomenon, which especially in recent decades has evolved from an exclusively regional phenomenon to become a global problem, necessarily involves a response both from individual jurisdictions as well as transnational coordination, in order not only to suppress the phenomenon but also to provide tools to support the victims of organized crime.[2]

The specific nature of this criminal phenomenon, however, necessitates different regulations to those aimed at protecting victims of other forms of crime. The need for an approach focusing on the protection of victims already becomes apparent when we examine the texts of criminal legislation dealing with such forms of crime. An emblematic case is Article 416-*bis* of Italy's Criminal Code (hereafter CC-Italy), which deals with mafia association and defines such criminal organizations on the basis of the fact that they rely on the power of intimidation and the associative bond—elements that necessarily have an impact on their victims.

The victims of organized crime are particularly vulnerable not only to harm resulting from the fact of the crime itself but also to so-called secondary victimization,[3] which is a second phase of personal harm committed by the institutions, social workers or unwanted media exposure. However, in our opinion, secondary victimization in the phenomenon of organized crime does not represent a secondary and eventual aspect of the offense, instead common to other crimes. Especially with regard to the crime of mafia-type criminal association, such harm not only stems from the fact of the crime but also occurs during the investigation. In fact, the intimidating strength of the criminal association may also emerge during the trial, in other words even when the crime itself has already been committed, making it necessary to protect the victim within the criminal process.

---

[1] Grasso and Sicurella (2007), p. 377.

[2] Michelini and Polimeni (2007), p. 5.

[3] See Fanci (2011), p. 53 ff.

The EU institutions have given attention to victims of crime since the Council Framework Decision 2001/220/JHA, which established minimum rules for the assistance of victims of crime before, during and after criminal proceedings. According to these, the Member States had to ensure that the victims' dignity was respected and that their rights were recognized throughout the proceedings.[4] We would have to wait, however, more than 10 years for the enactment of more comprehensive EU regulations, seen recently in Directive 2012/29/EU. The object of this study is to analyze the impact of the latter on the Italian legal framework.

2 Concept of a Victim of Crime

Preliminarily, we should start by focusing on the notion of the victim of crime and then try to highlight, in light of what was mentioned above, the features characterizing the victims of organized crime. In our view, it is crucial to establish a clear definition of the concept of victim, since this allows us to circumscribe the scope of legislation regarding their protection. In this regard, we find significant differences between international, supranational and national sources.

In fact, the concept of victim is very sensitive to the objectives from time to time targeted by each specific regulatory measure. Thus, Declaration A/RES/40/34, adopted by the UN General Assembly on 29 November 1985 with regard to the basic principles of justice for victims of crime and abuse of power, defines victims as

> persons who, individually or collectively, have suffered harm, including physical or mental injury, emotional suffering, economic loss or substantial impairment of their fundamental rights, through acts or omissions that are in violation of criminal laws operative within Member States, including those laws proscribing criminal abuse of power.[5]

This definition was also adopted in the Palermo Convention of 2000 against Transnational Organized Crime, which provides a general definition that does not distinguish between victims of organized crime and victims of crime in general.[6]

In Italian law, there is a tendency to equate the victims of organized crime to victims of other serious forms of crime such as terrorism. However, this equalization does not seem to be reflected in practice. Thus, in Italy, the Council of State, in an advisory capacity, in Opinion no. 1197/2012, stressed, with regard to the organized mafia crime, that

[4] Lupària (2011), p. 10 ff.

[5] UN Declaration 29 November 1985, 96th plenary meeting, A/RES/40/34.

[6] United Nations, General Assembly, United Nations Convention against Transnational Organized Crime signed during the Palermo Conference (12–15 December 2000).

> there are profound differences, both sociological and structural, between terrorism and organized crime, differences that influence the different type of protection given by the State to the victims of each phenomenon.[7]

In fact, solidarity with victims of the mafia is also seen as a preventive measure,[8] aimed at helping those who work in areas controlled by the mafia to come out of isolation, helping to break the conspiracy of silence and submission characterizing such areas and encouraging associates to "rebel" against Mafia pressure, in the belief that the state should not leave citizens alone but should provide support to families whose members are affected by mafia attacks.

In the European context, the definition of a victim of crime has undergone a dramatic evolution since the first definition was given in Framework Decision 2001/220/JHA. According to Article 1(a) of this legislative measure, the victim was solely

> a natural person who has suffered harm, including physical or mental injury, emotional suffering or economic loss, directly caused by acts or omissions that are in violation of the criminal law of a Member State.[9]

Directive 2012/29/EU considerably expanded the scope of protection by providing a definition of victim that includes not only an individual who has suffered physical, mental, emotional or economic harm as a result of crime but also the family members of a person whose death was caused directly by a crime and who have therefore consequently suffered an injury. In Directive 2012/29/EU, we can probably see the influence of the European Court of Justice's consolidated case law on the issue of the vulnerable victim.[10]

Already this extended scope of protection seems to pose problems of compatibility of the Italian system with recent supranational legislation. Therefore, while on one hand the definitions both of the Declaration of the General Assembly A/RES/40/34 and of Framework Decision 2001/220/JHA are very similar, since they are aimed at being adaptable to the various legal systems of the Member States, on the other hand, Directive 2012/29, albeit also structured to embrace more than one system, is innovative insofar as it also includes family members in the category

[7] Consiglio di Stato, Sezione I, 10 marzo 2012, n. 1197 in www.amministrativistaonline.it/giurisprudenza/cons-stato-sez-i-parere-10-marzo-2012-n-1197.

[8] *Ibid.*

[9] Lupària (2011), pp. 1–2.

[10] Cf. Court of Justice, Grand Chamber, Case C-105/03, Pupino, which ruled: "Articles 2, 3 and 8 (4) of Council Framework Decision 2001/220/JHA of 15 March 2001 on the standing of victims in criminal proceedings set out a number of objectives, including ensuring that particularly vulnerable victims receive specific treatment best suited to their circumstances. Those provisions must be interpreted as allowing the competent national court to authorise young children, who claim to have been victims of maltreatment, to give their testimony in accordance with arrangements allowing those children to be guaranteed an appropriate level of protection, for example outside the trial and before it takes place. The arrangements for taking evidence used must not, however, be incompatible with the basic legal principles of the Member State concerned, as Article 8(4) of that framework decision provides."

of victims. In fact, compared to the provisions of Article 2(1)(b) of the Directive, Italian criminal law, at both substantive[11] and procedural levels,[12] is based on a conception of family anchored to that of 1930, linked to "legally typed" rather than de facto family relationships. This concept is thus insensitive to changes in society and developments in European legislation.[13] To tell the truth, this limit with reference to relations of natural descendants has recently in Italy been subject to legislative intervention, in Legislative Decree no. 14/2013, aimed at eliminating the previous discrimination between legitimate and illegitimate children. However, differences in treatment remain between common law marriages or nontraditional forms of cohabitation and traditional families based on marriage. Pending legislative action to fill this gap, however, recourse can be made to a systematic interpretation that complies with EU principles, which have long been inspired by a more extensive protection for traditional and de facto family relationships.

3 Rights and Procedural Powers of a Victim of Crime

3.1 Foreword: The Procedural Role of the Victim

In order to assess the provisions in the Directive concerning the rights and procedural powers exercisable by the victim in criminal proceedings, we need to start with the role that the victim plays in these proceedings.

Also in this respect, Italian legislation does not seem entirely consistent with the approach followed by the Directive in question. In fact, the Code of Criminal Procedure of 1988, despite giving importance to the victim during the preliminary investigation, did not go so far as to assign him with a role as party to the trial,[14] i.e., as a person entitled to submit judicial requests to the criminal court. The victim of an offense is in fact only entitled to bring a civil action for damages within criminal proceedings.[15] The scope of the 2012 Directive is wider and extends protection to "a natural person who has suffered harm, including physical or mental injury, emotional suffering or economic loss, directly caused by a criminal offence"

[11] Pursuant to Article 307(4) CP-Italy, "For the purposes of criminal law, 'close relatives' are considered to be ascendants, descendants, spouse, brothers, sisters, in-laws in the same degree, uncles, aunts, nephews and nieces: nevertheless, close relatives do not include in-laws if the spouse has died and there is no offspring."

[12] Pursuant to Article 90(3) CCP-Italy, "If the victim has died as a result of the offence, the faculties and rights under law shall be exercised by the victim's close relatives."

[13] Cf. Tribunal 17 June 1993, case T-65/92, Arauxo-Dumay; Court of Justice 17 April 1996, case C-59/85, Reed; Judgment of the Court of Justice 22 June 2000, case C-65/98, Eyüp; Court of Justice 23 March 2006, case C-408/03, Commission v. Belgium.

[14] Parlato (2012), pp. 39 ff.; Tranchina (2010), p. 4055.

[15] Chiavario (2012), pp. 221 ff.

(Art. 2). This framework could make it possible to encompass those persons involved in the proceedings classified in Italy as parties injured by the offense.

Taking into account this difference in terms of definition, the following analysis focuses on two aspects, concerning the right to information and the victim's powers to react to a decision not to prosecute.

3.2 Balancing the Right to Information Against Requirements of Confidentiality

With regard to the first point, it is known that, especially during the preliminary phase of criminal proceedings, the right to information must be balanced against investigative requirements of confidentiality. This analysis aims to highlight the differences between the approach of Italian legislation and that emerging from the recent EU Directive with regard to the dialectical relationship between the right to information and investigative confidentiality.

The diversity of approach between the two standards is already clear with regard to the view of the right to information in the early stages of criminal investigations, a right recognized by Article 6 of the Directive. Meanwhile, Article 329 CCP-Italy does not include any right to information precisely in the initial stage of the investigation. The impact on the victim of the offense becomes more serious in the context of many forms of organized crime. This is due to the fact that Article 335(3) CCP-Italy establishes the confidential nature of the registration of instances of offenses covered by Article 407(2)(a) CCP-Italy, which also include the crime of mafia association. This in turn leads to a stricter form of investigative confidentiality, whereby the prosecutor is not permitted to inform the victim of a crime that a person's name has been entered into the register of criminal offenses, even when the victim submits a specific request for such information. The rationale for this is to avoid prejudicing the proper conduct of proceedings against persons suspected of serious (organized) crime. The rule, at first glance, does not substantially conflict with Article 6(2)(b) of the Directive in question, which provides, as a limit on the right to information, the need not to compromise proceedings still in the initial phase. However, the Italian provision, by establishing an absolute prohibition of communication, fails to achieve any logical balance between values, which is instead required by the supranational text. It is also worth paying particular attention to paragraph 1(a) of Article 6 of the Directive in question, which requires Member States to inform victims without undue delay of any decision not to continue investigations or not to prosecute the alleged offender. In the Italian system, the Code of Criminal Procedure obliges the prosecutor to notify the victim of any request he makes to the court to drop prosecution, if the victim has previously expressed his desire to be informed of such a request (Art. 408). However, if the court grants the application for the dropping of prosecution, no form of communication is envisaged, not even to the suspect, except when the latter is remanded in custody.

Another interesting aspect regards the right to be informed of the passing of a final judgment in a trial, a right provided for under paragraph 2(a) of Article 6 of the Directive. Here, we see even more clearly a discrepancy with Article 545(3) - CCP-Italy, which does not require the judgment to be directly communicated to the victim, who receives such information only through publication of the judgment. In our view, this system, based on the assumption that the publication of a judgment is equivalent to notification, is deeply disturbing on a substantial level, since it prevents the victim from responding quickly and effectively to a measure that is potentially unfavorable to him.

Ultimately, if we compare the requirements established under Article 6 of the Directive and the approach found in Italian criminal procedure, we see that the Italian system clearly gives priority to protecting the needs of the proceeding, at the expense of respect for the victim and his right to information in the various procedural phases. Here, however, the deficiencies are such as to make it difficult to intervene by way of interpretation. Rather, prompt legislative action aimed at eliminating these protective lacunae is desirable.

3.3 *Rights of Victims in the Event of Nonprosecution*

One aspect of particular importance among the victim's procedural rights and options as recognized under the recent Directive concerns the right to request the review of a decision not to prosecute. This right is dealt with in Article 11, which, speaking of "review," would thus seem to require the creation of a procedure designed to reevaluate the facts and legal grounds that led to the decision.

Also here, the Italian legal system has serious shortcomings. The victim has no real power to demand a review of the decision not to prosecute in the sense required by the Directive. In truth, the victim is able to oppose the decision to drop proceedings (Art. 410 CCP-Italy). The opposition has as its premise, under penalty of inadmissibility, the subject of the supplementary investigation and its evidence and therefore seeks to provide the judge for preliminary investigations with a wider range of sources of evidence to assess the validity of the charge. Since, moreover, it is an appeal made by the victim against the request, not the decision, to drop proceedings, the appeal does not satisfy the right to review required by the Directive or provide preventive protection.

The power to appeal against a measure to drop prosecution is instead provided for under Article 409(6) CCP-Italy, which grants the injured party the right to appeal to the Supreme Court against the order to drop prosecution. This action leads to a subsequent review, which the victim may however avail himself of only if he has had no chance to raise objections during the hearing that led to the adoption of the order to drop prosecution. Thus, control by the Court of Cassation is also limited and, insofar as it is limited to aspects of procedural legitimacy, does not fully satisfy the need for review in the full sense of the term. Here, then, the Italian system provides fewer guarantees even than those provided by systems still bound to the concept whereby the decision to drop prosecution is in the hands of the prosecutor. Thus, for example, in Germany, although the prosecutor can independently drop prosecution, the victim is given a dual possibility of reacting through the so-called *Klageerzwingungsverfahren*: he may apply to the officer above the prosecutor (usually the General Attorney) to reevaluate the merits of the request for dismissal of the case and the need to initiate trial proceedings [§ 172 (1) CCP-Germany]. If this appeal does not achieve the desired result, he may, within the period of 1 month, request jurisdictional review by the Superior Regional Court (*Oberlandesgericht*).[16]

In another aspect, the Italian procedural system proves incapable of implementing the rights emerging from Article 11 of the Directive in question. In the Italian system, there is in fact no instrument allowing a remedy to be sought against a decision to reject a request by the public prosecutor to reopen an investigation. Once again, therefore, the Italian legal system proves deficient in respecting the guarantees of the victim, providing a regulation that fails to meet the protection standards required by the EU, even with the aid of consistent interpretation.

4 Coordinating Support Services for Victims of Organized Crime

It is worth considering separately Articles 8 and 9 of Directive 2012/29/EU, which state that "Member States shall ensure that victims, in accordance with their needs, have access to [. . .] support services" [Art. 8(1)]. These services promoted by the Directive, however, can manifest themselves in various ways, in the sense that they can be "set up as public or non-governmental organizations, and may be organized on a professional or voluntary basis" [Art. 8 (4)]. Therefore, the main regulator of these services is the principle of subsidiarity in its two classical modes of expression: vertical and horizontal.[17] Vertical subsidiarity is seen in the distribution of administrative responsibilities between various levels of local government (supranational level: EU-Member States; national level: national state-regions; subnational level: state-regions-autonomous local authorities) and expresses the (subsidiary) action of the higher local authorities with regard to the lower ones. Horizontal subsidiarity is found in the relationship between authority and freedom and is based on the assumption that collective needs and activities of general interest are directly provided by private citizens, while public authorities intervene in a "subsidiary" function of planning, coordination and possibly management.

[16] In this regard, cf. Beulke (2010), para. 348.

[17] Fracchia and Casetta (2012), pp. 82 ff.

Dwelling on the content of these specific rights and the methods of their implementation, Article 8 of the Directive envisages the right to access specific free support services, set up and operating for the victims before, during, and for an appropriate period of time after criminal proceedings. This provision should be correlated with Article 9, which envisages a range of services, e.g., information, advice and assistance relating to the rights of victims; psychological support; advice relating to financial and practical aspects arising from the offense; advice relating to the risk and prevention of secondary and repeated victimization, intimidation and retaliation.

In Italy, all this is however guaranteed only through various nongovernmental microorganizations, or single offices at the municipal level, which are not, however, coordinated nationally. The Directive, in fact, proposes a system of cooperation and coordinated services, which is not reflected in the Italian context, unlike in other jurisdictions. For example, classic examples of countries that offer these types of services to victims, basically inspired by the principle of vertical subsidiarity, include Sweden and the UK, where we find a wide range of services available throughout the country, especially at the local level, showing extensive decentralization. In particular, in Sweden,[18] each office of the association is headed by an assistant: a professional figure, either from the police, the social services or a psychological support background. A similar, but at the same time much more developed system is that of Victim Support UK in the United Kingdom, which is a tertiary organization that works closely with the police and that, moreover, also coordinates with other associations at a European level. In other European countries, however, support services for victims are characterized by close interaction with institutions, such as in the Netherlands, where we find the National Organization for the Support of Victims,[19] which is mainly engaged in providing legal assistance and moral support to victims of crimes and acts according to suggestions made by the police. The last type of assistance, meanwhile, is found in highly institutional systems. An interesting case is that of France, where the CNAV (National Council for Assistance to Victims) has been set up at the Directorate of Criminal Affairs and Pardons. This is chaired by the Minister of Justice and is composed of representatives of the various ministries involved, local administrators, civil service and private professionals, representatives of the INAVEM (National Institute for Assistance to Victims and Mediation) and victim support associations. In Italy, we do not have, to date, any form of national coordination, since all the services are actually only local or, at most, regional and thus provide assistance that in terms of quality and quantity fall well below the standards of other countries, as well as differing from region to region. We may mention in particular

[18] *Brottsofferjourernas Riksförbund* (BOJ), the National Association for better working condition of victims, is a nonprofit organization. The work is based on international conventions on human rights. There are 93 local victim support centers around the country. See http://www.boj.se/.

[19] *Landelijke Organisatie Slachtofferhulp*. The association is committed to improving the position and rights of the victims in general and promotes the development of knowledge in this area. See www.slachtofferhulp.nl.

the establishment of offices in the Emilia Romagna region or in the cities of Turin, Milan and Genoa or the information service at the prefecture of Messina. If implemented, however, nongovernmental organizations promoted by the Directive would provide for coordination with the institutions, thus ensuring greater substantive protection than that currently available and creating a network of both state and private services. This approach, however, the so-called third sector characterized by the coexistence and partnership of the public and private sectors, is not unknown in Italy, where it is found in the health care and economic fields.

5 Conclusions

The analysis of the adequacy of the Italian system with respect to the legal framework resulting from Directive 2012/29/EU, and therefore of the impact of the latter on the national framework, has made it possible to highlight—disregarding minor differences related to individual institutions—a different substantial approach to viewing the role of the victim. The strengthening of the victim's procedural powers and the recognition of his effective rights would seem to suggest that he is viewed not merely as a person involved in the proceedings but likewise as a party to them. In fact, the degree of procedural power enjoyed by victims in the new supranational framework testifies to the EU's intention to entrust them with an active, propulsive role, while Italian legislature is still tied to the idea of the victim as merely a person involved in the proceedings. Moreover, this is situated in a wider framework, in which we see a revision of the very role of the criminal process, whose function is not limited to ascertaining the commission of a crime but extends to protecting subjective situations of individuals other than the defendant, including the victim, especially in cases of organized crime. Significantly, some recent criminal codes, such as in Hungary, have also developed the passive personality principle, in this case used as the basis for the extraterritorial extension of Hungarian jurisdiction.[20] Independently of the decision taken by individual systems to give importance to the role of the victim, to the point of legitimizing them to bring private charges, this change in perspective constitutes a cultural revolution that introduces into the balancing act between the needs of the authority and individual freedoms the need to respect the rights of the victim, as a "co-protagonist" in the proceedings and no longer as a person with extremely limited procedural rights.

References

Beulke W (2010) Strafprozessrecht, 11th edn. C.F. Müller, Heidelberg
Chiavario M (2012) Diritto processuale penale. Profilo istituzionale, 5th edn. Utet, Torino

[20] For a comment on this, cf. Karsai (2013), p. 490.

Fanci G (2011) La vittimizzazione secondaria: ambiti di ricerca, teorizzazioni e scenari. Rivista di Criminologia, Vittimologia e Sicurezza 5:53–66
Fracchia F, Casetta E (2012) Manuale di diritto amministrativo, 14th edn. Giuffrè, Milano
Grasso G, Sicurella R (2007) Lezioni di diritto penale europeo. Giuffrè, Milano
Karsai K (2013) La via ungherese alla soluzione dei conflitti: più paternalismo, meno flessibilità. La Legislazione penale 33:485–491
Lupària L (2011) Il concetto di vittima e la nozione di particolare vulnerabilità (Luca Lupària-Susanna Oromi i Vall-Llovera). In: Lupària L, Armenta Teu T (eds) Linee guida per la tutela processuale delle vittime vulnerabili. Working paper sull'attuazione della Decisione quadro 2001/220/GAI in Italia e Spagna. Giuffrè, Milano
Michelini G, Polimeni G (2007) Criminalità organizzata transnazionale e sistema penale italiano. In: Rosi E (ed) La convenzione ONU di Palermo. Ipsoa, Milano
Parlato L (2012) Il contributo della vittima tra azione e prova. Torre del vento, Palermo
Tranchina G (2010) La vittima del reato nel processo penale: Cassazione penale, pp 4051–4055

MIX
Papier aus verantwortungsvollen Quellen
Paper from responsible sources
FSC® C105338

If you have any concerns about our products,
you can contact us on
ProductSafety@springernature.com

In case Publisher is established outside the EU,
the EU authorized representative is:
Springer Nature Customer Service Center GmbH
Europaplatz 3, 69115 Heidelberg, Germany

Printed by Libri Plureos GmbH
in Hamburg, Germany